CRIME, THE POLICE AND CRIMINAL STATISTICS

An Analysis of Official Statistics for England and Wales using Econometric Methods

This is a volume of

Quantitative Studies in Social Relations

Consulting Editor: Peter H. Rossi, University of Massachusetts, Amherst, Massachusetts

A complete list of titles in this series appears at the end of this volume.

CRIME, THE POLICE AND CRIMINAL STATISTICS

An Analysis of Official Statistics for England and Wales using Econometric Methods

R. A. CARR-HILL
St. André de Majencoules
30570, Gard, France

and

N. H. STERN
Department of Economics
University of Warwick, Coventry, England

1979

ACADEMIC PRESS   London   New York   San Francisco

A Subsidiary of Harcourt Brace Jovanovich, Publishers

ACADEMIC PRESS INC. (LONDON) LTD.
24/28 Oval Road
London NW1

United States Edition published by
ACADEMIC PRESS INC.
111 Fifth Avenue
New York, New York 10003

Library of Congress Catalog Card Number: 78-66678
ISBN: 0-12-160350-4

Printed in Great Britain by
THE LAVENHAM PRESS LIMITED
Lavenham, Suffolk

Contents

List of Tables

Preface

Crime fascinates many people. The study of crime and the reaction of society to it, is an important feature of several academic disciplines: politics, sociology, the law and economics as well as criminology. We believe that this study has benefitted from the fact that each of us has a very different view of the world which is, at least in part, due to the different disciplines to which we are attached. R.A.C-H. was first a criminologist and then a social statistician and N.H.S. is an economist.

Criminal statistics are important. They are frequently used in popular discussion of crime and they form the basic raw material for the academic and the policy maker. The relationships between crime, the police and the criminal statistics are the central issue of our study.

But as well as being fascinating and important the study of these relationships is complex. The complexity is an unavoidable consequence of theories we have had to consider and in the techniques required when using the criminal statistics to study those theories. The complexity derives mainly from the fact that we have to examine many things at once rather than any overwhelming difficulty of particular aspects of our work. The resulting broad spread of our subject matter has led us to explain the theories and statistical procedures under discussion in some detail. Accordingly any one reader will find that some parts of the book appear laboured whereas others require extra concentration.

We hope that our work will be of interest to a variety of readers. It will be of special interest to criminologists, economists concerned with social problems in general and the economics of crime in particular, sociologists of deviance and of the law and to statisticians interested in the problems of social data. The only requirements are the willingness to become involved in the development of a formal model of the processes involved and in the discussion of the quantitative results from testing this model statistically.

The book can be considered a monograph in the sense that it is a report on a single study, and it is therefore best read as a whole. We think, however, that some readers may wish to concentrate on certain chapters.

For example, Chapters 2 and 3 contain a review of theories of crime, criminal statistics and some aspects of the police. Chapter 5 provides a description of the simultaneous equations techniques of econometrics which are used extensively in our analysis. An examination of the use of criminal statistics in public discussion is offered in Chapter 8, and in Chapter 9 we provide a critical review of recent attempts to provide a purely economic theory of punishment. Whilst each of the five chapters just mentioned is to some extent a review of an area none of them is intended to be exhaustive.

The study was planned and executed jointly and our work has been in 50-50 partnership. However, R.A.C-H. takes particular responsibility for Chapters 2, 3, 7, 8 and N.H.S. for Chapters 5, 6, 9 and the Appendices to Chapters 2 and 9. Responsibility for Chapters 1, 4 and 10 is equal. The Data Appendix was compiled by Jocelyn Kynch.

Our work on this project began in 1969 when we were graduate students together at Nuffield College, Oxford. During the course of writing this book we have published three reports: Carr-Hill and Stern (1973), Carr-Hill and Stern (1976), Carr-Hill, Hope and Stern (1972). We have presented various aspects of our work to a large number of seminars involving groups from a wide range of academic disciplines in universities and research institutes beginning with our first performance in Nuffield College in 1969. The first presentation at a public conference was at the Barcelona meeting of the Econometric Society in 1971 (see the summary of the papers published by the Organising Committee).

We intend this book to be the final statement of our results. It has several features which cannot be found in our earlier published work. Thus there is a thorough discussion of the criminological, economic and sociological assumptions (in Chapters 2 and 3) underlying the model which is developed in Chapter 4. This last chapter provides an extensive discussion of the measures used. We begin in Chapter 4, and develop at length in Chapter 5, the problems of identification and unobserved variables, which occur in our analysis. There are two particular aspects of the model itself which do not appear in our earlier work. The first is the discussion of unemployment as a possibly important factor (see Chapter 2) and the second concerns the question whether or not there is such an entity as the "real" or "true" offence rate. The relevance or existence of such an entity would be denied by most sociologists of deviance. Indeed, the academic debate in this area has been fruitful for our study. But for more of this see Chapter 3. Finally, this monograph contains, in Chapter 7, a thorough discussion of the implication of our results for substantive criminological theory. We made one last recheck of our data before performing the calculations for this final report and picked up some minor errors. We were able to use data on socioeconomic groups from the 1971 census which had not been available for our previous studies. We have presented a very wide range of results, not only to cover the range of arguments under examination but also to provide help to the reader who may have wished to pursue a line slightly different from our own. For all these reasons we hope that quotes will be made from, and issue taken with, this book rather than our earlier articles.

We have adopted certain conventions in the book which we should mention here. Equations are numbered from (1) for each chapter. Cross references to equations are to the same chapter unless otherwise stated. There is a list of works cited at the end of the book and we refer to works in the text by name of author, with the year of publication in brackets. "He" is used when referring to a person simply for convenience without connotation of gender. Standard data sources are not included in the list of works cited. A full description of data sources and formal definitions is contained in the appendix on "Definitions and Sources". Our main econometric model and notation are summarized in Table 5.1 on p. 138. Our data have been deposited at the S.S.R.C. Survey Archive at Essex University.

There are many individuals who have been both kind and helpful to us during this study; of most importance are the members of our families. We have been fortunate with many institutions as well. We mention below those whose help was of special importance and apologise now to those whom our forgetfulness has led us to omit.

We received financial support from the S.S.R.C. (Grant Number HR3733) and Oxford University. Academic Press have shown consideration and patience in waiting for this book for so long. We are grateful to all three.

We have been supported throughout our work by the respective institutions to which we have been attached. R.A.C-H. was at Nuffield College, Oxford from 1968 to 1971, at the University of Sussex from 1971 to 1974, at the OECD in Paris from 1974 to 1977, and from January 1978 has been unemployed in the South of France. N.H.S. was at Nuffield College, Oxford from 1968 to 1969, The Queen's College, Oxford from 1969 to 1970, St. Catherine's College, Oxford from 1970 to 1977 and from January 1978 has been at the University of Warwick. We are grateful to St. Catherine's College, Oxford and Oxford University for granting leave in the autumn 1977 thus hastening completion of the book, and special thanks are due to Claude Henry and the Laboratoire d'Econometrie of the Ecole Polytechnique in Paris for hospitality and to the French Government C.N.R.S. for providing finance.

Jocelyn Kynch and David Deans have worked with us on this project from time to time for several years and we are especially grateful to them. Jocelyn Kynch collected some and checked all of the data which are the basis of our empirical estimates. She kindly wrote an account of the data which has been included under her name as an Appendix. She has also compiled the subject and author indexes, and located many references. We are greatly indebted to her. David Deans carried out most of the programming with considerable expertise and good humour. Oliver Morgan did the remainder and thanks are due to both of them.

We owe an important debt to Cliff Wymer, then of the L.S.E., who made available his SIMUL package programme. The options available in this programme were a major influence on the econometric work we were able to do. Jerry Hausman adapted the programme for the Oxford University ICL 1906A computer, on which the estimates reported here were produced. Clive Payne provided patient advice over the years. We were also fortunate to be able to use the FAKAD package developed by Emil van Broekhoven and Kenneth MacDonald.

There are many individuals who have had an intellectual influence on the development of our work. We were particularly helped by the detailed comments of Art Goldberger on an early unpublished paper presented at the 1971 Barcelona meeting of the Econometric Society. Grayham Mizon was very helpful too on the econometric side. We benefitted from comments at various stages of our work by David Downes, John Flemming, Jerry Hausman, David Hendry, Al Klevorick, B. S. van der Laan, Gordon Wasserman and Nigel Walker. Mary McIntosh was kind enough to read and comment on Chapter 3, and Chapter 5 benefitted greatly from the comments of David Begg, Jerry Hausman and Kenneth MacDonald. Peter Rossi provided useful comments on most of the manuscript.

Seminar audiences have responded with vigorous and often constructive comments at a number of university and research gatherings too numerous to name. We must mention in particular, however, the comments by the group working on the econometrics of crime at the Hoover Institution at Stanford University and we are grateful to Michael Block for arranging a visit there in 1976.

We have been particularly fortunate in the kindness shown to us by the secretaries who have been involved in this work. These are Audrey Hiscock, Vera Kastner and Betty Wilbery at St. Catherine's College, Oxford; Marie-Louise Pouderous at the Ecole Polytechnique, Hazel Coleman, Lesley McIntosh, Irene Sinha at the OECD, Brenda Jeater and Kathy Thorpe at the University of Sussex, Ann Sampson, Kerrie Beale, Shirley Patterson and Yvonne Slater at the University of Warwick, and Yvonne Scragg.

Finally, and most important, is our debt to our friend Andrew Cornford. He commented in great detail on the whole manuscript and hunted down a large number of references for us.

In view of the long list above we must conclude by stressing that all errors are our own.

March 1978   *R.C-H.*
                                                                          N.H.S.

1

Introduction

The focus of our study is the relation between official criminal statistics and the activities which they are supposed to reflect. Theories of crime should be able to tell us something about the generation of criminal statistics and the analysis of criminal statistics should improve our assessment of theories of crime. Accordingly, we shall be interested in testing theories of the determination of the number of offences. Our concern is, however, much wider than this. One of the central interests of the criminal statistics is their relation with real events. The statistics are produced by official bodies, in particular the police force, and are to a large extent a function of the choices made by these bodies. Thus an examination of criminal statistics requires at the same time analysis of police activities. In other words, we shall be investigating theories of the generation of criminal statistics as well as of crime. It is unfortunate that many commentaries on, and academic studies of crime and deterrence, have been marred by a failure to appreciate and take account of the difference between offences as recorded and the number of illegal events. We shall see that this difference will be crucial to an understanding of criminal statistics and in the interpretation of our results.

But our interests do not, and we shall argue, cannot stop with theories of the level of offences, as officially recorded, and crime. Broadly speaking the problem is as follows. Simple deterrence theories suggest that the level of offences will depend on the probability of being caught. It is also reasonable to suppose that the number of offences which are recorded depends on the number of police. In turn one can argue that the probability of being caught, or the proportion of offences solved, depends on the number of offences to be solved and the strength of the police force; and again the allocation or recruitment of police officers would be determined in part by the recorded

1

level of crime and the "success rate" or proportion solved. We are faced, therefore, with a problem of simultaneous causation: a given factor or variable will simultaneously contribute to the determination of another and be determined by it (for further details see Chapters 4 and 5).

One cannot ignore, although it is all too common, these simultaneous relationships in a statistical investigation without producing biased or misleading results. Here, we are interested in the determination of all three variables—the offence rate, the proportion of offences solved and the number of police. But even if we are interested in just one of these, and the offence rate is a popular candidate, we could not omit some study of the other two.

Our first task is to present the theories we are to examine and to place them in the form of a particular model. There are, again broadly speaking, three groups of theories concerned with the determination of the level of recorded offences: deterrence theories which concentrate on the consequences, possible pay-offs and penalties of acts, in the determination of whether or not they are committed; the theories of traditional criminology which specify certain groups as being more prone to offending; and theories of some sociologists which concentrate on the recording of offences and the labelling of offenders. These three groups of theories are not necessarily competitive. Few commentators would argue that just one is relevant and that the other two can be excluded, but analysts differ considerably in their emphasis. We shall be examining all three groups of theories.

In modelling the determination of the second variable, the proportion of recorded offences solved, we shall, in addition to the number of recorded offences and the number of policemen, be including variables intended to capture various aspects of the difficulties in solving an offence. In the process of modelling the determination of the third variable, the number of policemen, we shall be discussing factors affecting both allocation and recruitment as well as the number of recorded offences and the proportion solved, as already mentioned.

Our data are for the cross-section of police districts in England and Wales and we examine this cross-section for the years 1961, 1966 and 1971. The police district is the lowest level at which the offence data are reported. Our measure of recorded offences is "all indictable offences known to the police" (see the annual Home Office publication *Criminal Statistics*). Indictable offences are, loosely speaking, those serious enough to allow the possibility of trial in front of a jury (for a full list of offence types included, see the appendix to Chapter 4). We must emphasize at the outset, particularly for readers from the U.S.A. who may associate indictable offences with their "felonies", that there is no monetary cut-off for an indictable offence. Thus the theft of an item, however small in value, is an indictable offence.

Our reasons for selecting such an aggregated offence class are as follows. First, police activity is an important factor in our analysis and cannot sensibly be allocated to different offence classes. Secondly, the overall level of crime and the proportion solved as measured by all indictable offences and the corresponding "clear-up rate" (see Data Appendix for the definition) are important issues in public discussion. Thirdly, theories of crime based on incentives form a major topic of this study and such theories are better applied to economic offences than to others (see, in particular, the appendix to Chapter 2). The overwhelming majority of indictable offences (over 90% in the years of our study) are thefts without violence against the person (see the appendix to Chapter 4 for a numerical breakdown of offences by different categories). And fourthly, sociologists of deviance would argue that it is the labelling of an act or person as criminal, rather than the particular offence type which is recorded, that is important to the subsequent development of the situation.

The number of indictable offences per year in any police district is large. In 1966, for example, there were 117 police districts in England and Wales and 1,199,859 indictable offences. There are, therefore, on average over 10,000 indictable offences per district. We are therefore aggregating across individuals as well as offence classes. Many researchers have preferred to work more closely to the level of the individual and have gathered their own data on the grounds that the detail they require is not available in the official statistics. Our analysis is in no way meant to be a substitute for these micro-level studies. Such studies have the following two advantages. First, they can examine theories of individual behaviour using data on individuals. Secondly, the data can be selected to concentrate on factors of particular interest.

However, aggregates across individuals are themselves of direct interest. Many policy decisions such as the allocation of resources to the police are strongly influenced by aggregate data on crime. They are commonly used, for example, by Chief Constables and politicians to argue for greater expenditure on the police force. Given this interest in understanding the determinants of the aggregate level of recorded offences and clear-up rates, the question arises of whether one can build an aggregate picture from a combination of micro-level studies. We believe that the nature of micro-level studies, together with the data on distributions of characteristics within the population which are available, are such that this method of constructing aggregate relationships would be very difficult. More importantly however, as we have just noted, to a substantial extent some of the influences at work, for example the allocation of policemen and police effort, would appear to be functions of the aggregates, such as the level of offences themselves. Further, at our level of aggregation we can rather easily take account of a wide range of variables, for example by using census data on the characteristics of the population, whereas the collection of data for a micro-level study over a corresponding range would require substantial resources.

Thus there are reasons for pursuing both aggregate and micro-level studies; such studies should complement each other. The theories embodied in the aggregate study would be in general based on suggestions from micro-level studies. An obvious example from economics is the consumption function. Predictions of the overall level of consumption in a community are usually based on other economic aggregates such as income. The discovery at the level of aggregate quantities, that the short-run marginal propensity to consume out of income was less than the long-run, was associated with the development of a number of interesting theories of individual behaviour.[1] And research on understanding the overall suicide rates in different communities draws on observations of different types of societies and has prompted many small-scale studies.

Similarly, in this study we shall be looking at the response of the aggregate recorded offences to overall probabilities of apprehension. A corresponding model of behaviour at the level of the individual is based on standard theories of choice under uncertainty. We argued above using the examples of the consumption function and the suicide rate, that the discovery or confirmation of certain aggregate effects can, in their turn, prompt micro-level studies. We think that a number of important suggestions for such studies follow from the interpretation of our results and we shall be making some suggestions in our concluding chapter.

The techniques of estimation we shall employ for our models will be those of the simultaneous-equations methods of econometrics. We have emphasized that the theories under study force the examination of several relationships at the same time; this consideration must be embodied in our estimation techniques (the argument is elaborated below). The techniques we have used, and similar ones, are known to research workers in other social and behavioural sciences but, it seems, not widely. Many of the theories under common discussion in sociology and criminology involve simultaneous relationships, yet in empirical studies of these theories ordinary single equation regression or analysis of variance techniques are often used. For reasons we have already intimated and we shall explain at length in later chapters, such single equation techniques are inappropriate and misleading: there is no reason to suppose that they yield results which

---

[1] For a review of such theories see Ferber (1966).

are even a first approximation to correct estimates of parameters. Our study is one of the first applications of the simultaneous-equations methods to criminology. Accordingly, we have gone to some effort to explain these techniques in detail and we hope that our study will be seen as informative and constructive in this respect.

There is a further respect in which our study differs from the majority of those in criminology. We take a given police district, with its population, and ask how many recorded offences, what clear-up rate and how many policemen will arise from a district and population with characteristics as incorporated in our independent variables. On the other hand, the more usual practice in criminology is to start with given offenders and ask about their characteristics. Thus whereas the usual procedure is to begin with convicted offenders and to ask who they are, we go from population to recorded offences.

The book is arranged in three sections: the first is the theoretical background, the second the empirical argument and the third certain implications of our study. The first section consists of Chapters 2, 3 and 4. Chapters 2 and 3 contain detailed discussion of the criminological, sociological and economic theories under consideration in the light of available evidence, and their relevance to the countries and period of our study: England and Wales in the 1960s. Chapter 4 summarizes the model we choose as the outcome of that discussion and the measures selected to test it, together with a brief description of the data. Detailed information on the sources of data are provided in the appendix to this book. The second section describes the techniques employed (Chapter 5) and the results obtained (Chapter 6) together with our interpretations (Chapter 7). We range more widely in the final section, Chapters 8, 9 and 10. Chapters 8 and 9 are prompted by what we regard as serious misuse of statistics, theory and results in this area. In Chapter 8 we examine the use of official criminal statistics in discussions of policy; and Chapter 9 contains a review of models designed to use relationships of the type estimated here to specify the appropriate or optimum punishment and deterrence. Chapter 10 contains conclusions and suggestions for further research. The remainder of this introduction gives a little further detail on each chapter in turn.

Chapter 2 is concerned with factors influencing the level of criminal activity. Indeed, the study was partially prompted by a revival of interest in theories of criminal behaviour which emphasize the importance of potential reward and the probability and severity of punishment in motivating or dissuading an individual in his decision whether or not to commit an offence. A well-known article by Becker (1968) indeed claims that ". . . a useful theory of criminal behaviour can dispense with the special theories of anomie, psychological inadequacies, or inheritance of special traits and simply extend the economist's usual analysis of choice'' (p. 170). Such a theory would suggest that one should analyse the choices facing an individual in terms of the probability and severity of punishment, and the alternative legal and illegal opportunities open to him.

Subsequent empirical work in the economics literature (see, for example, Phillips, Votey and Maxwell (1972)) has, however, recognised that some of the more traditional factors studied by criminologists and sociologists, such as age, sex, race, social class and type of residence, are also important. The "traditional criminological" and the "economic" approach have in common their concern to understand the determinants of the behaviour of the individual. One can distinguish the two by saying that the latter concentrates on the perceived costs and benefits of the decision to commit an offence for the individual (and their probabilities), whereas the former takes these for granted and focusses attention on the socio-demographic factors determining the weights which the individual attaches to the consequences of his actions and the way their costs and benefits are perceived.

The two types of theory of individual behaviour are set out in Chapter 2, and the technical detail of the relevant economic analysis of choice under uncertainty is provided in an appendix to that chapter. This analysis of choice will be used in Chapter 9 in a formal model of suitable or optimum strategies of punishment.

In order to test these behavioural hypotheses, we must take into consideration the institutional context within which they are located. At one level this raises the problems of simultaneous causation already mentioned —we argued that each of the recorded offence rate, the probability of apprehension and the number of policemen contributes to the determination of the other two. And the study of the latter two variables has considerable interest independent of the recorded offence rate. In Chapter 3 we consider theories and evidence relevant to the detail of the appropriate form of the relationships for the determination of the probability and severity of punishment and the intensity of formal social control (by which we mean the numbers of, and expenditure on, the police).

On a rather different level there is a rival body of sociological theory of recent origin, which becomes important when testing a theory of crime and criminal behaviour against criminal statistics. Any such test will have to rely on legal definitions of crime and criminal behaviour and on data which are nearly always collected by official agencies. Traditional criminologists, whose views remained more or less unchallenged until the late fifties, held that one could take the criminal statistics as a more or less accurate reflexion of the state of crime, as long as one realised that there was considerable under-reporting and that local conditions could cause particular distortions (see, for example McClintock and Avison (1968)). Researchers who have attempted to estimate the parameters in deterrence theories from aggregate statistics have also, usually implicitly, taken this view.

Sociologists of deviance, however, have claimed that official statistics are simply a product of the agencies of social control and should be treated as such. This is part of a broader theoretical argument about the processes involved in being and becoming an offender. And the implication that some of these theorists have drawn is that there is no point in using the criminal statistics at all. In the latter part of Chapter 3, where we develop this theory (or at least that part of it relevant to the production of data), we suggest that there are ways of examining the effect of agencies of social control on the aggregate statistics and we discuss the appropriate variables to capture these effects. The behaviour and attitudes of both the agencies of social control and the public can change quickly, particularly that of the former which depends, we suppose, rather sensitively on methods of organisation. Accordingly, we pay particular attention in Chapter 3 to changes in the organisation of the police and in the attitudes of public and police in England and Wales in the 1960s.

The wide range of theories that are discussed in Chapters 2 and 3 are pulled together into a formal model in Chapter 4. This model contains several equations as a result of the simultaneous causations which it embodies. Before turning to a discussion of the data, we must first ask whether it is possible to estimate such a model.

It is important, indeed crucial in a sense which will be made precise in Chapter 5, that the equations of the model should have features which distinguish them one from another—this is the "identification problem". This means that we must argue, for example, that some variables which should be included as contributing to the explanation of the clear-up rate should not be included as explanations of the recorded offence rate; thus our discussion of the model in Chapters 4 and 5 will include an examination of what should be left out of an equation as well as what should be included. It takes confidence, of course, to argue that some variable has no direct effect whatsoever on the offence rate, although it does have a direct effect on the clear-up rate. Without such assumptions, however, estimation of our relationships is impossible and if one believes that one can learn something of the relationships under study from official statistics, then one must also believe that such assumptions are justified.

Appropriate statistical techniques for estimating simultaneous-equations models are probably unfamiliar to many readers; we offer, therefore, in Chapter 5, a brief review of such techniques. We then take the model developed in the previous chapters and discuss the problems for estimation and testing which it poses. A particular difficulty is that through theories of individual behaviour, the model deals with both the "actual"[2] level of offences (recorded plus unrecorded) and the recorded level of offences. We examine ways of coping with this problem and justify the approach which we choose. We also pay attention to the identification problem just mentioned.

We have described briefly the theories under examination and said that appropriate techniques for testing these theories are available; we now turn to our choice of data. Because many of the theories emphasize the importance of socio-demographic factors, we were constrained in our cross-section analysis to use data from census years. A time-series analysis would have required a sophisticated body of (dynamic) theory and a yet larger number of parameters than are contained in the model which we use (see Chapter 5). This effectively ruled out the possibility of a time-series approach. The highest number of observations for such an analysis would have been for annual data since the Second World War. This would yield too few observations for such an exercise, even if the difficulties in specifying the more sophisticated theory could have been overcome.

We selected, therefore, cross-section data on police districts. In principle it would have been possible to use cross-section data from any of the census years since the publication of criminal statistics began, but we restricted ourselves to the analysis of the data for 1961, 1966, 1971. Our resources were limited and so we decided to select the three most recent census years to make our study as relevant as possible to current discussions. Moreover, this was a time of special concern with crime. The "crime wave" became a major topic of public discussion in the sixties and the debate between sociologists of deviance and other criminologists got under way. An added attraction of this period from our point of view, was that it contained an extensive reorganization of the police force, thus allowing the possibility of asking interesting questions connected with the role of official agencies in recorded statistics.

Our results are presented in Chapter 6. The arguments advanced in earlier chapters concerning the importance of police and public attitudes and police practice, for the official statistics, give strong reason to suppose that urban and rural areas differ significantly in the process of the generation of criminal statistics, and that there are significant differences between the years of our sample. We provide formal tests (developed in Chapter 5) for these differences and conclude that the differences are indeed strongly significant. A number of other hypotheses are tested, for example concerning

---

[2] There are severe problems with this notion; these are discussed in Chapter 3. We shall see in that chapter and at several points in the book that such problems present no obstacle to our statistical analysis.

the role of unemployment in the model, and we present results using different estimation techniques. The number of data sets and hypotheses under examination, together with the different techniques we use (properties and advantages vary across techniques—see Chapter 5) dictate a considerable quantity of estimates. But this is inevitable if one is to provide a careful analysis of a complex system for several different sets of data.

Such a set of results does not speak for itself and the task of Chapter 7 is the interpretation of our estimated coefficients variable by variable. We examine both the levels of coefficients for each data set and the way in which they vary across years and between urban and rural areas. We have already remarked that we expect to see differences across data sets and indeed we find that for only a few of the variables are the coefficients similar. The interpretation of these differences, in the light of the theories and the changing situation in England and Wales in the 1960s described in Chapters 2 and 3, provides the main focus and, we think, interest of this chapter.

We discuss also in Chapter 7 the possible role of our estimated coefficients in policy. It would appear that a model such as ours, which provides estimates of the parameters of the functions behind offence rates and clear-up rates, would have an immediate application in policy formation. There are important problems, however. Many of the effects captured in our offence function operate through the recording process rather than on illegal activity. And we shall see that our estimates of the determination of the clear-up rate indicate that it may be rather difficult to control. Whilst we think our results have interesting implications for both theory and discussions of policy, the coefficients themselves have no direct application to policy formation.

The third section of this work elaborates the lessons of the empirical analysis for theoretical development, policy and research. In Chapter 8 we examine the role of official statistics in public discussion and policy making. The argument of the sociologists of deviance about the process by which official statistics are produced, seems from our results to have considerable force and suggests caution in the use of such statistics.

The arguments and observations throughout the book on the recording problem are then integrated into a systematic description of the process by which criminal statistics are generated. We go on to examine, using examples from published analysis of recorded offences, the implications of recording for the use of official criminal statistics in policy discussions. In particular we discuss the possibility that the rapid rise in recorded crime rates in the 1960s, the so-called "crime wave", may be as much an artefact as real.

Chapter 9 is more explicitly theoretical and philosophical. We do find in our empirical analysis that the probability and level of punishment have significant effects on recorded offences in the direction described by deterrence theories. Recent discussion and recommendations of policy towards crime by some Chicago economists (see, for example Becker (1968)) has placed the deterrence function at the centre of the stage. If one knows this function, the cost of crime and the cost of achieving a given clear-up rate, then, they argue, the optimum policy is to manipulate the level of offences through expenditure on police, the clear-up rate and thus deterrence to minimise social cost. But the simple cost-benefit approach to crime and punishment they present has serious logical flaws. We shall establish this claim in Chapter 9 and go on to argue that the cost-benefit approach cannot be saved by tinkering with the model, in the sense that it can be used to explain neither punishment levels as they now stand, nor punishment levels that would be generally regarded as acceptable. The reason is that the approach leaves out any notion of the just punishment. Thus, as we fear the misuse of criminal statistics as described in Chapter 8, we fear also the application of erroneous and misguided theory.

In Chapter 10 we summarize the conclusions from our analysis. We stress the importance of the problems of simultaneous causation in the study of crime and that the official statistics cannot be understood without discussing the process of recording. Further, we claimed earlier that studies such as ours, using aggregate data, can suggest possibilities for further research using data at the level of the individual. We believe that there are several fascinating possibilities which arise from our results; some are set out in Chapter 10 and we hope that these may be explored by some of our readers.

But whether or not our work generates new research we hope that we shall have done something to stimulate the use of appropriate techniques in sociological and criminological research, to demonstrate the complexities involved in the analysis of deterrence, to promote caution in the use of criminal statistics, to counteract the crass application of misguided economic "solutions" to the problem of policy towards crime and punishment and finally, to help the understanding of the processes of the social production of criminal statistics.

2

The Factors Influencing the Level of Criminal Activity

2.0 INTRODUCTION

Theories of the determinants of criminal activity and deviance range from those in terms of congenital defects in the individual to Marxist explanations of crime as a product of a capitalist society. It is often argued against the former that criminal activity is not particularly abnormal, and against the latter that it suggests that deviance can be totally eliminated. Our question, which is relevant to the whole range of possible theories, is, however, somewhat different. It is whether they can, in a given society, be used to account for variations in the level of criminal activity.

The task of even describing the level of criminal activity, however, raises two problems. The first is that many types of offence are seen by most parties—offenders, victims and the state—as relatively trivial and are not the object of criminological theorising. Indeed, the distinction between minor and serious offences has been a part of English law for a long time, since the gravest of offenders could be tried only at Assizes and lesser offences could be dealt with by Magistrates' Courts. We have decided to restrict our attention to indictable offences: that is, those where the accused has the right to demand trial by jury.[1]

We describe briefly the broad distribution of offence types here. We must bear this distribution in mind both when we are considering the relevance or otherwise of certain theories to our study and in the discussion of the

[1] This right has been accorded because both the nature of the accusation and the possible consequences to the accused are considered sufficiently serious to warrant extra care being taken over the determination of the guilt or innocence of the accused. For details of precisely which offence types are included and their relative numerical importance, see the appendix to Chapter 4.

estimates later in the book. The preponderance of minor thefts is well illustrated by the following figures for 1966 taken from Table A of the Home Office publication, *Criminal Statistics, England and Wales, 1966*. Of the 1,199,859 indictable offences known to the police for 1966, 848,600 (or 70·7%) were Class III, "offences against property without violence"; of this 848,600, 775,990 (or 64·7% of the total of indictable offences) were larcenies, 50,934 (or 4·2%) were frauds and false pretences, and 21,676 (or 1·7%) were receiving. In addition, there were 83,615 (or 7·0% of the total of indictable offences) offences of house-breaking and 119,146 (or 9·9%) offences of shop-breaking in a total of 280,852 (or 23·4%) Class II offences, "offences against property with violence". Of the remaining 70,407 (or 5·9% of the total of indictable offences), 21,308 (or 1·7%) were sexual offences and 26,716 (or 2·2%) were offences of violence against the person. The figures refer, of course, to those offences which are recorded. We doubt whether, *on average*, (see § 3.5) the unrecorded offences are more severe. The footnote to Table A reads:

> In the 212,588 offences of Sacrilege, Burglary, Housebreaking and Shop-breaking a sub-sample of Class II, the value of the property is reported to have been: (i) Nil in 2,996 cases; (ii) under £1 in 21,439 cases; (iii) £1 and under £5 in 41,605 cases; (iv) £5 and under £10 in 28, 051 cases; (v) £10 and under £100 in 86,836 cases; and (vi) £100 and over in 32,201 cases. In the 691,594 Larceny offences shown against the Heads numbered 38-43 and 45-47 and 49 a sub-sample of Class III, the value of the property stolen is reported to have been; (i) Nil in 9,776 cases; (ii) under £1 in 132,510 cases; (iii) £1 and under £5 in 180,106 cases; (iv) £5 and under £10 in 110,722 cases; (v) £10 and under £100 in 231,805 cases; and (vi) £100 and over in 26,675 cases.

Clearly the typical (recorded) offence in England and Wales during this period was a theft and the amount (reported) stolen was, on the average, comparatively small.[2]

We thus have a sharp distinction between the offences of our sample and those used in most other recent econometric work on criminal statistics (see, for example, Ehrlich (1973), or Phillips, Votey and Maxwell (1972)). For the data in these studies are usually from the U.S.A. and involve some sub-sets of felonies and in the case of crimes against property this classification is restricted to property values above $100. This is roughly equivalent to excluding all thefts involving property below £36 (at the then, 1966, official exchange rate). Over half the property offences referred to above would be excluded by applying this cut-off. The consequences of this distinction for the kind of model we develop are considered in detail in § 2.2.5.[2]

---

[2] The implications of this for explanations of offending activity which include economic theories of choice and the particular role which unemployment is supposed to play, are examined in more detail in the appendix to this chapter.

The second problem is that it is known that there are a considerable number of incidents that are not reported, but which, if they were reported, would be recorded as unlawful. We call the total number of such incidents and recorded offences *the level of actual offences.*[3] We take it that most theories of the level of criminal activity refer to actual offences. This problem would not be very serious if we could assume that recorded offences accurately reflected the level of actual offences—for example, if they were proportional to each other. It seems plausible to argue that illegal property transactions, which constitute the majority of recorded offences, also constitute the majority of actual ones, but it is difficult to be any more precise about the composition of actual offences; similar difficulties apply to the total volume. Thus 896,424 indictable offences were recorded in 1961, 1,199,859 in 1966 and 1,646,081 in 1971; hence recorded offences nearly doubled in ten years. However, commentators disagree sharply over the extent of the increase in actual offending, if any. It certainly cannot be taken for granted that actual and recorded offences are directly proportional to each other. This problem of recording means that we have to be careful about the evidence advanced in support of theories (see § 2.1.1). The process of recording and the complexities it introduces form the major topic of the next chapter. For the remainder of this chapter, unless otherwise stated, we shall be discussing theories of the determination of actual, rather than recorded, offences.

We discuss in § 2.1 some methodological preliminaries: the problem of recording indicated above; some particular features associated with a macro-study such as ours; and the range of theories which we consider. The factors determining offences which follow from the "economic" or punishment and reward theories are discussed in § 2.2. Theories which have traditionally[4] been the focus of much attention in criminology, namely culture conflict, anomie, and family background, are examined in § 2.3. § 2.4 contains some concluding remarks.

We want to emphasize that the two types of theory discussed here can be seen as complementary rather than conflicting. The economic approach isolates the importance of the probabilities and magnitude of reward and punishment, and shows how they can be treated formally (see our account in the appendix to this chapter). The criminological approach takes these for granted and indicates how different groups might view and react to these probabilities, rewards, and punishments. Our model, the con-

---

[3] We suppose, for the sake of this argument, that incidents which are reported to the police and regarded as unlawful are recorded.

[4] For convenience we have grouped the theories discussed in § 2.3 under the heading "traditional criminology".

struction, testing, and interpretation of which is the main purpose of this work, will include both approaches and some others. We postpone both the presentation of these in the form of a model and a discussion of our precise choice of measures until Chapter 4 (until after we have discussed the other parts of the system), since both of these are best tackled in the context of the complete model.

Apart from the constraints imposed on our analysis by two problems described, we make one further restriction—to consider cross-sectional variations only. Our reasons for rejecting a time series analysis were mentioned in Chapter 1 and are discussed further in Chapter 5. For a cross-section analysis observations on a wide range of socio-economic variables are readily available only in census years. The basic unit of police data (both on the police and on crime) is, of course, the police district—to which census data can be matched—and, at least before the amalgamations of these districts in 1968, they provide a substantial sample (there were over 100 in 1961 and 1966). Constraints on the resources available to us meant that we had to limit the number of years for which we examined the cross-sections. We decided to select the three most recent census years, 1961, 1966 and 1971. Our basic unit of observation is the police district and our data on offences, the official recorded statistics.

The justification for macro-studies of this kind and their relation to micro-studies has been discussed in Chapter 1, and further comments are contained in Chapter 10. The implications of the use of macro-data for our consideration of the theories are examined in § 2.1.1 and § 2.1.2. The data themselves are examined in more detail in Chapter 4. The process of recording is examined more closely in Chapter 3. We emphasize again that in this chapter we are concerned with theories of the determination of the level of criminal activity which refer to the generation of *actual* offences. Given our data set, we are concerned to derive factors from these theories to account for the cross-sectional pattern in offending behaviour.

Our purpose in discussing the theories is to demonstrate that they have sufficient *a priori* plausibility to warrant testing, to examine any conceptual problems that arise, and to discuss previous empirical work. As well as identifying the theories to be incorporated in the model, this is important background to the selection of measures of variables and also provides the context of previous research in which our results can be interpreted. In this way this chapter contains a brief survey of theories of crime and their previous investigation, insofar as the theories refer to the determination of the cross-sectional pattern of criminal activity. We do not pretend to be exhaustive but merely to say enough to achieve the purpose just described.

2.1 SOME METHODOLOGICAL PRELIMINARIES

2.1.0 *The Problem of Recording*

The evidence from self-report studies, where individuals are asked whether or not they have committed any offences, and from victimisation studies, where individuals are asked whether or not they have been victims of an offence, show large differences between recorded and actual offences in both composition and volume. For example, Erickson and Empey (1963) found in the U.S.A. that a sample of 180 boys admitted to 122,471 offences, of which 2,596 were detected by the police. Ennis (1967), also for the U.S.A., found that only one-third of house-breaking offences reported by victims to interviewers had been reported to the police, and so on (for further discussion see § 3.4).

There are several methodological problems with both types of survey which, apart from sampling difficulties, boil down to questions of validity and reliability. These are whether the incident which the respondent reports (whether as perpetrator or as victim) was actually a crime, and how reliable the respondent is in remembering what happened. Several reviews now exist of both types of study (for example, Chapters 1 and 2 of Hood and Sparks (1970) and OECD (1976)), but the remark by Christie (1968), although referring only to self-report studies, still provides a good summary of the state of the art. As he concluded:

> This all leads us to the point where it has to be admitted that our present studies on self-reported crime have the same principal weakness as the official crime statistics. We have exchanged the official system of registration for some social scientist's system of registration" (*op. cit.*, p. 6).

Similarly in the field of victim surveys, although an interviewer asks directly about criminal activity rather than waiting for it to be reported, there is no reason to suppose that the respondent will tell all, and the interviewer, like a policeman, exercises discretion in recording—although the criteria applied would be different (see Biderman (1967)).

It is clear both that the resources involved in attempting to collect large samples of "actual" offences (on the supposition that an appropriate population of actual offences can be defined, see the discussion in the latter half of Chapter 3) for several years or over a wide cross-section of areas would be enormous, and that the recording problem would not be over-come, but merely altered. Furthermore, we shall argue, there is substantial interest and importance in trying to understand the process by which actual offences or incidents become recorded as offences in the official criminal statistics. We have, therefore, restricted our data on offences to those known to the police. The link between these data and any notion of actual offences is one of the main topics of this book and is discussed in detail in Chapter 3.

In discussing the empirical foundation of theories of the level of illegal activity or actual offences, we shall be concerned with arguments and evidence used by previous researchers based on the empirical investigation of identified delinquents or of recorded offences. By this we do not mean to imply that most criminologists would not admit the existence of unrecorded crime. Indeed, the majority of criminologists would probably accept a weak version of the arguments in Chapter 3 (§ 3.4). But to the extent that they believe that studies of recorded offences or caught offenders are a valid test of their own theories, then they suppose that the factors which intervene between actual and recorded offences (and also between those who commit offences and those who are caught offending) do not make sufficient difference to invalidate their tests. In many cases this seems unlikely and we shall, therefore, be paying special attention to the appropriateness of the evidence in this respect in our discussion in § 2.2 and § 2.3 of this chapter.

2.1.1 *The Macro Nature of Our Study*

(a) Population to Offences. We shall be testing a particular class of criminological theories—those which claim that "crime is more likely when X obtains", and not those which claim that "criminals differ from others in certain respects". Because of supposed methodological difficulties (for example, the ecological fallacy discussed in Chapter 5), the latter type of research, which moves from observations about present identified offenders to inferences about the potential populations of offenders, is more usual in criminology. The former type of research, moving from theoretical statements about the population to predictions about the level of offences, is, of course, a natural way of testing causal theories of the generation of criminal activity.

The difference is worth emphasizing because the two types of research, apart from requiring different kinds of data, are also likely to lead to different results and, at a further remove, different implications for policy. Say, for example, one finds that youth are in the majority among convicted offenders. If one then concludes that the young are particularly prone to offending, one might go on to search for factors which motivate the young to behave in this way. If it was believed that such factors had been isolated, certain policy conclusions might follow rather naturally. Yet there may well be good reasons why youth are more often convicted, regardless of their offending behaviour. Of course, sociologists often make this very point (see our discussion in § 3.4); its implications for the analysis of crime statistics are, however, rarely discussed.

We are not, thereby, denigrating studies which start from observations about identified offenders. Indeed, the majority of our discussion in this and the next chapter depends on such studies. We are, however, arguing that analysis of the kind we attempt here is a necessary complement to the more detailed studies of identified offenders.

(b) Aggregate Statistics and Particular Theories. We are operating on a more aggregate scale as regards offences and populations than is usual in criminological research. For our purposes, a theory can only be a candidate for accounting for the variations in the observed patterns of crime (and thus inclusion in our model), if it specifies the way in which a social phenomenon can influence the observed pattern of offending across different areas. Thus, although theories which are based on mental abnormalities might be instructive, by themselves they tell us nothing about the ways in which patterns of offending would be determined. As it happens, protagonists of such theories usually confine themselves to special classes of offences (or groups of offenders) which are in quantitative terms insignificant when compared to 1 or 1½ million indictable offences. The same is true of theories based on, for example, birth order or physical deformities, so that, even though some theorists do refer to certain background factors as predisposing people to delinquency, these theories will not be considered in any detail.

Several theories of delinquency make use of the notion of maladjustment. This is often based on psycho-analytic concepts, and divides into an explanation of the delinquent act itself and an explanation of its genesis in terms of the delinquent's defects of character. Inasmuch as the story goes no further than this, the theories are not at issue here, but often the inference is made that families of delinquents and non-delinquents differ in such a way that delinquency should be associated with broken homes, deprivation of parental care, and so forth. We shall therefore be discussing factors of this kind (see § 2.3).

(c) Ceteris Paribus *and Interactions.* Our arguments for the inclusion and interpretation of any factor will be *ceteris paribus* arguments. This is necessary, since we shall be considering a number of different factors. Thus, when we say that one factor (A) should affect another (Y) *ceteris paribus*, we are saying that we are looking for the effects of a change in A on Y, when all the other factors are held constant.

The problem of *interactive effects* arises when the effect of one factor (A) on (Y) depends on the actual value of another factor (B). It is not easy (though not impossible either) to allow for the analysis of interactions within the simultaneous-equation techniques we have used (for more detail see § 5.6). We think, however, that it would be extremely difficult to specify hypotheses about the form of interactive effects on the basis of the theories. The problems of selecting single variables to be included on the basis of the theories is already difficult enough. We have therefore not attempted to allow for any interactions.

2.1.2 *Omissions*

There might appear to be two serious omissions from the following review. There is no discussion of the differential association or ethical learning groups of theories, both of which purport to explain how individuals learn to act criminally.

The first type of theory, attributable to Sutherland and Cressey (1966), pp. 77-80, claims that "A person becomes delinquent because of an excess of definitions favourable to violations of law over definitions unfavourable to violation of law" (*op. cit.*, p. 78), and that the important factors in the process are the frequency, duration, priority and intensity of a person's associations. The definitions thus learnt include:

(a) techniques of committing the crime, which are sometimes very complicated, sometimes very simple; and
(b) the specific direction of motives, drives, rationalisations, and attitudes.

Furthermore, Sutherland and Cressey (1966) claim that the theory should explain crime rates.

The second associated with Eysenck (1957) and Trasler (1962) concentrates on cognitive processes involved in learning to be a criminal. Trasler (1962, Chapter III) sets out the theory formally as follows:

I   The acquisition of values and attitudes of respect for the property and persons of others is mediated to a considerable extent by conditioning reactions of an autonomic kind (anxiety);
II   The anxiety reaction so conditioned acts as a learned drive, having the effect of inhibiting or motivating certain kinds of behaviour.
III Extroverts are resistent to conditioning; introverts are readily conditioned (all from p. 63).

He goes on to argue that "the two important variables in the socialisation of the individual are his responsiveness to conditioning and the efficiency of the methods which are employed to train him" (p. 85).

Both of these theories, although important and possibly the most broadly accepted theories that have emerged in criminology, do not, *by themselves*, account for the observed differences between police districts in the level of offending. For each theory is used more as a vehicle for organising certain observations rather than to account for patterns of offending, so that little attention is paid to collecting evidence or even measuring the crucial variables. Thus, in the case of Sutherland's differential association theory, the crucial variable for distinguishing between population groups turns out to be the measurement of the intensity of one's associations:

> 'Intensity' is not precisely defined but it has to do with such things as the prestige of the source of a criminal or anti-criminal pattern and with emotional reactions related to the associations (*op. cit.*, p. 78).

Similarly, in the case of the ethical learning theory, although the factors are specified very precisely, they distinguish only between individuals rather than between groups. However, the crucial variable is the quality of upbringing. It is true that Trasler ((1962), Chapter IV) and Eysenck ((1964) Chapter 5) do adduce some evidence about the social context of learning and conclude that "a higher proportion of individuals reared in Class V families will become criminal than [others]" (p. 82). But equally Trasler (1962) uses the observed distribution of (recorded) criminality to make predictions about the quality of upbringing. In any event, authors see this quality as being important from many different standpoints, so that we shall discuss possible factors and variables which might indicate its areal variations.

2.2 THE INCENTIVES TO OFFEND

2.2.0 *"Rational" Behaviour and Economic Hypothesis*

The earliest theories of criminal behaviour supposed that individuals made choices about how to act which depended on the likely consequences of their acts as perceived by them, and on the alternative opportunities that were available. Thus, Beccaria (1769) and Bentham (1948) both argued that the best way of controlling crime was a judicious application of the pleasure-and-pain principle, on the assumption that individuals maximised their own pleasure or happiness within the options available to them. A special feature of their arguments was that they assumed that all individuals reacted in the same way to possible consequences and opportunities. They deduced from this that there should be a rigid penal code: thus Beccaria (1769), (Chapter IV, pp. 14-16) wrote:

> There is nothing more dangerous than the common axiom: *the spirit of the laws to be considered* . . . we see the same crime punished in a different manner at different times in the same tribunals.[5]

[5]Moreover, it was essential that the consequences were understood by everyone in order that they would decide rationally. This partly accounts for their advocacy of public justice.

It was this inflexibility which turned the attention of criminologists away from the treatment of the offender as "rational economic man" (Vold (1958)) and toward treatment of individual peculiarities. For the moment, however, we shall discuss the revival of interest in the deterrence argument by certain economists. The theories of traditional criminologists are considered in the next section.

Some economists have argued recently that crime is just like any other activity and have applied the standard economic theory of choice under uncertainty. The potential offender evaluates all possibilities within the limits of the information that he possesses and chooses that activity which maximises his expected utility, that is to say the sum of the utilities in the various possible outcomes weighted by the probability of those outcomes. The basic argument (elaborated in the appendix to this chapter) in a utility-maximisation approach is that an individual decision-maker explicitly or implicitly considers all benefits and costs—whether monetary or non-monetary—which he expects to result from any decision which he takes about action. As Becker (1968) has written:

> Some persons become 'criminals', therefore, not because their basic motivation differs from that of other persons, but because their benefits and costs differ (p. 176).

Decision-makers are, in this sense, meant to act rationally—that is, to choose that action which maximises their expected utility—within those limits set by their own perceptual and information-processing apparatus and according to their particular circumstances and history. In the model a potential offender behaves as if he has a view about, and is responsive to, both the probabilities of detection and the possible punishments as well as the range of opportunities available to him for both illegal and legal activities. It is these perceptions which determine his behaviour and which need to be modelled and measured if the economic approach to deterrence is to be tested.

2.2.1 *The Concept of Deterrence*

There has been considerable discussion in the criminological literature over exactly what is meant by deterrence. It is usual to distinguish between "specific" and "general" deterrence where the former refers to the extent to which individuals upon whom a penal sanction has been imposed are discouraged by the experience, and the latter the extent to which people in general (including potential offenders) are discouraged by the imposition of penalities. Although in most cases the effects work in the same direction, it is possible that the imposition of a penal sanction may increase the chances of the person offending again whilst at the same time deterring others.

In this study, we are primarily concerned with "general" deterrence. Gibbs (1972) argues that the general deterrent effect is notoriously difficult to demonstrate mostly because the phenomenon of deterrence itself (as distinct from its causes or effects) is inherently unobservable. We shall be discussing Gibbs' contribution at length at the end of this section; here we take as a typical definition that given by Bedau (1970):

> . . . a given punishment P deters a given population H from a crime C to the degree D that the members of H do not commit C because they believe that they run the risk of P if they commit C and, *ceteris paribus*, they prefer not to suffer P for committing C (p. 541).

Depending on the exact meaning of "believe" this definition is quite close to that employed in the utility-maximisation model.

Despite the intuitive plausibility of "the deterrence doctrine", (Gibbs (1975) p. 5), several authors in the past have doubted whether there is such an effect. Thus Barnes and Teeters (1959) say:

> The claim for deterrence is belied by both history and logic. History shows that severe punishments have never reduced criminality to any marked degree (p. 286).

In fact, for a long period since the war, Andenaes (1974) was one of the few to argue consistently that punishment and the threat of punishment deter. He relies on obvious examples such as the Scandinavian experience with drunken driving, where drivers with more than 0.05% of alcohol in their blood are sentenced to short terms of imprisonment. He says:

> A person moving between Norway and the United States can hardly avoid noticing the radical differences in attitudes towards automobile driving and alcohol. There is no reason to doubt that the difference in legal provisions plays a substantial role in this difference in attitudes (p. 60).

Zimring and Hawkins (1968) emphasize the importance of considering the varying reactions of different groups in the population. They argue that deterrence is probably irrelevant to the substantial majority of the population because most individuals have (and here they quote from Toby (1964) p. 333) ". . . introjected the moral norms of their society [and] cannot commit crime because their self-concepts will not permit them to do so" (*op. cit.*, p. 101). One could translate this into the terms of the economic hypothesis by saying that, for most people, the subjective cost of illegal activity is very high, although of course direct measurement of such subjective cost would be difficult. They argue that, if one is considering the level of a particular criminal activity, one should consider deterrence policies for the marginal group, that is the group which is next most likely to offend. If such a group can be identified, then deterrence policies should be adjusted to the characteristics of members of the group.

They go further and claim that:

> The predication of the existence of criminal and marginal groups significantly different from the general population suggests as a corollary that normal patterns of responses to threats should not necessarily be anticipated from such groups (*op. cit.*, p. 108).

We assume this means either that such individuals do not behave as if they calculate their potential benefits and costs, or that their perceived benefits and costs are different. The first interpretation would run counter to the economic hypothesis, but their choice of examples to illustrate their argument suggests the latter. And in their recent book (1973) they quite clearly see the threat of punishment and the levels of penalties as affecting the behaviour of potential offenders.

Zimring and Hawkins (1968) also emphasize the importance of identifying the nature of the deterrent. Thus, they discuss the Chambliss (1966) study of the effect of a change in parking regulations at a mid-western university which had increased the fine for second and third parking offences and provided, for the first time, that:

> . . . if a faculty member failed to pay his fine, his right to park on campus would be automatically revoked, and if he parked on campus his car would be towed away at his own expense (*op. cit.*, pp. 111-12).

Chambliss (1966) himself concluded that "an increase in the severity and certainty of punishment does act as a deterrent to further violation." (p. 70). But Zimring and Hawkins (1968) argue that his data better support the inference that "the change in behaviour of the frequent offender group [is] attributable to the removal of what we have called 'information and attention deficiencies' and to increases in credibility of the threat rather than to the upward shift in the punishment level". Whether they or Chambliss are correct, both can be fitted within the framework of the economic approach.[6] The difference is that, with Zimring and Hawkins' interpretation, we have to consider the extent to which people *believe* that they are likely to be caught, and the perceived severity of possible

[6]Unless if, by "information and attention deficiencies", Zimring and Hawkins (1968) mean that, once someone really knows that a particular activity is illegal, he refrains without considering the consequences. However (im)plausible in principle, this is irrelevant in our study when the bulk of offences are larcenous; most people know that theft is an offence.

punishment, rather than the level and likelihood of punishment themselves. But Zimring and Hawkins are making a further, and we believe important point: the subjective cost of offending is increased by public concentration on, and condemnation of, particular behaviour.

Previous discussions of deterrence theories have, therefore, been in terms of the following factors: the likelihood and perceived likelihood of punishment; and the level and perceived severity of punishment. We shall argue that for both the likelihood and severity of punishment, the perceptions are crucial and these are the subject of the next two sections. We shall, however, be discussing the relationship between the perceived and objective variable in each pair in the next two sub-sections.

Before we do this, however, we should comment on the nine properties of legal punishment which Gibbs (1975) argues "are possibly relevant in contemplating a deterrence theory" (p. 144). Apart from the four above, these are the knowledge, level and severity of prescribed punishments, and the objective and perceived celerity of punishment. The first three relate to the punishments as fixed by statute, and so are only of interest indirectly insofar as they affect the severity of punishment as perceived by the potential offender. In jurisdictions like some States of the U.S.A. where there are many mandatory or minimum penalties, the actual punishment is likely to be quite close to these fixed penalties which may therefore affect perceived penalties. But, in England and Wales, the only fixed penalties are for murder (which is rare) and for some driving offences (which are numerous but mostly excluded from the category of indictable offences), and there are no minima, whilst the usual range of penalties is considerably below the statutory maximum. The last two relate to the delay between offending and eventual punishment which is not explicitly included in the economic approach. However, the delays are unlikely to vary much between police districts and, in any case, no data for individual police districts was available. We have not, therefore, considered these other five properties.

2.2.2 *The Likelihood and Perceived Likelihood of Detection*

Any empirical examination of the deterrent effects of different likelihoods of detection is complicated by the fact that not all offences are recorded. Indeed, it is likely that the most effective way to avoid detection is to ensure that the incident is not recorded as an offence in the first place. It is difficult to see how to obtain evidence about the actual likelihood of detection, since that supposes we know the number of actual offences. Therefore, apart from very specific categories of offence, the only possible source is self-report or victim surveys of the population. Both have their problems (see § 2.1 and § 3.4), but both clearly suggest that the actual probability of detection for most of the offence types considered here is very low.

The relevant variable for our analysis is, however, the perceived likelihood of detection and some of the self-report studies have examined this issue. We discuss briefly two such surveys which have been conducted in England and Wales. The first of these studies investigates the perceived probability of being caught, whereas the second study attempts to relate the perceived probability to the commission of offences.

Willcock (1974) reports the results of interviewing a representative sample of 808 youths aged 15-21 by showing them descriptions of 40 typical offences on cards. They admitted to a mean of 3.9 different types of offences per head by the age of 15, although some of these were admittedly quite trivial. They were then asked what they thought the chances were of "getting away with" nine different (fairly serious) offences. The response broken down by the offence score (number of different offence types to which they had admitted) is given below.

Table 2.1
Expected chances of "getting away with"
each of nine prompted offences by offence score

No. of offence types out of 9 for which expected chance of escaping detection is:		Offence-Score			
		0-3	4-5	6-8	Over 8
			Percentages		
75%	0-1	33	30	23	17
or	2	23	30	15	16
more	3-4	38	30	43	46
	5 or more	6	9	19	21
		(100)	(100)	(100)	(100)
25%	0	23	24	24	30
or	1	27	26	32	27
less	2	16	19	22	19
	3	16	14	10	15
	4 or more	17	17	11	9
		(100)	(100)	(100)	(100)
Population base		229	229	212	138

From: Willcock (1974), Table 34, p. 102.

In his summary of the results, Willcock (1974) says:

For five of the nine offences the *average* estimate of getting away with it favoured the offender, and only for 'starting a punch-up in a dance hall' was less than a 40% chance estimated. Moreover, for those offences which are similar to the ones described on the offence cards [used in the question on which types of offences they admitted committing], the 'average' tendency was to *underestimate* the actual chances of those who had committed the offence described not being taken to court (p. xxiii).[7]

And, commenting on the table, he says:

The proportions thinking there was a *very good chance* of getting away with none or only one of the nine offences declined progressively . . . with increasing personal offence-type score (*op. cit.*, p. xxiv).

He therefore concludes: ". . . young people in general are more inclined than those among them who have committed a given offence to over-estimate their chances of detection" (*ibid.*).

The second study by Belson (1975b) found that:

. . . all of the 1,425 London boys in the sample had admitted to at least some stealing and there was no class of theft behaviour amongst the 44 that was endorsed by less than 5% (p. xii).[8]

Belson also asked these boys whether or not they were likely to be caught by the police. The replies are given in the following table.

Table 2.2
Confidence about not getting caught by the police

	If I went in for stealing	If I kept on stealing
	Percentages	
Sure they would not catch me	5	2
Don't think they would	27	4
They might catch me	40	12
There is a good chance they would catch me	22	36
Sure they would catch me	6	46
	(100)	(100)

From: Belson (1975b), Table 3.1, p. 107.

Belson's hypothesis is that "Boys take up stealing or continue partly because they think they won't get caught by the police" (p. 140). He finds (*ibid.*) that:

[7] The actual chances were calculated from the experience of those in the sample who had committed the offence.

[8] "Endorsed" here means "ticked the appropriate box" and thus having admitted to the offence.

. . . boys who think they won't get caught by the police for stealing, do more stealing than other boys . . . [and] . . . tend to continue with relatively serious stealing over a longer period than other boys.

The conclusion from these studies, therefore, is that the perceived likelihood of being caught does seem to be an important variable in the determination of offences. While it may be related to the actual likelihood of being caught, its value seems to be very different.

The problem is that the possible determinants of the perceived probability of being caught, apart from the actual likelihood, are not easy to identify. We have seen that it seems to depend on the experience of the individual in committing offences. But what prompts the less experienced to rate the probability so highly (see Table 2.1 above)? One possibility is that because of their inexperience they may have little confidence in their own techniques. Whilst this explanation has some plausibility it is not wholly convincing, since the "techniques" involved in a minor theft are minimal. And it is not easy to model the way in which this lack of confidence might vary across areas.

An important, and measurable, determinant of the perceived probability is, we suggest, the conspicuousness of social control. Recorded crime has risen sharply when the police have been temporarily immobilised. A classic example is the 7½ month period towards the end of the German occupation of Denmark in the Second World War, when the Danish police went underground or were deported. The numbers of robberies and thefts increased enormously (see Christianssen (1975)), even though a "Community Guard" was organised, the prosecution authorities expanded their function, and the courts gave out stricter punishments.

A further example is given by Buikhuisen (1975). He reports on a study in Groningen where the police announced that they were going to check for worn tyres in the following week. Samples of cars were compared in Groningen and another town and it was found that 27% more had replaced their tyres in Groningen than in the other town. Of course, it is likely that the actual probability of being caught had changed in both these examples, but it is also likely that the behaviour and presence of the police had something to do with the changes in the offending observed.

A study which avoids the difficulty of simultaneous changes of the actual probability of capture is provided by Schwartz and Orleans (1961). They took a sample of 400 taxpayers in the Chicago area and randomly assigned them to four groups. One group received a threatening appeal, the second group a message appealing to conscientious motives for tax paying, the third group received a neutral message and the fourth no message at all. Data on the subsequent tax year showed that the first and second groups tended to pay more tax than the third and fourth.

We conclude then that the number, behaviour and conspicuousness of the forces of social control do play a role in determining the perceived probability of apprehension, which is in addition to any effect through the actual probability. We return to the problem of modelling this perceived probability in Chapter 5.

2.2.3 *The Severity of Punishment*

Most research on the deterrent effect of punishment has focused on the rates of recidivism amongst individuals who have already been subjected to a penal sanction. It has thus been concerned with the question of specific deterrence (see above, § 2.2.1). This is not the place for a full critical review of the many hundreds of studies involved (see, for example, Wilkins (1969)). Methodological defects, such as varied follow-up periods, and interpretative difficulties, such as the separation of deterrent effects from socialising effects (for example, "learning the trade" in prison), have always plagued these kinds of studies. For example, the review by Bailey (1966) of 100 such evaluative studies found that the more rigorous the research design, the higher the percentage reporting either "no change" or detrimental effects from the treatment.

Furthermore, a valid test of the specific deterrent effect of legal sanctions would involve comparing the offending behaviour of those already punished with those who have not been so punished.

The case of capital punishment for murder is of interest for two reasons. First there has been intensive discussion of the effect of different degrees of severity of punishment on offence rates and, secondly the argument runs in the same direction as for our study—from the population or policy variable to offences. We should not be surprised, however, that there is no unambiguous answer, for as N. D. Walker (1968) argues, anecdotal material suggests that capital punishment sometimes operates as a deterrent, sometimes as an incentive (for example, to martyrdom) and is sometimes irrelevant (see N. D. Walker (1968) for further discussion of the evidence).

A more interesting set of studies for our immediate purpose of establishing the *a priori* plausibility of the deterrence theorists is the survey research that has been conducted both here and in the U.S.A. of the extent to which, in a population sample, individuals are deterred by the possibility of different punishments. Willcock (1974), pp. 78-82, reports the results of asking his sample of 808 adolescent youths the specific question "Which of these things would worry you most about being found out by the police?". The results were as shown in Table 2.3. Even those offenders (in the sample of adolescents) who had committed a wide variety of offences marked the worries in roughly the same order.

Table 2.3
Ranking of deterrents to crime

	Mean rank	Percentage placing item first
1. What would the family think about it	2·38	49
2. The chances of losing my job	2·96	22
3. The publicity or shame of having to appear in court	3·88	12
4. The punishment I might get	4·40	10
5. What my girlfriend might think	4·72	6
6. Whether I should get fair treatment in court	6·07	2
7. What my mates would think	6·08	1
8. What might happen to me between being found out and appearing in court	6·20	2

From: Willcock (1974), Table 22, p. 79.

As Willcock says:

> To a marked extent court appearance *in itself* seems to be an important part of the penalty. We described a hypothetical case in which the informant had committed an offence for which the maximum penalty was a fine of £20, was sure he would be found guilty, but knew that he might get off with a very much smaller fine if he appeared in court . . . Half our informants said that if they had the choice they would prefer to pay the maximum fine and not have to appear in court ((1974), p. xxi).

Thus, from this point of view of the offender, there is probably a substantial fixed element in any punishment, associated with appearing in court *per se* irrespective of the level of punishment. We return to this point in Chapters 7 and 8, as well as the appendix to this chapter.

It does seem rather unlikely that the actual level of offences does not depend on the perceived severity of punishment. Indeed, at certain levels punishments are effectively seen as a cost of doing business (for example, illegal loads and road haulage, or libellous articles in newspapers), and so are normally taken into account in business calculations. We shall therefore include in our model a measure of the severity of punishment. In the light of the above discussion its role must operate through perceptions. We shall not, however, be using any variables to portray these perceptions other than our measure of severity itself (compare our treatment of the perceived probability of detection), for it is very hard to think of feasible and useful variables.

More recently there have been direct attempts to test whether or not there is a deterrent effect in respect of certain types of offences. There have been several statistical studies in the United States (see, for example, Ehrlich (1973)) following the article by Becker (1968). With varying levels of sophistication they have examined the interrelationships between the recorded crime rates and the probability and severity of punishment. Most of them have concluded that there is an (in some cases quite substantial) effect. Because our results will be directly comparable to the results of such studies, detailed discussion is deferred until Chapter 7.

Before we go on to examine other factors in the generation of offences, we should comment on the contribution of Gibbs (1975). He has argued at length that the problems with the formulation of deterrence theories and their empirical testing are so large that there should be "a moratorium on conventional research" (p. 2). In the course of his critique, he supplies a useful survey and bibliography of studies on deterrence and the reader who wishes to follow the literature further would find his book a good place to start. While agreeing that some of the problems he raises are real, we find his conclusion too rigid and pessimistic.

This is not the appropriate place to examine in detail the arguments which Gibbs makes at book-length, but we shall briefly consider his main objections. First, he argues that, whatever the individual does (commits or omits an illegal act) it is not evidence of deterrence since, "if the individual refrains, the omission could be attributed to (1) the dictates of personal conscience, (2) the individual's recognition of and respect for the social (extralegal) condemnation of the act, and/or (3) the fear of some extralegal consequences (e.g. stigma)" (p. 12). Thus he argues that statistical relations between properties of punishment (see above) and crime rates could simply reflect the dependence of both on the social condemnation of crime. We suggest that it is implausible that this consideration could account for an observed statistical relation to the exclusion of an argument in terms of precautionary reactions to changes in perceived punishment.

Secondly, he argues that there are nine possible ways in which punishment might prevent crime which do not involve notions of deterrence. These are: "incapacitation, surveillance, enculturation, reformation, normative validation, retribution, stigmatisation, normative insulation, and habituation" (pp. 92-3). Gibbs (in Chapter 3) shows how these are analytically distinct from a pure concept of deterrence—using this term to denote instances where someone refrains from a particular type of criminal activity because of the fear of punishment. This is much narrower than the definition we have employed which, put simply, says that a person acts according to the consequences he perceives. Within our definition most of the effects to which Gibbs draws attention are incorporated as determinants of the person's perceptions, either through the punishment of others or through his prior experience of punishment. The exceptions are incapacitation and, to a lesser extent, punitive surveillance where the individual is physically prevented from committing criminal acts. This situation does not fit easily within the framework of the economic approach because of the particular nature of the way in which the person's opportunities are restricted. However, for our study we do not think that the problem is as severe as for some others. Remember that we are dealing in the main with a very large number of recorded minor property offences (over 1½ million in 1971) and a prison population (in England and Wales) of around 40,000. It seems unlikely that the differences in the numbers of people from each district being imprisoned could be of sufficient magnitude to explain *directly*—that is simply because those imprisoned are prevented from offending—differences in offence rates. This is a matter of judgement, of course, and depends on our view that 1½ million recorded offences are sufficiently many to be viewed as every-day occurrences (even forgetting about the much greater number of "actual" offences) and attributable to a substantial offending population. It is worth noting, however, that the appropriate variables for these incapacitating effects would be the actual likelihood and severity of punishment rather than the perceived.

His third general criticism is that "virtually any finding in deterrence research is subject to all manner of interpretations" (p. 93). We tend to agree and shall be cautious about interpreting our findings. However, we would also argue that our research has been designed so as to avoid most of the criticisms he makes of other studies. Thus, we are careful to control for a wide range of what he calls extralegal generatory and inhibitive conditions (see § 2.3 below): moreover, we have explained why we have chosen the perceived likelihood and severity of punishment out of the many possible properties of punishment as the crucial variables in this study. The determination of the perceived likelihood of punishment is discussed in Chapter 4. An alternative interpretation of a relation between the offence rate and the severity of punishment is considered in Chapter 3. The magnitude of the effects that we find are presented in Chapter 6 and discussed in Chapter 7.

2.2.4 *Opportunity*

An economic approach to the theory of crime generation should take account of the range of opportunities or rewards open to an individual to act legally as well as the sanctions imposed and potential rewards for acting illegally. Although in principle, arguments about opportunities are applicable to all sorts of offence behaviour, the major emphasis in the literature in the case of crimes whose impact is mainly of an economic kind has been placed on alternative sources of income and wealth. Similar sorts of theories are used to argue that the provision of youth clubs and sports activities forestalls violence on the streets, or that the screen portrayal of violence is cathartic. However, since the majority of recorded offences are economic, we shall concentrate on the economic opportunities open to the individual. We begin with the illegal opportunities.

There seem to be clearly established relationships between the opportunities for, and the recorded rate of, economic offences. In an early study of British data, Burt (1944) examined seasonal variations in offending between 1900 and 1909 and observed marked peaks for violence against the person, suicide, and sexual crimes in the summer months (when more people were outside) and less marked peaks for property crimes in the winter months (under cover of darkness). He then correlated the rates with recorded temperature, daylight, sunshine, and rainfall for each month, and found that the first three factors were strongly correlated with such crimes but showed negligible correlations with forgery. Walker (1968) suggests: ". . . theft and housebreaking are facilitated by the long nights of winter . . . Forgery, on the other hand, is an all-weather pursuit" (p. 92). And at a more detailed level, Burt (1944) found that Sunday was notable for juvenile delinquency.

The same effect has been observed over longer time scales. Wilkins (1964) found that the number of thefts of unattended motor vehicles from 1938 to 1961 was very closely correlated with the number of motor vehicles registered. Similarly, offences related to horse-drawn vehicles dropped dramatically after the First World War and, we presume, the decrease in number of poachers is related to the availability of game.

It seems reasonable to suppose that the relative rarity of theft in rural areas is connected with opportunities. Thus, large supermarkets in towns present tempting targets, and indeed it is said that some stores evaluate the attractiveness of their counter displays (to shoppers) by the rate of "unexplained loss".

At a different level, there have been several studies of the relationships between economic growth, the business cycle and the rates of economic crimes. The results are usually interpreted in terms of intervening variables such as unemployment and poverty (which we consider below). One exception is McClintock and Avison (1968) who, after comparing the value of property reported to police as stolen in England and Wales in 1955 and 1965, say that "it is also important to ascertain to what extent these trends reflect a decline in the value of money over the decade" (p. 52). They adjust the average value of property stolen for each theft by the Retail Price Index and conclude that this adjusted value rose from £22.8 to £30.5 between 1955 and 1965. They estimate that the adjusted total value of property stolen rose from £7.2 million to £26.0 million. They conclude that the "increase in prices therefore only explains part of the very great increase in the value of property stolen" (*op. cit.*, p. 56).

They go on to say that the "real problem of an increase in criminality against property clearly exists . . . however, affluence itself may be producing a significant growth" (*ibid.*). Thus, changes in the value of real wealth or property may have been part of the story. It is impossible to judge the magnitude of the increase, however, without taking account of the recording phenomenon (which was ignored by McClintock and Avison (1968)). For example, the growth in insurance over the period could have led to an increased propensity to report thefts (for further discussion, see Chapter 8). But whatever are the deficiencies of their study, it does seem clear that offending increases with opportunity.

2.2.5 The "Alternatives" of Employment and Crime

The relationship between offence behaviour and the alternative legal opportunities is much less clear. In recent empirical work the rate of unemployment has been the most common variable used to capture the (lack of) alternative legal opportunities. There are, however, different interpretations of the role of unemployment in this context. One can view the occupations of a legal job and a life of crime as mutually exclusive, or alternatively see the two sources of income as different but non-exclusive, so that an individual can engage in both kinds of activity.

In recent U.S. literature, the individual is pictured as splitting his time between legal activities (often with certain pay-offs) and illegal activities (with uncertain pay-offs)—see, for example, Ehrlich (1973) or Block and Heineke (1975). And in much discussion of unemployment or labour force participation and crime one is encouraged to think of the legal-illegal choice as dichotomous—one opts either for a life of crime or a legal job (see Phillips, Votey and Maxwell (1972)).

We should suggest that these models of the allocation of time, or of the dichotomous choice (legal versus illegal activities) are not particularly helpful for the analysis of the types of offence discussed in this book. Minor thefts without violence to the person or forcible entry (and these are the majority of recorded offences) take very little time and are not inconsistent with a legal job. Indeed, casual empiricism suggests that a large number of offences are committed on the job, in particular the theft of company property. We presume that many such offences go unrecorded. Of course, a sufficiently large number of such offences or one sufficiently complicated offence would take enough time to rule out legal employment, but it is reasonable to suppose that a substantial proportion of property offences are committed by people with full-time legal jobs.

The interpretation of the role of unemployment in empirical work is obviously affected by whether we view employment and crime as mutually exclusive or not. If not, then an increase in unemployment could decrease offences since fear of unemployment would affect behaviour both at work and outside if dismissal was a consequence of conviction. On the other hand, if we view the choice as dichotomous, the rate of unemployment would be a consequence of, as well as a factor in, the decision to offend. These causation problems are discussed further in Chapter 5. Representative studies are discussed below.

The evidence from several studies about the work habits of caught offenders is clear. Whilst job changing and unemployment prior to being caught are good predictors of subsequent reconviction, a large proportion of those caught have a steady job. A typical study is that of Mannheim and Wilkins (1955) who examined the careers of 720 boys who were sentenced to Borstal training in 1946/7. Of these 720, only 46 had not retained any job for more than three months, whilst 274 had retained at least one job for more than one year (p. 100).

An American study which has followed the line of argument that unemployment leads to criminal activity because of poverty, is that by the criminologists Glaser and Rice (1959). They correlated age-specific arrest rates with unemployment rates in Boston, Chicago, Cincinnatti, and the U.S.A. as a whole between 1930 and 1956 for property offences, crimes against the person, and a miscellaneous group of misdemeanours.[9] In respect of all three types of offence they found high positive correlations for the age groups between 21 and 45, somewhat lower correlations for older age groups, and negative correlations for the 10 to 17 age group. Glaser and Rice (1959) suggest that one explanation of this latter finding is that unemployment keeps fathers at home which, in turn, keeps their teenage sons out of trouble. (The difficulties of incorporating such interaction effects—in this case between an age variable and unemployment—into our model are described in Chapter 5, § 5.6).

An old study by Dorothy Thomas (1925) of the relationship between crime and economic conditions showed clear correlations between various social statistics and fluctuations in the business cycle. She found that prosecutions for drunkenness increased with prosperity, whilst burglary and other forms of breaking and entering showed a strong tendency to increase in the lean years. Similar correlations are observed by Henry and Short (1954) between burglary and robbery and down-swings in the business cycle in samples of American cities during the periods from 1929 to 1941 and 1946 to 1949.

[9]See also the work of Fleisher (1966).

Some American authors have discussed the different career opportunities available in different areas in terms of criminal organisation. Cloward and Ohlin (1961) argued that there were opportunity structures available to a teenager in areas with an established criminal network which could offer a stable "employment". However, as emphasized above, the recent literature has focused on the importance of legal opportunities. Thus, Phillips, Votey and Maxwell (1972) found a strong relationship between the rising arrest rates of young males and lower rates of labour force participation (after allowing for the influence of some other variables), and advocate the creation of job opportunities as a method of combating higher crime rates.

The difference in the two views of the role of unemployment raises problems as to the best indicators to use in the relation modelling the determination of the offence rate. The approach which suggests that illegal activity is an (exclusive) alternative to a legal job would appear to require some index based on labour force participation,[10] probably by adult males. But where non-participation arises from the choice to lead a life of crime, participation rates are a result not a cause of decisions to offend (see Chapter 5 for further discussion).

The other approach would suggest that if unemployment is important it is because it indicates the lack of alternative sources of income and wealth so that some index of poverty is required. It is not, however, clear that the unemployment rate is the best indicator of poverty. Even if the unemployment is a good measure of the wealth of an area, it would be capturing (at least) two effects: more wealth producing more offending because of more opportunities, and less wealth producing more offending because there are more poor individuals motivated to offend. Furthermore, it is not obvious that the standard economic theory of choice under uncertainty would imply that the poor offend more. The case has to be argued carefully. This is something which is taken up in the appendix to this chapter. And there are additional problems of interaction: for example, the poor in rich areas may be particularly tempted to offend.

It is clear that there are many difficulties of both theory and measurement in introducing unemployment as a variable to explain the level of criminal activity. Some of these difficulties are taken up in the appendix to this chapter, and Chapters 4 and 5—and in Chapter 3 we discuss the relation between being unemployed and the recording of offences—but they should not be forgotten when we come to interpret the results.

---

[10]Labour force participation of a given age and sex group is the number holding or seeking a job divided by the size of the group. The unemployment rate is the number seeking divided by the number holding or seeking. Definitions of unemployment vary across countries, but it is usually the case, in principle anyway, that to be classified as unemployed you must be both out of work and looking for (legal) work.

2.2.6 *Income Distribution*

We have up to now in this chapter said nothing about the effect of the distribution of income on the propensity to offend. This issue has been largely ignored in the recent economic and econometric literature. Measures of the dispersion of incomes were not used in this study, since they are not available at the level of the police district. Statistics for the class structure and level of unemployment were, however, incorporated in our model (see Chapters 4 and 5). There is one interesting econometric study using U.S. data which does incorporate statistics on the dispersion of incomes— Danziger and Wheeler (1975). They use time series data for the U.S.A., 1949-1970, and cross-section data for U.S. cities in 1960. There are some problems with their estimation techniques—to give one example, they do not look at recording problems, see our Chapters 3, 4, 5—but there does seem to be a strong association between recorded offence rates and income inequality in their samples.

They remark (p. 125) that recorded offence rates in the U.S.A. rose through the 1960s when aggregate income was rising and declined in the 1930s when income was falling, in support of their argument that it is low relative incomes and not low average income which generate offences. The evidence is interesting but must be viewed with circumspection, since many changes other than those in incomes were happening during the periods in question (and, in particular, we should speculate on recording phenomena —Chapters 3, 4 and 5).

We do not offer here any theoretical development of the Danziger and Wheeler model. Indeed they do not really develop it themselves beyond the remark that inequality may imply crime. However, it is a statement which we find convincing and which should be elaborated. We turn now to some of the factors that have been the concern of more traditional criminology and sociology.

2.3 TRADITIONAL CRIMINOLOGY AND SOCIO-DEMOGRAPHIC FACTORS

2.3.0 *The General Theories*

The three main groups of explanations in criminology for how individuals come to have the dispositions they have (excluding theories of differential association and ethical learning), rest on anomie, culture conflict and the family. As explained in 2.1.5, the omission of theories of differential association and ethical learning from our work is partly borne out of necessity because of the lack of appropriate data on the patterns of an individual's association or upbringing respectively. But it is likely that if these theories were used to account for the variations in observed crime rates, the factors so identified would overlap with the factors that are suggested by some of the theories considered below. In particular the differential association theory overlaps with the hypotheses about criminal neighbourhoods (see § 2.3.3), and the ethical learning theory with hypotheses about the effects of family background.

The theory of anomie is based on the observations that modern societies differ from mediaeval ones in the extent to which an individual's status is ascribed or achieved. In mediaeval societies a person's status was determined within very narrow limits from birth; but in modern western societies there are few formal barriers to social mobility, and ideologies and mythologies emphasize the possibilities. Thus individuals are expected to try to "get ahead" and may well incur disapproval if they do not do so. Moreover, in modern societies as compared to older more stable ones, the change in a person's social situation may occur rapidly and this is likely to cause stress. Durkheim's theory of anomie (Durkheim (1966)) showed how rapid economic and social change would lead to certain level of deviance.[11] In so far as he specified particular groups or individuals in this argument, he suggested that those groups who were subject to the most violent change either in terms of a deterioration in their economic situation or in terms of their value patterns, were the most likely to deviate.

Therefore people whose social situation had suddenly deteriorated and for whom no social support was provided, would be in an anomic and deviance-prone situation. The obvious candidates, at least in economic terms, are those who suddenly become poor in a relatively affluent area through a change in family or personal circumstances. Since during the sixties the general economic situation was reasonably stable, the main source of sudden economic change for an individual was unemployment. Moreover, this was likely to vary systematically between areas so that the theory might suggest that individuals who became unemployed in an area with a relatively low unemployment rate would be prone to the anomic effects described by the theory.

Anomie theory lay dormant for several decades but was taken up again by Merton (1938). He took a different approach from Durkheim (1966) and concentrated on the responses of individuals in a static situation, whereas Durkheim (1966) emphasised more the dynamics of the process. Merton

---

[11]He went on to argue that this deviance might have a role to play in maintaining social order, partly because it provided an outlet for frustrations, but also because its characterisation could demonstrate the limits of (legally) acceptable activities and thus make the norms of society clear. Although this is perhaps the more interesting part of his argument, it is not germane to our study.

(1957) based his argument on the observation that societies differ in the relative emphasis which they place on the importance of individuals achieving the goals which are socially prescribed and on the importance of abiding by the institutionalised methods for attaining them. An individual can accept or reject the institutional means and the goals, and he can try to change them. Merton (1957), p. 140, labels the solution adopted by individuals as in the following table. He argues that the most frequent form of adjustment is "innovation" where the goals are accepted and striven for, but institutionalised means are discarded in favour of unorthodox ones. He sees this as a consequence of the high premium on economic affluence and social ascent in a situation where large groups of people lack the formal education and financial resources to attain these ends by institutionalised means. They therefore resort to innovation on a large scale: where material wealth is concerned, innovation eventually means fraud and theft.

Table 2.4
A typology of modes of individual adaptation

Modes of adaptation	Culture goals	Institutionalised means
Conformity	+	+
Innovation	+	—
Ritualism	—	+
Retreatism	—	—
Rebellion	±	±

Note
The acceptance (rejection) of culture goals or institutionalised means is signalled by +(—), and the rejection of prevailing values and the substitution of new ones is signified by ±. The behavioural outcome is denoted in the first column. Source: Merton (1957) p. 140.

The theory is supplemented by Cloward and Ohlin (1961) and later Spergel (1964) who argue that the choices of a given individual are determined partly by the opportunities that are available in the locality and partly by his or her psychological type. This version of anomie theory would suggest that groups that are disadvantaged in their access to institutionalised means would turn to illegal activity. One might therefore single out ethnic minorities, females, immigrants, lower social classes, and the poor as especially likely to turn to offending. Appropriate indicators will be discussed later.

The theory of culture conflict was developed from the suggestion that, when one group imposed its own code of conduct on another by force, there was likely to be a large increase in crime (Sellin (1938)). Even in societies which are fairly homogeneous in their ethical beliefs, there are obviously some individuals who are opposed to these beliefs. For us, of course, the main question is the identity of such groups if they do in fact exist. In a society whose belief system is dominated by males, whites, and the middle aged, the main candidates are females, blacks and immigrants and youth.

We argue below that the representation of blacks and immigrants in the population of different areas in our sample is not sufficiently large to be important for our study. Further, the variation in the proportion of each sex in the population of an area is too small to be useful in our analysis. Thus we shall consider only the position of youth. The main questions here for criminologists have been whether there is a tendency towards the formation of particular groups or sub-cultures among youth, the majority of whose members are opposed in this way, how the opposition arises and the gangs or groups form, and how these groups are maintained. A. K. Cohen (1955) argues that young working-class boys find themselves being judged by middle-class standards—especially at school—which they cannot meet; they therefore resort to reaction formation. They not only reject the dominant value system, they "stand it on its head" by exalting its opposition. As Cohen (1966) admits, the theory has been severely mauled by its critics. But the exploration of delinquent gangs or subcultures has continued and the best treatment in the context of England and Wales is probably that of Downes (1966). Here we simply note that young working-class males are assumed to be more delinquent than others in order for theorising to begin.

Most theorists who point to the influence of family background are working in terms of psycho-analytic or psychological concepts of maladjust-ment or psychopathy. We have explained why we have not included a review of these theories and also how the theory of ethical learning is insufficiently specified in terms of what precisely affects the efficiency of social training, for it to be used as a source of hypothetically important factors or variables between localities. Nevertheless, one can turn the theories around and argue that, if they were true, then the families of delinquents and non-delinquents would differ in certain, observable, respects. The conditions most often discussed are broken homes, parental care and birth order (see, for example, N. D. Walker (1968)). The first two are meant to be associated with the way in which the ego or super-ego develops, and the last with the special treatment accorded those children in special positions.

Of the three groups of theory, those of anomie and culture conflict over-lap considerably in terms of the social factors which are identified as providing the context for delinquency. The former suggests that the groups which are most likely to offend are those permanently or temporarily disadvantaged in their access to institutional means for attaining valued social goals, and such groups are ethnic minorities, females, immigrants, the poor, the unemployed, and the working class. The latter suggests that females, immigrants, particular neighbourhoods, the working class, and youths are most likely to offend. Indeed, in many important ways the theories provide mutual support for each other with the latter filling out the context of the former. The theories associated with the type of family background are clearly of a different kind from anomie or culture conflict. However, the factors selected because they differentiate areas in terms of the type of families in them may well be similar to, or even depend on, those named above. Therefore, we first present the arguments for incorporating variables relating to each of these different groups into our model and finally we look at the effect of family background.

2.3.1 *Ethnic Minorities and Immigrants*

It was the condition of immigrants in the United States which prompted Sellin (1938) to relate crime to cultural differences. He found that the crime rate was lower among first-generation immigrants than among the general population—possibly because of the fear of repatriation—but highest among their American born children. There are, however, very few types of offence whose genesis can plausibly be ascribed to an individual's membership of different national or racial groups, and the concentration in this study is on the overall level of offences. There is a stronger case for suggesting that such groupings are prone to innovatory behaviour because of their relative lack of access to institutionalised opportunities; indeed much of the literature in American criminology stresses the social position of the black minority as a causal factor in their relatively high representation in the crime statistics.[12]

In the British context, McClintock (1963) claimed that West Indians were heavily over-represented among violent offenders. However, his analysis is marred by his failure to standardize the rates of offending for either age or sex which is particularly serious, since he was talking about a young, male immigrant population. The phenomenon, real or otherwise, is however not of great importance for our purposes since most (more than 90%) of indictable offences do not involve violence against the person. Moreover, during the period of our study an ethnic minority constituted a substantial proportion of the population in only a few police districts, so that it seemed superfluous to include such a variable.

---

[12]See, for example, Curtis (1975) who discusses a survey finding that over two-thirds of violent offences recorded by the police involve both black offenders and victims.

2.3.2 *Females*

At first sight, females ought to offend more since they are denied access to institutionalised means and they are an oppressed cultural group. But there are very few women among the population of caught offenders. The anomie theorist could argue that they have less motivation to strive after the goals of material wealth (since that is their husband's role) and that in fact they have every interest to conform, whilst the culture conflict theorist could argue that the female is oppressed by the male rather than by property. More typical explanations are that women have different capacities and opportunities for offending and, more importantly their offences are less likely to be reported, recorded and prosecuted. But, regardless of the explanation, the variation between our areas in the proportion of women in the population is so low that it is unnecessary to include the sex ratio in our model.

2.3.3 *Neighbourhoods*

Numerous studies of particular areas have found that the residences of known adult or juvenile offenders tend to cluster in small areas. This observation was developed into a systematic theory of cultural transmission by the Chicago School in the first half of this century (see, for example, Shaw and McKay (1942)). Morris (1957) found a similar phenomenon in Croydon, Surrey. The explanation has usually been in terms of the relatively fluid social and cultural structures which can develop in interstitial areas, producing a classically anomic situation for the residents at the same time as a loosely knit subculture. Such neighbourhoods develop in highly industrialised or urbanised areas. The appropriate variable to capture such effects is discussed in Chapter 4, § 4.1.2.

2.3.4 *Poverty and Unemployment*

Poverty and unemployment are being discussed together not only because the poor and unemployed overlap to a considerable extent, but also because the same (often rather confused) arguments are relevant to both. Considerable research has been devoted to examining the relation between crime and poverty and unemployment, some of which has been discussed in § 2.2.5, where we considered the "purely economic" reasons which might prompt the unemployed to offend (see also the appendix to this chapter). Here we discuss the more sociological arguments and look at the evidence which links poverty to offending.

In Durkheim's model of anomie a deviance-prone situation was one in which one's life chances had changed or were about to change. Thus on this theory areas of stable continuing poverty and high unemployment would not necessarily have high crime rates. On the other hand the turnover rate might be an important variable: the turnover rate is defined as the rate of unemployment divided by the average length of a period of unemployment; thus it measures the average rate at which jobs are lost. We illustrate with a numerical example. Suppose that there are one million unemployed in a work force of 25 million, and that the average length of a period of unemployment is three months. The unemployment rate is 4%. In a year, four million jobs are found (the number of unemployed divided by the average period—1/4 year—out of work). Thus, in a steady state, four million jobs are lost. There are 24 million jobs, so 1/6th of jobs are "turned over" in the year, and 16% (4 divided by 25) of people are "turned over". This last figure is the turnover rate as we have defined it.

Hence, if in an area a high unemployment rate goes with a high turnover rate, one would expect, according to the theory, a high crime rate: but there are arguments the other way. If the crucial factor in motivating individuals to criminal activity is a sudden change in their situation (presumably relative to what they can expect), areas with little poverty and low unemployment may generate more crime because someone who found himself either poor or unemployed in such an area would not have a stable reference group and would feel isolated, so that his commitment to general societal values (such as obeying the law) would diminish.

Merton's (1938 and 1957) static model of anomie, with its stress on reactions to a situation of disjunction between means and ends, would suggest unambiguously that individuals who were poor and unemployed amidst a society of plenty would strive to compensate for their situation by innovating. It is certainly true that the poor male is more often caught offending than the rich. Thus the study by Ferguson (1952) shows how the percentage of boys between 8 and 18 with convictions decreases according to the quality of their home district. This result does not, however, apply to a comparison between the actual level of offending of the poor and the rich. Self-report studies indeed, suggest that the ranking might even be inverted. Thus Christie, Andenaes and Skirbekk (1965) concluded: "Instead of any concentration of high degrees of self-reporting at the lower ends of the class scale, we found a slight but persistent tendency in the opposite direction" (p. 105). Possible explanations of results such as those of Ferguson (1952) are either that a higher proportion of offences committed by the poor are reported, or that the poor offender has a higher probability of his offence being detected.

2.3.5 *Working Class*

Several investigators have emphasized the disadvantaged position of working-class males in attempting to achieve status. Thus Cohen (1955) maintains that working-class boys are negativistic, anti-utilitarian and aggressive in reaction to their inability to conform to a middle-class school system. Within a culture-conflict framework, Miller (1958) argued that the working-class community generates an alternative culture whose social concerns "centre around the need to be tough, to be smart in outwitting opponents, to experience excitement, to try your luck and to be free from too close supervision and restraint, rather than from a reaction to status and economic frustration" (p. 9), so that their male offspring are more likely to offend. It is not surprising that the evidence is voluminous.

If we simply look at the representation of the different social classes among caught or convicted offenders, the differences are staggering. As J. Q. Wilson (1968) says "assaults and at least minor thefts are much more likely to be committed in lower status areas and by lower status persons" (p. 141). Similarly, a national sample of children born in England and Wales in 1946 showed that by the time they were 17 nearly 25% of the lower working class had been convicted for an offence, compared to less than 3% of the upper working class (Douglas *et al.* (1966)). Self-reporting studies, which have proliferated on this question, are more equivocal. The series of studies by Short and Nye (1958) found no significant difference between the delinquencies of boys from high, medium, or low status backgrounds. Similar conclusions have been reached in other countries and at other times (see Vaz (1966)), but some authors have argued that lower status boys were more frequently delinquent and commit more serious offences (see, for example, the study by Gold (1966)).

English self-reporting studies are sparse, but those that exist tend to lead to conclusions similar to that of Gold (1966). Willcock (1974) found that lower class boys admitted to more frequent delinquencies. MacDonald (1969) studying both the official and self-reported delinquency of a sample of 800 children from three different schools in three different areas, claimed that the social classes showed significantly different rates of delinquency, even when the sample was broken down by type of school and area. But the extent of difference which she observed was very small and not sufficient to account for the differences in the delinquency rates between the areas which she studied.

It is unclear from the discussion above just how great is the importance of social class as a variable in the determination of the rate of actual offences. We have seen the dangers of passing from observations on the class background of convicted offenders to inferences about offending behaviour. However, the class factor is of sufficient *a priori* interest to the above theories to warrant its inclusion as an explanatory variable for actual offences. Measures are discussed in Chapter 4, § 4.1.1, and § 4.1.2. It also appears that membership of the working class is possibly an important mediating variable between the commission and recording of offences. This phenomenon is discussed in Chapter 3, § 3.4.

2.3.6 *Youth*

A criminological favourite for explaining the mass of offences is the delinquent adolescent. It is fair to say that some criminologists (see, for example, West (1967)) have taken youthful adolescent delinquency as the most important topic to be explained. In fact the peak age for caught offenders has hovered around 15 or 16 for the last 20 years in England and Wales. Most theoretical explanations have been a variant on the rather general claim that youth is a transitional period between childhood and adulthood when the societal values are being questioned, but attempts to be more specific have not been particularly successful.[13]

In view of this concentration it is rather surprising that so few attempts have been made to test the proposition that, *ceteris paribus*, more adolescents imply higher offence rates. One exception is Willmer's (1968) study of the trend in breaking-and-entering offences over a twenty-year period. He found a close correlation between the rising recorded offence rate and the proportion of the population in two youthful age groups.[14] Since he assumed that most breaking-and-entering offences are reported (an observation whose implications for our model we shall consider in Chapter 5, § 5.3) and noted that adolescents are found to be responsible for most of the breaking and entering offences for which convictions are recorded, Willmer (1968) felt able to conclude that the age structure of the population explained the overall trend (in that a constant and high proportion of individuals in these age groups were committing the offences).

It is clear that there are strong reasons for including in our model a variable which captures variations in the age structure of the population. In our time periods (1961, 1966, and 1971) particular age groups are of interest because of the relation between their infancy and the Second World War period. Our attempt to investigate this relation using our model is mentioned in Chapter 7.

[13]Compare, for example the maturation hypothesis of Glueck and Glueck (1950) and Matza's (1964) techniques of neutralisation.

[14]In fact, his predictions for the trend, after 1968, do not correspond at all with actuality.

2.3.7 *Family Background*

Another popular candidate for explaining the genesis of the bulk of offending, is family background, on the argument that its quality determines the quality of the upbringing received by the individual and therefore his emotional and ethical reactions. Although there are several studies which purport to identify the different psychological types of offenders that one would expect individuals with defective upbringing[15] to have, our interest is more in the extent to which particular family or home environments produce future delinquents. The conditions most discussed are broken homes, quality of parental care and birth order.

Glueck and Glueck (1950) studied 500 delinquent matched with 500 non-delinquent controls; 60% of the delinquents came from homes which had been "broken by separation, divorce, death or prolonged absence of a parent", as against 34% of the non-delinquents. However, they studied delinquent boys in correctional institutions—a situation which may have been the consequence of the absence of a parent. The study by Carr-Saunders *et al.* (1942) is superior in that their samples of delinquents were not biased in this fashion. Out of 1953 delinquent boys and 1970 non-delinquent controls, 28% of the former and 16% of the latter came from families where one or both natural parents were missing.

The quality of parental care is the central concept in the kind of theory that focuses on family background. Most studies which attempt to look at this directly, however, depend crucially on the judgment by the investigators of the quality of parental care. One study which may have partially escaped this problem is that by Andry (1960) of 80 London boys aged 12-15 with more than one conviction for theft, since in about one-third of his sample he interviewed the parents as well as the boys to see the extent to which the two versions of their relationships tallied. Although he claimed to find several differences between delinquents and controls in the quality of the relationships they had with parents and especially with their fathers, he found no evidence for an association between stealing and physical separation in childhood from either parent.

No conclusive results have been obtained as to the relationship between birth order and delinquency, but most investigators have agreed that delinquents tend to belong to larger families than do controls. For example, Ferguson's (1952) study indicated this association in a sample of Glasgow boys in that 8% of boys in one-or-two children families as compared with 20% in families with 8 or more children, were convicted between the ages of

---

[15]See, for example, Hewitt and Jenkins (1947) who identify unsocialised aggressive behaviour, socialised delinquency, and over-inhibited behaviour in a sample of 500 children seen at a child guidance clinic.

8 and 18. He went further, however, and sub-divided large and small families according to the extent of overcrowding with the results given in Table 2.5.

Table 2.5
Incidence of delinquency and crowding in the home

Delinquency rates	Number of children in family	
Number of persons in room	1-4	5 or more
1-2	7·0%	6·3%
4 or more	11·2%	19·2%

(Taken from Ferguson (1952) p. 22.)

These suggest that overcrowding is more closely associated with delinquency than is family size.

Three factors have been suggested in this subsection which may monitor the relationship between the quality of upbringing and delinquency: broken homes, quality of parental care, and family size. The first two variables seem to have an independent importance, but the influence of family size seems to be spurious and better captured by the degree of overcrowding.

2.4 CONCLUDING REMARKS

We have been concerned in this chapter to examine theories of offending behaviour in order to identify the determinants of the level of actual offences. We judged the importance of the theories not only in terms of their logical structure and supporting evidence, but also in terms of their relevance to explaining cross-sectional variations in England and Wales in the 1960s. The factors identified will be integrated into a formal model in Chapter 4 where we also discuss the problems of measurement.

Theories have been considered under two headings: incentives to offend (the economic approach) and socio-demographic factors (traditional criminology). Despite the longevity of deterrence ideas, we found that the identification of appropriate factors to include in our model was not straightforward. On the other hand, the problems of selecting variables to capture the theories of traditional criminology were not so severe. This explains the relative brevity of our discussion of the latter theories.

We raised at the beginning of this chapter, the problems of recording and in Chapter 1 the difficulties associated with the interdependence of some of our variables. These problems and difficulties provide the focus of the next chapter.

Offending as Behaviour Towards Risk

2.A.0 INTRODUCTION

An important part of the discussion in the body of this chapter has been the examination of the decision whether or not to commit an offence as a function of perceived probabilities of gains and losses. Such a treatment portrays the decision in terms which are close to the economist's usual model of behaviour towards risk. The choice of whether or not to offend is thus seen as "normal" in the sense that one employs the same descriptive model as for other choices. The usual economic examples are the purchase of insurance or bonds. In this appendix we give a version of this conventional choice theory as applied to the decision whether to offend.

One can show (see, for example Green (1976)) that under some simple assumptions on individual's preferences over strategies or actions with risky outcomes, that he would behave, *as if* he maximised expected utility. In other words, as if he appraises a strategy by forming a weighted sum of utilities across different prospective situations which may follow from the strategy, using as weight on the utility in a given situation its perceived probability under the particular strategy. This weighted sum is the expected utility and, in the model, he chooses the strategy with highest expected utility.

Consider now a person who is trying to decide whether or not to commit an offence. If we apply the general model just described he looks at his expected utility if he commits the offence, at his expected utility if he does not and then chooses to commit the offence if the former expected utility exceeds the latter. If different people take different decisions it is because they differ in their perceptions of probabilities or their evaluation of outcomes.

We must be clear at the outset as to the kind of offence we have in mind when applying this theory. We shall be thinking of the offences which contribute the vast majority of those analysed in this empirical study—minor thefts. We emphasized the importance of such offences in our total "all indictable offences" in § 2.0. Further detail on offence types is given in the appendix to Chapter 4. That our offences are mostly minor thefts has important consequences for the kind of model we shall be discussing. We argued in § 2.2.5 that models of the allocation of time between legal and illegal activities, popular in recent U.S. studies, were inappropriate for such offences.

We shall not, therefore, give a formal presentation of models of the offence choice which involve the allocation of time. We shall concentrate on a model in which expected utilities with and without an offence are compared for a given starting level of wealth. The analysis proceeds in terms of perceived potential gains and losses, together with their probabilities, from committing an offence. Before examining the model in detail, however, we must emphasize that we do not intend to press the model as one of the decision whether to commit a violent offence. This caveat is necessary because there have been recent and well-known applications in the U.S.A. of this kind of model to violent crime and particularly to murder (see, for example, Ehrlich (1975) and (1977)). The determinants of the different levels of violence in different communities are, we presume, many and complex. And amongst these determinants it is quite possible that one may find the probability and level of punishment. But the interpretation of an expected utility model becomes banal in the case of violent offences because of the difficulty in providing a sensible measurement of the gain from an offence. One is quickly reduced to the statement that an individual commits an offence when the "pleasure" he perceives from carrying through the assault or murder, say, outweighs the expected losses. This view does not involve any claim as to whether violent offenders respond to punishment or not. What we are saying is that the attempt to derive response functions for violent offences from expected utility maximisation is likely to be futile.

In the next section of this appendix we set out the model of choice under uncertainty. The subsequent section (§ 2.A.2) contains a discussion of the proposition that offenders' preferences will be such that crime does not pay. This will lead naturally to problems of measuring punishment and some of these are discussed in § 2.A.3. The relation between poverty and offending in the model is discussed in § 2.A.4, unemployment in § 2.A.5 and concluding remarks are contained in § 2.A.6.

2.A.1 THE MODEL

[The notation in this appendix has been chosen to allow easy comparison with the literature. It is not consistent with our discussion of our econometric models—Chapters 4 to 7. We shall use the same notation, as for this appendix, in Chapter 9 and its appendix.]

Let us now turn to the analysis of our formal model. We are to think of an individual with given starting wealth W who is to decide whether or not to commit an offence, a theft. To keep matters simple we suppose the possible punishment is by fine. If punishment is by imprisonment the issues become more complex (we say a little more about this below). The probability of being apprehended is p and we make here no distinction between apprehension and conviction. The gain from the offence, measured in monetary terms is G and the loss, if apprehended, is L. We assume that if the individual is apprehended he not only loses the proceeds G, but in addition incurs the loss. This does not imply that all "loot" is actually recovered or that there is any confiscation of an equal amount if it is not recovered, but is merely a convention for the measurement of L. From the formal point of view the convention for the measurement of L is of no great significance, but it does become important when we come to interpret results and we return to this point below (§ 2.A.2). The model is one of the individual decision and all variables are thus as perceived by the individual *ex ante* or whilst contemplating the offence.

After an action has been taken and any consequence has occurred, the individual will have some level of wealth. Utility is a function $U(\ )$ of this "terminal" level of wealth. The utility function embodies all aspects of individual preferences which are a consequence of wealth. Thus if the rich have a penchant for fast cars, utility which results from the purchase of fast cars is included in $U(\ )$.

The expected utility EU from committing the offence is

$$(1 - p)U(W + G) + p\,U(W - L) \tag{1}$$

If he gets away with the offence he has wealth $W + G$; if he does not $W - L$, and the two outcomes have probability $(1 - p)$ and p respectively. If he does not commit the offence he has utility $U(W)$ with certainty; thus if he chooses the option with higher expected utility he will commit the offence if

$$U(W) < (1 - p)U(W + G) + p\,U(W - L) \tag{2}$$

and he will not commit the offence if the inequality in (2) is reversed. It is clear that expected utility decreases as p increases and as L increases. Thus the number of people and the number of offences for which (2) holds, decreases as p and L increase and we have that the number of offences committed is a decreasing function of the probability of apprehension and the severity of punishment in accordance with the theory as expressed in the main body of the chapter.

It is important to note that we have used the same utility function in the above regardless of whether an offence has been committed or not. Thus we look only at consequences in terms of wealth and not any utility or disutility from the act itself. Hence we have not embodied the views of individuals as regards codes of conduct. It is possible to include the utility of the act itself as part of the consequences. For example, an individual's dislike for illegal acts would form part of his evaluation of the illegal acquisition of goods. This would complicate the model considerably and it is rare to see it done.

2.A.2 DOES CRIME PAY?

It is a standard result in the economic theory of choice under uncertainty that if the marginal utility of wealth declines with wealth then an individual will reject all "unfair" gambles; by an unfair gamble we mean a bet where the expected monetary value of the gains is less than that of losses. Such an individual would also reject all fair gambles (where expected money gains equal expected money losses) and even favourable gambles if the expected gain did not exceed the expected loss by a sufficient amount. Intuitively the individual, because he has diminishing marginal utility of wealth, is more concerned about the possibility of losing a given amount, than he is attracted by the possibility of gaining that amount and will therefore reject the offer of a 50-50 chance of winning or losing £ X.

Similarly individuals for whom the marginal utility of wealth increases with wealth will accept some unfair gambles. If an individual accepts a large number of unfair gambles on average he will lose.

In the theory of choice uncertainty it is usual to call those with decreasing marginal utility of wealth risk-averters and those for whom it increases risk-preferrers; the language is justified by the implied behaviour towards unfair gambles just described.

Thus, if it can be shown that offenders are generally risk-preferrers, then they will in their offending activities accept unfair gambles and eventually become less wealthy. In this case one might say that "crime does not pay". In his 1968 article, Becker claimed to have shown that if we have optimum fines and expenditure on police (the model and sense of "optimum" is discussed in Chapter 9 and its appendix—see in particular § 9.A.3) then offenders will indeed be risk-preferrers and thus, at the optimum "crime does not pay". The conclusion was deduced from the condition that, at the optimum, offenders will be more responsive to the probability of apprehension than the level of punishment, in the sense that a 1% increase in the level of the former would have a greater impact on the level of offences than a 1% increase in the latter. (The condition itself will be examined in the appendix to Chapter 9.) And one often hears the empirical claim that the probability of apprehension is more important than the level of punishment. It is therefore of interest to ask whether one can indeed infer that a greater responsiveness to the probability of conviction implies risk-preference by offenders and hence that "crime does not pay".

We shall examine the question in terms of the responsiveness of expected utility to proportional changes in the variables p and L. Differentiating (1) with respect to p and L we have

$$-p\frac{\partial EU}{\partial p} = p(U(W + G) - U(W - L)) \tag{3}$$

$$-L\frac{\partial EU}{\partial L} = L p U'(W - L) \tag{4}$$

If Δp is a change in p then $\Delta p/p$ is the proportional change. Thus the left hand side of (3) denotes the increase in expected utility in response to a (proportional) reduction in p holding L constant and of (4) to L holding p constant. Comparing the right hand sides of (3) and (4) we have that the responsiveness to p is greater than that to L if and only if

$$U(W + G) - U(W - L) > LU'(W - L) \tag{5}$$

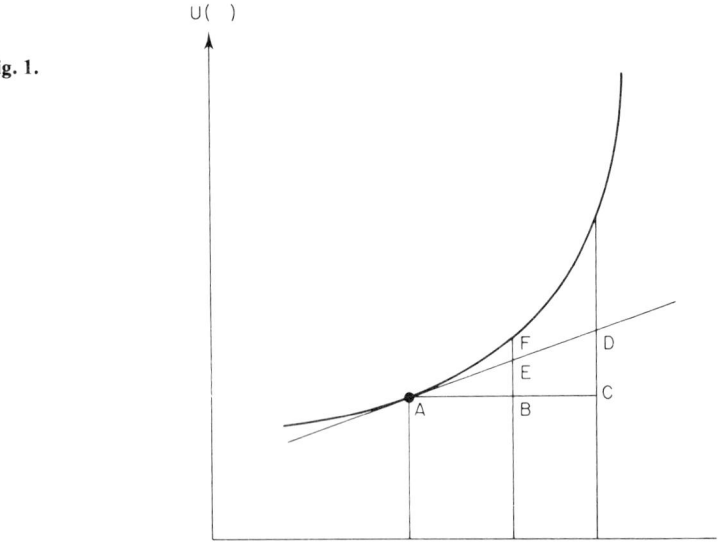

Fig. 1.

Condition (5) can most easily be investigated using a diagram illustrating properties of concave and convex functions: $U(\ )$ concave corresponds to decreasing marginal utility of wealth and convex to increasing marginal utility. A convex function $U(\ )$ is sketched in Fig. 1.

We can see from Fig. 1, and it is a standard property of convex functions, that

$$U(W) - U(W - L) \geq LU'(W - L) \tag{6}$$

The reverse inequality holds for concave functions. For the convex function of Fig. 1 the l.h.s. of (6) is the distance BF and the r.h.s. BE (since AB is length L and $U'(W - L)$ is the gradient of the tangent at A). For the case of convex functions then, we have (5) immediately from (6), since $U(W + G) > U(W)$. We therefore have that risk-preference (convex U) implies the responsiveness to p will be greater than that to L. Thus an individual who accepts unfair gambles will be more responsive to changes in the probability of gains than changes in possible losses.[1]

We are not, however, justified in the claim that risk-preference is implied by the observation that the responsiveness to p is greater than that to L. If we could deduce equation (6) from equation (5) this would, for the case of differentiable functions, be sufficient to give convexity of $U(\ )$ and thus risk-preference; but we cannot deduce (6) from (5). Equation (6) does follow from (5) if assert that (5) holds for all $G \geq 0$. If we have individuals who are more responsive to p than to L for offences involving articles of high value but not for those of small value, so that (5) holds for large G but not for small G, then the inequality in (6) is reversed so that $U(\ )$ is concave and they are risk-averters.

The analysis in this sub-section has followed Brown and Reynolds (1973) in their demonstration that the Becker proposition, deducing that "crime does not pay" from the assertion that offences are more responsive to the probability of apprehension than the level of punishment, does not follow if punishment is measured by L. Becker derived his proposition by adopting a different convention for the measurement of the individual's loss from apprehension from that given above. He uses a measure of loss which is equivalent to $G + L$ in the above. His definition is implicit only and contained in footnote 16 of Becker (1968) where punishment f is the difference between wealth with and without apprehension. Substituting $L = f - G$ in the definition of expected utility (equation (1)) and re-

---

[1] Avinash Dixit has made the following important point to us. We have examined the choice whether or not to commit a particular offence. If the individual can commit many such offences he must choose how many. If the utility function is everywhere convex then the individual problem has no solution—he would try to commit an infinite amount. One would have to abandon the assumption that the utility function is everywhere convex.

working the above analysis in terms of proportional changes in f rather than L, one can verify that Becker's proposition is valid if expressed in terms of his f. Brown and Reynolds (1973) have argued, we believe plausibly, that Becker's notion of punishment does not accord with common usage. This argument is, essentially, accepted by Heineke (1975) in his comment on Brown and Reynolds (1973) although he (and we) would quarrel with any suggestion that L corresponds to punishment as imposed by the courts. He argues that this would only be the case if the proceeds of the crime, or loot, were always confiscated in full before imposition of sentence.

2.A.3 THE MEASUREMENT OF PUNISHMENT

The argument at the end of the previous section implies that the judgement of Becker's proposition that offenders are risk-preferrers becomes empirical. If the assertion that individuals are more responsive to the probability of apprehension than the level of punishment is based on a measure of punishment which involves the whole difference between wealth with and without apprehension, then Becker is justified. We should suggest, however, that it is most unlikely that such assertions, where they are documented, could be based on such a measure. Published punishment levels, for example, are usually in terms of sentence only and not in terms of any other punishment, confiscation of loot or otherwise, imposed by the court.

We have argued from the very beginning of our work on this subject (see Carr-Hill and Stern (1971) and (1973)) that the severity of punishment as measured by the sentence imposed by the court misses a very important element of the perceived cost of punishment—the shame attached to apprehension and, particularly, to appearance in court. Evidence in support of the claim that this aspect of the perceived cost is substantial was offered in the main body of this chapter. Writing J for this perceived cost, f' for the penalty imposed by the court and B for resource costs to the individual involved in apprehension other than those measured in J (for example, time and money costs of court appearance and any confiscation, partial or total) we have that the full punishment, Becker's f (our $G + L$) is $J + B + f'$. We have assumed for the sake of this argument that the costs can be written additively. Their combined effect is likely to be more complicated than this.

Empirical investigations would in general work with proportional changes in f'. It is clear that these will be greater (and we should suggest, substantially greater) than proportional changes in Becker's f. Empirical estimates of the responsiveness of offences to punishment levels will therefore seriously underestimate responsiveness to Becker's f, since they associate given changes in offences with proportional changes in punishment that are "too large". The kind of evidence on which Becker appears to base his claim (see his remarks on pp. 178-9 of Becker (1968) where he refers, *inter alia*, to Ehrlich (1967)) cannot therefore be used, without substantial argument which is absent in his discussion, to support his conclusions.

2.A.4 POVERTY AND OFFENDING

Evidence on the relation between wealth and offending has been discussed in the main body of this chapter (see § 2.2.5). We saw that while statistics on arrests show a higher proportion of the poor and unemployed than in the population as a whole, the self-report studies show little difference between offending behaviour, at least for juveniles, between the poor and the rich.

The models of the allocation of time between legal and illegal activities generally arrive at the conclusion that the poor are more likely to offend. Intuitively the argument is that the opportunity cost of indulging in illegal activities in terms of the income forgone from legal activities is higher for those facing high legal wages than those facing lower. If the pay-off from illegal activities is similar for different wage groups, one would expect to find proportionately more of those with low potential legal wages opting for illegal activities.

It does not seem to be recognised that, in general, the prediction from models of the kind used in this appendix would be that the poor are less likely to offend. And given the conflict between the evidence from the self-report studies and the predictions from the allocation of time models, it is fortunate to have an argument that goes in this direction. Let us examine the proposition in more detail.

Consider a collection of individuals with differing wealth but with the same utility function and the same perception of the probability and magnitude of punishment and pay-off from an offence, who are contemplating an offence with gain G and loss L. We assume the gamble is fair in the sense that $(1 - p) G = pL$. Each individual is asked to specify the maximum he would be prepared to pay rather than be forced to commit the offence. The response, α, will, in general, depend on the wealth of the individual and we write it $\alpha(W)$. The formal definition of α is that

$$(1 - p) U(W + G) + pU(W - L) = U(W - \alpha) \tag{7}$$

Let us suppose that both the gain and possible loss from the offence are small, so that we can use a second order approximation to $U(W + G)$, $U(W - L)$, $U(W - \alpha)$ around $U(W)$. We have

$$(1-p)\left[U(W) + G\,U'(W) + \frac{G^2}{2}\,U''(W)\right] + p\left[U(W) - LU'(W)\right.$$

$$\left. + \frac{L^2}{2}\,U''(W)\right] = U(W) - \alpha U'(W) \qquad (8)$$

where terms higher than the second order in G and L have been ignored.[2] Using $(1-p)\,G = pL$ we have

$$-M\frac{U''(W)}{U'(W)} = \alpha \qquad (9)$$

where $M = (1-p)\dfrac{G^2}{2} + \dfrac{pL^2}{2}$ and is the same for all individuals since it is

independent of W. The quantity $\dfrac{-U''(W)}{U'(W)}$ is called the index of absolute

risk-aversion and we call it $R(W)$. It is commonly suggested that $R(W)$ will decrease with wealth. Indeed the above argument is the direct application of the standard analysis (see Arrow (1971)) and merely relabels the gamble of that analysis as an offence. The argument that decreasing absolute risk aversion is the natural assumption is indeed, based on the proposition that the rich are more likely to accept a given gamble than the poor. If I have only £50, so the argument goes, I am less likely to accept a 50-50 bet of £5 than if I have £500.

If individuals do become less risk-averse as they become more wealthy, in the above sense, then the premium the poor person will be prepared to pay to avoid being forced to commit the offence will be higher than for a rich person.

We can extend the standard analysis and show that, if we consider a given small (in the sense used in the derivation of equation (8)) offence with non-zero expected monetary value, then all individuals in our collection with wealth above some given level ($\hat{W}$ say) would commit the offence and all with wealth below $\hat{W}$ would not, provided only that absolute risk-aversion is decreasing around $\hat{W}$, that is $R'(\hat{W}) < 0$.

Let the difference, $EU - U(W)$, between the expected utility from committing the offence (for a person of wealth W) and the utility of wealth W be $F(W)$. If $F(W) > 0$ the offence will be committed and if $F(W) < 0$ it will not. If we can show that $F(W) = 0$ implies $F'(W) > 0$, it will follow that $F(W) > 0$ for all $W > \hat{W}$ and $F(W) < 0$ for all $W < \hat{W}$. This last implication

---

[2] We check below, see equation (9), that α is of second order in G and L so that we are justified in ignoring α^2 and higher powers of α.

is a general proposition for differentiable functions and is clear if one sketches the graph of $F(W)$ against W.

Expanding $F(\ )$ and $F'(\ )$ in a series to the second order in G and L it is straightforward to verify that, to second order in G and L

$$F(W) = \left[(1-p)G-pL\right] U' + \left[(1-p)\frac{G^2}{2} + \frac{pL^2}{2}\right] U'' \qquad (10)$$

$$F'(W) = \left[(1-p)G-pL\right] U'' + \left[(1-p)\frac{G^2}{2} + \frac{pL^2}{2}\right] U''' \qquad (11)$$

where derivatives are evaluated at W.

Then $F(\hat{W}) = 0$ implies

$$F'(\hat{W}) = M \left[-\frac{(U'')^2}{U'} + U'''\right] \qquad (12)$$

where M is as defined following equation (9) and functions are evaluated at $\hat{W}$. But differentiating the definition $R(W) = \dfrac{-U''}{U'}$ we have

$$R'(W) = \frac{(U'')^2}{(U')^2} - \frac{U'''}{U'} = -\frac{1}{U'}\left[-\frac{(U'')^2}{U'} + U'''\right]$$

Substituting in (12) we have

$$F'(\hat{W}) = -MU'R' \qquad (13)$$

where derivatives are evaluated at $\hat{W}$. Hence $F(\hat{W}) = 0$ implies $F'(\hat{W}) > 0$, provided that at this point $R' < 0$. This is the result we require to establish that all individuals with wealth above $\hat{W}$ will commit the given (small) offence and all with wealth below will not.

There are arguments which lend some support to the opposite conclusion. That concerned with the allocation of time has already been mentioned. Higher status or income groups may be more worried about loss of status or income from the notoriety of court appearance — thus they may, in the language of the previous subsection, have J's which are higher and hence a higher perceived punishment. It may be that different income groups face different probabilities of apprehension too. If anything we should guess that this would lead to the proposition that the rich are more likely to offend. The evidence from self-report studies suggests that the effects captured in the above arguments may cancel themselves out. We must recognise, however, that there are important issues concerned with the formation of attitudes and preferences which are not contained in the above models. Thus membership of a different family, group or class, can lead to different attitudes to offending. In the language of the theory presented here, these different attitudes would have to be represented by different subjective utility functions for the case where offences are committed. The relevant effects are too subtle to be captured merely by letting U depend on W, since the membership of a group or class involves more than just wealth, and the attitudes are to the actions themselves and not just the consequences for wealth. Extending the arguments of U would, in our view, contribute little to an analysis of these issues.

2.A.5 UNEMPLOYMENT AND PARTICIPATION

Unemployment has been for some time, a popular variable in the explanation of crime (see § 2.2.5). Recently some of the U.S. literature, influenced by the view that the choice between a legal job and a life of crime is exclusive, has concentrated on participation rates as a more appropriate measure (see Phillips, Votey and Maxwell (1972)). The participation rate is the labour force (employed plus unemployed) divided by the population, whereas the unemployment rate is the number of unemployed divided by the labour force. The definitions of labour force, employment and unemployment vary across countries but it is usually the case, in principle anyway, that to be classified as unemployed you must be both out of a job and looking for (legal) work.

A problem with using unemployment or participation rates as an explanatory variable, based on the models of allocation of time, is that the unemployment rate or participation rate is determined simultaneously, in such models, with the offence rate by the collection of choices in the community between the life of crime and legal employment. One should not, therefore, if one follows such a model, use the unemployment or participation rate as an explanatory variable for the offence rate. We have already argued that such models are not relevant for our data. We did test for the inclusion of the unemployment rate in the explanation of the recorded offence rate in this study (see Chapters 4, 5 and 6) but in the light of the argument just given and the complex inter-relation between unemployment, age distribution and poverty in an area (discussed in Chapter 2), we regarded the inclusion as interesting for comparison with other studies rather than justified on the grounds of theory or substantial prior evidence.

2.A.6 CONCLUDING REMARKS

We have examined in this appendix economic theories of choice as applied to offending behaviour. We emphasized that our interest here is confined to property offences without violence against the person and cast doubt on the usefulness of utility maximisation as a model of violent crime. In addition we argued that the standard choice under uncertainty models was more appropriate for the data of our sample (that is, small thefts) than those which examine the allocation of time between legal and illegal activities. We emphasized the difference between the data of our sample, which include *all* thefts however small and the U.S. data on felonies which have a monetary cut-off below which a crime is not seen as a felony. We note here that if an individual has a different, in particular a lower, view of the value of the property he is stealing than the recording police officer, he may commit a felony "unintentionally". This means that one should use results from data which involve a cut-off with caution if one wishes to make inferences from them about individual behaviour.

It was shown that one is not justified in making the claim that "crime does not pay" on the basis of the observation that offence rates are more responsive to the probability of apprehension than to the severity of punishment as imposed by the court. We emphasized in particular that there was an important element of punishment in addition to that imposed by the court, namely the perceived shame or loss of status or income attached to court appearance *per se.*

We showed that the usual assumptions about risk-aversion and wealth implied that the poor were less likely to offend than the rich. A factor which may be of substantial importance to the propensity to offend is the distribution of income. We have not offered a formal analysis here, but see § 2.2.6.

In conclusion we should like to make two points about the model as applied here. The first relates to the consequentialist approach of the expected utility model; and the second to the extension to punishment by imprisonment. By the consequentialist approach we mean that the individual evaluates only the (perceived) consequences of the act of offending and compares them with the consequences from not offending. Now one *can* incorporate attitudes towards the act itself in the definition of the individual's evaluation of the consequence of that act. In other words, for example, if an individual dislikes doing something illegal, one can incorporate that dislike in his evaluation of the possible outcomes of the offence (whether or not he is caught). But the analysis would become much more complex and the neat, simple results of standard theory would be lost. It is all too easy to use the same utility function for the evaluation of states which result from offending and those which do not. Thus the individual's attitudes to codes of conduct, which might be very important to him, are omitted (Block and Heineke (1975) is a notable exception).

In an extension of the model to the case where punishment is by imprisonment one can replace prison sentences by money punishments if a monetary equivalent of the individual's time in prison is used; this may cause problems in application, but is a possible way to proceed. There is an important difference between fines and imprisonment, however, when it comes to the estimation of functions representing the response of offences to punishment levels. Where individuals are incarcerated they may find it physically very difficult to commit certain offences, even though their expected utility if not incarcerated would be improved by the offence. Thus one must in principle be wary of making inferences about expected utility from an empirical study where imprisonment is an important punishment.

3

The Social Reactions to Criminality

3.0 INTRODUCTION

In the previous chapter we examined various explanations which have been proposed to account for the genesis of criminality at the level of the individual. Within the framework of the economic approach, important explanatory variables are the probability of detection and the level of punishment. The relevant probability is that perceived by the individual, and we showed that this, in turn, could be affected by the manpower of and the expenditure on the police force. Furthermore, the propensity to offend might be influenced by the last two factors not only through the perceived probability of being caught, since the individual's awareness of inappropriate or unsocial behaviour might be sharpened by the presence of extra police and thus his subjective cost of offending (whether or not the person is caught) might be increased.

There are, however, good reasons for supposing that the recorded clear-up rate[1] depends, *ceteris paribus* on the recorded offence rate if only because a certain number of policemen can deal only with a limited number of offences. Similarly, the numbers of (and possibly the expenditure per officer on) policemen are likely to be a function of the offence rate. Indeed, the previous year's offence rate probably forms a basis for the budget submission. Further some people argue that the severity of sentences depends on the apparent prevalence of offending. We explained intuitively in Chapter 1—and the reasons are elaborated in Chapter 5—that in order to reach well-founded empirical conclusions as to the magnitude and direction

[1] For a definition of the clear-up rate see Chapter 4 and the Data Appendix. Loosely, it is the proportion of recorded offences (effectively) solved.

of the effects posited in the previous chapter, these mutual relationships must be taken into account. Otherwise we cannot tell whether we are examining, for example, the effect of offences on the probability of detection or clear-up rate, or the effect of the clear-up rate on the level of offences.

The object of the first half of this chapter is the examination of these mutual relationships. Thus we try to analyse the determination of the variables just mentioned (excluding the offence rate). Just as in Chapter 2, where we scrutinised some of the theories which might explain the geographical pattern of offences, we present and critically discuss theories which could account for the variations between police districts of the detection rate, the number of and expenditure on the police, and the severity of punishment. We shall also be examining some of the evidence relevant to these theories. Thus we shall be providing a survey of theories and evidence on a wide range of aspects of the social system. The same qualifications advanced in Chapter 2 are relevant here. Our survey is not intended to be exhaustive. We wish to say enough to justify the inclusion in the model we are building of a variable to capture the determinant under consideration.

Ever since criminal statistics were collected on a routine basis, there has been a considerable debate as to whether they faithfully reflect the real crime rate.[2] In the last quarter century, there has been a flood of literature discussing the problem of what meaning should be attached to the official statistics on crime and deviance. The general theme is that, in order to understand official statistics on crime, we have to look at the institutions surrounding their production.

The second half of the chapter therefore takes a sociological view of the generation of recorded offences themselves. We consider the position of conflict theorists who argue that the nature and level of social control, including the recording of offences, is determined ultimately by the holders of power. We also look at the related position of labelling theorists who study the effect of the specific interactions between individuals and the agents of social control on the assignation of the criminal label (we shall sometimes use the term "interactionist" to describe these positions). This involves an examination of the social institutions controlling the production of criminal statistics in general, and of the specific variables which intervene between "criminogenic" factors and both the observed crime rates, and the apparent efficiency (measured by the clear-up rate) of the police force.

The end product of the discussion of Chapters 2 and 3 will be a model containing several relations or equations, each modelling a different process. Each relation will include a certain number of variables whose inclusion will have been justified by recourse to prior theory and evidence as

---

[2] For an outline history of the debate see Sellin and Wolfgang (1964) who have traced the controversy back to Quelelet.

explained above.[3]. The equations which are the algebraic equivalent of these relations are presented formally in Chapter 4, where we also discuss data problems. In Chapter 5, we discuss in detail the problems of estimation and testing to which we have alluded above.

The argument in this chapter proceeds as follows. In the next section we discuss three types of factors which might enter into the determination of the detection rate: characteristics of individuals or groups; organisational characteristics of the police force; and social structural features of the locality. In the second section we look at the possibility that the level of punishments—which we postulated was a factor determining the offence rate—is in turn determined by the offence rate. Our discussion suggests that, whilst a wide range of social factors (including the amount and pattern of offences) affect the severity of punishment imposed on an individual and the average level of sentences countrywide over time, it is difficult to believe that areal variations in the severity of punishments are signifcantly related to variations in the offence rate between areas. In the third section, we examine the factors which affect the supply of police and demand for police on a local level. We discuss the possibility that we should include two separate relations, one for demand and one for supply, but conclude that, during the period under consideration and in a sense to be made precise, supply factors dominated. In the fourth section, we introduce the views of sociologists of deviance and what these imply for the analysis of criminal statistics. In particular, we discuss whether or not a real offence rate can be said to exist and how our model should be formulated in either eventuality. The fifth section reviews those studies which have isolated factors affecting both the reporting of incidents by the public to the police and the way in which the police go about recording incidents (whether or not reported to them) as indictable offences. Finally, we consider the changes in police organisation which took place in the sixties in England and Wales and their likely effect on the recorded criminal statistics.

3.1 THE DETERMINATION OF THE DETECTION RATE

3.1.0 *Introduction*

In this section we examine the determination of the likelihood of detection as measured by the clear-up or conviction rate. We first set out our reasons for supposing that the likelihood of detection, or detection rate, depends on the offence rate. We then examine other factors which might enter into the determination of the detection rate—which will be defined more closely in Chapter 4.

[3] The notions of "including a variable in a relation" or "including a variable in the model" will be used frequently in this chapter. We trust that the intuitive explanations given above and in Chapter 1 suffice for the purposes of this chapter; a more formal treatment is given in Chapter 5.

Why should the likelihood of detection depend on the number of offences? In principle, the chance of someone being detected for an offence that he commits depends on the care which he takes to conceal what he is doing. Indeed, prior to the existence of organised police forces in 1829, when the apprehension of a felon depended on the vigilance of the citizenry, the likelihood of detection may have been independent of the offence rate. But in the last 150 years, although the public still report offences and likely culprits, and a large number of people are in positions of social control, the police have become the major institutional means by which offenders are apprehended. The police not only decide what counts as a clear-up and who should be prosecuted, but they also have the task of collecting the evidence and finding the person, all of which takes time. It is for this kind of reason that we argue that the likelihood of detection depends on the number of offences. The argument just described refers to the probability of solving a recorded offence and it is this recorded detection rate which is at issue in this section.

For a given number of police, in a given area at a given time, with existing detective skills and under existing legal constraints, cannot solve an indefinitely large number of offences. That is, if the offence rate is higher in that area than an otherwise comparable area, we should expect the proportion solved to be lower. Thus we have to include, in an explanation of the determination of the detection rate, the factor which measures the weight of work, the recorded offence rate. Thus the recorded offence rate and the detection rate are mutually interdependent.

We have spoken, without being very precise, of the detection rate meaning by this either the number of recorded offences cleared-up divided by the number of recorded offences (the clear-up rate) or the number of convictions divided by the number of recorded offences (the conviction rate). As analytic variables, both have disadvantages. The police may be sure that a particular person is responsible for an offence but there may be some obstacle to proceeding: for example, a chief witness may refuse to give evidence.[4] In these circumstances the police, from their point of view understandably, regard the case as "cleared-up" even though this may mean that no offence is ever proved. However, we shall use the clear-up rate (it is defined precisely in the Data Appendix) as one measure of the detection rate. The alternative measure is the number of convictions in relation to the number of offences. The problem here is that we have, by police district, data on the number of people convicted but not on the number of offences for which they are convicted. A measure of the "conviction rate" must, therefore, be somewhat hybrid.

[4] Indeed for Turk (1969), an offender's ability to stop a major witness from appearing may be an important tool in resisting the process of criminalisation. We shall be discussing the way in which we are going to take Turk and related positions into account in § 4, 5 and 6 of this chapter.

We postpone until Chapter 4 the detailed discussion of the appropriate measures of the rates of conviction and detection. We shall be using the alternatives of the clear-up rate and the number of people convicted divided by the number of offences. Both these variables are determined inside the system but, since they are capturing the same process, we should not include both in the model at the same time. We give results for each alternative and draw some conclusions from the comparisons of these results. To ease the discussion we shall speak in the remainder of this chapter mainly of the detection rate. We return to the issue in Chapter 4.

We turn now to the determinants of the detection rate. First we examine the way in which the police go about apprehending offenders and those characteristics of individuals or groups which make them vulnerable to detection; secondly the organisational characteristics of the police force which affect its likely efficiency, and finally the social factors which might impose local constraints on the efficiency of the police in detection.

3.1.1 *Apprehending Offenders*

There has been some discussion in the literature of the factors which affect the likelihood of conviction given that a suspect has been apprehended (see, for example, Chapman (1968)). But there are very few studies of the factors affecting either the likelihood of detection for an individual or the recorded clear-up rate for a specific offence. We therefore have to rely on our knowledge of how the police go about their business.

The police develop internal specialist units for collecting, processing and using information about potential suspects. Willmer (1970), who worked with the Police Research and Planning Branch of the Home Office, says: "The police can be viewed as an organisation which receives and responds to information . . . All sections are encouraged to get to know their local criminals, where they meet, what they are doing and with whom they are associating" (p. 7). He shows how police form the smallest possible suspect set with a good probability that it includes those responsible. "From information received from all these different sources (e.g., enquiries, local knowledge, records and informants) the police form a useful suspect set for a given crime or a pool of general suspects, i.e. people suspected of being active criminals" (*op. cit.*, p. 14).

To understand the likely effect of these search procedures, it is important to see what kind of information gets recorded, and about whom. Willmer (1970) says that ". . . examples of intelligence type information are the registration of a criminal's latest car, the names of his companions, and of the places of entertainment that he normally patronises" (p. 24): and he suggests ways in which these might be even further developed: "Computers could . . . be of considerable benefit to police when applied to such problems as the searching of *modus operandi* (MO) files, vehicle index files, missing persons and finger-prints." (*op. cit.*, p. 15).

Russell's (1973) study of the Sussex police found that information is compiled for all persons perceived by the police to be involved in, summonsed, cautioned, or arrested for a crime (meaning here an offence for which fingerprints can be taken). This information is used to build up six different files in the main criminal records. The main nominal index contains 300,000 names of persons accumulated from the daily information inputs. The others are a conviction card index, which includes information about police prosecutions for acts not in the main schedule of offences; a vehicle index of all cars reported stolen, abandoned, broken down or in possession of persons who have been disqualified from driving; a cheque index of all cheque books reported stolen, missing or lost in Sussex and any known to be at present in the use of "fraudsmen"; a "spoke-of" index recording the various social identities assumed by systematic "fraudsmen"; and a formalised and systematic *modus operandi* index of sufficiently distinctive methods used in breaking-and-entering offences.

We can assume that all police forces have a corresponding set of files. Thus, the police have a large amount of information about those with whom they already have some contact[5] and very little about anyone else. It is, therefore, considerably easier for them to link a known person to a given reported crime than an unknown one. This, however, distinguishes only between individuals and not between social groups or areas. We might, however, surmise that areas better endowed with numbers of police and equipment would have more and better organised information and therefore higher clear-up rate. We consider this further below.

3.1.2 *The Police as an Organisation Producing Detections*

The rate at which an organisation can produce usually depends on the manpower involved in production; in the present case, we therefore need to measure the effective police manpower which is actively used in producing detections. Possible measures are the total amount of police time spent in detective work and the number of CID officers. Martin and Wilson (1969) showed in their survey of eight police districts in England and Wales, however, that police forces in the early sixties spent only about 8% of their time on explicit detective effort and a further 12% on the procedural aspects of justice. Similarly, the proportion of detective officers in the force is of the order of 5%. Both these numbers are small and may not yield a very good measure of the variations in the allocation of detective effort between forces.

[5] We take up the question of whether the police tend to collect information about certain types of people rather than others in § 3.4 where we discuss Russell's results in some detail.

Moreover it is arguable that tracing the culprits is, or should be, one of the main goals of the police force. The police themselves perceive the ritual of search, chase and capture as "real crime work" (see Skolnick and Woodworth (1967)), and this view is reflected in police organisation (see Cain (1973) see § 4.2). But the study by Martin and Wilson (1969) showed the difficulty of dividing the time the police allocate to different functions. In an important sense, therefore, the whole police force is a unit "producing" apprehensions or detections.

We therefore decided to use the number of serving policemen in a district as the best proxy indicator of manpower available to produce apprehensions. Our main reason, apart from problems with other measures, is that police presence can, by itself, substantially influence the clear-up rate. A good example of this is the study by Maguire[6] of all burglaries in dwellings in the Thames Valley Police Authority during 1975. He divided the burglaries into police reported and public reported and found that the clear-up rate for the former (at 75%) was much higher than for the latter (at 24%). Another is a study carried out for the President's Commission on Law Enforcement and the Administration of Justice (1967) in Washington, which was investigating the speed with which the police arrived at the scene of the incident after a call. They found that precincts with faster reaction times (which would depend on the number of policemen available to answer calls) had higher clear-up rates.

However, the number of policemen (*per capita*) is not by itself capturing sufficient information. Man hours worked vary between areas: for example, in general, city and borough forces work more overtime than country forces. The seniority structure and the number of supporting staff will vary from district to district. Also the equipment available to different forces varies and this, we presume, affects their detective efficiency. Salaries are the major element in police expenditure (roughly 65%), and they are uniform throughout the country. Thus, a higher expenditure per policeman must reflect a different seniority structure, more overtime, more supporting staff, or more expensive equipment. We therefore decided to use expenditure per policeman together with the number of policemen *per capita* to represent police input.

3.1.3 *The Social Context of Police Work*

We have so far understood the process by which the detection rate is determined as a "production function", a relationship describing the output or detection rate as a function of the work load, recorded offences

[6]Private communication from Michael Maguire of the Oxford University Institute for Criminological Research.

and input, police activity. Thus, our model of the production of detections as developed so far says that two areas with the same number of offences per head of population and with given police resources per head of population should produce the same detection rate regardless of the relative size of the police districts. It is common, however, to suppose that the *size* of an organisation will affect its efficiency. Big organisations can reap economies of scale. We suppose, in particular, that in the case of police districts, there may be advantages to a more precise division of labour. However, there are also disadvantages of scale. Apart from the problems of bureaucratic growth, larger police forces and more advanced equipment (for example, cars rather than bicycles) can put the officer out of touch with the local population. Hence, there is a serious empirical question to examine.

The size of police operations in terms of the area or population covered would be an appropriate measure of scale. And the inclusion of such a measure as an explanation of the detection rate seems reasonable in the light of the Home Office's stress on the efficiency of larger (in either population or area) police districts: see, for example, Her Majesty's Inspector of Constabulary Reports during the sixties (and also McClintock and Avison (1968) p. 120). We can measure size by many indices whether related to population or to area; they are all highly inter-correlated. The most convenient for our purposes, was the residential (night-time) population of the police district.

It is worth remarking that the examination of scale is especially interesting in the period of our study, since the first major change in the administrative boundaries of police districts for over a century was planned in the first half of the decade as a result of the report of the Royal Commission (Willink Commission (1962)) and took place in 1967/8. Moreover, other changes, intended to promote efficiency, also took place over this period. We should expect, therefore, that, in general, larger forces should be more efficient, and that the form of the relationship between size and efficiency in terms of clear-ups or convictions would also change across the years.

A further factor, which we include as having an important effect on the "production function", is the nature of the task and the clientele confronting the force in different areas. Different crimes indicate a different strategy of investigation. We might thus expect a crime-mix variable to affect the overall "efficiency" of police work, or the detection rate.

The most common division which is used in the literature is between personal, property and public order offences. That, for example, is how Sellin and Wolfgang (1964) approach the classification of offence types in order to construct an index of delinquency; similarly McClintock and

Avison (1968) propose an area "criminotype" based on the same trichotomy. The official criminal statistics themselves identify five main classes of indictable offences: violence against the person, sexual offences, breaking and entering offences, larceny offences, and others (see the appendix to Chapter 4). However, from the point of view of affecting the strategy of investigation in an area, violent offences are probably the most important. First, the public is probably more concerned about solving violent offences (consider reactions to "waves of mugging"); secondly, the extent to which an area is "violent" may well affect the morale of the police and therefore the vigour with which they pursue their investigations; and thirdly, the clear-up rate for violent offences is nearly double that for all other offences (in 1961, 84·5% of offences against the person were cleared up as compared to 45% of all indictable offences; see appendix to Chapter 4) because the offender is more often known to the victim. The latter effect is not, however, as important as it might appear, since the ratio of offences against the person to all indictable offences is less than 10%, so that a large increase in the number of offences against the person would not change the overall detection rate very much. We decided, therefore, to view the ratio of offences against the person to all indictable offences as the best *indicator* of the effect of the overall pattern of offences on the success of investigation in an area.

We have, therefore identified the following factors as determinants of the detection rate: the number of policemen *per capita*; the expenditure per officer, the offence rate, the population of a district, and the crime-mix (as described above).

There is also the possibility, when we measure the detection rate by the conviction rate, that the level of punishments may affect the likelihood of the public prosecutor obtaining a conviction. For witnesses may be reluctant to give evidence and juries to convict if they perceive the penalties to be unjustly high. Thus in the nineteenth century, when nearly 300 different types of offences were deemed capital, including some quite minor offences, juries would refuse to convict in the face of apparently overwhelming evidence. A recent phenomenon, on a slightly different scale, seems to account for the low rate of convictions for motoring offences where the person charged pleads not guilty.[7]

Two reasons made us decide against including the level of punishments as a determinant even of the conviction rate. First, such phenomena are likely to be most relevant on a national scale and in respect of particular types of

---

[7] One might also argue that the change in the requirement of juries to reach a unanimous verdict was an example of this effect. It is possible, however, that this change was prompted more by the belief that some potential jury members were reluctant to convict, whatever the penalty.

offence; secondly, if there are variations across areas they would be between the catchment areas for Quarter Sessions which are not the same as police districts (see § 3.2 for the problems of measurement this would involve). We note here only that the level of punishments might well be an important determinant of the likelihood of conviction, in general, and indeed we shall refer to this effect when discussing the social choice of punishment levels in Chapter 9. We do not, however, include it in as a factor influencing variations in the detection rate between areas.

3.2 THE LEVEL OF PUNISHMENTS

It might appear that there are quite good grounds for supposing that the level of punishments meted out by the courts—which we included as one of the "deterrent" variables affecting the behaviour of offenders (see Chapter 2, § 2.2.3)—might in turn depend on the existing level of recorded crime. For judges have been known to make reference to existing levels of crime in justifying what they call "exemplary" sentences. For example, each of a group of youths with no previous convictions who attacked and wounded blacks in Notting Hill was given a sentence of four years imprisonment in 1958 at a time when the usual punishment for a comparable offence would have been a heavy fine or, at most, six months imprisonment (see *The Times*, 16th September, 1958). Similarly, Lord Chief Justice Parker claimed that vandalism in damaging telephone kiosks would be detered by custodial sentences (*The Times*, 5th February, 1966).

There are some criminologists who claim that the level of offences affects the pattern of punishments by area. Thus, Arnott and Duncan (1970) discussing the change in use of detention in Scotland for different types of offences between 1954/5 and 1961/2 say that ". . . it is seen that consistently severer sentences are imposed in the cities. Whether this indicates that city crimes are of a more serious nature and therefore the perpetrators receive sterner penalties, or whether the sterner penalties are simply a matter of policy, the criminal statistics as presently constituted make it impossible to determine" (p. 137). We note here that they believe that sentencers react to offence rates but we shall be commenting further on their inferences from data in Chapter 8.

If, in order to correctly estimate the parameters of our model, we have to take into consideration the process by which the level of punishments is determined, then we must consider which other variables, apart from the offence rate play a part in this process. We have suggested above that individual sentencers might react to particular types of offences—normally the violent ones—with increased punishments. This would suggest that the same crime-mix variable which has already been proposed, the proportion of total indictable offences involving offences against the person, should also be included as a factor affecting the level of punishments.

Secondly, if sentencers do respond to social pressures because of the level of recorded criminality, one might expect that a social class variable would be important. It could be argued that the offending behaviour of a predominantly working-class area would be viewed severely by the sentencing body because of the social distance between it and those sentenced; whilst middle-class magistrates in a predominantly middle-class area might tend towards leniency. Although our prior belief is not very strong, we therefore suggest that the proportion of middle-class people in an area is another factor which affects the level of punishment.

Finally, it is frequently argued that sentencers are influenced by the prison capacity (see N. D. Walker (1968) p. 210). It is certainly true that some forms of disposal cannot be ordered unless the court has been told that corresponding facilities exist in their area. The clearest examples are attendance centre and detention centre orders; these were being introduced during the sixties and so were not everywhere available. Remand homes also often become full, and hospital or restriction orders cannot be imposed unless a hospital or out-patient clinic is willing to accept the offender as a patient. Only prisons, borstals, the special hospitals, probation officers and children's departments have to accept offenders—however overloaded they are.

The capacity of penal institutions does therefore seem to be an important variable. However, it is very difficult to construct an appropriate measure within the context of our study. For penal institutions are not linked to police districts: not only are they directly administered by the Prison Department of the Home Office, many of them are specialist institutions whose inmates may have been sentenced anywhere in a large region. Thus for our model, capacity constraints contribute to random effects and noise but do not provide an argument for the inclusion of an extra relation.

Note that were the capacity constraint to be relevant to our model, increases in recorded offences, for a given conviction rate, would imply a reduction in the proportion of convicted offenders who are imprisoned. In this sense the severity of punishment would decrease with the level of recorded offences; this, of course, would run counter to the effect described previously.

Finally, Gibbs (1975) suggests that the level of punishments in a community is determined by the social condemnation of offending behaviour (he also suggests that this determines the offence rate—see the previous chapter, § 2.2.3). Once again, it is difficult to decide what would be an appropriate measure of social condemnation and Gibbs himself is not precise. Inasmuch as social condemnation might vary between areas, this might be captured partly by the proportion of middle class in an area. If Gibbs (1975) is also right in supposing that the level of social condemnation influences the level and pattern of offences, then variables which capture variations in the level and pattern or offences (which we have already included) might serve as surrogate measures for the social condemnation. We have not, therefore, searched for another variable.

Thus the determinants of the level of punishment, if it is to be explained inside the system, have been identified as the recorded offence rate, the proportion of the population that is middle class, and the ratio of offences against the person to all indictable offences.

On a national level the overall level of punishments meted out in the courts is affected by the prevailing social conditions, and the perceived amount and pattern of crime is almost certainly a very important element in any assessment of these social conditions. Similarly, sentencing patterns over time in England and Wales have been heavily influenced by the institutional capacity which the executive is prepared to provide (see Walker (1968)). Equally, on an individual level, the sentence imposed on an individual offender is influenced not only by the type of offence for which he is convicted but also by his social characteristics (see Thomas (1970)). Moreover, individual sentencers have their own idiosyncracies and, where these are large enough, they will affect the average level of sentence imposed by the bench of which he is a member, so that one observes variations between the pattern of sentences imposed at different courts. Indeed, we argued in the previous chapter that these variations would affect the behaviour of a potential offender.

It is not, however, plausible that these variations between courts can be related to variations between the police districts in the level and pattern of offences and the social structure of an area. First, there is the problem of the non-alignment of the police district and the sentencing authority of a particular bench. Secondly, the cases we cited where judges remarked on the level of offences in justifying particular sentences, concerned relatively rare offences. Finally, a study by Carr-Hill (1979) of the variations in sentences imposed on individuals by nine Courts of Quarter Sessions in England and Wales in 1963, showed that it was impossible to distinguish between benches according to their social characteristics and that variations in crime rates had only a small effect on variations in the severity of punishments. Our investigation of this possibility is therefore conducted with our prior beliefs tilted against rather than for the hypothesis that such a relation is an important part of the system.

3.3 THE SUPPLY OF AND DEMAND FOR POLICE

3.3.0 *The Problem*

We have argued that an important variable determining both the recorded offence rate (in Chapter 2) and the recorded detection rate (in the previous sections) is the level of social control. This has been measured, in both cases, by the police manpower and the expenditure per officer. We must decide whether or not to treat either (or both) of these variables as being determined inside the system.

We concentrate here on the number of policemen (see § 3.3.3 for expenditure). A standard economic approach would be to analyse the determination of the number of policemen in terms of a *demand* from the public for police and a *supply* from individuals who wish to be policemen. One would then, following the standard procedure, go on to suppose that supply and demand were in equilibrium. There would be two relations to be incorporated into the model simultaneously, supply and demand. However, it is not obvious in this case that supply does equal demand for policemen. The examination of the issue requires a preliminary discussion of the process of allocation of police strength to different areas.

The bulk of spending on the police is incurred by the local police forces. Despite reorganisation in 1968, the system of financing has remained structurally the same. Each police force is controlled by a police authority two-thirds of which consists of councillors and one-third of magistrates, with slight variations for police authorities covering two or more local councils and the City of London. The police service is partly financed by a direct grant representing 50% of approved police costs from central government, the remainder coming from rates and the Rate Support Grant. The main instrument of central control is that the Special Police Grant is dependent upon the Home Secretary being satisfied that the force is efficiently and properly maintained and equipped. In addition, the Home Office controls spending on capital programmes and fixes national pay and allowances. Subject to all this, police budgets are a matter for local police authorities.

Central government control seems, at the moment, to be encouraging recruitment rather than imposing a ceiling on it. Thus the 23 December 1974 Joint Circular on Rate Fund Expenditures and Rate Calls in 1975-76 said: "It is the Government's intention to strengthen the police and the forecast allows for 1,000 additional police officers compared with the number in post at the mid-point of the current financial year. If this increase is exceeded, within the limits of authorised police establishments, specific grants will be paid on the additional expenditure". Establishment strengths, decided jointly between local police authorities and the Home Office, are rarely met (see Table 3.1). Thus the local police authority seems to have considerable freedom in determining the level of manpower. The problem appears to be in finding more policemen and keeping those already in the force. In other words, supply falls short of demand.

We can demonstrate this by comparing the male establishment numbers authorised with the manpower available to obtain the corresponding shortfalls in strength during the decade in which we are interested (Table 3.1).

Table 3.1
Aggregate shortfall in police numbers

	Establishment authorised	Available manpower	Shortfall
1 January 1961	57 179	53 126	4 053
1 January 1966	69 965	62 119	7 846
End 1971	79 289	71 150	8 139

*Source:*Reports of Her Majesty's Inspector of Constabulary for 1961, HMSO, 1962, p. 6; for 1966, HMSO, 1967, p. 12; for 1971, HMSO, 1972, pp. 14-5.

There was a rapid increase in establishment of between two and four thousand a year between 1960 and 1967, which changed after reorganisation in 1968 to a lower yearly increase of around 500. In the case of the majority of forces there was a deficiency in strength (in the sense of the shortfall in Table 3.1) as can be seen from the following table for 1966.

Table 3.2
Shortfall in police numbers in detail in 1966

Deficiencies in strength	County forces	City and Borough forces
Less than 2%	2	2
2 — 5%	6	9
5 — 10%	14	15
10 — 20%	17	32
20 — 25%	5	4
25 — 30%	1	3
Over 30%	4	2

Source: Report of Her Majesty's Chief Inspector of Constabulary for the year 1966, H.M.S.O., 1967, page 12.

We have seen that it is illegitimate to view demand for and supply of police as being in equilibrium, and it is supply that is the effective constraint on the number of policemen in the force. Thus our relation for the number of policemen in an area should be interpreted as modelling the determination of supply. We shall allow what are apparently demand factors to enter the relation, however, since the enthusiasm with which recruitment is pursued in an area will depend on demand, and we suppose that recruitment drives do affect the numbers coming forward to be policemen.

3.3.1 Factors Determining the Level of "Demand"

At central government level, the establishment strengths of police forces are determined by a number of factors including "population growth or decline, crime rates, road mileage and road accidents, also the length of the police working week" (Report of Her Majesty's Chief Inspector of Constabulary for the year 1973, p. 9). In 1966 the House of Commons Estimates Committee felt strongly that a much more clear-cut method was required for rational planning (First Report, Session 1966-67, *Police*, HMSO, 1966, (HC145) paragraph 18), but a follow-up inquiry (Second Report, Session 1968-69, *Police*, HMSO, 1969, (HC89), paras. 6, 7) reported that it was unlikely that "any single comprehensive formula" could be found. The Expenditure Committee (Seventh Report, Session 1974, *Police Recruitment and Wastage*, HMSO, 1974, (HC310), para. 10) concluded "We find it unsatisfactory that there is no clear explanation how an establishment is in practice decided", but the Home Office replied that "a formula capable of general application is not a practical possibility" (Home Office, *Police Recruitment and Wastage* (Observations on the Seventh Report of the Expenditure Committee), HMSO, 1974, Cmnd. 6016, para. 7).

Whilst it may be difficult for the Home Office to construct a precise formula, one can identify certain factors as being important in determining demand. Consider the list described at the beginning of the previous paragraph. *Population growth and decline* are largely irrelevant in a cross-sectional analysis, but we should note that our form of analysis already takes the size of the population into account, since the criterion variable is police *per capita*. It seems obvious that the Home Office's view of police requirements in an area will be influenced by the recorded *crime rate*; indeed, the power of the central authority to draft policemen from one area to another, although used sparingly, was one main reason for supposing that the number of police per capita was determined within the system. Information on the *police working week* was not available by area so we have had to omit consideration of this variable. Finally, it would have been possible to collect information on *road accidents and road mileage*, but we decided instead to include a more general measure of the type of area being policed. We chose population density partly because it is a convenient proxy for urbanisation (and therefore for road accidents and road mileage) partly because more densely populated areas almost certainly require more police-men *per capita*, but also partly because of conversations with a Home Office economist.

We have decided to include, as factors affecting the Home Office's view of police requirements, two other variables. First, we suppose that, even though clear-up rates are not published by police district because they are seen as unreliable (McClintock and Avison (1968) p. 120), they in fact, affect an assessment of need. Secondly, it seems likely that local pressure to increase authorised establishment strength, will at least affect recruiting drives. We decided to include that proportion of the population which is middle-class. For we can suppose that areas with high concentrations of middle-class people, and therefore with a more than ordinarily middle-class police authority, will be more concerned by a given offence rate than others, partly because they have more to lose in terms of property and partly because they value more highly a sense of stability and security.

3.3.2 *Factors Influencing Supply*

The actual daily strength of the typical police force usually varies between 80 and 90% of the establishment strength (see Table 3.2, p. 72). In fact, these shortfalls have often been perceived as sufficiently serious for there to be intensive recruiting campaigns in schools and in universities, and big increases in pay. In late 1960, the Interim Report of the Royal Commission on the Police (1960) recommended substantial increases in the salary scale for constables. These were to vary with length of service and amounted to more than 30% for those with nine or more years' service (*op. cit.* paragraphs 170-85 and Appendix V). The increases were implemented in the following year. It is significant that 1960 was a year in which the Report of Her Majesty's Inspector of Constabulary (1960) shows that there was a decrease in available manpower of 168. The corresponding Reports of Her Majesty's Inspector of Constabulary for the following three years show an increase during this period of 5,939.

A labour economist would discuss the effectiveness of recruiting in terms of the comparative advantage in terms of wages and benefits of taking and keeping a job as a policeman, compared to other similar occupations in that area. Without a special study of relative wage rates and comparative working conditions, it is difficult however, to see how to construct an index which would be sensitive enough to discriminate between areas. Even if we can disaggregate an industrial wage index by area, we should still have to decide which occupations compete for labour with the police and this is problematic.

We decided to opt for a global index of conditions in the local labour market in an area on the grounds that occupations with recruitment problems would benefit in a slack labour market. The most natural index is the rate of unemployment. For, although the choice of the police as an occupation is unlikely to be in response to short-term conditions in the labour market, areas with higher unemployment rates at a given point in time would usually have had a recent history of relatively high unemployment rates. In other words, although the unemployment rate in an area fluctuates over time, relativities are generally preserved so that recruitment to the police will be easier in an area with higher current unemployment.

Many people have argued, however, that the problem is not one of recruitment but of resignations from the force. Thus, according to Sir Robert Mark, Commissioner of the Metropolitan Police (April 1972 to March 1977), the effects of an intensive recruiting programme in London in 1972 were more than offset by the large numbers of men leaving the force (see Borrell and Cashinella (1975), p. 6). Similarly, David McNee, Chief Constable of Glasgow, said to his Police Committee: "I am persuaded that the main causes are unsocial hours, the consequent disruption to family life, and the inadequacy of the pay offered to young men embarking on a career in the force" (quoted on p. 3 in Borrell and Cashinella (1975)). These factors apply equally to all police forces but the extent to which a police officer would be tempted to resign would be influenced, in part, by conditions in the local labour market.

If, on the other hand, it is low morale in a police force that leads to more resignations than otherwise, then there are several possibilities to account for low levels of manpower in certain areas. Thus, if there is a high offence rate in an area or if it is difficult to clear up reported crimes, then serving policemen may begin to think that their work load is too high and their results disappointing. Somewhat similarly, a high rate of violent crime in an area may make a policeman believe that his job is too dangerous. Thus an explanation of the number of police *per capita* in an area based on supply-side factors should include the offence rate, the clear-up rate, and an index of violent crime.

It should be noted that the three factors just mentioned would influence demand in the opposite direction, but we have argued that it appears to be supply effects which dominate. Our list of factors modelling the supply of police *per capita* then becomes the following: those directly influencing the decision of the individual to become or remain a policeman are the rate of unemployment, the offence rate, the clear-up rate, and the proportion of offences that are violent; and those influencing the intensity of recruitment in addition to these factors mentioned above are the population density and the proportion of the population that is middle-class (see § 3.3.2).

3.3.3 *Expenditure per Officer*

We have just discussed the appropriate explanatory variables in modelling the determination of the number of policemen *per capita*. One might suppose that similar arguments applied to expenditure per officer; however, there is no supply equation for expenditure per officer as there is for a police officer. Expenditure per officer is determined as the outcome of a complicated decision process involving the local authority and the Home Office. The factors influencing the result would be similar to those involved in the determination of the demand for policemen. Given that we suppose the discussion in and between local authority and the Home Office concentrates on the number of policemen, we decided not to attempt to model separately the determination of the expenditure per officer. We suppose that it is determined outside the model.

3.4 THE NATURE OF CRIMINAL STATISTICS

3.4.0 *Introduction*

The review of theories in Chapter 2 looked at a variety of claims which have been made for according one variable or another causal primacy in explaining crime. In these types of theory, the focus has often been on understanding the problem which is causing crime—whether it be lack of employment, poor integration into society, or faulty upbringing—and on the offending behaviour of the individual. Law and sanctions are seen as having developed in response to the problems posed by criminal behaviour although of course they would in turn influence behaviour.

In this section we look at the major challenge to this view—sometimes called a consensus view—which has developed on the basis of conflict theory. Theorists differ but their general position is that crime is a product of the social order, and consequently any attempt to explain observed criminality must take into account the way in which those who hold economic and political power (variously defined) affect the nature of crime through criminal legislation and its enforcement. Early conflict theorists tended to concentrate on poverty and inequality[8] caused by the development

---

[8]These factors are the same as those considered in the previous chapter under the heading "traditional criminology". There is no contradiction here, since the causal chain for the conflict theorist goes from the distribution of power through poverty to criminality; whilst for a present-day consensus theorist the causal chain begins with poverty.

of capital, in opposition to the then (19th century) dominant belief that poverty was a consequence or a symptom of criminal activity which itself was caused by idleness, intemperance or physical or mental defects. However, the arguments of the recent group of sociologists of deviance have concentrated on the capacity of official agents of social control to define certain actions and people as deviants and not others.

Inasmuch as the early conflict theorists recognised the existence of a real level of criminality and acknowledged *immediate* causes very similar to those which we considered in Chapter 2, we consider them no further here. Moreover, such theories tend to be on a grand scale and so would not be relevant to an explanation of areal variations in the pattern of recorded offences. Instead we examine the writings of sociologists of deviance who have been suggesting that a wide range of factors determine whether or not an act is labelled criminal. Some of the theorists go on to deny the existence of criminal behaviour *per se* and claim that the official statistics can only be seen as a record of sanctions and are therefore of limited interest. Others simply emphasize the importance of taking into account organisational features of the social-control apparatus in discussing the meaning of variations in crime rates. These different views are presented below in § 3.4.1 and their implications for the model we shall be constructing are discussed in § 3.4.2.

3.4.1 *Sociology of Deviance and Criminal Statistics*

We first of all consider the position that, since official statistics are merely sanctions and since the system of law and order determines what is a crime, then the criminal label which is imposed on an offender is arbitrary (in a sense to be explained). Turk (1969) states: "Thus anyone who is defined officially as a violator . . . is criminal in the *generic* sense, whatever he may be called in a word with the terminologies and assumptions currently in vogue. That there are differences in the ways in which authorities perceive and process violators does not negate the fact that . . . our observations are of the sanctioning process" (p. 22).

Turk's position is that the only characteristic which is common to incidents recorded as offences is that they have been recorded—we cannot therefore assume that they share any other features. This would mean that the official crime statistics are covering a very wide range of possible activities or situations, so that the attempt to account for variations in them would be forlorn. Douglas (1967) in discussing suicide rates, appears to agree: "The term 'potential suicide rate' is used here, rather than the more normal term 'real suicide rate', simply because it is a fundamental part of the argument throughout this work that there does not exist such a thing as a 'real suicide rate'. Suicides are not something of a set nature waiting to be correctly or incorrectly categorised by officials. The very nature of the 'thing' is itself problematic so that 'suicides' cannot be correctly said to exist (i.e. to be 'things') until a categorisation has been made'' (p. 196).

Further, Cicourel (1968) who relies on a general theory about social measurement, appears sometimes to argue that delinquency rates are unusable because of the arbitrary way in which decisions about the dispositions of individual juveniles are taken.

When researchers seek the 'underlying patterns' to manifest materials, they employ an implicit abstracting procedure for discovering a few ideas to explain large masses of unintelligible manifest data, rather than develop a theoretical apparatus that would explain and generate everyday behaviour (pp. 332-3).

We should agree that the relation between recorded criminality and actual behaviour is very problematic and that one cannot use recorded rates of criminality in any direct sense as indices of the processes by which actual behaviour is generated. We should, however, argue that the question of how recorded crime rates are produced is an interesting and sensible one. Indeed, many authors take this as the problem for research: thus Kitsuse and Cicourel (1963) say ''Our primary aim is to explain the *rates of deviant behaviour* . . . [this explanation] would be concerned specifically with the processes of rate construction'' (p. 135). When examining the treatment of juvenile delinquents, Cicourel (1968) concludes ''each successive stage of legal decision-making transforms the object or event so that the contingencies, the situation in which the actor interprets what is going on, the kind of 'theorising' or thinking employed, are progressively altered, eliminated and reified as the case proceeds up the legal machinery and reaches the stage of a hearing, trial or appellate jurisdiction'' (pp. 50-3).

Hindness (1973) emphasizes the extent to which the recorded official statistics depend on a theory of society and are thus a direct reflexion of the class structure of society. He states: ''. . . the evaluation of (official statistics) for scientific purposes must never be restricted to a concern with more or less deliberate misrepresentation or with the identification of technical errors or inadequacies . . . In addition to these considerations, the rational evaluation and utilisation of statistics for scientific purposes must take account of the conceptual means of their production, that is, of the system of categories together with the instructions and elaborations in which they are specified'' (Chapter 3, pp. 44-5). For him it is irrelevant to make any statements about the extent to which particular categories of individuals will be involved in criminal behaviour. Thus, ''the evaluation of social statistics is always and necessarily a theoretical exercise and, further, different theoretical problematics must produce different and sometimes contradictory evlauations of any given set of statistics" (p. 47).

This view is taken further by Taylor, Walton and Young (1975) when they say "It is clear that a proper examination of the statistics is helpful in revealing the class-organised practice of criminal and legal systems" (p. 36-7). Indeed, in some ways, our study in examining the factors determining the official criminal statistics is a test of these propositions.

3.4.2 Is there a Real Crime Rate?

There remains however, one problem posed by these arguments for the development of our model. Insofar as the social order has defined certain actions as criminal and has provided procedures which are more or less followed in determining whether or not any particular action can be classed as criminal, the effect of these procedures can be modelled. But Cicourel (1968) and Douglas (1967) seem, at some points, to argue that the outcome— the identification of a particular event as an offence or person as an offender, is an arbitrary decision of the agents of social control. It is unclear what these authors mean by "arbitrary"[9] but it could imply they believe that it is not possible, even in principle, to identify any particular type of behaviour as being criminal, of which recorded criminality is a subset. Turk's position is less rigid in that he believes that the only quantity of interest is the recorded crime rate and how it is produced. Taylor, Walton and Young (1975), seem to take it for granted that there is a real crime rate. "Both working-class and upper-class crime (whether reported, apprehended and prosecuted or not) are *real* features of a society involved in a struggle for property, wealth and economic self-aggrandisement" (p. 34).

The differences between the theoretical positions in respect of the meaning of the official criminal statistics have not usually been seen as important. All sociologists of deviance can agree that the official criminal statistics do not reflect actual behaviour and since, for other reasons (see, for example, Taylor, Walton and Young (1975) Chapter 1), they are not interested in quantitative analysis, there is no need to be more precise.[10]

[9] Indeed, at other points, Douglas (1967) seems to believe that this arbitrariness eventually leads to consistency—thus "the probabilistic nature of the categorisations is sufficient in itself to account for the regularity of official suicide statistics in any given society or, at least, most of the regularity. But, if the suicide deaths [i.e. before categorisation] are themselves probabilistics so that we have a two-stage probabilistic process, then we can expect even greater regularity than would otherwise have been the case".

[10] Indeed, since many writers in this vein avoid any reference to criminal statistics at all, they give the impression that such statistics are of no interest whatsoever. Obviously we hold a different view—which is summarised at the end of this section.

However, our problem is to model the effects indicated by these theorists: two approaches are possible. The first argues that there is a well-defined and finite actual crime rate. We have discussed in Chapter 2 some of the theories which try to explain its level and the above authors may have some other theories in mind. If we accept this position, we must then try to specify a relation between the recorded rate and the actual rate. The second approach states that the social structure provides that any situation can be defined as involving criminality and that those incidents which are reported are some subset of all actions which is defined by those in power and authority. Thus one cannot sensibly speak of the actual crime rate and our task should be to model the process determining the recorded rate.

It is indeed possible that people could be indicted for transgressing less serious laws in a very large variety of situations: for example, in England there is no speed at which one can walk without being open to either a charge of loitering or disorderly behaviour likely to cause a breach of the peace (running). On the other hand, even if we allow that the particular definitions of criminality can be manipulated in a number of ways, it seems difficult to believe that a similarly large variety of circumstances can be defined as involving what are considered to be the most serious crimes such as homicide, aggravated assault, rape and robbery.

Thus, in a poignant passage about the findings of his survey of officially recorded crime in the United States, Curtis (1975) says that "the attack on 'traditional criminology' is insensitive to the commonsense reality of the contemporary American ghetto-slum and is really just designed for debate among white theorists" (Curtis (1975) p. 126). His attack is perhaps a little misplaced, in that sociologists of deviance were specifically concerned with the criminalisation of people for "minor deviations", but the point is well taken.

The consequences of the two approaches for our study are as follows. Under the first we suppose that, if we choose those crimes which are regarded as more serious and refer to identifiable incidents, then the true crime rate, though possibly very large indeed, can be defined and is finite. From the point of view of this study that is all that is necessary.[11] If it is acknowledged that there is a true crime rate, the issue becomes one of determining what are the factors which transform it into the observed official statistics. If we follow the second approach, we suppose that there is no "actual" crime rate and that the recorded crimes are the result of the social interaction between individual actors, the agents of social control and the members of the public involved. In this case, from the point of view of

---

[11] We must also suppose under this interpretation, that an incident which is recorded as an offence is also an actual offence.

this study, we are concerned to model the factors which determine whether or not an incident is recorded as a crime by the authorities. In other words, we have to look for social characteristics of the incident or individual which affect the likelihood of labelling.

It is not only the characteristics of the individual that determine the likelihood of his being labelled as an offender. For he can take action himself to decrease the probability of being so labelled. It is particularly likely that he will choose to take such action where the probability of being labelled is high and the consequences severe. Thus one can argue that the probability and severity of punishment affect the recorded offence rate whether or not they affect the actual and, indeed, whether or not one accepts the notion of an actual offence rate.

Whichever view is taken of the status of the recorded offence rate an understanding of the process by which it is produced is both important and interesting. We therefore reject the implication that seems to arise from the argument of some sociologists of deviance that the difficulties with the notion of actual offences renders the recorded offence rate unworthy of study.

The remainder of this chapter concentrates on the social characteristics of the incident or individual which affect public reporting and police recording practices.

3.5 RECORDING AND REPORTING

3.5.0 *Introduction*

The literature on the ways in which the organisation and strategy of social control affect the observed crime rate is vast but insufficient for our purposes. Thus there are several studies showing that the attitudes of some person (often an official agent of social control) has affected the labelling of an action or an individual as criminal. Although these studies are often very precise about the way in which this has happened, it is very difficult to make them the basis for generalisations which can be used in other situations and which make it possible to say that the occurrence of certain factors or situations is likely to increase the recorded crime rate for a given actual crime rate. The review of the literature which follows is, therefore, very selective in choosing only those studies which point to the importance of a factor which could be included in our model. We show first, however, that there is wide scope for reporting and recording effects.

3.5.1 *The Magnitude of the "Dark Number"*

It is important to emphasize the possible magnitudes of the effects that we have to consider. Studies of self-reported delinquency or criminality, where a random sample of respondents are asked whether or not they have ever—or in a fixed period of time—committed a delinquent act, suggest that there is an enormous "pool" of unrecorded and unreported delinquency. Thus, Short and Nye (1957) seemed to show that nearly every juvenile in the United States had, within the last year, committed an offence. And although respondents do report trivial incidents, the recording problem exists for every major type of offence. Thus, Erickson and Empey (1963) obtained the results given in Table 3.3 from a sample of 180 adolescent males in the United States aged 15-17 who were asked about whether they had committed 22 types of violations and if so, how often. The responses indicate quite prodigious powers of recall.

Table 3.3
Extent of violations and per cent undetected

Category of offence	Entire sample		Sub-samples			
	Total (offences)	% Unde-tected	Non-delinquents		Incarcerated delinquents	
			Total (offen-ces)	% Unde-tected	Total (offen-ces)	% Unde-tected
Traffic	23,946	98·6	3,885	98·9	11,953	99·0
Theft	24,199	96·3	1,031	91·3	8,472	94·5
Alcohol and Narcotics	21,773	99·1	237	100·0	15,580	99·1
Property violations	12,278	96·8	546	96·7	5,374	96·4
Offences against the person	9,026	99·6	354	100·0	6,340	99·5

Source: Erikson and Empey (1963), pp. 460-1.

Note: an offence was defined as detected if the offender was detected by the police, a parent or any adult.

The American studies suggest that some of the non-reported delinquencies are relatively serious. In England and Wales, however, studies tend to emphasize the triviality of reported but non-recorded delinquencies. Thus West and Farrington (1973) report the results of a questionnaire on possible delinquent acts administered to 405 boys at the ages of 14-15 and 16-17 (as part of a longitudinal survey of the development of juvenile delinquency) in the following terms:

. . . the overwhelming majority of our boys had committed the more trivial acts such as letting off fireworks in the street (93·2 per cent), going to 'X' films under age (91·7 per cent), travelling without a ticket (89·5 per cent) and riding a bicycle without lights (88·3 per cent). On the other hand, only a small minority claimed to have indulged in the more seriously delinquent acts such as planned housebreaking (7·1 per cent), unplanned housebreaking (9·3 per cent), store-breaking (9·5 per cent) and shop-breaking (12·7 per cent) (p. 154).

On the other hand, when they ranked the boys on their self-reported delinquent behaviour, they found that the 80 boys with the highest self-report scores—all of whom had admitted at least 21 acts—included only 41 of the 84 boys who were officially registered as delinquents.

Finally, although the majority of studies have been concerned with the activities of juveniles, there is no reason to believe that the results would be substantially different with adults. Indeed, one of the first studies which demonstrated the prevalence of deviance was by Wallerstein and Wyle (1947), who distributed questionnaires naming 49 offences which, under the penal law of New York, were sufficiently serious to draw a maximum sentence of not less than one year. Questionnaires were returned by 1,698 individuals from New York City and showed that the mean number of offences committed in adult life ranged from 8.2 per person for ministers to 20.2 for labourers (with a mean of 18 for all men).

In other words the volume of incidents or events which could be classed as indictable crime must be several times the recorded annual figure of one and one-half million (England and Wales, 1971), and the same is true for each major class of offence. In this situation, since it seems highly unlikely that the apparatus of official social control acts randomly, it is curious that we should ever have to argue that the incidents actually recorded (and therefore the individuals involved) are a biased subset of actual offending. Nevertheless, it is remarkable how many studies have ignored this problem.

The argument that, although police statistics are not a statistically random sample of all offences, the offences which are *not* reported or recorded are trivial and certainly not as serious as those which are, cannot be sustained as a universal claim. For indictable offences of property include any theft or embezzlement however small the amount involved so that, for example, many thefts of objects of low value are recorded in the criminal statistics as indictable offences (see § 2.0). So only if unrecorded thefts were predominantly of articles of negligible value could the argument be taken seriously. That this is not the case can be seen from the results obtained by Belson (1975) from an interview survey of 1425 London boys aged between 13 and 16, on the extent to which they had committed 44 classes of theft behaviour. A large number of offences in each class were unrecorded and some classes involved serious offences. He observes: "All of [them] admitted to at least some stealing and there was no class of theft behaviour . . . that was endorsed [admitted to] by less than 5 per cent" (p. xii).

An examination of the factors which affect public reporting and police recording behaviour is therefore central to the construction of our model. This is the task of the next two sections.

3.5.2 *Studies of Reporting to the Police*

Until recently, the evidence on what influences reporting to the police by the public as distinct from the evidence of respondents in self-report studies has tended to be limited to special circumstances. Martin's (1962) survey of companies in Reading showed that, among the six most recent cases of theft or embezzlement which each company could recall, more than half were not notified to the police, the most frequent reasons being that the result would not have been worth the unpleasantness or publicity, that the offender was regarded as a good worker or a "decent chap", that it would have been a "waste of time", or that the loss was not serious enough. None of these reasons provides useful ways of distinguishing between the mass of unrecorded and recorded offences, for a cross-sectional analysis such as ours.

McClintock (1963) in his study of crimes of violence, reports the police as stressing that there was a increasing tendency on the part of the victims and members of the public to report crimes of violence.[12] He goes on to estimate that "in many areas it would be quite easy to find four or five times as many crimes of violence that had not been reported to the police as had actually been recorded by them" (p. 72). He goes on to explain that the police accounted for this either because some violence was accepted as normal, or because of lack of sympathy with the police, or because the victims wanted to avoid unwelcome publicity. Once again this does not provide us with ways of distinguishing between areas in their patterns of recording.

However, victim surveys carried out in the last decade have often asked respondents, who had reported being victims of offences and who had not notified the police, why they did not do so. The main English study (by Sparks, *et al.* (1977)) at the Cambridge Institute of Criminology has not yet been published.[13] However, American studies suggest variously that the propensity to report depends on the public attitude to the police (Biderman

---

[12] It is interesting that in the light of these statements he says "it is generally agreed that in the last ten years there has been an increase in crimes of violence". But more of this in Chapter 8.

[13] We learnt of the eventual publication of this study too late to include it in our discussion.

(1967)), the perceived threat of victimisation (Hawkins (1973)), and the likely pay-off from reporting (Schafer (1968)). For example, Hawkins (1973) interviewed 1,411 subjects in Seattle and found that 744 had been the victim of at least one criminal act in the last year. Of the most recent incidents (for any given individual) 345 (45%) had been reported to the police—interestingly enough only 263 (34%) by the victims themselves. He found that those victims who did report, perceived the threat of property victimisation to be, in general, high. Among victims who did not report, 33% said that nothing would have been done and another 29% said they did not want to get involved.

The American studies we have quoted above do not show a clear demarcation of seriousness between those incidents which are reported and those which are not. There is the suggestion that victims who make reports to the police perceive offending behaviour more seriously than others. But since the argument of sociologists of deviance is that definitions of evil—and specifically of criminality—depend on who is doing the defining, this finding is both unsurprising and inadequate for distinguishing between groups of incidents.

Other important clues can be drawn from the survey of the relations between the London public and the Metropolitan Police Force conducted on behalf of the Metropolitan Police in 1972, reported in Belson (1975). Belson reports the responses of the 1,200 adults, 503 young people and 1,000 police officers interviewed (who constituted 81%, 97% and 93% of the respective populations who were eligible and available).

Belson (1975a) obtained the following results when respondents were asked if they would contact the police in each of a range of situations:

Table 3.4
Willingness of the public to contact the police in different situations

	%
If your home was burgled	99
If a child of yours was lost	99
If you saw teenagers damaging a telephone kiosk	80
If you were the only person to see a car accident	80
If you lost your purse or wallet	75
If a stranger made an indecent suggestion to you	60
If you saw a stranger hanging around for a long time in your street	58
If you knew someone had a gun that he had not got a licence for	48
If you knew one of your neighbours was driving a stolen car	46
If you saw a fight in a cafe	39
If you knew someone was selling something that had been pinched	33

Source: Belson (1975a) p. 45.

The reasons for being unwilling to contact the police were principally that the respondent felt:

(a) It is somehow wrong or unfair to report people to the police.

(b) There might be retaliation by the person reported.

(c) No useful purpose would be served because the police are too busy or would not be interested or the trouble would be over before the police arrived.

(d) The incidence was not important enough or "happens all the time".

Then the interviewer evoked a series of different ways in which people might help the police. When asked if they would be willing to help in the future "the great majority (97 per cent) claimed that, given a chance, they would be helpful to the police" (Belson (1975a) p. 46). However, when asked if they had ever helped in specific ways there was more variation "with 64 per cent claiming that they had at sometime told their children to look on the police as their friends and 1 per cent saying that they had reported a motorist going through a red light" (Belson (1975a) p. 47). The contrast between past and potential helpfulness is quite marked.

The results he obtained with young people were quite different. The interviewers asked not only whether young people would contact the police, but whether they would contact anyone at all with the results shown in Table 3.5. The percentage willing to contact the police did not rise beyond 68% for any of the ten situations considered. Furthermore, it was well below 50% with respect to "if someone had drugs on them". In addition, there was a similar contrast between past and potential helpfulness as with the adult sample.

Table 3.5

Willingness to contact anyone/the police in different situations: youth sample

Hypothetical situation	Proportion willing to contact	
	The police (%)	Anyone (%)
If a gang of boys was beating someone up	68	87
If there was a car accident and someone got hurt	66	99
If you found a bunch of keys in the street	64	84
If some boys were breaking up a telephone kiosk	59	73
If something of yours was stolen	58	92
If you lost your purse or wallet	57	85
If someone you know had pinched a car	46	58
If someone was hanging around some parked cars	32	38
If someone had drugs on them	30	43
If a strange man followed you home at night	22	74

Source: Belson (1975a) p. 49.

Other indirect, evidence does, however, suggest that public reporting discriminates systematically between different classes of offender. Researchers interpreting the almost equal distribution of self-reported delinquency across the social classes, attribute part of the wide disparity between self-reported and officially recorded middle-class juvenile delinquency to varying public perceptions of deviant behaviour by different social groups. (See for example, Gold (1966), Short and Nye (1957).)

Hood and Sparks (1970) summarize their comparison of the findings of self-report studies and official prosecutions as follows: ". . . the police and the public have definite sterotypes about the kinds of offence and offender which should be dealt with by the criminal law: seriousness of offence is certainly a major criterion for official action, but so also are persistence in offending, lack of family support, membership of street corner groups, and dress and demeanour . . ." (p. 78).

It is indeed plausible that, where the victim knows the offender, the likelihood of the incident being reported depends on the victim's attitude to the particular person involved. It is more usual, except in the case of offences against the person, however, for the offender to be unknown to the victim (and there is not always a victim). In this situation one can hazard a guess that reporting behaviour partly depends on the victim's image rather than his knowledge of the offender.

This brief survey suggests that the factors which influence the public to report incidents with which they are involved as offences to the police depends on their view of the offender, the incident, the likelihood of police action in respect of the particular offence type, and their attitude to the police. We turn in the next sub-section to police discretion in the recording offences. We shall see that variables which one might be able to derive to measure public willingness to report would be similar to those we shall be using to measure the operation of police discretion. We refer in particular to the age and class structure of the neighbourhood. The effects of these two variables appear to be more straightforward and better substantiated in the case of police discretion.

3.5.3 *Police Discretion in Recording*

As far as law breaking is concerned, virtually all of what is generally regarded as crime by large areas of society only emerges in court as a result of the police at some point in the process. (Russell (1973) p. 2.)

As Davis (1969) points out, the police in the U.S.A.:

. . . make far more discretionary determinations in individual cases than any other class of administrator; I know of no close second . . . the amount of governmental activity through the police, measured in man hours, is more than forty times as much as the amount of governmental activity through all seven of the independent federal regulating agencies [such as the Food and Narcotics Bureau]; those agencies in the aggregate have about 10,000 employees but the nation has about 420,000 policemen, exclusive of supporting personnel (pp. 222-3).

In England, Steer's study (1970) documents the fact of discretion in the decision to administer a caution (see also Rainton (1973)). But because "the police department has the special property . . . that within it discretion increases as one moves *down* the hierarchy" (Wilson (1968) p. 7), this discretion is both pervasive and relatively hard to identify in detail.

What is important to us here is the general way in which this discretion is used. Numerous American studies document the way in which the treatment received by black and young offenders differs from that received by the remainder of the offending population (see Piliavin and Briar (1964) and Skolnick (1966)). More important from our point of view is the way in which the police choose possible suspects. Chambliss and Seidman (1971) cite an article by a police inspector (Adams (1963)) on field interrogation (referring to the American system) which lists *Subjects who should be subjected to field interrogation* as follows:

1. *Suspicious persons known* to the officer from previous arrests, field interrogation and observations.
2. Emaciated-appearing alcoholics and narcotics users who *invariably turn to crime* to pay for the cost of habit.
3. Persons *who fit description* as wanted suspect.
4. Any person observed in the *immediate vicinity* of a crime very recently committed or reported as 'in progress'.
5. *Known trouble-makers* near large gatherings.
(p. 273.) (The italics are ours.)

The only innocuous item in the list appears to be point 3. On the other hand, the study by the Task Force on the Police for the President's Commission on Law Enforcement and the Administration of Justice (1967) cites an instructor in a training session:

(It) is a poor policeman who cannot find a description to fit the suspect, as you officers have at least 30 days of daily bulletins in your notebooks (p. 186).

Hence the criteria suggested during training mean that from the police point of view, there exists a group of *prime suspects*. They are identified either because of their suspicious appearance or associates or because they have been recently arrested or convicted. Stinchcombe (1963) suggests that the crucial variable is the social location of different types of crime—that is, whether in "private" or "public" places. He illustrates this argument by reference to the variations in police practice with respect to different types of crime. He goes on to argue that when a person does not have control over a "private place" he or she often has to produce special evidence of legitimate activity. This would point to the homeless and unemployed as being specially liable.

The only parallel English study[14] seems to be Russell (1973) who interviewed police officers about the most recent occasion on which they had questioned someone. He found that the police developed quite clear stereotypes on the basis of the various types of information collected by their divisional police force. Moreover, most policemen on the beat knew "their local criminals" and kept close watch on them (see Russell (1973).

One would naturally expect that the development of the police as a specialised bureaucracy to enforce society's norms and rules would lead to particular stereotypes of the criminal. First, a bureaucracy tends to develop a fairly well-defined set of parameters (from the information available to it) for internal use for the fulfilment of its tasks, in this case the pursuit and apprehension of offenders. Secondly, if the police do develop fairly well-structured and stable parameters for what counts as crime, this has the advantage that they can ignore the conflict of different possible interpretations which would otherwise be proposed by different groups in society. A bureaucracy is a formal organisation for making decisions according to a set of rules (see Gerth and Wright Mills, 1947). The argument above is but a natural extension of this.

Russell (1973) interviewed 96 police officers stationed in Brighton about their last check with SUSCRO (the information repository described above, § 3.1.1) to examine the situations where this social knowledge was used, why it was requested, and about whom. He also analysed a sample of over 2,000 of these checks at SUSCRO. In his interviews he found that over half of the 77 checks by uniformed officers were on persons whom the officer knew to be previously involved in crime, and that the remainder were relatively precise social categories (the Roadster, persons of No Fixed Abode, and Deviant Youth) seen to be marginal with respect to the normal community in and around Brighton.

There were two main purposes quoted by police for referring to SUSCRO: "getting to know who has a criminal record in the area"— usually checks of persons not previously known to the officer; and finding out whether a person was wanted—usually checks of previously known criminals.

Russell (1973) found that two thirds of the checks were of suspects aged 17 to 32, and that most available information concerns the criminality of

[14] We learnt of the publication of the study by McCabe and Sutcliffe (1978) too late for discussion of it to be included. They sat in police stations in Oxford and Manchester and observed the process of reporting to, and recording by, the police.

this group. Another of his findings was that, in general, younger people were more often checked in groups, rather than alone, which reinforces the view that the police see the young as a particular sub-culture. We conclude, from this study, that in areas with a high proportion of young people, incidents are more likely to be recorded as offences.

Further detail on attitudes to the young comes from the study of West and Farrington (1973) who examined the characteristics of boys who were classified differently according to self-report and official criteria with the results shown in Table 3.6. Thus group B (the boys who are self-reported but not official delinquents) are in the "better" category on nearly every factor than either group A (both self-reported and official) or group C (not self-reported but official). West and Farrington (1973) suggest that the most likely inerpretation is that "because the official processes are biassed towards labelling as delinquents those who possess the characteristics of the delinquent stereotype, the group B boys tend to get 'left out'" (p. 161).

Table 3.6
Differences between official and self-reported delinquents

Factor	A Official and self-reported (N = 41)	B Not official self-reported (N = 41)	C Official, not self-reported (N = 43)	D Not official, not self-reported (N = 286)
Troublesomeness	56·1	20·5	41·9	14·7
Daring	34·2	20·5	23·3	6·7
Dishonesty	54·8	27·8	43·2	18·2
Parental criminality	53·7	23·1	30·2	18·5
Poor parental behaviour	47·5	21·1	32·4	20·1
Low family income	48·8	15·4	25·6	19·6
Large family size	48·8	18·0	27·9	21·0
Clumsiness	43·9	23·1	34·9	21·3
Parental unco-operativeness	17·1	10·3	23·3	7·7
Separations	39·0	28·2	30·2	17·5
Low intelligence	48·8	23·1	27·9	21·3
Poor parental supervision	36·8	35·1	25·0	13·7
"Catholic" families	38·7	25·7	25·7	17·3
Parental authoritarianism	44·4	15·4	29·6	22·6
Delinquent older brothers	42·9	21·1	25·0	16·5

The figures in each cell represent the percentage of each group falling in the "worst" category in each factor. Source: West and Farrington (1973) p. 160.

If this latter interpretation is correct, then it is interesting to note that, apart from several personality features, the factors which discriminate between official and non-official but self-reported delinquents are low family income, large family size, and separations. In general, therefore, variables representing these factors should be included as explanations of the recorded offence rate, regardless of their effect on the actual offence rate. It should be noted that these three variables correspond to some of the factors that were discussed in Chapter 2 as distinguishing between offenders and non-offenders. The results reported above show that we should exercise caution before inferring an association between a factor and actual delinquency from an observed association between a factor and recorded delinquency.

We conclude from the work of West and Farrington that in areas with a high proportion of poor or working-class people, incidents are more likely to be recorded as offences.

Cain (1973), who carried out her research into the policeman's role in society in 1960, is also of interest here. She examined the relative influence of four groups of potential role definers. The local community in which she was working; the family; colleagues on the police force; and directions from her or his senior officers. She found:

> . . . the county policeman, in particular the man working a one-man rural beat, was highly motivated to accept the community's definition of reality and of his role (p. 224);

they saw themselves in a peace-keeping role and resented pressures from senior officers to report rather than caution non-indictable offences. On the other hand, in the city "there were insufficient men for a peace-keeping role to be adopted" (p. 229). The average beat patrol in the city tended to be both unpleasant and monotonous and the serving officers developed several means of compensating for this such as "'booking' members of 'rough' categories" (p. 229) which would also enhance their status and "job earning" both official (the sports facilities made available) and unofficial (after hours in cafés, pubs and clubs). She argues that:

> Because the definition of good police work in the city was more closely linked with thief taking [the officially encouraged way of preventing boredom by] 'working up' a beat . . . did not necessarily give a man status (p. 229).

She concludes that:

> The police force [in the city] is a tight, integrated whole facing a community, which is seen as segmented and in part undesirable" (p. 232).

City police officers saw themselves in an enforcement role.

Cain (1973) is therefore arguing that the police played very different roles in city and county police forces in the early sixties. These differing roles would have a large effect on their approach to recording incidents as crimes known. Indeed, insofar as the police played a peace-keeping role in the counties, more and better equipped police would make it easier for the police to cover up an incident and so avoid confronting even a part of the community by recording an offence; whilst in the city forces, more and better equipped police would lead to more offences being recorded. These arguments were part of the evidence which made us think that urban and rural areas were better treated separately (see the next section and Chapter 4, § 4.0 and § 4.6, Chapter 5, § 5.0).

3.6 CHANGES IN POLICE ORGANISATION AND POLICE PUBLIC RELATIONS AND THE EFFECT ON CRIMINAL STATISTICS

3.6.0 *Introduction*

The previous section has summarized what is known about reporting by the public and recording by the police of incidents as crimes. These studies demonstrate that there are important effects which must be taken into account. However, since we have data for three different years, we also have to ask whether there have been significant changes in the way in which these effects operate in the model. This is especially interesting for our study because the 1960s was the occasion for the first major reorganisation of the English police since their foundation.

3.6.1 *Trends since the War*

The modes of operation of the English police force and its organisational imperatives remained roughly the same from its creation in the first half of the 19th century until the middle of the 20th century. These included the accent on the police force as part and parcel of the community, representing their respect for law and order without having any extra powers; the emphasis on foot patrols establishing not only a continuous presence but human contact with the resident population; and the integration of the police force with the structure of local authorities.

Pressures began to mount after the war for a more professional police force. Thus McClintock (1963) found that during the period 1950 to 1960 there was an increasing emphasis on completeness and uniformity in the way in which crimes of violence were recorded. He estimates that the number of crimes of violence recorded in 1960 was 6% higher than the police return in 1950 due to this cause alone. He says: "The overall effect of these administrative changes means that there has been an appreciable increase in crimes of violence recorded which is statistical rather than real" (p. 66).

From his interviews with older policemen, McClintock (1963) also suggests that "more of the borderline cases are today recorded as crimes than were so listed ten years ago" (p. 67). One older policeman said "the post-war generation of policemen are more form and paper minded than we used to be" and that "minor indecencies and certain acts of violence used to be regarded as part of everyday life; these things were not recorded as crimes". [15]

The recording of assaults on the police is a special case but does show what a tremendous difference recording practices can make. Thus an officer of senior rank said that there "is a smaller toleration of violence all round and that quite a lot of the increase in crime recording reflects this". He illustrated his point by telling a story of what happened soon after he joined the police force. "I was on beat duty and saw a burglar leaving a house; I gave chase and came to grips with him. We both rolled over in the dust; after a struggle in which I received a cut lip and several bruises I was able to get him back to the station, where he was put in a cell. I made my report to the station sergeant and dwelt upon the fight and the injury received. When I was finished there was silence for a few minutes and then the sergeant said, "You've done well my lad, but don't expect burglars to be gentlemen. You'd better brush your uniform, wash your face, have a cup of tea and get back on your beat". There was no question of recording a crime of violence or even an assault. Today this would be recorded as an indictable offence of assault, either causing actual bodily harm or with intent to resist apprehension" (all quotes from McClintock (1963) p. 68).

The way in which such incidents are now treated by the police can be seen in the following report which appeared in the *Evening Argus* (the Brighton local paper) of December 6th 1977 on a case heard in the Crown Court: "X was taken to the police station after urinating [in public]. As he was turning out his pockets he kicked out at the police officer." The offender was jailed six months for assault.

McClintock (1963) also discusses the way instructions affect the recording of crimes of violence by the police. He shows how a revision of instructions

---

[15] The forms and paperwork became systematised in 1963 with the introduction of the Offenders Index at the Home Office Statistical Department in Tolworth Towers. This is a computer listing of all persons who have, after the age of 18, been convicted of any one of the offences on the Home Office Standard List (which is slightly wider than the definition of indictable offences). It includes details of their previous convictions (including those before the age of 18) and disposals.

in 1950 led to an artificial statistical increase in this class [of approximately 7 per cent (p. 64)]. This was because, after 1950 all crimes, with the exception of murder have been classified according to the initial assessment made by the police and this classification is not altered as a result of the judicial process, as had been the practice prior to 1949. For example, under the early system a crime initially recorded by the police as an assault occasioning actual bodily harm but where the offender was convicted of only common assault, no indictable crime of violence would have been recorded; whereas since 1950, irrespective of the verdict of the court, the crime recorded remains an assault occasioning actual bodily harm.

3.6.2 *The Royal Commission and Subsequent Changes*

Real changes were heralded by the Final Report of the Royal Commission in 1962 which advised the establishment of the Police Research and Planning Branch:

> . . . a central government unit charged with the planning of police methods, the development of new equipment . . . and to study new techniques so as to enable police services to deal promptly and effectively with changes in the pattern of crime and the behaviour of criminals.

Cain (1973) linked this shift to increased rationalism on the part of the police forces of England and Wales with its emphasis on the force as a profession to what she called our "city manager" style of government.

In her concluding chapter, Cain (1973) speculates about the likely effect of changes in police organisation during the sixties; first of all, she suggests that the

> . . . pay rise of 1961 played a not inconsiderable part in freeing men from the area they policed . . . it was more common for the men to own cars and to have a more active social life outside their area . . . the changes will signify the end of peace keeping as we have defined it (p. 241-2).

In this way police serving in county forces will become more like the police serving in city forces. Further, the introduction of unit beat policing means that:

> . . . the informal structures of county police forces will henceforth approximate more closely to that of cities . . . the change will signify the end of peace keeping as we have defined it (p. 242).

In the cities "the new system will make possible more control from above" (p. 243). On the other hand, peace-keeping will become an officially defined part of the role of the unit beat men, yet since:

> . . . the urban [often working class] community will lack the power over its beat officer which the rural community have . . . in the event of discrepancy in role definitions senior officers or colleagues will still 'win' (p. 243).

She goes on to argue:

> . . . the range of ways in which the police role is conceived [will be] progressively limited [so that] thief taker and policeman become synonomous (p. 245).

She concludes:

> In the earlier type of consensus . . . people approved of policemen who worked one way and not of policemen who worked another and they made efforts to ensure that they got what they wanted. In the new style consensus everyone knows what is meant by the police, and people can take a stand for or against this unitary thing (p. 266).

This implies that some social groups develop antagonisms for the police—or vice versa. In fact, newspapers of the times suggest that the youth were becoming actually alienated from authority and its first line of defence, the police. And indeed Belson's (1975) study reported in the previous section shows that by the end of the decade there was a great deal more mistrust between the youth and the police than adults and the police. Given that the changes in the 1960s were towards a more formal approach to recording incidents as offences, this would suggest that the offences committed by juveniles were more likely to be recorded as offences later in the decade than earlier (and this effect would be independent of any general variance in the recording of offences). The separation of the police from the community in this way is also more likely to affect the position of working-class people, since they are more vulnerable than others; we might therefore expect offences committed by working-class people to be recorded more more often later in the decade. Indeed this was the result that West and Farrington obtained (see the previous section).

The police forces were led to introduce new procedures for dealing more efficiently (quickly) with the volume of crime and these procedures involved increased formality and routine. There were the initial attempts during this period to experiment with more "effective" styles of policing which generated a plethora of specialist units and the setting up of centralised information stores, for example, with regional criminal record offices (see Willmer (1970) for a description of other innovations in this style).

The changes were not necessarily seen as positive. Thus, one Chief Inspector Brooks, lamenting the deterioration in police-public relations, said: "We have found that through increased mobilisation and mechanisation they are getting out of touch with the public" (see television programme quoted below). Indeed, the innovation of unit beat policing[16] in 1967 was welcomed more for the promise of restoring the neighbourhood "copper" than for its supposed administrative efficiency.

From our point of view, what is important is that a change in the style of policing means that for the same quantity and sophistication of illegal activity, different—and possibly different numbers of—incidents get recorded and reported; and, as a corollary, different individuals are liable to be arrested. Commenting on the increased mobility, Sir Douglas Osmond (Chief Inspector of Hampshire) said on television (15th February, 1971, BBC 2, *Crime and the Criminals*, No. 6):

> The motorised policeman means more criminals are caught and probably sets up a deterrent.

Specifically an increased amount of information means that people who have once been caught and processed are more likely to go through the process again (see § 3.1.1). This means that the same individuals will be arrested more frequently. Although this is a very important phenomenon from the individual's point of view, it is not an effect which will appear in a cross-sectional study such as this. It does imply that the recorded crime rate will increase over time (see Chapter 8, § 8.4).

More important from our perspective is that the emphasis on more formal and "rational" conduct has the specific consequence that individual police officers are more conscious of the requirement to report and record incidents which they encounter during their work. We think it is reasonable to assume that many of the marginal offences now recorded for the first time would, *ceteris paribus*, be among the less serious legal infractions—less serious in the eyes of both the public and the police.

3.6.3 *Implications for our Model*

In Chapter 2 (§ 2.2.2) we argued that variables representing the number of, and expenditure on, the police should be included as factors determining the offence rate. There we were concerned with perceived probabilities of apprehension. We have seen that these variables also have effects on the

---

[16] Briefly, it involves assigning to each patrol area a team which provides, for each of three daily shifts, two area constables, one small conspicuously marked police car (the "Panda" car) and driver, a detective and a collator. The collator is the hub of the system in that he records and sifts all information sent in by the police teams.

recorded offence rate which operate through the public willingness to report and police discretion in recording.

One can now distinguish three ways in which the number and technical efficiency of the police affect the recorded offence rate and detection rate:

(a) If there are more policemen on the street, or in evidence, then they are more likely to "catch someone in the act" and also more able to charge them with, e.g. a public order offence. Both these sorts of offences are almost certain to be solved, so that we should expect *a priori* that an area with more policemen would have both more recorded offences and that more of these would be solved. This will be called the "creating" effect.

(b) The presence of policemen on the street means that it is easier for a member of the public to report an offence that they have just witnessed, and also that the community as a whole is more conscious of formal social control and the role of policemen in maintaining law and order. In urban areas, "marginal" crimes reported in this way would probably be left unsolved, since the police would consider them as less important. In rural areas, however, it is more likely that the reporter would know the identity of the culprit. *A priori* one might expect that in this way a larger police force would have a positive effect on the number of recorded offences in both urban and rural areas, but a negative effect on the proportion of those which are solved in urban areas and a positive effect in rural areas. These will be called "reporting" effects.

(c) The presence of a larger number of policemen or their possession of better equipment can act as a deterrent. Note, however, that we shall be including a measure of the probability of apprehension in our equations, as a variable distinct from the number of policemen. Thus the deterrent effect of an increase in the number of policemen in the equation explaining the offence rate in our model will be through perceived probabilities of apprehension. We should expect potential offenders who are deterred by increases in the number of police for a *given* detection rate to be less professional, and thus would have been more easily detected than the average offender if they had in fact committed their offences. Such deterrence would lower the detection rate. We shall suppose this effect operates mainly in urban areas. It depends on poor knowledge amongst potential offenders of circumstances in their area and we suppose that in rural areas individuals have better information on their surroundings. These will be called "deterrent" effects.

We suggest, therefore, that more policemen *per capita* will effect the criminal statistics in the following ways:

Table 3.7
Effects of extra police on criminal statistics

		Offence rate	Detection rate
Creating effect		+	+
Reporting Effect	Urban	+	—
	Rural	+	+
Deterrent effect	Urban	—	—
	Rural	0	0

Note: + denotes an increase, — a decrease and 0 no change.

We cannot *a priori* specify the relative strengths of these various effects and, in the absence of an empirical examination such as we propose, it is difficult to see how the issue could be sensibly discussed. We have indicated differences that might be anticipated between urban and rural areas (see, in particular, the discussion of Cain's study at the end of 3.5.3) and that the strength of these effects would have changed considerably over the 1960s. And we have seen in the previous section that similar arguments apply to other variables in our model, such as the age and social class structure. From several points of view, it therefore appears that we should treat urban and rural areas differently and we should not pool data for different years. We have, in general, followed this practice in the presentation of our results (see Chapter 6) but we have provided specific tests of the hypothesis that urban and rural data come from the same underlying structure, similarly for different years (see Chapters 5 and 6). To anticipate our results we find emphatic rejection of the hypothesis that the data should be pooled in either of the ways indicated.

Further discussion of the shifting magnitudes of the three effects just described will be postponed until § 7.3 when our results will have been presented.

3.7 CONCLUDING REMARKS

This chapter completes the review of theories which are intended to explain, or have some bearing on, the explanation of the variation in recorded rates of offending between areas. In the first part of the chapter we looked at the processes which we must model in order to satisfactorily test the hypotheses of Chapter 2, because certain variables suggested therein as determinants of the offence rate are themselves partly determined by the same offence rate. We first discussed the determination of the detection rate and suggested that appropriate explanatory factors were the numbers and technological proficiency of the police, the size of the area, the offence rate in the area, and the age and social class structure of the area. We then discussed the determination of the numbers of police *per capita* in an area and showed how this was probably dominated in the sense we described by supply considerations. We went on to argue that the supply depends on the offence rate and the clear-up rate, population density, proportion of middle class in an area and the offence mix. Lastly, we considered the possibility that the level of punishments also depends on the offence rate and argued that it was unlikely in an inter-areal analysis such as ours.

In the second half of the chapter we briefly reviewed a very extensive literature and the available evidence on the recording phenomenon. It can be summarized as follows: the actual rate of offending, if it can be said to exist, is very large and a variety of factors determines whether or not an action or a person is recorded as an offence or offender. One of the main factors is the tendency for the police to develop stereotypes, partly because of their organisation and training, and partly to facilitate their own job performance. During the sixties these stereotypes were mostly cast in terms of a youthful, working-class sub-culture.

This discussion of the recording phenomenon thus points to several variables which differ between areas and which may affect the rate of reporting and recording offences: the proportion of young males in the population, and the proportion of the population that is working-class. It is clear that the number of policemen *per capita* and their visibility will have an important effect on both the number of offences reported to and the number of offences recorded by the police. These are all variables identified in Chapter 2 as important possible determinants of the offence rate, so that our interpretation of the results in Chapter 7 will have to allow for more than one effect of these variables; this is made more explicit in Chapter 5.

Moreover, the arguments for including age and social class as important factors in the recording and reporting of offences clearly imply that these variables should also be included in an attempt to explain the clear-up rate.

Although each theory taken in isolation has not been difficult to explain or to take into account when considering these variations, the problem is more complicated when all the theories are considered together. Many interdependences have been discussed in this chapter, and these will force the use of fairly sophisticated techniques in estimation. These techniques are discussed, and the results of using them presented and interpreted, in the next section of this monograph. Before we can proceed, we must summarize the relations which we have described in terms of a formal model, and describe the measures which are to be used, so that the factors included can be represented as numerical variables. That is the task of the next chapter.

4

The Model

4.0 INTRODUCTION

A major purpose of this monograph is to develop and test a model of the determination and generation of criminal statistics. The preceding chapters have been concerned with the relevant theories and the next section of the monograph is concerned with testing such a model, given the available techniques and data. In our exposition and evaluation of the theories and our discussion of the processes at work in our system, we have isolated relationships and specified certain factors as important in those relationships.

In this chapter we present the outcome of that lengthy discussion concisely in the form of a model. Because there are several processes, we have several equations; their precise interrelationships will become clear in Chapter 5. We have three main purposes here: to crystallise the earlier discussion into precise equations; to provide variables which will measure the factors involved in those equations; and to discuss difficulties associated with the model we have written down. We discuss in particular certain aspects which were important features in our earlier chapters but which present insuperable difficulties in measurement—notably those factors associated with recording practices. We introduce the identification problem—that of telling one equation from another in a simultaneous system. And we explain briefly why certain variables which play a role in the theories and which were used at some stages in our estimation were eventually discarded.

The set of equations which is the outcome of our presentation in this chapter will form the basis of our discussion of techniques of estimation in the next chapter, and provides the framework of our results, which are presented in Chapter 6. Some of the variables and data have already been presented in preceding chapters but we discuss the full list for completeness. Formal and precise definitions are contained in the Data Appendix and the data themselves are available at the S.S.R.C. Survey Archive at the University of Essex.

In the next section of this chapter we examine the equation intended to model the determination of the number of actual offences per head. Section 4.2 is devoted to the equation for the proportion of recorded offences solved and in § 4.3 we discuss the determination of the number of policemen per head. We raised the possibility in Chapter 3 (§ 3.2) that the severity of punishment might depend on the offence rate and we consider a possible equation in § 4.4. The process by which an event becomes a recorded offence is the subject matter of § 4.5.

The several equations of the model are presented as a simultaneous system in § 4.6. In § 4.7 we discuss problems associated with aspects which are important but omitted for difficulties of measurement; and in § 4.8 we introduce the identification problem. The final section is devoted to concluding remarks and there is a brief appendix giving means of variables and a breakdown of offence types for 1966 to give the reader a feel for the numbers involved.

Before we show how the argument of the previous chapters is transformed into a model, we describe briefly the data sets we are considering. Our first choice was between time series and cross-section data; the former can quickly be ruled out. Leaving aside the question of stability of the parameters of the system over time, estimation of a system as complex as ours, with 30 observations (annual data since the war) is obviously out of the question (some brief further remarks on time-series analysis are contained in § 5.6). We have therefore restricted ourselves to a cross-sectional analysis. For this purpose the natural unit of observation is the police district, since this is the unit both for police organisation and official statistics. The individual police districts in 1961 and 1966 corresponded in most cases to a local authority area, and in 1971 to a combination of local authority areas. 1961 and 1971 were full census years and 1966 a 10% sample census year. There are census units which correspond to local authority boundaries so that census data can be matched with police data.

We confined attention to police districts in England and Wales. The legal structure and thus offence statistics in Scotland are rather different from those in England and Wales (see, for example, N. D. Walker (1968)). Northern Ireland too, has its own particular characteristics, legal definitions and data problems which imply its exclusion from our sample. A few areas in England and Wales were excluded, however, because of difficulties in allocating census data to police districts. Specifically we were forced to drop the police districts of London (Metropolitan Police District, (MPD)) and five adjacent counties. The MPD includes parts of these counties and thus boundaries are situated in a manner which makes the allocation of data impossible. Note that the inclusion of the MPD had it been possible, would have added just one observation to a sample of over 60 urban police districts—see below.

By taking a police district into the sample we are, of course, supposing that for this district (apart from random factors) the relations underlying the processes we examine are the same as for the others in the sample. Thus we implicitly assume that we have incorporated in our list of explanatory variables the important measurable factors accounting for differences across districts in offence rates, clear-up rates and number of police.

If there are important regional differences in the behaviour of public and police then parameters of the system would be different for those regions. We should, therefore, estimate for different regions separately. We argued in Chapters 2 and 3, particularly the latter (§ 3.6), that one would expect to find differences between areas which are 100% urban and those which are, to a large extent, rural. We had in mind the character of police work and the network of local knowledge and social relations. Accordingly we treat urban and rural areas differently and provide explicit tests for the hypothesis that they should be treated differently (see Chapter 5, § 5.4). We trust that urban areas for a given year provide a sufficiently homogeneous set so that, after allowing for the differences which we measure directly and excluding the MPD and adjacent counties (for data reasons beyond our control), it is reasonable to assume that those offences and police statistics are generated by the same underlying structure.

Our two main data sets are urban police districts in 1961 and 1966 and for these we have 72 and 66 observations respectively. In addition, we have 47 rural districts in 1961 and 44 rural districts in 1966. Large amalgamations took place between 1966 and 1971, and in 1971 we have only 41 districts, some urban and some mixed urban and rural. The question whether we should pool urban and rural areas is one of the hypotheses to which we apply a specific test (see Chapters 5, § 5.4, and 6, § 6.1), and in the cases where we do pool them we include the proportion of the area that is urbanised as an explanatory variable in each relation—thus the model is slightly different from that for urban areas (see § 4.6). For the moment, to keep matters simple, we construct our model so as to refer to a cross-section of urban police districts.

4.1 THE DETERMINATION OF THE RATE OF "ACTUAL" OFFENCES

The first problem is to decide on an appropriate measure for offending behaviour. This was considered at some length at the beginning of Chapter

2 (§ 2.0). Although clearly there are differences between types of offences, the problem of partitioning the effect of certain variables, such as police effort, meant that we were forced to use a global measure of offending behaviour (for further discussion see Chapter 10). And there are direct arguments for examining the determination of aggregates—see Chapter 1 and Chapter 3, § 3.4.

We decided to restrict our attention to indictable offences and, as we have emphasized previously, and see the appendix to this chapter, the overwhelming majority are property offences. Theories of the level of offences refer mainly to property offences and the inclusion of, for example, regulatory and traffic offences would require a rather different model. We are, of course, restricted to the number of offences recorded by the police (Y). The relation between Y and the "actual" level of offences (Y^*) was the focus of much of Chapter 3 (especially § 3.4).

In Chapter 2 we discussed the theories which bear upon the relationship between offending behaviour and, on the one hand, variables determining the individual choice of whether or not to offend (§ 2.2) and, on the other hand, variables describing the social influences on individuals which affect their choice (§ 2.3). These are theories of the determination of Y^*. In this section we write down the factors assumed to determine Y^* in the form of an equation. A summary of our notation is provided in Table 5.1 of the next chapter.

4.1.1 *The Incentives to Offend*

Our discussion of the economic or deterrence theories of offending behaviour led us to suggest that

    (i) — the perceived severity of punishment
    (ii) — the perceived likelihood of the detection of an offence
and (iii) — the opportunity for offending

should all affect the individual's propensity to offend.

(i) *Perceived Severity of Punishment.* From the point of view of the potential offender, the total penalty for being caught or convicted for an offence involves not only the sentence likely to be imposed at the court, but also the immediate costs of court appearance and defence, and the social consequences of publicity, conviction, and the sentence served. These last are likely to vary considerably between individuals, and may be seen by a particular individual as of greater importance than the sentence imposed at the court. But this kind of penalty is very hard to measure and may not vary systematically between areas. There are also no data, by police district, on the costs of court appearance and defence. Further, there are no theories or empirical studies which would help us in modelling the perceived sentence. Thus we had to fall back on measuring the severity of penalties as imposed by the court (F).

We should have liked to use some index combining the level of fines and of imprisonment. However, breakdowns by amount of fine and length of sentence are not available by area. We concentrated instead on the difference between custodial and non-custodial measures. Although some institutional measures are imposed to serve humanitarian or reformative ends, there is no reason to suppose that they are perceived as other than punitive by the offender. (The exception might be that some psychiatric institutions are perceived as "soft" options.) The index used (F in Table 5.1) is the ratio of convictions of male offenders resulting in the imposition of custodial penalties to all convictions.

Local sentencers have considerable discretion on the sentences they pass and, in particular, on whether they impose a custodial punishment. And there appear to be considerable local variations (for standard deviations of variables see Table 7.1). We have argued in Chapter 3, § 3.2, that it seems reasonable to regard our index as an exogenous variable, and we trust that it reflects the overall severity of sentencers across the broad range of sentencing options. And one might expect potential offenders to be better informed of and more sharply influenced by variations in the likelihood of imprisonment than in the level of fines.

We consider in § 4.4 the possibility that sentencers might be systematically influenced in their choice of punishment by other variables in the system. We should record here that we do not regard the possibility, for our data set, as particularly likely and the results (see Chapter 6) § 6.4, lend support to this view.

(ii) *The Perceived Likelihood of Detection.*   From the individual's point of view a "detection" of a transgression involves a range of responses from peer group disapproval to incarceration. Thus in a very detailed analysis one might have a list of consequences (together with no punishment at all), each with its own probability. The severity of punishment would not then appear as a separate explanatory variable since the relevant information is the probability of each consequence. This kind of detail is impossible, however, and instead we include an index of severity and an index of probability.

Just as the index of severity involved an attempt to incorporate perceptions of severity, so also our probability index should relate to perceptions. We saw in § 2.2.2 that, whilst there is evidence that more experienced offenders are better informed about the probability of apprehension, the evidence is unclear as to precise determinants of perceived probability $(\tilde{P})$. One can, however, make certain suggestions.

Thus in Chapter 2 we examined certain studies on the relation between $\tilde{P}$ and the actual probability of the detection (P^*). In addition we suggested that the numbers and efficiency of the police in an area would be likely to affect people's perceptions. In the models examined in further detail in Chapter 5, however, we begin, for simplicity, by supposing that offenders are well informed about the actual probability of apprehension. Thus, we suppose the perceived probability $\tilde{P}$ is equal to the actual probability P^*. This assumption is relaxed fairly quickly and we incorporate the additional effects mentioned above.

Of course P^* is not itself measurable, and must be related to other variables. There are two official statistics of particular relevance. The first is the reported clear-up rate (defined in the Data Appendix). It should be noted, however, that the Home Office do not publish area clear-up rates, apparently on the grounds that they may be misleading (McClintock and Avison (1968) p. 92). An important reason is that they include offences "taken into consideration" (t.i.c.) about which policies vary widely between areas. Moreover, t.i.c.s can only affect the perceived probability of detection indirectly, since they are admitted *after* apprehension. Though the clear-up rate is the best available approximation to the likelihood of a recorded offence being solved, it may not be the most appropriate variable to use in a model of the perceived likelihood of detection for actual offences.

The alternative official statistic is the conviction rate, that is the ratio of the number of convicted *people* (where the convictions may involve any number of charges) to the number of recorded offences. A ratio of people to offences seems awkward. On the other hand, it may be well correlated with the actual likelihood of an individual who commits one or more offences being convicted in a given time period. Moreover, a potential offender may well be more aware of the number of individuals who have been convicted (or otherwise caught) than of the number of incidents for which someone has been apprehended. If one knew the total number of offenders involved in illegal incidents, it would then be possible to construct the proportion of offenders who are convicted. Such data are, of course, unavailable.

The probability variable is of central importance in our analysis. Both measures have their advantages and disadvantages not only as variables relevant to individual choice, but also where the probability of apprehension occurs elsewhere in the system. And we shall learn something from a comparison of results using the two different measures. We therefore decided to carry both, as alternatives, through the analysis. We call the ratio of convicted people to recorded offences P convictions and the clear-up rate P clear-up.

We argued in Chapter 2 (§ 2.2.2) that the perceived likelihood of detection may depend on the visible presence of social control, and that the presence of police officers may have an independent effect on offences, emphasizing the notion of legality and thus increasing the subjective cost of offending. The appropriate measure of police presence is unclear. It involves such questions as which of foot or vehicular patrols has the greater effect and whether more expensive equipment makes a difference, and so on. We decided to include both the simple measure of police presence, that is the number of policemen per head of population (C), and the expenditure per serving policeman (E). The latter measure would be a combination of expenditure on equipment, overtime and a variety of other things. We shall interpret cross-section variations in E in terms of equipment and overtime.

The problem of modelling the perceived probability is discussed further in Chapter 5 (§ 5.3).

(iii) *Opportunity for Offending.*   We wish to find a variable to capture the incentive to commit an offence in terms of the available "swag" or possible booty. Thus it would be nice if the measure captured not only wealth but also ease of theft—for example, portability. The only systematic source of data on variations in local wealth are the ratings of the value of the property in the area compiled by local authorities. Thus valuations of business property may well reflect the level of economic activity and thereby come close to the concept we require. Obviously local valuation traditions will distort inter-area comparisons of wealth, especially perhaps in respect of domestic property. However, given that many recorded incidents do involve domestic property, we decided to accept these difficulties and use the total rateable value (domestic plus other) as the main index of wealth in the area.

We decided to measure wealth per unit of land area. It is reasonable to suppose that most offences occur at or near work or the home, particularly in view of the small monetary value of most thefts—see, for example § 2.0. One would not travel great distances to steal an item of value £5. If most offences are committed near the home or work of the individual, then our index should measure available property in the area frequented. Our index of available "swag" is the total rateable value per acre (RV).

The "incentive" variables in the explanation of the rate of actual offending, Y^*, are therefore P^*, F, RV, C, and E, and we write

$$Y^* \sim P^*, F, RV, C, E \qquad (1)$$

The notation $\sim$ indicates that the left-hand side variable is a function of those of the right-hand side. We have here supposed that P^*, C, E combine on the right-hand side to produce as part of their joint effect a perceived probability of detection $\tilde{P}$. We could in principle model this process separately. For the reasons mentioned above C and E can have an effect on

Y^* other than through $\tilde{P}$. We return to the issue in Chapter 5 (§ 5.3), since it raises problems of estimation which are best discussed when we have introduced our statistical techniques.

4.1.2 *Socio-Demographic Variables*

The discussion in Chapter 2 (§ 2.3) suggests that several socio-demographic factors may be important in influencing the individual propensity to offend such as:

the prevalence of ethnic minorities,
the sex ratio,
the type of neighbourhood,
the extent of poverty or unemployment,
the concentration of working-class people,
the proportion of young people in the population,
the number of broken homes,
lack of parental care, and
the amount of overcrowding in the home.

For two of these variables the argument in Chapter 2 (§ 2.3.1 and 2.3.2) was that they varied so little between areas as to be irrelevant for our problem. Thus, since we have excluded London (see above in § 4.0), in the three years under consideration, ethnic minorities were only a very small proportion of the population in the vast majority of areas. Similarly, the sex ratio varies only very slightly between areas.

For two others, the number of broken homes and lack of parental care, it is very difficult to obtain reliable data for each area and they are not considered further in the model. The remaining five factors, the type of neighbourhood, the extent of poverty or unemployment, the concentration of working-class people, the proportion of youth in the population and the amount of overcrowding in the home, are considered in turn below.

The importance of the *type of neighbourhood* was suggested by theories of cultural transmission (see § 2.3.3) based on the observation that the residences of convicted offenders tend to cluster in certain localities. Whilst these localities are generally in urban areas, it is not easy to present a measure which will predict where such localities will be. Several variables are possible here and we chose initially for our urban data sets, population density D. The decision will be reviewed in § 4.6.

The introduction of the extent of *poverty or unemployment* as a factor was based both on the economic theories of crime and on the various theories of anomie. The problem with measuring the extent of poverty is that apart from special area studies there is no information on the distribution of income by local authority areas. For several reasons the extent of poverty may be an important explanatory factor for the "actual offence rate". However, its quantitative impact would be closely (inversely) related to the impact of the variable indicating the level of wealth in the area (which has been included to capture the opportunity effect). Since we have included the total rateable value per area (RV), we have not included a variable on poverty. We must, of course, be careful about the interpretation of the role of RV in the equations of our model.

The question of an unemployment variable is, however, a little different. To start with, unemployment rates are available by local authority area, at least for census years. Moreover, the problem of overlap with the wealth variable is less acute. There are theoretical problems, however, with the use of unemployment as a determinant of the offence rate (see § 2.2.5 and §2.3.4). We are not convinced that it should be included as a distinct determinant of the offence rate. We include the rate of unemployment (Q) at this stage because of the prominent role it has played in previous discussion. We return to this point in § 4.6.

We have suggested in Chapters 2 and 3 (for example, § 2.3.5 and § 3.4.4 and 3.4.5) that the evidence as to the relationship between *working class* concentration in an area and the rate of "actual" offending in that area is not clear cut. However, because of its theoretical importance we decided to include a measure (W). There is no agreed definition of what constitutes a working class population, and what is more important, the theories in which we are interested give no clear leads as to which of the many definitions correspond to the concepts in question. Thus a conflict model would require a Marxist definition of class, whereas an opportunity model would suggest a definition in terms of strata. Since the only source of socio-economic data by police district was the census, we chose a (strata) definition based on the Registrar General's Socio-Economic Groups (S.E.Gs). We selected S.E.Gs 7, 10, 11, 15, and the variable W is the number in these groups as a proportion of the population.

The SEG 7 is personal service workers, SEG 10 semi-skilled manual workers, SEG 11 unskilled manual workers and SEG 15 agricultural workers. A full description of the 17 SEGs is contained in the Data Appendix. The standard classifications of social class into I, II, III, IV, V are based on these SEGs but are not identical to sub-sets of the SEGs (for example a foreman in a particular SEG may be put in a different social class from the individuals, in the same SEG, who work under him). We have based our definition of W on the kind of occupations indicated where one finds claims about the connection between the working class and crime. The precise selection is, of course, a subjective one. In 1966 for example, in

England and Wales as a whole the proportion of the population in SEGs 7, 10, 11, 15 was 25·9%.

As was shown in Chapter 2 (§ 2.3.6), the criminological literature is almost indecently enthusiastic in assigning the responsibility for offending behaviour to male *youths*. The theories vary, however, between assigning the responsibility to school leavers and to young adults. In earlier work, reported in Carr-Hill, Hope and Stern (1972), we included two separate age variables—the proportion of males aged 15-19 and the proportion aged 20-24. The two variables were highly correlated and it proved difficult to disentangle their separate effects. We have therefore used the sum of these two variables in the analysis presented here (we call this sum A). See the work cited above for further discussion.

Finally, the theories in Chapter 2 (§ 2.3.7) suggested that the amount of *overcrowding in the home* may be an important variable independent of any effect of population density. A convenient variable from the census data which corresponds (inversely) to this concept is the percentage of households with less than ½ person per room (H).

The socio-demographic variables in the explanation of the rate of actual offending are therefore A, W, D, Q, H and we write

$$Y^* \sim A, W, D, Q, H \tag{2}$$

4.2 THE DETERMINATION OF THE PROPORTION OF OFFENCES SOLVED

We argued in Chapter 3 (§ 3.1) that the recorded offence rate, Y, and the number of serving policemen, C, should be included as explanations of any measure of the proportion of recorded offences solved or the recorded detection rate P—the first because it is a good measure of the work load of the police force, and the second because it is policemen who have to do the work in apprehending and processing suspects. We explained above ((ii) in the previous section) that there were two measures of P that were available—the ratio of convicted offenders to recorded offences, P convictions, and the clear-up rate, P clear-up.

Apart from Y and C, the other factors considered important in the "production" of clear-ups or convictions were the size and crime mix of the area and the technological proficiency of the police. There is a number of variables for which data are avaialable for both the size and crime-mix of the area. For the first we have chosen the night-time (residential) population of the area (N). For the crime-mix we require a measure which can indicate the ease with which recorded offences are solved. We chose the proportion V of offences which involve violence both as an indicator of the character of offences and of offenders in an area. Recorded offences against the person are easier to solve than others, because the offender is known to the victim, and we suggest that to a certain extent this may be true of other offence types in areas where violent offences form a higher proportion of total offences.

As a measure of the detective proficiency of the police force we included, at an early stage in our analysis, the percentage of CID officers in the force (*CID*) (see § 4.6 for further discussion). However, many clear-ups are not the result of work by detectives but result from the reaction time of the police and we therefore also included expenditure per officer (*E*) as reflecting hours worked, the mobility and technical back-up to the force.

We therefore have

$$P \sim Y, C, N, V, CID, E \tag{3}$$

4.3 THE DETERMINATION OF THE NUMBER OF POLICEMEN *PER CAPITA*

We presented in Chapter 3 the determination of the number of policemen as an interaction between demand for police as set by the authorities and supply in terms of average daily strength of the existing force. There is, however, no variable, such as price in economic models, to bring demand and supply into equilibrium in each region—the wage rate for police is set nationally. And since we argued that established daily strength (an indication of demand) was in general above the average (or actual) daily strength of the force, we took supply as the constraining factor. Thus we eventually have just one equation for the determination of the size of force, and that equation models supply (see § 4.6). Demand factors are, however, relevant, since they will determine the intensity of recruitment campaigns and, for the moment, we keep two separate equations—one for demand, the other for supply.

The reader is reminded that demand in the form of established daily strength is set by negotiation between the local authority committee in charge of the police force and the central Home Office (see § 3.3). We discuss demand factors first.

In Chapter 3 (§ 3.3.1), we argued that the recorded offence rate and the clear-up or conviction rate should be included as explanations of the demand for policemen. Other factors which were seen as affecting the numbers of serving policemen on the demand side were the rate of recorded violent crime and the social composition of the area. We used, to capture the former effect, the ratio of indictable offences against the person to all indictable offences (V) (we use the proportion rather than the rate, since the offence rate is already in the equation). And on the grounds that the major local pressures on the police come from those who feel strongly about law, order and the defence of property, the appropriate variable for social composition would seem to be the proportion of the population that can be considered as belonging to the middle class. Once again there are several possibilities for the measurement of this class variable. Since we were considering census years, we chose a definition based on the Registrar-General's classification of the population into Socio-Economic Groups. Thus we included M the number in S.E.Gs 5, 6, 8, 9, 12, 14 as a proportion of the population.

The titles of these SEGs are as follows: 5, intermediate non-manual workers; 6, junior non-manual workers; 8, foreman and supervisors—manual; 9, skilled manual workers; 12, own account workers (other than professional); 14, farmers, own account. In 1966 the proportion of the population in these groups in England and Wales was 56·7%. For further comments and detail, see § 4.1.2 and the Data Appendix.

At one stage, the Home Office tried to develop a formula for calculating establishment strengths (see § 3.3.0) based on the socio-demographic characteristics of the area. We explained in Chapter 3 (§ 3.3.1) how this attempt was eventually abandoned. The Home Office did indicate to us, however, that population density (D) was of importance and we decided to include this variable as an influence on demand.

On the supply side, one would expect the recorded offence rate in an area to influence the readiness of members of the public to present themselves as prospective policemen. Similarly, the success rate or the clear-up or conviction rate would be an important determinant of morale; and both would be influences on a decision to remain in the force. We consider two further factors. One is the amount of recorded violent crime in the area; this could influence the level of morale. We included the measure V, defined above. The other is the level of unemployment as a measure of the (relative absence of) alternative opportunities of the labour market and therefore of the relative ease of recruitment. We used, from the census data, the numbers reporting themselves as unemployed as a proportion (Q) of the economically active population.

We have therefore derived the two relations

$$C_{\text{demand}} \sim Y, P, V, D, M \tag{4}$$

$$C_{\text{supply}} \sim Y, P, V, Q \tag{5}$$

4.4 POSSIBLE DETERMINANTS OF THE
LEVEL OF PUNISHMENT

In the first part of Chapter 3 (§ 3.2), we discussed a possible relationship between the level of punishments (measured by the proportion of convictions for indictable offences which resulted in a custodial penalty) and the recorded rate of indictable offences (Y). There are two others which, because of their effect on the judiciary, may intervene in the process determining the level of punishment. The first is the amount of recorded violent crime, which as before we measure by the ratio of offences against the person to total indictable offences (V). The second is local pressure on the judiciary for stiffer punishments which we are supposing might emanate from the middle classes. We measured this as above, M.

This relation, if it entered the system, therefore, would look as follows

$$F \sim Y, V, M \qquad (6)$$

In fact we did not include this in our final system (see § 4.6).

4.5 THE RECORDING PROBLEM

The second half of Chapter 3 (§ 3.4), was concerned with the arguments of sociologists of deviance insofar as they impinge on the relationships we have been discussing. The main argument is that an offence is a legal label attached to an event and can therefore only be properly known as such when it has been recorded by the police authorities. Some authors claim that the concept of a real rate of offending (Y^*) is meaningless and that the recorded offence rate (Y) is a function of a set of interactional and socio-demographic variables. Others argue that it may be meaningful to talk of the real rate of offending, but that recorded offences are not simply a random sample of actual offences in that systematic biases are introduced by a similar set of interactional and socio-demographic factors. The argument is therefore that $Y \sim X, Z, (Y^*)$, where Y^* is not in the former version but in included in the latter and X, Z represent a list of socio-demographic variables and, in principle, interactional variables.

The interactional variables referred to, such as the characteristic reactions of particular individuals to their immediate social environment or to representatives of agencies of social control, are, however, much too complex to be included directly in a cross-section analysis of this type. We have to find variables to capture the possible prevalence of certain interactions. The sex of an individual is an important factor affecting whether or not a person is convicted of an offence but, as was remarked above, the sex ratio varies very little between areas. Other variables of the type required which are worth considering, are the proportions of working-class and youth in the area, and the rate of unemployment. There are similar reasons for considering each of the three variables. First, the police have certain stereotypes of offenders and, secondly, it is easier to gain knowledge about and interrogate individuals from some social strata rather than others. Thus young people are more visible or accessible than older, working-class people more so than middle-class, and the unemployed more so than the employed, in each case partly because they live less private lives and partly because they have less power.

The number of serving policemen will affect recording not only because the more police there are the more offences will be seen and recorded, but also because those offences which are reported personally to officers on the beat will depend directly on the density of their presence. It is possible that this personal-reporting effect depends also on expenditure per officer (E). We have omitted (E) here because while we regard it as likely that the ease of reporting and incentive to report depend on the number of officers in evidence, the effects of increased mobility through the greater use of cars, for example, or other expenditure, are unclear.

It is possible, inside these theories, to include the probability of apprehension and the level of punishment as explanatory variables for recorded offences. The argument would be that individuals take more care not to have their offences recorded when the perceived penalties are greater. We have not included this effect formally; it could, however, be incorporated. Equation (7) below would be changed but not the equations eventually estimated (see § 5.3).

Although the processes referred to above act most powerfully before an incident is recorded as an offence, the same arguments apply in some measure to whether or not a "solution" is recorded for a recorded offence. First, many clear-ups occur at the same time as the recording of an offence and, secondly, the considerations of visibility and accessibility discussed above, which suggested the variables A, W, Q, are also likely to play a role in the identification of "culprits". The number of policemen *per capita*, C, would also play a role in the determination of P in interactionist theories— see § 3.5 and Chapter 7.

We have, therefore, two relations which follow from our discussion of recording

$$Y \sim A, W, Q, C, Y^* \tag{7}$$

$$P \sim A, W, Q, C \tag{8}$$

We shall be testing explicitly (see Chapters 5 and 6) for the status of the unemployment variable, Q, here partly because it has been a subject of much discussion in connection with crime. In addition the *a priori* arguments for its inclusion in (7) and (8) seem weaker than the other variables. For the proportion of the population that was unemployed in our years (1961, 1966, 1971) was very low (around or just less than 2% of the work force, hence around 1% of the population). Unless crime is quite extraordinarily concentrated on the unemployed, variations in the rate would be unlikely to have large effects on the variables under consideration.

4.6 THE MODEL

As a first step let us collect and represent formally as equations, the relations which have been developed in the previous two chapters and the above sections of this chapter. We now write the relations in the form functions $f_i(\ )$.

$$Y^* = f_1(P^*, F, RV, C, E) \tag{1}$$

$$Y^* = f_2(A, W, D, Q, H) \tag{2}$$

$$P = f_3(Y, C, N, V, CID, E) \tag{3}$$

$$C = f_4(Y, P, V, D, M) \tag{4}$$
demand

$$C = f_5(Y, P, V, Q) \tag{5}$$
supply

$$F = f_6(Y, M, V) \tag{6}$$

$$Y = f_7(A, W, Q, C, Y^*) \tag{7}$$

$$P = f_8(A, W, Q, C) \tag{8}$$

The system (1) — (8) is not yet in a form suitable for estimation. Equations (1) and (2) refer to different sets of factors, according to different kinds of theory, all of which influence the "actual" rate of offending Y^*. Thus we amalgamate equations (1) and (2). We do the same for (3) and (8).

We argued above (§ 3.3.1 and § 4.3) that the number of policemen which is observed is essentially constrained by supply and that supply and demand are not in equilibrium. We argued that demand factors may influence

supply through the effects of recruitment campaigns. Therefore we regard the relevant equation as (5) but adjoin to it the demand variables D and M.
We thus have:

$$Y^* = f_9 (P^*, F, RV, C, E, A, W, D, Q, H) \tag{9}$$

$$P = f_{10} (Y, C, N, V, CID, E, A, W, Q) \tag{10}$$

$$C = f_{11} (Y, P, V, D, M, Q) \tag{11}$$

$$F = f_{12} (Y, M, V) \tag{12}$$

$$Y = f_{13} (A, W, Q, C, Y^*) \tag{13}$$

At an early stage in the development of the model we discarded CID which seemed to be completely insignificant in all data sets which we tried. The arguments in favour of including equation (12) were not considered strong (§ 3.2) and early results using (12) were not promising, so we decided to omit this equation, although some examples of these results are given in Chapter 6 (§ 6.4). The variable H, intended to capture variations in overcrowding, did not perform particularly well and was abandoned fairly early (examples of results are presented in § 6.8). Our tests for the appropriate specification of the role of unemployment in the model led us to include it in the third equation only (see § 6.2). This decision is in general in accord with the arguments advanced in § 2.2.5 and § 4.5. Finally, D and RV are highly correlated for all our data sets. We decided to accept the one for which the prior theory and research were the stronger—RV (see Chapter 2).
We have arrived eventually at the model represented by equations (14), (15), (16), (17).

$$Y^* = f_{14} (P^*, F, RV, C, E, A, W) \tag{14}$$

$$P = f_{15} (Y, C, N, V, E, A, W) \tag{15}$$

$$C = f_{16} (Y, P, V, D, M, Q) \tag{16}$$

$$Y = f_{17} (A, W, C, Y^*) \tag{17}$$

When estimating the model for pooled urban and rural data sets we include the percentage of the area urbanised in each equation. The argument is that there will be differences in each process between urban and rural areas. The percentage of the area urbanised (R) is highly correlated with RV and D. These last two variables were therefore dropped from (14) and (16) respectively. The correlation coefficients are in the appendix to

Chapter 6 and they are briefly discussed in Chapter 7 (§ 7.0). Further comments on the model with pooled urban and rural data are given in Chapter 5 (§ 5.3).

The equations (14) — (17) do not at present contain any stochastic error terms. The structure of such random terms is an important question, but one which can be discussed more easily when we have presented the estimations procedures and some more formal aspects of our model in the next chapter (see, in particular, § 5.5).

4.7 MISSING VARIABLES

The problems connected with the appearance of the unobserved variables Y^* and P^* in the system (14) — (17) will be discussed in the next chapter. There are, however, important influences which were discussed in Chapter 3 (§ 3.5) but which have been omitted from (14) — (17) and these concern in particular equations (15) and (17). We argued in Chapter 3 (§ 3.5) that police practices and police-public relations exert important influences on whether offences are recorded. At the same time these practices and relations will also affect the proportion of offences solved. It is clear that the measurement of such factors would be extremely difficult. Thus we have unmeasured factors missing from equations (15) and (17).

We argued further in Chapter 3 that the influence of these missing factors would be substantially different in the different years. Our alternative to any attempt to include direct measures is to test for a difference between the coefficients in these models in the different years. We then examine and discuss such changes as we discover in terms of these missing variables. That we have presumed a substantial change in the effects of the missing variables leads us to the *a priori* supposition that the models in different years will prove to have significantly different coefficients. The tests are described in Chapter 5 (§ 5.4) and the results reported in Chapter 6 (§ 6.4) and discussed further in Chapter 7 (§ 7.3).

4.8 AN INTRODUCTION TO THE
IDENTIFICATION PROBLEM

In the next chapter we shall explain in detail (§ 5.2) the formal problem of identification. We give a very brief intuitive introduction here, because the decisions taken in constructing the equations presented in § 4.6, are crucial to the problem of identification, a solution of which is itself crucial to estimation.

The problem of identification is, crudely speaking, the problem of distinguishing one equation from another. In a simultaneous system we wish to argue that there are several equations but the first, for example, represents the determination of the offence rate, and the second the clear-up rate. Equations are not distinguished one from the other by which variable we happen to put on the left-hand side as the variable to be explained. The issue turns on which variables are included and which are not included in an equation. Thus for example in a simple economic model of supply and demand for wheat, we have two equations both of which contain quantity and price of wheat. We might recognise the demand equation because it contains a variable measuring the income of consumers but excludes rainfall, and the supply equation because it includes rainfall and excludes the income of consumers.

The point here is that the decisions on the variables to be excluded from an equation, matter just as much as the decisions on the variables to be included. If both rainfall and the income of consumers were included in each of the equations in the example given above we should be unable to distinguish one equation from the other.

One needs to have confidence to assert that some variable has no affect whatsoever on some other. Our theories and previous experience usually suggest that certain variables affect other variables, but are rarely of a kind which allow one to dismiss completely other possible connections. However, as we shall see in detail in the next chapter, if we are to estimate we must be prepared to grasp the nettle of these exclusion decisions.

Let us look briefly at $(14) - (17)$ and ask which variables included in the system as a whole have been excluded from particular equations. From (14) we have excluded V, D, M, Q, N; from (15) F, RV, M; and from (16) F, RV, E, N, W. It thus appears that our three main equations do look radically different one from the other (discussion of the problems associated with the appearance of P^* and Y^* in these equations are postponed to the next chapter, § 5.3). But can we be so sure? For example, it is conceivable that the unemployment rate, Q, effects the clear-up rate, P. It is possible that the size of police district (the district is usually co-terminus with a city, at least in the 1961 and 1966 urban data sets) affects the offence rate and so on.

We have tried to justify those variables that have been included as those which are most important in relation to received theory, previous research and common sense: that was the major task of Chapters 2, 3 and this chapter. Where a variable is excluded the implied judgement is that the arguments for including it are weak or non-existent. We have no alternative to making such judgements if we are to estimate. We return to the issue in the next chapter (§ 5.3).

4.9 CONCLUDING REMARKS

We have now presented the theories which are to be examined in the form of a particular model, equations (14) to (17). We have described briefly the data and measures which are to be used in estimation. Full detail is in the Data Appendix. We have also discussed some of the difficult decisions in the construction of that model. It is time to turn to the statistical problems of estimating our model, and then to our results. These are the subjects of the next section of this monograph.

Appendix to Chapter 4

Table 4.A.1
Indictable offences 1966

Offence	Known to the police	Cleared up	Rate %
CLASS I: Offences against the person:—			
1. Murder:			
1. Of persons aged 1 year and over	160	144	90
2. Of persons under 1 year of age	9	3	33
2. Attempted murder	268	257	96
3. Threats or conspiracy to murder	78	67	86
4. Manslaughter:	172	168	98
4a. Infanticide	23	21	91
4b. Child destruction	—	—	—
4c. Causing death by dangerous driving	646	644	100
5. Felonious wounding	2,275	1,851	81
6. Endangering railway passengers	39	18	46
7. Endangering life at sea	1	1	100
8. Malicious wounding (misdemeanour)	22,204	18,592	84
9. Assault	548	426	78
10. Intimidation and molestation	—	—	—
11. Cruelty to children	—	—	—
12. Abandoning children under 2 years	17	10	59
13. Child stealing	28	20	71
14. Procuring abortion	208	189	91

Table 4.A.1 *continued*

Offence	Known to the police	Cleared up	Rate %
15. Concealment of birth	42	16	38
16. Buggery	575	521	91
17. Attempt to commit buggery, etc.	3,317	2,551	81
18. Indecency between males	947	903	95
19. Rape	644	472	73
20. Indecent assault on a female	10,938	7,439	68
21. Unlawful sexual intercourse with girl under 13	301	278	92
22. Unlawful sexual intercourse with girl under 16	4,156	3,776	91
23. Incest	237	224	95
24. Procuration	68	65	96
25. Abduction	64	62	97
26. Bigamy	241	228	95
TOTAL OF CLASS I:	48,024	38,948	81
CLASS II: Offences against property with violence:			
27. Sacrilege	801	337	42
28. Burglary	9,026	3,374	37
29. Housebreaking	83,615	26,615	32
30. Shopbreaking	119,146	40,646	34
31. Attempts to break into houses, shops, etc.	17,134	6,748	39
32. Entering with intent to commit felony	44,556	15,861	36
33. Possession of house-breaking tools, etc.	1,691	1,678	99
34. Robbery	4,474	1,662	37
35. Blackmail	409	324	79
TOTAL OF CLASS II:	280,852	97,245	35
CLASS III: Offences against property without violence:			
37. Embezzlement	4,347	4,248	98
38. Larceny of horses and cattle	424	89	21
39. Larceny from the person	8,219	1,634	20
40. Larceny in house	53,639	12,132	23
41. Larceny by a servant	20,157	19,605	97
42. Larceny of post letters	848	662	78
43. Other aggravated larcenies	1,828	939	51
44. Larceny of pedal cycles	60,007	8,256	14
45. Larceny from unattended vehicles	186,407	38,592	21
46. Larceny from shops and stalls	68,288	59,814	88

Table 4.A.1 *continued*

Offence	Known to the police	Cleared up	Rate %
47. Larceny from automatic machines and meters	46,805	14,948	32
48. Thefts of motor vehicles	20,042	6,563	33
49. Other simple and minor larcenies	304,979	99,736	33
50. Obtaining by false pretences	38,361	31,572	82
51. Frauds by agents, etc.	3,978	3,821	96
52. Falsifying accounts	2,334	2,308	99
53. Other frauds	6,261	5,352	85
54. Receiving stolen goods	21,676	21,606	100
55. Offences in bankruptcy	—	—	—
TOTAL OF CLASS III:	848,600	331,877	39
CLASS IV: Malicious injuries to property:			
56. Arson	1,546	794	51
57. Other malicious injuries	8,525	3,443	40
TOTAL OF CLASS IV:	10,071	4,237	42
CLASS V: Forgery and Offences against the currency:			
58. Forgery and uttering (felony)	10,698	8,839	83
59. Forgery (misdemeanour)	370	341	92
60. Coining	12	10	83
61. Uttering of counterfeit coin	5	4	80
TOTAL OF CLASS V:	11,083	9,196	83
CLASS VI: Other offences not included in the above classes:			
Offences against the State and Public Order:			
62. High treason	—	—	—
63. Treason (felony)	—	—	—
64. Riot	7	6	86
65. Unlawful assembly	1	—	—
66. Other offences	127	122	96
67. Perjury	251	245	98
68. Libel	41	20	49
69. Attempted suicide	—	—	—
70. Suicide, aiding and abetting, etc.	5	5	100
99. Other indictable offences	798	651	82
TOTAL OF CLASS VI:	1,229	1,050	85
GRAND TOTAL:	1,199,859	482,553	40

Source: Criminal Statistics 1966 Table A pp. 2-7.

Table 4.A.2
Crimes known and cleared-up in England and Wales for the main classes of indictable offences

| | 1961 | | 1966 | | 1971 | |
	Known	Cleared-up	Known	Cleared-up	Known	Cleared-up
Class I	38,005	32,256	48,024	38,948	70,657	56,479
Class II	167,540	65,485	280,852	97,245	459,002	168,366
Class III	584,858	250,524	848,600	331,877	1,087,809	501,102
Class IV	5,606	3,178	10,071	4,237		
Class V	6,924	6,176	11,083	9,196	28,613	21,518
Class VI	174	171	1,229	1,050		
Totals	803,107	357,790	1,199,859	482,553	1,646,081	747,465

Notes
(i) Offences cleared-up in a given year include all offences cleared-up in that year irrespective of the year in which they were committed.
(ii) 1961 *Criminal Statistics* Table I pp. 20-25
1966 *Criminal Statistics* Table A pp. 2-7
1971 *Criminal Statistics* Appendix I(a) pp. xlix-li.
(iii) The classes I-VI are as in Table 4.A.1. The last three for 1971 have been grouped together following the treatment in Appendix I(a) of the *Criminal Statistics* for 1971.

Table 4.A.3
Means of each variable

Variable name	Symbol	Unit	1961 Urban	1961 Rural	1966 Urban	1966 Rural
Recorded indictable offences *per capita*	Y	Offences per 1000	18·4	11·5	28·0	17·7
Proportion cleared-up	P clear-up	per cent	54·1	57·0	48·2	47·6
Numbers of convictions divided by number of offences	P convictions	per cent	23·1	22·9	22·4	20·9
Policemen per capita	C	officers per 1000	1·8	1·4	2·1	1·5
Severity of Punishment (proportion of convicted who are incarcerated)	F	per cent	17·4	15·1	19·2	17·5
Proportion of males aged 15-24 in population	A	per cent	6·6	6·2	7·1	7·0

Table 4.A.3 continued

Variable name	Symbol	Unit	1961 Urban	1961 Rural	1966 Urban	1966 Rural
Proportion of working class in population	W	per cent	27·5	27·0	28·1	26·9
Total rateable value per area	RV	£ per acre	1993	674	5274	2080
Population	N	1000's of people	134	332	148	405
Proportion of middle class in population	M	per cent	58·0	51·4	56·9	52·3
Expenditure per officer	E	£ per officer	1507	1902	1902	2137
Proportion of violence in total offences	V	per cent	4·9	6·8	4·4	5·0
Population density	D	persons per acre	13·3	0·6	13·6	0·6
Rate of unemployment	Q	per cent	2·2	1·7	1·8	1·5

Symbol	1961 Urban & Rural	1966 Urban & Rural	1971 Urban & Rural
Y	15·2	23·3	32·3
P clear-up	55·2	48·0	49·8
P convictions	23·0	21·8	20·0
C	1·6	1·8	1·8
F	16·5	18·5	14·7
A	6·4	7·0	7·3
W	27·3	27·7	24·2
R	35·2%	77·0%	18·5%
N	192	221	761
M	55·3	55·0	55·9
E	1559	1992	3388
V	5·6	4·7	4·9
Q	2·0	1·7	3·2

Notes:
(i)   The means are geometric means across police districts for the cross-section indicated. We take the anti-logarithm of the mean of the variables to be used in estimation (which were logged).
(ii) For full definitions see the Data Appendix.
(iii) The proportion of the area urbanised replaces RV and D for the pooled urban and rural runs (R above).

5

The Strategy of Testing a Social Theory

5.0 INTRODUCTION

The choice of statistical technique must depend on the theory under examination. For example, for some theories the technique of single equation multiple regression will be appropriate but for others, and our model is such a case, it will not. The purpose of this chapter is to justify the choice, and describe the procedure of, the estimation methods which we used and the approaches to hypotheses testing which we adopted. The estimation techniques were the simultaneous-equations methods of econometrics. Parts of this chapter may, therefore, seem laborious to econometricians but we hope that even they will find some of our estimation problems intriguing. Doubtless these simultaneous equations techniques will be completely new to other readers, and they might find this chapter a little difficult. We have tried to make it intelligible to someone who understands the technique of multiple regression in a model with one dependent variable and several explanatory variables, but as far as possible have avoided assuming much more than this. Our aim is to give sufficient intuitive feel for the techniques to allow an understanding of what we have done and why, and to enable the reader to understand and appraise the results which are presented in the next chapter. Our presentation will not be thorough from the theoretical point of view and neither will it be a manual on how to do applied econometrics. There are excellent textbooks for both these purposes and for the reader who wishes to go deeper into the subject we shall be giving several references.

We cannot begin to discuss the appropriate technique until we have a model. We express our model in the form of equations and these can be specified only by appealing to theories or prior knowledge. Our discussion of received theories in Chapters 2 and 3 led us to the model of Chapter 4, where we wrote down the explanatory variables corresponding to the main theories of the determination of offence rates (actual and recorded), clear-up rates and the number of policemen, which we want to test. The precise form of the equations of the model will be made specific in this chapter (for a full description see § 5.3). There must, of course, be some knowledge or theory preceding any statistical investigation or else that investigation could not take a particular form.

5.1 THE ESTIMATION PROCEDURES

The theories described in the preceding chapters, when written down formally, provide a model with several equations. We wish to estimate the parameters in these equations. We shall explain why the simple single equation multiple regression technique, applied to each equation, would be inappropriate and describe the simultaneous-equations techniques of econometrics which have been developed to meet the situation. We shall then discuss the problems of identification, or how to tell one equation from another, and of unobserved variables. We shall conclude with a description of the techniques we used for testing hypotheses inside our models.

Before proceeding to our full model (in § 5.3) we explain the simultaneous-equations techniques of econometrics, using a simple example which is a sharply limited form of our model. We shall be examining several problems using this simple model and have tried to keep it as small as possible without eliminating the problems which we wish to discuss. It will, of course, be more complex than is necessary for the discussion of any one of the problems but we did not wish to present a special model for each particular issue.

Suppose we begin by writing down the simple theory that the number of offences *per capita* (of the population), Y, in a police district is determined by the probability of detection, P, the severity of punishment, F, in that district, and the proportion, A, of young males in the population. Thus, for the moment, we assume away difficulties of knowing the actual or "true" level of offences (and we assume Y measures that level). This is the problem of "an unobserved variable" where we have a variable which plays an important role in the theory but for which we can find no satisfactory measure. This is a central issue in our study and we postpone treatment of the problem to § 5.3, after we have presented the full model. We ignore also other possible determinants of Y or, at least, we lump them into an error term. We shall suppose that our equations are linear in the logarithms of our variables—this assumption is discussed further in § 5.3. We denote the logarithm of a variable X by the lower case x. We have, therefore, described, in our simplified model, a first equation, with random term ε_1

$$y = \alpha_0 + \alpha_1 p + \alpha_2 f + \alpha_3 a + \varepsilon_1 \qquad (1)^0$$

where the α_i are coefficients or parameters which we want to estimate. We discuss the form of the errors below.

We have also argued in preceding chapters that the probability of detection depends on the number of policemen (*per capita*), C, and the number of problems or offences (*per capita*) Y, the police have to solve. There may, in addition, be economies or diseconomies of scale for a police district and we shall measure the size of the district by the population N. One could argue that the proportion of young males in the population might also affect the ease with which problems are solved. We again neglect other factors in the determination of p and, assuming the equation is linear in logarithms, we have in our simplified model a second equation

$$p = \beta_0 + \beta_1 y + \beta_2 c + \beta_3 n + \beta_4 a + \varepsilon_2 \qquad (2)^0$$

We have now written down two equations, one modelling the determination of y and one the determination of p. Given values of the variables f, a, c, n, and of the random terms ε_1 and ε_2, we have two equations for y and p which must *both* hold. Such a system is called a *simultaneous-equations system* and y, p *endogenous* variables. In general, we have as many equations as we have endogenous variables and in § 5.3 we shall be examining a full model of the processes described in the earlier chapters which will include more endogenous variables. In particular, we shall in § 5.3 be supposing that c is determined in part by p and y and hence is also endogenous.

Both equations $(1)^0$ and $(2)^0$ contain y and p. We have claimed, however, that $(1)^0$ represents the determination of y and $(2)^0$ the determination of p. We distinguish $(1)^0$, for example, by arguing that y is determined in part by f but not by n and $(2)^0$ by arguing that p is determined in part by n but not by f. Thus we can "tell the difference" between equations $(1)^0$ and $(2)^0$. The isolation of this difference is the so-called *identification problem* which was raised in § 4.8 and which will be explained in more detail in § 5.2. In § 5.3, when we have presented our full model we shall see that there are difficulties which cannot be dismissed.

Now suppose we applied the standard single equation multiple regression ordinary least squares technique to equation $(1)^0$. We know that, provided the right hand side variables p, f, and a are independent of the random disturbance ε_1 the simple ordinary least squares technique will provide unbiased estimates of the parameters α_i. [The argument can be illustrated by the simple regression case. Suppose the model is $z = \beta x + v$. The population (as opposed to the sample) estimate of β is $\dfrac{\text{cov}(x,z)}{\text{var } x}$, where we suppose the variables have zero means. But

$$\text{cov}(x,z) = \text{cov}(x,\beta x + v) = \text{cov}(x,\beta x) + \text{cov}(x,v) = \beta \text{ var } x + \text{cov}(x,v).$$

Hence our estimate, for the population would give β only if $\text{cov}(x,v) = 0$].

But is it possible in our two equation model for p to be independent of ε_1? The answer is negative because y depends on ε_1 and p depends on y through equation $(2)^0$. Formally substituting for y from $(1)^0$ into $(2)^0$ we have

$$p = (1 - \alpha_1\beta_1)^{-1} \times$$
$$\{(\beta_0 + \beta_1\alpha_0) + \beta_2 c + \beta_3 n + (\beta_4 + \beta_1\alpha_3) a + \beta_1\alpha_2 f + (\beta_1\varepsilon_1 + \varepsilon_2)\} \quad (3)^0$$

(equation $(3)^0$ is the *reduced form* equation for p—see next section). We see that p must be dependent on ε_1 if $\beta_1 \neq 0$. And our theory has led us to suppose, *a priori*, that $\beta_1 \neq 0$. Hence the ordinary least squares technique will, *a priori*, give biased estimates. Furthermore, the error in estimating the parameters will not tend to disappear for large samples, since the correlation between p and ε_1 will persist, however many observations we have. More formally we say our estimates are inconsistent. Technically an estimator $\hat{\alpha}_i$, of the coefficient α_i is unbiased if the expectation of $\hat{\alpha}_i$, or the average $\hat{\alpha}_i$ across possible samples, is α_i. It is consistent if it tends to α_i (in probability) as the sample size goes to infinity or plim $\hat{\alpha}_i = \alpha_i$. The notions are distinct. By "in the limit" or "in large samples" or "plim" we shall be referring to probability limits as the size of sample tends to infinity.

We saw that the bias and inconsistency arise from the correlation of p and ε_1. This correlation can occur *even if* p is not dependent on y in the second equation, since ε_1 and ε_2 may be correlated. This can occur if we have omitted a variable x_1 from the first equation and a variable x_2 from the second and x_1 is correlated with x_2 (as for example, when x_1 and x_2 are the same variable). We shall have a little more to say about this possibility when we discuss the variance-covariance matrix of residuals in § 5.5

The simultaneous-equations techniques of econometrics correct for the inconsistency. They do not correct for bias but it appears that for medium size samples the bias with these techniques may not be large (see discussion of Monte Carlo studies at the end of this section). The simplest of the techniques is two-stage least squares (2SLS). This replaces p, for the purpose of parameter estimation by $\hat{p}$, a "measure" of p which is close to p but which is independent of ε_1. This is done by the OLS regression of p on all the variables in the system except y. By omitting y we produce a measure $\hat{p}$ which is, in the limit, uncorrelated with ε and by including all the other variables we obtain a measure as close as possible to p. We use as $\hat{p}$ the fitted value in this "first stage" regression. This use of a fitted value implies that in the limit the stochastic element ε_2 disappears, thus avoiding any problems of the correlation between ε_1 and ε_2. The second stage involves the OLS regression of y on $\hat{p}$, f, and α. The estimated coefficient of $\hat{p}$ in this second stage regression is a consistent estimate of α_1. In other words, if we went on increasing the number of observations, our estimate would tend to α_1.

We have so far described the estimation of the parameters of the first equation. In this estimation we have used information from the second equation only to the extent of specifying which exogenous variables it includes which are not included in the first equation. Thus, for example, we have not used the information that f is not included in the second equation. And if there were further endogenous variables and further equations the 2SLS procedure would remain the same: there would merely be more regressions in the first stage (one for each right-hand side endogenous variable), and more exogenous variables to be included in the set of "all exogenous variables" for this first stage. We should not need to know which of the exogenous variables, in addition to those in the first equation, came from which of the remaining equations. For this reason the 2SLS procedure is called a *limited-information* technique.

We should expect to do better in the sense of obtaining sharper, or more efficient, estimates if we used the extra information from the other equations (there are problems, of course, if this information is not correct —see the end of this section). Techniques which use all the information embodied in the full equation system are called *full-information* methods. We shall be discussing the two most important methods: *three-stage least squares* or *3SLS*, and full-information maximum likelihood or *FIML*.

Suppose we have carried out 2SLS estimation for both equations (1)[0] and (2)[9]. Then for each equation we have fitted values of the left hand side variable and a set of residuals. We can, therefore, use the residuals to estimate the covariance of the random terms in the two equations. Let us suppose that the residuals are positively correlated—thus districts with "randomly" high offence rates also have "randomly" high detection rates. Knowledge of the outcome of the second equation would give us information on the first. The random terms capture the effects of many small omitted influences and these factors may be relevant for both equations. There will be further discussion of the residual or error terms in § 5.5. The first and second stages of 3SLS, therefore, are those of 2SLS, and the third stage uses the estimated covariance of the residuals derived from 2SLS to give sharper estimates; since both are consistent, in the limit they give the same parameter estimates. We have to know the structure of *each* equation in the system in order to measure the error terms from 2SLS. The method, therefore, uses "full-information". Note the procedure gives us estimates of the variance-covariance matrix of the residuals in addition to the coefficients of the variables in the equations.

The precise manner in which we use the estimated variance-covariance of the residuals in the equations of 2SLS in order to generate the 3SLS estimates is rather technical, and we leave it to the interested reader to pursue the matter in one or more of the many text-books on econometrics: see (for example, Dhrymes (1970), or Malinvaud (1970) or Johnston (1972)).

We can help the reader who is familiar with Aitken's method (see Dhrymes (1970)) in the single equation case by saying that the relation between 3SLS and 2SLS is similar to the relation between Aitken's method and OLS for the single equation. In that case Aitken's method uses an estimate of the variance-covariance matrix of the error terms to transform variables so that the error structure is of the usual kind, with errors for different observations independent and with the same variance (see Dhrymes (1970), p. 150 and p. 209).

We have explained 3SLS by describing three stages in the computation. In fact, one can compute the estimates at one go without performing three separate regressions, since they are a relatively straightforward function of the observations on the endogenous and exogenous variables. The programme will be described briefly after we have discussed our main estimation method which is *full-information maximum likelihood* or *FIML*.

We shall explain the FIML estimates in terms of our simple two equation model. Let us suppose that $(\varepsilon_1, \varepsilon_2)$ has a bivariate normal distribution with the means of ε_1 and ε_2 both zero. The variance of ε_1 is σ_{11}, and of ε_2, σ_{22} and the covariance between ε_1 and ε_2 is σ_{12}. We suppose that the errors for different observations, or areas, are independent (see § 5.5). The σ's will be estimated along with the coefficients α_j and β_j.

Given the observations on the exogenous variables, equations (1)^0 and (2)^0 tell us that there will be a probability density function (loosely, the function describing the probability that y and p together take particular values) for the observations on y and p for any given parameters (α_i), (β_i) and (σ_{ij}). The probability is called the likelihood of (y,p), given the observations on the exogenous variables. We shall choose our estimates of the parameters in order to maximise this likelihood, given the observations on y and p. In other words, our parameters are selected so that the probability of (y,p) occurring is larger than for any other possible values of those parameters, or we suppose that the parameters are such that the observed values of y and p are more likely than for any other parameters.

The method has considerable intuitive appeal. A given body of data provides a set of observations and we assume that the underlying structure is such that amongst all possible structures these observations were the most likely. In the absence of some prior information on the possible values of the parameters, it would be unnatural to suppose that the structure makes the set of observations that actually happened less likely than does some other structure. Of course, we can imagine some set of prior beliefs or hunches about the parameters but it is difficult to make these precise, given the number of parameters involved, and not particularly easy to incorporate these beliefs into the estimation exercise (see, however, Zellner (1971)).

The FIML technique also has considerable advantages in the testing of hypotheses. Suppose, for example, we want to test the hypothesis that the proportion of young males in the population does not affect the detection rate, in other words (see equation $(2)^0$) that $\beta_4 = 0$. We can estimate assuming $\beta_4 = 0$ and obtain a maximum likelihood. We can then make a second estimate allowing β_4 to vary in the maximisation, and thus obtain a second maximum likelihood. The second likelihood must be at least as great as the first, since the set of possible structures over which we search for the maximum include those available in the first search. We can construct tests which enable us to decide whether the increase in the likelihood is sufficiently large to be significant. We shall describe these tests in more detail in § 5.5 and make considerable use of them in Chapter 6, when we present our results.

We shall now describe briefly the state of knowledge concerning the properties of the four estimation techniques we have mentioned: OLS, 2SLS, 3SLS and FIML. In a simultaneous equations situation OLS estimators are inconsistent, whereas the other three are consistent. One can also show that 2SLS, 3SLS and FIML estimates are asymptotically normal. In other words, as the number of observations increase, the distribution of our estimators approaches normality. Formally, if ∂ is the vector of parameters to be estimated and T is the number of observations, an estimator $\hat{\partial}$ is asymptotically normal if $\sqrt{T}(\hat{\partial} - \partial)$ tends in distribution to the multivariate normal distribution $N(O, \Sigma)$, where Σ is a positive definite variance-covariance matrix (and $N(\alpha, \Delta)$ denotes the multivariate normal distribution with vector of means α, and variance-covariance matrix, Δ). We say, informally, that $\hat{\partial}$ is asymptotically $N(O, \Sigma)$. One can show that FIML and 3SLS are equivalent and more efficient than 2SLS in the following sense. If the FIML estimator is asymptotically $N(O, \Sigma_1)$, the 3SLS is also and if the 2SLS estimator is asymptotically $N(O, \Sigma_2)$, then $\Sigma_2 - \Sigma_1$ is a positive definite matrix. Indeed, amongst (uniformly) asymptotically normal estimators, FIML is the most efficient (see Dhrymes (1970), p. 130). The superiority of 3 SLS over 2SLS is demonstrated in Dhyrmes (1970), p. 219, and a particularly clear demonstration that FIML and 3SLS are asymptotically equivalent is given in Hausman (1975). Hausman also shows that an infinite number of such equivalent estimators exist.

Given that FIML is efficient compared with other estimators, provides convenient likelihood-ratio tests and has intuitive appeal, the arguments for using it are strong, and indeed this is the estimator which we have used the most. There are two disadvantages, however. The first is computational. One cannot derive explicit expressions for the estimates in terms of the observations on the variables. Thus the search for the optimum is numerical, and the task of designing efficient computational procedure is not easy. Most programmes use an iterative procedure and convergence problems can occasionally arise. We were fortunate that Cliff Wymer of the LSE made his SIMUL programme available. This provides an efficient and convenient package.

The second disadvantage arises from its use of full information, and this disadvantage is shared with 3SLS. In justifying the 3SLS estimator relative to the 2SLS we argued that the 2SLS estimator of equation $(1)^0$ was inefficient because it did not use all the available information on the structure of equation $(2)^0$. But what if our assumed information on $(2)^0$ turns out to be mistaken? If we use a full-information system such as 3SLS or FIML we have carried this mistake into our estimates of the first equation. Experiments with Monte Carlo studies have shown that this problem may be serious in that specification errors in other equations can cause misleading estimates of the equation under consideration, if a full-information technique is used. Of course, any estimation of a single equation, be it limited or full information, will suffer if mistakes are made in the specification of that equation.

Hendry and Srba have shown in a recent Monte Carlo study (1977) that the bias using the simultaneous equations estimators discussed here may be quite small (see also Hendry and Harrison (1974)). Recall that one can in general establish the large sample or limiting property of consistency for these estimators but not unbiasedness, a property unrelated to size of sample.

We regard the FIML estimators as in general superior on the grounds of intuitive appeal and convenience of hypothesis testing. However, given the asymptotic equivalence and the relative ease of computation of 3SLS the preference is not a strong one. The choice between FIML and 2SLS depends on our trade-off between tight estimates and fear of errors. If we are very worried about the latter (for example, if the consequence of errors in a policy decision are large), we might choose 2SLS. Accordingly, whilst our main attention is on FIML (which has the other advantage of easy hypothesis tests), we give a selection of 2SLS results in Chapter 6 (§ 6.7.2).

One would regard the worry about errors in FIML with less seriousness the "closer" were 2SLS estimates to FIML. We have not used any formal tests of proximity and the reader is left to judge "by eye" in Chapter 6. For a further discussion the reader is referred to Dhrymes (1970), Ch. 8, and to Summers (1965). Some formal tests are provided in Hausman (1977).

Cliff Wymer's SIMUL programme provides 2SLS, 3SLS and FIML estimates. OLS estimates were obtained with the FAKAD programme of E. van Broekhoven and K. MacDonald. Computations were carried out on the Oxford computer—the ICL 1906A. The SIMUL programme computes 2SLS first, then 3SLS, and then uses the 3SLS estimates as a starting point for the iterative procedure which searches for the maximum of the likelihood function in FIML. At each step the current values of the parameters are revised so that the likelihood value is increased and an attempt is made to choose the step in the direction of the steepest slope of the likelihood surface. The process is terminated when the changes in the parameters at each step have become small or the increases in the likelihood at each step are small. The time required on the 1906A to compute 2SLS, 3SLS, and FIML estimates on a model with 110 observations with our specified degree of accuracy[1] was between 30 and 60 seconds.

5.2 THE IDENTIFICATION PROBLEM

The identification problem arises in our simple two equation model $(1)^0$ and $(2)^0$ in the assertion that it is $(1)^0$ that models the determination of the offence rate and $(2)^0$ the determination of the clear-up rate. Both are equations relating *y and p* and we have to use our knowledge of the *other* variables which should enter the two equations in order to tell one from the other. We shall explain the problem in detail in this section. In the following section, when we have presented our full model we discuss the particular difficulties that arise in our analysis; they are not negligible.

The following diagram illustrates the problem. Plot y, the (log of the) number of offences, and p the (log of the) detection rate on the horizontal and vertical axes respectively. Let the curves $S_1 S_1$, $S_2 S_2$, $S_3 S_3$ represent the dependence of y on p through equation $(1)^0$ and the curves $D_1 D_1$, $D_2 D_2$, $D_3 D_3$ the dependence of p on y through equation $(2)^0$.

We suppose that the curves $S_i S_i$ and $D_i D_i$ ($i = 1, 2, \ldots$) depend on other variables. For the moment, we suppose we do not know what these are, but that they do vary across police districts. The curve $S_1 S_1$ will represent the y,

---

[1] Iterations were terminated when no coefficient in the model changed at the last step by more than 0.001.

p relation of the first equation for police district one, $S_2 S_2$ for police district 2 and $S_3 S_3$ for police district three. Similarly, for $D_1 D_1$, $D_2 D_2$ and $D_3 D_3$. For police district one we actually observe X_1, the point of intersection of $S_1 S_1$ and $D_1 D_1$, since, if our model is correct, the observed values of y and p must lie on both curves. Similarly, for district two we have X_2, and for district three X_3.

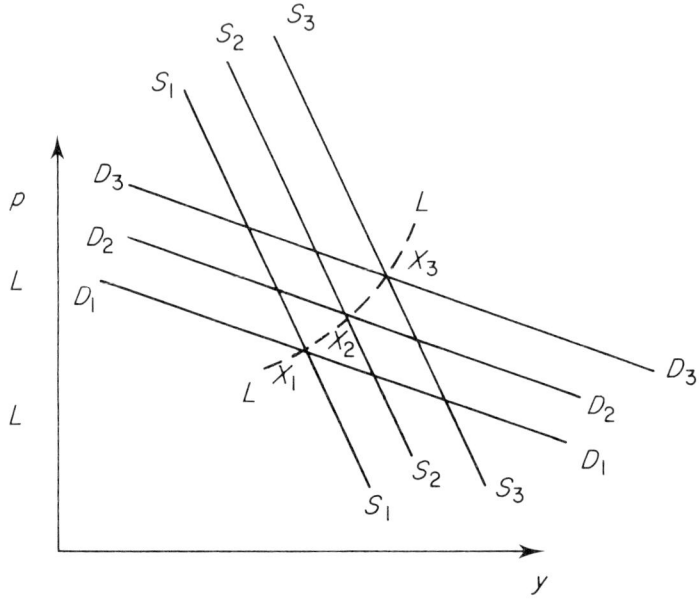

Fig. 5.1.

Suppose now that we had failed to notice that there was a second equation and we had set out naively to estimate the dependence of y on p by a simple one equation regression. In the situation expressed in our diagram we should have concluded that the regression line is LL and a higher clear-up rate generates more offences. It might then have occurred to us that there was another relation between p and y through equation $(2)^0$. And it could be argued, and such arguments are common, that we could not tell whether y is driving p or p is driving y. In other words we would have the "horse-and-cart" problem; but the situation would be worse than that. In both equations $(1)^0$ and $(2)^0$ the relation between y and p, we suppose, is an inverse one, yet we have seen that our regression can yield a positive relation between y and p. Thus the estimated equation would not be either $(1)^0$ or $(2)^0$, and is, in fact, something that looks completely different from each of them.

It should be clear that an analysis of the variance or co-variance of y

would not help us in the understanding of the first equation. The analysis of variance technique is essentially that of multiple regression where the right hand side variables are all of the zero-one variety (that is, any particular variable can take only the value 0 or 1)—see Scheffé (1959). Thus its use would involve a mistake analogous to that involved in examining the line LL. The analysis of covariance involves a mixture of zero-one and continuous variables and is subject to the same problems.

How then do we proceed? Suppose we knew that there were factors in equation $(2)^0$ affecting the determination of the detection rate which did not directly affect the determination of y and so were not part of equation $(1)^0$? Then as the $D_iD_i(i = 1, 2, \ldots)$ curve varied from district to district because of these factors we should discover the SS curve—see Fig. 2—since in district i we should observe p and y given by Z_i, the point of intersection of S and D_i.

For example, we have supposed that the size of the district affects the detection rate but not the offence rate. Thus if we selected observations from districts of different size, but similar in all other respects, we should have points on the same SS curve but on different DD curves. Thus we "trace out" the SS curve. We should, therefore, have succeeded in identifying our first equation. Similarly if there were factors affecting $(1)^0$ but not $(2)^0$ we could trace out the DD curve and we should have identified both equations.

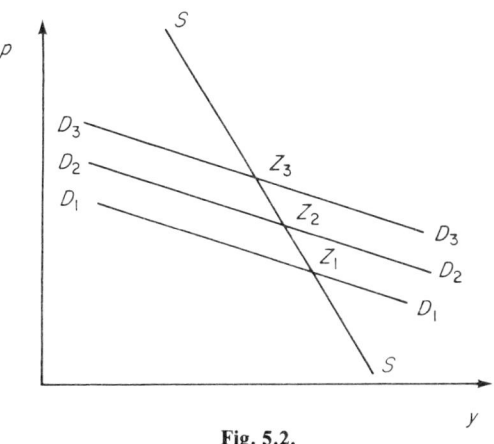

Fig. 5.2.

We can see now that equations $(1)^0$ and $(2)^0$ are indeed identified, since each contains a variable which does not appear in the other equation: f appears in $(1)^0$ but not $(2)^0$, and n appears in $(2)^0$ but not $(1)^0$. We have thus solved the "horse-and-cart" problem.

Note that it is quite possible for one equation to be identified but not the other. For example, suppose $(2)^0$ were also to contain f. There would then be a shift in the SS curve associated with any shift in the DD curve because all factors affecting DD also affect SS. To put the matter another way, we could not distinguish equation $(2)^0$ from an equation $(\dagger)$, say formed by adding $(1)^0$ and $(2)^0$, since $(2)^0$ and $(\dagger)$ would contain the same variables. This second way of expressing the failure of identification is in the spirit of the rank condition (see Fisher (1966)) which is necessary and sufficient for identification (see below).

We should emphasize that the feasibility of our estimation techniques depend crucially on the equations being identified. Consider 2SLS estimates for equation $(1)^0$. At the first stage we regress p on all the exogenous variables of the system. If these are *all* contained in equation $(1)^0$, we should run into an insuperable problem at the second stage. The value p which we should be using at the second stage, would be a perfect combination of the other right hand side variables and we should have exact multi-collinearity preventing us from carrying out the second stage. This problem must arise if we attempt to estimate an equation which is not identified: it cannot arise if the equation is identified. We now turn to formal conditions for identification.

In our discussion above we have demonstrated one sufficient condition for the identification of each equation: each equation should contain an exogenous variable unique to it. Our procedure to check for identification (in § 5.3), therefore, will be as follows. We shall write down the endogenous and exogenous variables entering each equation. We shall then look at the equations to check that each one has an exogenous variable unique to it. Whilst the model we estimate will satisfy this condition, it is difficult to be completely confident about the specifications which lead to the condition being satisfied.

The above sufficient condition for identification is a special case of a more general sufficient condition (which is also necessary) stating that each equation of a system is identified if no one of them can be reproduced by taking a scalar multiple of each of the other equations and adding them together. This is the rank condition—for further discussion see Fisher (1966) and Malinvaud (1970) and the next section. Identification is achieved by imposing *restrictions* on the model. For example, to say that some exogenous variable is unique to a given equation is to say that its coefficient in each of the other equations is restricted to zero. It is the pattern of such restrictions which is crucial to identification and the problem is usually discussed in terms of such restrictions. Restrictions on the coefficients may be of many kinds and are not necessarily of the type where a coefficient is assumed to be zero—for example we might restrict two coefficients to be equal.

An alternative statement of the identification problem is that of passing from the *reduced form* to the structural model. In our simplified model the *structure* is represented by equations $(1)^0$ and $(2)^0$, and the coefficients therein are described as *structural coefficients*. These equations describe the behavioural and institutional characteristics of our system and each equation is intended to model one particular process. The system $(1)^0$ and $(2)^0$, however, determines y and p simultaneously and, given levels of the exogenous variables and disturbance terms, we can calculate both y and p. Indeed, we saw in equation $(3)^0$ how to do this calculation for p. We can obtain an equation for y analogous to equation $(3)^0$ by substituting from $(2)^0$ into $(1)^0$

$$y = (1 - \alpha_1\beta_1)^{-1}\{(\alpha_0 + \alpha_1\beta_0) + \alpha_2 f + (\alpha_3 + \alpha_1\beta_4)\alpha + \alpha_1\beta_2 c + \alpha_1\beta_3 n + (\varepsilon_1 + \alpha_1\varepsilon_2)\} \tag{4^0}$$

For ease of reference we repeat equation $(3)^0$

$$p = (1 - \alpha_1\beta_1)^{-1}\{(\beta_0 + \beta_1\alpha_0) + \beta_1\alpha_0 f + (\beta_4 + \beta_1\alpha_3)\alpha + \beta_2 c + \beta_3 n + (\beta_1\varepsilon_1 + \varepsilon_2)\} \tag{3^0}$$

Equations $(3)^0$ and $(4)^0$ are the *reduced form* of our system. We could estimate these directly by regressing y on all the exogenous variables and p on all the exogenous variables; we should then have coefficients from these regressions. Our next step would be to try to reconstruct our structural equations $(1)^0$ and $(2)^0$. In other words, we calculate estimates of the α_i and β_i from the estimated coefficients of $(3)^0$ and $(4)^0$. The importance of the conditions for identification given above is that they ensure that we can, in fact, achieve this.

The coefficients in equations $(3)^0$ and $(4)^0$ are the *impact multipliers* (see for example Dhrymes (1970) p. 508). They describe the total effect of a change in some variable, say a, on y after all the indirect effects working through the other endogenous variables, here p, have been taken into consideration. For short term prediction and policy they are the coefficients of importance.

However, a knowledge of the economic, criminological, or sociological processes in the system is equivalent to a knowledge of the structure; also we need to know the structure if we wish to discuss changes in our system. For a claim that some change in behaviour has occurred would involve a shift in some structural coefficient; this can be specified only in terms of the structural equations. A shift in one structural parameter, however, would affect many coefficients in the reduced form (see equations $(3)^0$ and $(4)^0$), and it would be complicated to conduct the discussion of such a change using only the reduced form.

We now turn to the question of *over-identification*. We saw that a sufficient condition for identification of each structural equation was that each should contain one exogenous variable unique to it. If each equation in a system does contain at least one exogenous variable unique to it but some equations have more than one variable unique to them, we have more restrictions than are necessary for identification: we have an example of *over-identification*. Equation $(2)^0$ contains two exogenous variables c and n, which, in our simple system $((1)^0, (2)^0)$ are unique to it and $(1)^0$ contains one variable f and we have therefore such an example. This over-identification implies that there is a restriction on the reduced form. We can see that in $(3)^0$ and $(4)^0$ the ratio of the coefficients on n and c in the two equations must be the same. We say that a system is *exactly identified* if the specification of the structure places *no* restrictions on the reduced form, but yet we have enough information to pass from the reduced form to the structure. Our definition of *over-identification* is the existence of restrictions on the reduced form, and the degree to which it is over- identified is measured by the number of such restrictions.

These considerations enable us to consider tests for our model specification. We shall obtain a better fit in our reduced form if we estimate it by regressing y and p on all the exogenous variables paying no attention to restrictions imposed by the structures, than if our estimation does recognise these restrictions. We can construct a test (see § 5.4) which attempts to measure whether the improvement in fit obtained by the relaxation of the over-identifying restrictions is significant. If it is not, then we can accept our over-identifying restrictions as justified. In this sense we shall be testing our model specification. Since we cannot estimate the structural model unless it is identified, we cannot test a particular restriction in an exactly identified model.

The estimation techniques 2SLS, 3SLS and FIML described above, allow for any over-identifying restrictions, since the structure is estimated directly. We can then solve for $(3)^0$ and $(4)^0$ to calculate the coefficients of the reduced form. To emphasize that the restrictions of the structure are carried through, we call $(3)^0$ and $(4)^0$ the *derived* reduced form (to contrast with the *unrestricted* reduced form). Examples are given in Chapter 6, § 6.5. We turn now to a presentation of our full model.

5.3 THE FULL MODEL, UNOBSERVED VARIABLES, AND FURTHER DISCUSSION OF IDENTIFICATION

5.3.0 *The Full Model*

In the preceding sections we have used a simple two-equation model to explain our estimation techniques and to examine the identification problem. Furthermore, we drew attention to the distinction between recorded offence and clear-up rates and actual rates. The system described in Chapters 2, 3 and 4, however, involves more than two equations and much space was devoted to the discussion of the difference between the recorded number of offences and the actual or "true" number. We shall now write down the model of Chapters 2, 3 and 4 in full and discuss the problems of identification and unobserved variables that it raises. We shall have to deal with a system with several equations but the only mathematics we shall use will be the substitution from one equation into another.

We begin by writing down the five equations of our full model and then discuss the variables and each equation in turn. The variables are defined in Table 5.1.

$$y^* = \alpha_1 p^* + \alpha_2 c + \sum_{i=3}^{7} \alpha_i x'_i + \alpha_0 + \varepsilon_1 \tag{1}$$

$$p = \beta_1 y + \beta_2 c + \sum_{i=3}^{7} \beta_i x_i^2 + \beta_0 + \varepsilon_2 \tag{2}$$

$$c = \gamma_1 y + \gamma_2 p + \sum_{i=3}^{6} \gamma_i x_i^3 + \gamma_0 + \varepsilon_3 \tag{3}$$

$$p^* + y^* = p + y \tag{4}$$

$$y = y^* + k(\ ) + \varepsilon_5 \tag{5}$$

This system of equations is based on equations (14)-(17) in Chapter 4 which were in turn the outcome of a lengthy discussion in Chapters 2, 3 and 4. We shall not, therefore, dwell on the underlying economic, criminological and sociological theories. The system (14)-(17) in Chapter 4 embodied general functional forms. We have chosen here the particular functional form where the equations are linear in the logarithms of variables. This choice will be discussed below. With this functional form equations (1)-(3) here are equations (14)-(16) of Chapter 4. The fourth equation (4) here is an identity which will be explained below. Equation (5) represents equation (17) of Chapter 4. We suggested specific arguments for the function $k(\ )$ in Chapter 4—namely, c, a, w. For the moment we remain agnostic about those arguments, since the recording process embodied in equation (17) is a difficult one to capture and we wish to carry through the analysis a description of the effects of introducing additional variables into

Table 5.1

Variables in the full model

Endogenous Variables

Y^*	"True" number of offences per capita
Y	"Recorded" number of offences per capita
P^*	"True" probability of detection
P	"Recorded" probability of detection
C	Police officers per capita

Exogenous Variables

Equation 1:

X_3^1	:	F	Proportion of males convicted given custodial treatment
X_4^1	:	A	Proportion of young males (15-24) in population
X_5^1	:	W	Proportion of population that is working class
X_6^1	:	RV	Total rateable value per acre
X_7^1	:	E	Total police expenditure per officer

Equation 2:

X_3^2	:	A	See equation 1
X_4^2	:	W	See equation 1
X_5^2	:	N	Population
X_6^2	:	E	See equation 1
X_7^2	:	V	Proportion of offences that are violent

Equation 3:

X_3^3	:	M	Proportion of population that is middle class
X_4^3	:	V	See equation 2
X_5^3	:	D	Population density
X_6^3	:	Q	Unemployment

Notes:

1. The equations are justified in Chapters 2, 3 and 4.
2. Measurement of the variables is explained in Chapters 2, 3 and 4 and precise sources are given in the Data Appendix.
3. Lower case letters represent the logarithms of the upper case letters.
4. In our estimates we use two alternative measures for P, the clear-up rate and the conviction rate.
5. The equation numbers 1, 2, 3 refer to equations (1), (2), (3) presented in this subsection and the included endogenous variables in each equation are given in (1), (2), (3).
6. $\tilde{P}$ is the perceived probability of detection.

that equation. We note here that the model would not be acceptable to some sociologists of deviance (see Chapter 4 and below). We give, as a recap, a brief explanation of each equation and then we turn to the choice of appropriate functional form.

Equation (1) models the individual behaviour which determines the "true" level of offences. We assume that individuals have a perception of the "true" probability $p*$ of being caught, and that this is the variable which affects behaviour (some of the difficulties with this assumption were discussed in § 2.2.2, and in § 4.1.1). We suppose for the moment that we do not need a separate equation to model the determination of the perceived probability $\tilde{p}$ of being caught. Such a procedure is possible and it is examined later in this section; it gives a further endogenous variable and requires specification of the determinants of $\tilde{p}$. We shall return to this point below (see equatioin (1b)), and shall discuss the effect which the additional equation has on the interpretation of the estimated parameters. At present, however, let us suppose that the perceived probability $\tilde{p}$ is given by $p*$, the actual or "true" probability of detection.

The second equation models the process of solving recorded crimes. We suppose this detection problem results in some recorded detection rate, which depends on the number of recorded problems or offences which the police have to solve.

The process by which the number of police officers is determined is represented in equation (3). We explained in Chapter 3 (§ 3.3) and in Chapter 4 (§ 4.3) that we see this as a supply equation modelling the willingness to become or remain a policeman. The supply is in turn influenced by certain demand factors, through recruitment drives.

We turn now to equation (4). If the number of recorded offences counted by the police as solved is G, then $PY = G$. We take as a formal definition of the "true" probability of detection $P*$, G divided $Y*$. Thus equation (4) becomes an identity. It is important to consider the relation between this particular definition of $P*$ and the perceived probability of punishment—see equation (1b) below. Since we are working with the logarithms of variables (where $p = \log P$ and similarly the other variables— see Table 5.1) we have $p* + y* = p + y$. We shall see that it is very convenient to have this identity in linear form and this is one of our reasons for using the logarithm, rather than some other transformation of the variables (for further discussion of the logarithmic form see below).

Finally, we have the fifth equation which states that the number of reported offences is a fraction of the number of true offences where this fraction has logarithm $k( ) + \varepsilon_5$ where k is a function of as yet unspecified variables and ε_5 is a random term with mean zero. For some sociologists of deviance the question of the fraction $Y/Y*$ would not arise since $Y*$ is not admitted as a concept. They might also wish to include additional variables from the list included in equation (14) of the previous chapter. We shall see below that elimination of Y^* and P^* from the model will not change the equations to be estimated but will change their interpretation.

We have already indicated one advantage of the logarithmic form—it makes the identity (4) linear. And it is not unnatural as a functional form in this context, since it involves diminishing marginal effects in the following sense. Let us take an example from the first equation: a given increase in the severity of punishment would have a smaller effect on the level of offences at a higher than a lower punishment level. Similarly, a given increase in available "swag" would have a smaller effect on the number of offences, the greater the amount of available swag already available. These diminishing returns take a particularly neat form with the logarithmic specification— a given percentage change in an explanatory variable produces a percentage change α times as large in the variable to be explained where α is the coefficient in the equation. We call α the *elasticity* of the variable to be explained with respect to the explanatory variable.

We tried at an early stage two alternative functional forms for the estimating equations (see below) which do not carry with them the two advantages of the logarithmic form which have been mentioned. We tried a linear specification (that is substituting upper case letters) and the use of the $\log \dfrac{P}{1-P}$ instead of p for those variables that are proportions. Neither showed any superiority over the logarithmic form. Our judgement of superiority here was informal since there is no widely accepted rigorous criterion for comparing the performance of alternative functional forms. We looked for "reasonable" parameter values in terms of the theory and high likelihood values (see § 5.4).

The rationale for using $\pi = \log \dfrac{P}{1-P}$ where P is a proportion is that it provides the possibility of values of π spreading from $-\infty$ to $+\infty$. The use of $p = \log P$ implies that p must be less than zero (since $P<1$). This does not live very happily with the assumption of normality of errors. The advantages of the logarithmic form are such that we chose to ignore this particular problem.

We turn now to the problem of unobserved variables and we begin our discussion with equation (5). In the same spirit as the rest of the model we assume that k is linear in the logarithm of its arguments. The problem, of course, is to know what the arguments of the $k(\ )$ function are; in other words, what determines the proportion of offences that is reported? We gave our best guesses in Chapter 4, based on the discussion of Chapter 3 but, for our analysis here, let us for the moment remain agnostic and substitute from equations (4) and (5) into (1). We have

$$y = \alpha_1 p + \alpha_2 c + \sum_{i=3}^{7} \alpha_i x_i^1 + \alpha_0 + (1 + \alpha_1) k_1() + (1 + \alpha_1) \varepsilon_5 + \varepsilon_1 \qquad (1)'$$

We now see that if any of the variables on the right hand side of (1)′ are among the arguments of $k()$, then the corresponding parameter α_1 is unidentified as a parameter of (1). For example, suppose k depends on c (and it is reasonable— see Chapters 2, 3 and 4—to suppose that it does) then we write $k() = \eta c + k_1()$ and (1)′ becomes

$$y = \alpha_1 p + (\alpha_2 + (1 + \alpha_1)\eta)c + \sum_{i=3}^{7} \alpha_1 x^1{}_i + \alpha_9 + (1 + \alpha_1) k_1()$$

$$+ (1 + \alpha_1) \varepsilon_5 + \varepsilon_1 \qquad (1)''$$

Suppose we know k_1 is constant. We can estimate the system (1)″, (2) and (3), since it is a three-equation system in 3 endogenous variables y, p, c. It is easy to check that the system (1)″, (2), (3) satisfies the condition for identification given in § 5.2. The point is that although we can estimate $(\alpha_2 + (1 + \alpha_1)\eta)$, we cannot isolate α_2 and η.

The estimation procedure which we used was to include as explanatory variables in the first equation p, c, and the five exogenous variables given in Table 5.1. In other words we have

$$y = \alpha'_1 p + \alpha'_2 c + \sum_{i=3}^{7} \alpha'_1 x^1{}_i + \alpha'_0 + \varepsilon'_1 \qquad (1)'''$$

The system estimated was (1)‴, (2) and (3). We thus have a three-equation system with three endogenous variables y, p, c and ten exogenous variables. There are 23 coefficients (including 3 constant terms) and 6 distinct entries in the variance-covariance matrix. It satisfies the condition for identification given in § 5.2 (the problem is discussed further at the end of this section).

We can assert that α_i is a parameter of equation (1) as well as (1)‴ only if we are convinced that the corresponding variable is not an argument of $k()$. If we are not so convinced, then we should interpret the parameter as a product of two processes: the first determining the actual or "true" level of offences, the second determining the number of these offences which reach the record book. We shall make liberal use of such interpretations in Chapter 7. It should be noted that if y or $p*$ is an argument of $k(\ )$, then none of the α'_i will be equal to α_i (examine $(1)'$). Further we have assumed that $k(\ )$ does not depend on any of the exogenous variables that were excluded from (1) (see Table 5.1), so that the incorporation of the $k(\ )$ function does not imply that we have to include extra variables in $(1)'''$.

Until now we have, for simplicity, made the assumption that the perceived probability of detection $\tilde{p}$ is equal to $p*$. It is time to relax this assumption. We shall let $y*$ depend on $\tilde{p}$ rather than $p*$ in (1), and use a separate equation to model the determination of $\tilde{p}$. We then carry out a procedure of substituting for $\tilde{p}$ from this separate equation, just as we eliminated $p*$ using (4) and (5). Suppose that following the discussion in Chapter 2, § 2.2.3, we can write

$$\tilde{p} = p* + \delta_1 c + \delta_2 e + \varepsilon_{1b} \qquad (1b)$$

so that the perceived probability of being caught is a multiple of the true probability, where that multiple depends on the number of police *per capita c* and on e, and that the new version of (1) depends on $\tilde{p}$.

The way in which $\tilde{p}$ depends on $p*$ depends on how the latter is defined. We chose to define $P*$ as the number G of recorded offences actually classified as solved in police statistics, divided by $Y*$. This definition provided equation (4) as an identity. The individual's view of the probability of a sanction depends on which events he himself sees as unpleasant. It is clear that such events are more numerous than G. We are thinking in particular here of informal sanctions such as a reprimand by a policeman or other adult to a juvenile. The example indicates both that p will depend on the attitudes of those in authority and will vary systematically across individuals. Such effects are hard to measure directly but will form part of our interpretations in Chapter 7.

We can now substitute from (1b) into (1) and arrive eventually at a modified version of $(1)''$ with a coefficient of c, for example, of $(\alpha_2 + \alpha_1 \delta_1 + (1 + \alpha_1)\eta)$. We must, therefore, interpret α'_2 the coefficient of c in the first equation (see $(1)'''$), as embodying this further process of the determination of $\tilde{p}$. Indeed, as we stated in Chapter 2 (§ 2.2.2) the main reason for including c and e in the first equation from the point of view of the determination of actual offences, is their effect on the perceived probability of being caught. If this were their only effect then α_2 and α_7 in equation (1) would be zero.

By this stage the reader may have become somewhat exasperated by all the equations we have inflicted. It must be emphasized, however, that the equations described above are no more than a formal statement of the arguments contained in Chapters 2 and 3 and derive their complexity solely from those arguments. We hope that by now the reader will be able to specify such equations as he or she thinks that we may have omitted, or to carry out any other modifications which might be regarded as necessary. We should guess that, given the data, the equations which would be specified would be close to the ones that we have used but there may be a different interpretation of some of the coefficients.

Some sociologists of deviance, as we have emphasised at several places, would drop Y^* and P^* altogether from the system. Such a position, in fact, makes derivation of the estimating equations much easier. If deterrence variables are included in equation (17) of Chapter 4, Y^* is dropped from that equation, and equation (14) is eliminated, then we can immediately reproduce the system estimated here. Thus the new first equation becomes a model of how police and the public interact to produce recorded crime rates. Our preference for the system described above is because it allows explicit consideration of deterrence theories. Note that the interpretation of p and f in the first equation if Y^* is eliminated, becomes that individuals take care to make sure their actions are not recorded as offences if the likelihood and severity of punishment for a recorded offence are high.

We shall not discuss the data at length here. Our measures of variables have been discussed in Chapters 2 and 3 and summarized in Chapter 4. A detailed description is given in the Data Appendix and the data are on file at the SSRC Survey Archive at the University of Essex.

5.3.1 *Alternative Procedures for the Problem of Unobserved Variables*

Given that we had unobserved variables in our model, we chose the option of manipulating the equations to eliminate these variables. We then interpreted our three-equation system as a *partial reduced form*, where we have substituted out the unobserved endogenous variables. Recall (§ 5.2) that a full reduced form involves substituting out all the endogenous variables— we take as a definition of a partial reduced form the system obtained when just some of the endogenous variables are eliminated by substitution. The coefficient of c in the first equation, for example, is then not "pure", as we noted above, but involves several possible effects. We should record here, however, an alternative procedure which we tried at an early stage. This was to look for a variable which is closely correlated with y^* that we could use as a surrogate.

It is sometimes argued (see Willmer (1968)) that the reporting rate for breaking-and-entering offences is very high (mainly for insurance reasons). Suppose we add to our system

$$y^*_{BE} = y_{BE} \tag{6}$$

$$y^* = y^*_{BE} + b + \varepsilon_7 \tag{7}$$

where y^*_{BE} is the logarithm of the true number of breaking and entering offences, y_{BE} is the logarithm of the reported number, b is a constant and ε_7 a random term with mean zero. So we assume all breaking-and-entering offences are reported and that true breaking-and-entering offences are a fraction (with random component) of total indictable offences. Suppose also that we decompose (4) into (4a) $p = g - y$ and (4b) $p^* = g - y^*$, where g is the logarithm of the number of clear-ups. Then the system (1), (2), (3), (4a), (4b), (5), (6), (7) is an eight equation system in the 8 endogenous variables y, y^*, y_{BE}, y^*_{BE}, p, p^*, c, g. We can form the partial reduced form

$$(1 + \alpha_1) y_{BE} = \alpha_1 g + \alpha_2 c + \sum_{i=3}^{7} \alpha_i x^1_i + \alpha_0 - (1 + \alpha_1) b$$
$$- (1 + \alpha_1) \varepsilon_7 + \varepsilon_1 \tag{8}$$

$$g = (1 + \beta_1) y + \beta_2 c + \sum_{i=3}^{7} \beta_i x^2_i + \beta_0 + \varepsilon_2 \tag{9}$$

$$c = (\gamma_1 - \gamma_2) y + \gamma_2 g + \sum_{i=3}^{5} \gamma_i x^3_i + \gamma_0 + \varepsilon_3 \tag{10}$$

$$y = y_{BE} + b + k( ) + \varepsilon_5 + \varepsilon_7 \tag{11}$$

These are four equations in the four observable endogenous variables y, y_{BE}, g and c. If we assume further that $k( )$ has no arguments apart from those included in equations (8)-(11), then a limited information technique such as 2SLS would allow us to estimate the first equation and identify the α_i.

All this depends, however, on our accepting equations (6) and (7). Our attempts to use breaking-and-entering offences have lead us to believe that either the reporting rate for breaking-and-entering offences is not sufficiently high (so that (6) does not hold), or that crime patterns are not sufficiently fixed (so that (7) does not hold) for the purpose of the above procedure. The results from estimation using breaking-and-entering offences are contained in Chapter 6, § 6.4.2, and the view just mentioned is discussed further there. It is corroborated, at least for the USA, by the research of the National Opinion Research Centre (Chicago) which found that only 31% of the burglaries (similar to our breaking-and-entering offences) of their sample were reported—see p. 8 of Ennis (1967). Furthermore, we are interested in more than just the estimation of the determinants of y^*, even accepting its existence.

5.3.2 *The Model for Pooled Urban and Rural Areas*

There are modifications which we make to our model for the estimation using the data sets which pool data on urban and rural areas. We shall be discussing in the next section tests for whether we should, in fact, pool urban and rural data but, on the assumption that we should, we need some minor alterations to our model. The changes which we make are to include in each equation a variable which distinguishes urban from rural areas: the proportion of the area that is urbanised. (As for our other variables, we continue to take the logarithmic form.) For urban areas this variable takes the unlogged value $1 \cdot 0$ or 100%. Suppose, for example, the coefficient of this variable in the second equation is λ. If R were the proportion of an area that was urbanised, then we would be asserting that the impact of changes in the other variables in the second equation would be the same for differing R's, for example, the same for rural and completely urban areas. Comparing an urban and a rural area with the same value of all variables other than R, the only (non-stochastic) difference would be the additive effect of $\lambda \log R$. The treatment of urban and rural data sets separately, of course, allows *all* the parameters to be different for urban and rural areas. One can view the two treatments, on the one hand the inclusion of $\log R$ and on the other, separate estimation, as polar cases. The former allows differences only in the constant terms and the latter in all the parameters. Intermediate approaches would constrain some parameters to be the same and allow others to be different. Since it would have been hard to specify which parameters had not changed, we made no attempt to do this.

As explained in Chapter 4, the inclusion of percentage urbanisation in the first, second and third equations forces us to drop rv (total rateable value per area) from the first equation and d (population density) from the third equation, since $\log R$ is highly correlated with both (correlation coefficients for all the data sets above 0.8). We call the model the *% urb model*. It has one more coefficient than the model of $(1)'''$, (2), (3).

5.3.3 *A Further Discussion of Identification*

Those who differ from us over the relevance or importance of certain theories might wish to see changes in the specification of the full model (1)–(5). We should suggest, however, that many reasonable changes would involve at most small additions or deletions to the estimated equations $(1)'''$, (2), (3), and often only the reinterpretation of coefficients. Thus one would not encounter estimation problems or a set of equations radically different from our own. There are two important exceptions: first, if one of the variables we classify as exogenous is deemed to be endogenous and second, if the changes suggested lead to the model becoming unidentified. We discuss these possibilities in turn. Our discussion is based on the model relevant to our main data sets, those for urban areas.

If we were to decide that one additional variable of our system $(1)'''$, (2), (3), should be endogenous we should have to add a new equation. An examination of the exogenous variables in Table 5.1 shows that there is one variable for which this problem might be thought serious, and that is the severity of punishment variable f. Indeed, in Chapter 3, § 3.2 and Chapter 4, § 4.4, we went as far as specifying a possible equation for the determination of f. Since we did not regard the *a priori* arguments in favour of the endogeneity of f as strong and results using the additional equation did not look promising, it was dropped from the system (for examples of such results see Chapter 6, § 6.4.1).

At the time the computations were performed there appeared to be no test of the hypothesis that a variable should be deemed to be exogenous. Such a test has, however, recently been proposed by Hausman (see Hausman (1977), and in particular, the version to be published in *Econometrica* in 1978). The proposal appeared too late to be incorporated in our analysis. Thus we adopted the informal procedure of using our judgement of the plausibility of theories and estimated coefficients.

A second possible class of modifications to our model which would raise radical difficulties would be those which destroyed identification. Indeed without identification, as we have already explained, estimation of the structure is impossible. Let us examine, therefore, the nature of our identifying restrictions and ask whether we can have sufficient confidence in them to proceed with estimation.

The restrictions giving identification of our model, equations $(1)'''$, (2), (3) were of the exclusion variety, that is we stipulate *a priori* that certain variables do not appear in certain equations. From the first equation $((1)''')$ we excluded v, d, m, q, n, from the second, f, rv, m, q, d and from the third f, a, rv, e, n, w. The included variables (in unlogged form) are set out in Table 5.1. It is the combination of these restrictions which provides identification of each equation of our model. We explained in the previous section that we have identification of each equation of our system if each equation contains one variable unique to it. This condition is a special case of a more general sufficient condition, called the rank condition, which is also necesssary (see Fisher (1966)). This rank condition is too technical to be explained in detail here, but it can be expressed intuitively (for the case where we have only exclusion restrictions and where each equation contains all the endogenous variables—as we have here) by saying that the list of exogenous variables included in any one of our equations should not be the same as, or a subset of, those included in another, and further it should not be possible by combining the lists of exogenous variables from any two of our equations to generate a list of variables which is the same as, or a subset of, those included in the remaining equation. We gave an intuitive explanation of this condition in the discussion surrounding Figs 1 and 2 in the previous section and it should be clear that the sufficient condition we employed above to idenfity the system $(1)'''$, (2), (3), is indeed a special case of the rank condition.

The (general) rank condition as just described provides for identification of each of the equations of a system. A given single equation is identified if no combination of other equations yields a list of exogenous variables which is the same as, or a subset of, those included in the given equation.

It is easy to check using the rank condition that for each equation in our system $(1)'''$, (2), (3) we have more than is required to provide identification. Thus each equation is over-identified. For example, is both m and q were included in the first equation, we should still have identification of all equations—our condition that each equation has a variable unique to it is still valid. And if m, q, and n were included in the first equation, whilst the special condition we employed would not guarantee us identification, the rank condition tells us that we do indeed have identification of each equation. The list of exogenous variables in the first equation would have grown quite long with the additional variables, but note that no combination of (2) and (3) could provide a list of exogenous variables which was the same as, or a subset of the list in the first equation, because even after the additions, the first equation still does not contain v, which is in the second equation, or d, which is in the third equation. Note, however, that if we included m, q, n, *and* either v or d or both in the first equation, then the first equation would no longer be identified since it would fail to satisfy the rank condition (which is also a necessary condition). For example, if v were included in addition to m, q, n the second equation has a list of exogenous variables which is a subset of those in the first.

By adding to and deleting from the three equations, one can produce a very large number of examples of models some of which would have all three equations identified, some just two, some only one and others none. We must ask ourselves, however, which of these examples merit serious consideration. We have, of course, already offered the model $(1)'''$, (2), (3) as the one we regard as the most appropriate, thus we shall be considering models which have been implicitly or explicitly rejected. But it is rare in the social sciences for prior theory to be so strong that one can with complete confidence rule out other possible models, and in our case prior theory and knowledge is no stronger than is usual. It is pointless to repeat all the arguments which led up to the formulation of our model and we shall concentrate on just a few points.

There would appear to be two serious issues. The first involves distinguishing between the second equation (for the detection rate) and some combination of that and the third equation (for the number of policemen *per capita*), and the second issue concerns the problem that the inclusion of extra variables in the first equation (for the recorded offence rate) might lead to that equation failing to be identified (see the examples above). We assume that there can be no confusion of the second and third equations with some combination of themselves and the first, since the first equation contains the distinguishing variables severity of punishment f, and available wealth rv. We examine the two issues just described in the order given.

One can see from (2) and (3) that the only exogenous variable the equations have in common is v. It would appear, therefore, that there is no problem in telling one equation from another. One might argue however, that q, m, and d should all enter the second equation and in that case the second equation would not be identified (we should not be able to distinguish (2) from an amalgamation of (2) and (3) since (2) and the amalgamations would contain the same variables). The arguments for including the rate of unemployment q in the equation for the determination of the apprehension rate (equation (2)) were set out in Chapter 3 (§ 3.4) and Chapter 4 (§ 4.5). We took them sufficiently seriously to test for the presence of q in the second equation (see § 4.6, § 5.4 and § 6.2). Our prior reasoning was, however, against including q in the second equation because unemployment rates were low (see § 4.5) relative to the population as a whole; and whilst the unemployed do appear to be more visible and therefore more vulnerable, variations between districts affecting relatively small numbers would be unlikely to produce significant variations in the detection rate. The same argument does not apply to the use of q in the third equation (it provides an indication of the state of the labour market). Note that if the second equation would not be identified if it contained q, then we could test the restriction which excludes q from that equation (the reason will become clear when we have presented the tests in § 5.4).

The arguments for including m in the second equation are not strong. We saw in Chapter 3 (§ 3.4) and Chapter 4 (§ 4.5) that previous criminological work concentrates on the working class as being particularly vulnerable to arrest. The correlation between w and m is not close to 1.0 for any of the data sets (see the appendix to Chapter 6) so the inclusion of w does not involve the implicit inclusion of m. And note that the distinction between w and m can contribute to identification provided w and m are not perfectly correlated.

It is possible that the population density has some effect on the detection rate. One can imagine arguments which say that the character of police work in very dense cities is sufficiently different from less dense cities to have an important effect on the proportion of offences solved. But one could argue that the effect was either positive or negative. And it would not be easy to tell whether the effect was genuinely in terms of density of population or whether it is associated with other variables—for example social class. The absence of previous work and the theoretical uncertainties imply, in our judgement, that we can maintain the exclusion of d from the second equation.

Provided it is correct to exclude at least one of the variables q, m and d from the second equation we have identification of that equation.

We turn now to the first equation. It is in principle possible that any given variable affects the offence rate. We have tried to include only those variables for which the arguments in terms of prior theory and previous research are strong. We can include, in addition to the variables in $(1)'''$ any three from q, m, d, n and v (but not both n and v) and retain identification of the first equation. Note that if both n and v are included we lose identification, since the variables in the second equation become a subset of those in the first.

Whilst it is possible that the size of district n affects offences *per capita*, one cannot be confident that the effect operates through size *per se* rather than, for example, available swag which is captured in our variable rv. The arguments for excluding v from the first equation appear to be strong—one does not expect the mix of offences to have an important effect on the overall number. Let us suppose then, that either n or v can be excluded from the first equation. We need then exclude only one of q, m, d. There are possible arguments for including population density d and rate of unemployment q and these were considered and eventually rejected in Chapters 2, 3 and 4 (see § 4.6 for a summary). There do not seem to be any strong arguments for including the proportion of the population that is middle class m. Self-report and victimisation studies give little or no class difference in actual offending and where criminologists or sociologists of deviance have concentrated on a class group as being, respectively, more criminogenic or more liable to attention from the authorities, it is the working class. We repeat that m and w are not particularly strongly correlated (see appendix to Chapter 6).

We believe then, that reasonable changes in the model would leave the first equation identified. We should have been happier, however, if there were another exogenous variable which clearly does affect the detection rate p, but which clearly does not affect the offence rate y. In retrospect we should perhaps have included the number of road accidents, or the number of road accidents per police officer, in the second equation (it would have been possible to obtain such data). Road accidents are an important burden on the police and thus are likely to affect p, but it is less likely that there is a strong effect on y (although if the police have more time to solve offences they will also have more time to record offences).

The above arguments on identification have been conducted in terms of the model for our main data sets—the urban areas. One can perform an analogous exercise for the % urb model for the pooled urban and rural data sets.

The importance of the identification problem in studies of crime has recently been stressed by Fisher and Nagin (1976). They reach the conclusion that identification will not, in general, be possible in cross-section models because, and here we summarise their arguments, anything which affects the detection rate could also affect the offence rate.

Whilst Fisher and Nagin are right to assert the importance of the identification problem and the requirement to use prior theory and research to impose any identifying restrictions, we do not follow them in their nihilistic conclusion. The reason is that their stress on prior theory and research is accompanied by what appears to be a decision to ignore or dismiss prior criminological work—for example on social class variables. Certainly such work is not discussed. On the other hand, we have presented this work at length and have used it to construct a model which, we have argued, is identified. Each equation in the resulting model is, in fact, over-identified and we have shown how some additional variables can be included whilst retaining identification.

In the end, however, identification is a matter of judgement. It would be idle to pretend that prior theory and research guarantees that some particular variable does not affect, say, the offence rate. We have to decide whether we shall regard such an effect as important, or not. If we are not prepared to be sufficiently confident in our restrictions to provide identification, then we have to abandon the idea of learning anything of the determination of the offence rate, the clear-up rate and the number of policemen from an analysis of the official crime figures. The assumption that certain variables do not affect certain others is a precondition of estimation in many situations in the social sciences and ours is no exception.

5.4 HYPOTHESIS TESTING

We describe several different hypotheses which are to be tested but we use a single technique for testing. For a given model we compare two sets of estimates. For the first we place no restrictions on the coefficients and the second we constrain certain parameters to be zero or to be equal to other parameters. The maximised likelihood value for the first estimation will be at least as high as that for the second, since the coefficients chosen in the second case are candidates in the search for a maximum in the first case. We must decide whether the increase in the likelihood when we relax the restrictions and pass from the second estimation to the first is significant. Let us call L_u the maximised likelihood in the first case and L_r the maximised likelihood in the second, and suppose m restrictions are relaxed in passing from the second estimation to the first. For our models it is agreed that

$2 \operatorname{Log} \dfrac{L_u}{L_r}$ is distributed asymptotically as chi-square with m degrees of free-

dom.[2] We now describe how this test was used for six different kinds of hypotheses. We have chosen a particular order in which to carry out our tests. The outcome of our tests is, in principle, dependent on this order and we shall discuss our choice when we have presented all the tests.

We argued in Chapter 3 (§ 3.5) and Chapter 4 (§ 4.7) that we expected the structure and particularly those elements affected by the recording process, to change across the years. It is therefore important to test the hypothesis that the observations for different years came from the same sample, that is the coefficients in the models for the different years are the same. We examined this hypothesis for 1961 and 1966 using the data on urban areas only, since, as we shall see in Chapter 6, § 6.1 we came to the conclusion that urban and rural areas are best treated separately. We pooled the data for the two years so that we had 138 observations on urban areas (72 from 1961 and 66 from 1966). We estimated our model using this data set and found a maximised log-likelihood value ℓ_3 ($\ell_3 = \log L_3$). We estimated the model for the two years separately and found a log-likelihood value of ℓ_1 from the 72 observations for 1961 and ℓ_2 from the 66 observations for 1966. The log-likelihood value ℓ_3 corresponds to $\log L_r$ in the above discussion since, by pooling the data sets, we restrict the parameters for the two years to be the same. The log-likelihood value $\log L_u$ corresponds to $\ell_1 + \ell_2$, since the unrestricted assumption is that the two data sets came from different independent populations (so that the likelihood values are multiplied and thus the log-likelihood values added). Hence $2(\ell_1 + \ell_2 - \ell_3)$

---

[2] It has been known for a long time (see Hood and Koopmans (1952) p. 178) that, in certain examples, $2 \log \dfrac{L_u}{L_r}$ is distributed asymptotically as chi-square. The view has also been taken that the class of models and tests for which such a result holds is quite wide. The literature has, however, been rather casual on properties of FIML estimators in simultaneous models—see, for example, Berndt et al. (1974). But recently the class of cases for which rigorous results are available has been extended (see Amemiya (1977)). We are grateful to Jerry Hausman and Alberto Holly for helpful discussion of these issues.

is asymptotically chi-square on the null hypothesis that there is no structural change between 1961 and 1966. The number of degrees of freedom in this test is equal to the extra number of restrictions in the more constrained model. The extra restrictions in the more constrained model (here corresponding to estimation using the pooled data) reflect the assumption that the coefficients are the same in 1961 and 1966. Thus there is one restriction corresponding to each coefficient, and there are 23 coefficients (counting constant terms). In addition we estimate the 6 entries in the variance-covariance matrix of residuals, and in the estimation using the pooled 1961 and 1966 data these entries are restricted to be the same in 1961 as they are in 1966. Thus there are altogether 29 extra restrictions, and $2(\ell_1 + \ell_2 - \ell_3)$ is asymptotically chi-square with 29 degrees of freedom. A similar procedure for testing for a structural break was followed in examining whether there was a change between 1966 and 1971. Since the data set for 1971 is based on a pooling of urban and rural areas, we compared the 1971 results with those from 1966 urban and rural. The model used, therefore, was the % urb model—see § 5.3—where there is one extra coefficient and so 30 degrees of freedom in the test.

The above two tests, comparing 1961 and 1966, and 1966 and 1971 are the only tests for structural breaks or differences in structure across the years which are presented in Chapter 6. We could, of course, have compared 1961 and 1971 or have pooled data sets for the three years and examined the hypothesis that the coefficients are the same for all three years. However, the results in favour of a structural break between 1961 and 1966 and between 1966 and 1971 were so conclusive, that we decided further testing for differences across years was unnecessary. The results are presented in § 6.1. We are grateful to Grayham Mizon for this test for a structural break— see Mizon (1972). There is one line of testing which might have been interesting but which we did not pursue. In the test just described, for differences between the years, we have tested the hypothesis that all the coefficients are the same for the two years against the hypothesis that they may all be different. We might have been able to learn something more about the origins of the structural break by testing the hypothesis that some coefficients stay the same whilst others may change. From what we have already described it should be clear how such a test would be formulated. But there is no theory to tell us, neither is it obvious, which coefficients should be assumed constant (although one can point to those particularly likely to change).

A similar test to that described above was performed for the hypothesis that the urban and rural data sets for each year came from the same population. In exactly the same way we estimated separate models for the urban and rural pooled data (giving log-likelihood value ℓ_3), the urban data (giving ℓ_1), and the rural data (giving ℓ_2) leaving us with $2(\ell_1 + \ell_2 - \ell_3)$ distributed as chi-square with 29 degrees of freedom. We used our main (see § 5.3.0) model (since we obviously cannot use R as a variable for the urban data sets, when each area is by definition 100% urbanised) and were able to do the test only for 1961 and 1966. The 1971 data had too few purely urban areas to estimate the model.

We have not tested for possible geographical interactions for example, between urban areas and the surrounding rural areas. A test would involve writing down an explicit form for the geographical correlations. This would be difficult to do convincingly and would make the whole estimation process much more complicated. The issue is postponed to the next section where we discuss the stochastic structure of the model.

Our next series of tests concerned the way in which unemployment was included in the model. We explained in Chapter 2 (§ 2.2.5, and § 2.3.4, and the appendix to that chapter) that we do not regard the arguments in favour of including unemployment in the first equation as particularly strong. It would, in part, be representing effects which are already included elsewhere, for example the opportunity and social-class variables. Further-more it has been argued, particularly for the first equation, that it interacts with other variables, for example the age structure, in such a way that its aggregate effects are difficult to assess; and we came to a similar conclusion concerning the inclusion of unemployment in the second equation (see § 4.5). However, we recognise that it is a variable of some interest (see, for example, Fleisher (1966) or Phillips Votey and Maxwell (1972)), and we have, therefore, tested hypotheses concerning where unemployment should appear in the model. We have estimated and so have likelihood values for models where unemployment is included in all three equations, the second and third equations only, the third equation only, and nowhere in the system. We can then test, for example, the model with unemployment in all three equations against that with unemployment in the third equation only. Here twice the difference between the log-likelihood values is asymptotically chi-square with two degrees of freedom, since in the second case two coefficients are constrained to be zero. The tests tend to support our view, expressed in earlier chapters, that unemployment plays a role in the third equation only (see Chapter 6).

Having estimated our three equation model with twenty-three coefficients (including unemployment in the third equation and three constants) we attempted, for each data set, to find a model with better fits by discarding some of the variables from equations where they seemed to be of little significance. This is equivalent to imposing restrictions which involve putting certain coefficients equal to zero and can be tested in the manner which should by now be familiar. We tried two such restricted exercises, labelled "Restricted" and "Severely Restricted" for each data set. We chose to present "Restricted Results" (see Chapter 6) for which, on the whole, we succeeded in raising the significance levels of coefficients somewhat without disturbing the results from the full model very much.

We explained in the appendix to Chapter 2 that, in the analysis of crime using the usual economist's approach to choice under uncertainty, much emphasis has been placed on the apparent observation that individuals are more responsive, in their decision whether to commit an offence, to changes in the probability of being caught than to changes in punishment levels. We tested the hypothesis that in the first equation the coefficient of p is equal to the coefficient of f, (although the arguments of Chapters 2 and 3 should caution against any simple interpretation of our coefficients as directly relevant to this choice theory). This is an application of our standard test. We run the estimation with and without the restriction and twice the difference in the log-likelihoods is distributed as chi-square with one degree of freedom.

Our final test is for the overall specification of the model. When we discussed the conditions for identification in § 5.2 and § 5.3, we saw that we should often use received theory and a priori reasoning to place more restrictions on our structure than are necessary for identification (see Chapter 4). We can, therefore, look at the log-likelihood value of a just-identified model and compare it with the log-likelihood value of an over-identified model. Twice the difference will be distributed as chi-square with degrees of freedom equal to the number of over-identifying restrictions. All just-identified models have the same likelihood value. The reason is that they are equivalent in the sense that they pose no restrictions on the reduced form. In each set of results in Chapter 6 we present the "chi-square value of the log-likelihood ratio", and this corresponds to the test of all the over-identifying restrictions just described. It is generally the case in a three-equation model such as ours, that identification will require a minimum of two restrictions per equation, thus $3 \times 2 = 6$ (and more generally $n(n-1)$) restrictions overall. Those readers who are aware of the order condition (see, for example, Johnston (1972)) necessary for identification will understand the reasons behind these numbers. Thus the number of restrictions in the test described is the total number of exclusion restrictions less six; this number is the degrees of freedom for the test.

There is no single correct order for doing these tests and the sequence we have followed is not dictated by a clear simple rule. We have, however, loosely speaking, tried to go from the general to the particular. Thus we have tested the hypothesis involving all the coefficients (that is, those concerning breaks between years and the split between urban and rural) before those involving just one or two—such as for unemployment or that the elasticity of offences with respect to the probability of detection is the same as that with respect to the probability of punishment. The outcome for the tests for breaks between years and differences between urban and rural areas were so conclusive, that we find it hard to believe that any other procedure would have given a different result. Note that the test for overall model specification (that is all the over-identifying restrictions) is, in a sense, outside the sequence since it is performed each time a model is estimated.

It is clear that we cannot use the kind of procedure described above to test particular restrictions in a just-identified model. For if we relax one restriction in such a model we produce a model that is not identified and the structure cannot therefore be estimated. If we cannot estimate we cannot compare likelihood values. One can estimate the reduced form in an unidentified model but the likelihood value will be the same as for the just-identified model, since the relaxation of the restriction on the structure does not relax any restriction on the reduced form in an unidentified model.

We should emphasise that the provision of likelihood values in Cliff Wymer's SIMUL programme makes hypothesis testing particularly easy and was an important factor in our choice of FIML as estimation technique. It would have been possible to derive tests, based on sums of squared residuals, for other techniques, but this would have involved extra statistical work and extra programming. Given the other attractions of the FIML technique it would not have been worth the trouble.

5.5 THE VARIANCE-COVARIANCE MATRIX OF RESIDUALS

The residuals in the three equations of our models represent the random terms in each equation or the effects of the many factors which we have omitted from the model. Two important considerations arise in a simultaneous-equations context which do not appear in the simple ordinary least squares, single-equation model. The first is that there is no guarantee that the variance of the residuals from a simultaneous equations technique in an equation will be less than the variance of the variable the equation is intended to explain. For example, suppose y is the vector of observed values and $\hat{y}$ is the vector of fitted values in the first question (where we measure both quantities as differences from the mean). The vector of residuals $\hat{u}$ is defined by $y = \hat{y} + \hat{u}$. Now the procedure of the single equation OLS technique guarantees that $0 = \sum_i \hat{y}_i \hat{u}_i$, where i runs over the observations.

We say that $\hat{u}$ is perpendicular, or orthogonal to, or uncorrelated with $\hat{y}$; but $\hat{y}$ depends on p and we saw in § 5.1 that p is correlated with the error term. Indeed it was this correlation which led us to abandon the OLS technique. Thus we should not expect to find on using, say FIML, that $\sum_i \hat{y}_i \hat{u}_i$ vanishes.

But $\sum_i y_i^2 = \sum_i \hat{y}_i^2 + 2 \sum_i \hat{y}_i \hat{u}_i + \sum_i \hat{u}_i^2$. Hence if $\sum_i \hat{y}_i \hat{u}_i$ is sufficiently

negative, we can find $\sum_i \hat{y}_i^2 < \sum_i \hat{u}_i^2$. It is, therefore, pointless to measure how

well we explain y by comparing its variance and the variance of the residual in the structural equation. Thus the R^2 technique, standard in simple OLS application which uses the "explained" variance divided by total variance as measure of goodness-of-fit, cannot be applied sensibly to structural equations.

The reduced form of a simultaneous system, however, describes how the exogenous variables of a system determine the endogenous. And since endogenous variables do not enter the right hand side of a reduced form, we do not have the problem of a correlation between fitted values and residuals. The reduced form is, therefore, the natural place to look for measures of goodness-of-fit and a division into explained and unexplained variance. Where we cite measures of the goodness-of-fit, we shall compare the residual variances from the *derived reduced form* (that calculated from the structure and embodying such restrictions as the structure implies— see, for example equations (3)^0 and (4)^0) with those of the (endogenous) variables to be explained. These variances tell us how well the variations in the exogenous variables account for those of the endogenous (although we do not offer a distribution for this statistic and have not seen one displayed elsewhere).

The second issue which arises is the correlation between the residuals from different equations in the structure. Our estimation procedure provides estimates of the variance-covariance matrix of the residuals. We have said that these residuals may arise from the effects of factors which we have omitted from the equations. However, the correlation between errors in different equations can give us a clue as to what these omitted factors might be. For example, if areas with more police than would be predicted by the third equation (a positive residual there) also had a higher detection rate than would be predicted by the second equation, we should have a positive correlation between the errors in the two equations. We can then ask how this could come about. One explanation could be that areas better endowed with police than others of similar characteristics had higher morale and a higher detection rate (than would be explained by the higher number of police). We examine such considerations in Chapters 6 and 7.

We turn now to an issue which can arise in both single and simultaneous-equations contexts—the problem of correlation between the error terms in different observations. In time series analysis this is called auto-correlation. Here we must discuss geographical correlations.

Our explicit assumption on the residuals in our three-equation model was the usual one that $(\varepsilon_{1t}, \varepsilon_{2t}, \varepsilon_{3t})$ is $N(0, \Sigma)$ and $\text{cov}(\varepsilon_{it}, \varepsilon_{it'}) = 0$ for $t \neq t'$, where ε_{it} is the error term in the tth observation (here the tth area) on the ith equation. The assumption $\text{cov}(\varepsilon_{it}, \varepsilon_{it'}) = 0$ rules out interactions between areas. The alternative would be to specify explicit forms for the interactions between areas (or geographical correlations of errors) and estimate the parameters of these interactions.

We have stressed frequently in this book that the offences we are analysing are mainly thefts of objects of small value. It is unreasonable to suppose that offenders will travel large distances in pursuit of such objects. We have therefore been assuming that crime as measured by our offence variable is primarily a local phenomenon. There would not be, therefore, to any important extent, switching of offences from one area to another. Thus there are *a priori* grounds for supposing that geographical correlations of errors is negligible. A possible exception to this claim would be an inter-action between a city and the surrounding countryside—this would be relevant only for pooled urban and rural data.

It is hard to see how one could provide a convincing model of those geographical interactions, supposing they do exist. Note that there is no special order linking one area to the next as in time series. And the whole estimation procedure would be made much more complex if such inter-actions were included—we should have to estimate all the (numerous) parameters of such a system. Given the difficulties of these procedures and our prior belief that such interactions could be ignored, we feel justified in not testing our assumption of "no interaction" any further.

5.6 SOME CONCLUDING REMARKS ON OUR ESTIMATION PROCEDURES

We have described in some detail the model which we have estimated and have attempted to justify, building on the earlier chapters, the estimation procedures adopted as well as the model itself. We shall not attempt to summarize these procedures but shall devote this sub-section to an explanation of why we rejected some alternative specifications or procedures which others might suggest as preferable, and to an attempt to anticipate some possible misunderstandings of what we have done.

We have used the techniques and language which are standard in econometrics for our model and estimation. Many of the techniques and problems appear in other disciplines in the social sciences under different names. Fortunately it is unnecessary for us to compare these techniques in detail, since a recent publication has done just this. We refer the interested reader to the valuable and illuminating collection of articles edited by Goldberger and Duncan (1973) and, in particular, the introduction by Goldberger. Path analysis, for example, a technique with which sociologists will be familiar, can include the problem of simultaneous causation. Similarly some of the more modern forms of factor analysis (such as confirmatory factor analysis) popular with psychologists are close in spirit to the techniques used here. We shall concentrate however, on the particular problems raised by our model and estimation technique.

The first concerns *ceteris paribus* and the role of interactions in our model. Let us consider, for example, the coefficient α_6' of rv in the first equation of our model (see Table 5.1). This number gives us the proportional change which would occur in the number of offences *per capita* given a 1% increase in RV the total rateable value per area, when all other variables are held constant. We deal in percentage changes since we have used the logarithmic form of the model. (A change of 0·01 in $\log_e X$ corresponds to a 1% change in X). The model involves the assumption that this percentage change is the same whatever the level of RV, Y and all the other variables; in this sense we have no interactions between variables. More complicated forms of the relationships are certainly possible. For example, we might argue that a higher rateable value (or extra "booty") in a predominantly working-class area would cause more crime than a similar increase in middle-class areas; this effect could not be captured in the simple form of the model we have used. However, we have already seen that there are difficult questions involved in knowing merely which variables to include. The detail of the specification of interactions would have been still more problematical. Given the extra estimation problems of non-linear models, it did not seem worth embarking on complications in this direction.

A second set of issues is the choice of cross-section rather than time-series data and changes in structure. The great advantage of the use of cross-section data is that it provides, for our case, many observations and at the same time allows the assumption that economic, political, social, and cultural factors not captured by our variables did not vary across a given sample of districts. Thus we are in a position to argue that our observations are generated by an underlying social process that is the same for different districts. We discussed the problem of geographical auto-correlation in § 5.5. A time series analysis using national data would allow only few observations, since one could reasonably apply such analysis only to annual post-war data. Furthermore, it would be hard to argue that the underlying structure remains constant. Indeed our tests for structural change across the years, described in § 5.4 and reported in Chapter 6, § 6.1, will lead us to the conclusion that there have been significant changes over even short periods of time. Thus, for example, the impact of extra police per head on the offence rate in the first equation may vary for a sample taken from a time series, and hence the coefficient α_2' in the first equation could not be assumed constant for the sample. We should have to modify the model to describe how the process of change occurs; this would raise severe difficulties.

The assumption of an invariant underlying structure is more justified the more homogenous the sample. Thus we have concentrated in Chapters 6 and 7 for many of our conclusions on the results derived from urban areas and we conclude from our tests for the difference between urban and rural areas that urban and rural data sets are better treated separately.

A third problem concerns the role of *time lags* in our model. We have, for each data set, used observations on all the variables for the same year. Our structural equations involve behavioural relationships and we must, therefore, argue that the relevant behaviour is determined by variables operating in that year. It is reasonable to suppose that there are at most only a few cases where problems may arise (the reader is referred to Table 5.1 for a summary of the model). Thus, in the first equation, if it is claimed that the young commit more offences than the old, then for the determination of the number of offences in an area in one year we shall want to measure the age structure for that year. A further, but slightly different example, concerns rv, the measure of available "booty" in an area. For the determination of the number of thefts in an area we shall require the booty in that area in the year in question, since the estimate by a potential offender of what is available for theft would, we suppose, involve current information.

The variables for which there might be difficulties resulting from time lags would appear to be p and f in the first equation. We do not know how long it takes a population to become aware of changes in the probability of being caught and in the level of punishment. We are supposing that the lag is less than a year so that current values are appropriate. If the cross-sectional pattern of p and f does not vary very much from year to year, then we are unlikely to be in great error. If, however, the lags are slow and the cross-sectional pattern changes quickly, we may be in trouble; this is something of interest for further research. We should hazard the guess, however, that for those who are liable to commit offences, information on the consequences may pass on the grape-vine fairly quickly. If more of your friends are being caught and punished, it is unlikely to take more than a few weeks to find out.

There would be a problem with the third equation if it were interpreted as an allocation process. For then the central authority might react only after seeing last year's figures. This problem does not really arise if it is interpreted as a recruitment equation. True there is a lag involved in training a policeman but it is not more than six months.

We should mention a pitfall which is known amongst sociologists as the "ecological fallacy". This is the assertion from the observation that, say, abortions are more common in areas with many Roman Catholics, that it is the Roman Catholics that are having the abortions. One could not feel confident about such an assertion until one had examined the population at a much less aggregated level. Our procedure has a logically different structure. We begin with certain hypotheses about behaviour of individuals and the police force which are embodied in our model. We then examine the data using the model, and accept or reject or revise our opinions about the hypotheses. Thus basically we begin with the hypotheses rather than the data. We should emphasize, however, that just as in the example of the abortions and Roman Catholics, the mechanisms which we suggest do require examination at a much less aggregated level and this is one of our suggestions for further research in Chapter 10.

We have discussed the identification problem at length. We argued that a combination of previous theoretical and empirical work and commonsense provides sufficient information for us to be able to specify structural models which can be estimated using our data (thus are identified). The specification of an econometric equation is, however, always an act of faith and we must leave the reader to form his own judgement. If one decides that, in the light of such prior knowledge as one has been able to accumulate identification is impossible, then one gives up the idea of learning anything from the crime statistics about, for example, the determination of recorded offence rates.

Finally, we should emphasize that we are following a procedure which is conceptually distinct from that used in many criminological studies. These studies often start with convicted offenders, examine their characteristics, and then make inferences about the sort of people who commit crimes. We start with characteristics of the population, age-structure, wealth, social class, unemployment, and so on, and model the process by which offences and detections are generated. Thus we start with the population and go to offences, rather than starting with offenders and forming conclusions about the offending population.

6

Results

6.0 INTRODUCTION

We present in this chapter the results of estimating the models and carrying out the tests of hypotheses using the techniques described in Chapter 5. Our model consists of three equations $(1)'''$, (2), (3) of § 5.3.0 of Chapter 5. The first equation $((1)''')$ explains the recorded offence rate, the second ((2)) the detection rate, and the third ((3)) the number of policemen *per capita*. Detailed interpretation of the results from the standpoint of various criminological, sociological and economic theories is the subject-matter of the next chapter. Our concern here is with the description of what the results turned out to be.

We begin in the next section of this chapter with our tests of how the data from different areas and years should be pooled: there are two major decisions to take. First, we must decide whether we should pool the data for separate years, and thus make the assumption that the underlying processes generating the data were identical for the different years, 1961, 1966, and 1971, of our sample. Secondly, we must decide whether to pool the data for urban and rural areas; in other words, whether we should suppose that there is sufficient detail in the model to justify the claim that all relevant differences between urban and rural areas are measured and included, so that the structure and coefficients of the model are the same for both types of area. These tests were described in § 5.4. We suggested in § 3.6 that we should expect to find significant differences both between years and between urban and rural areas.

Once the decisions on how to pool the data have been taken, we examine in § 6.2, for each data set, specific hypotheses concerning certain coefficients. We take first the issue of where unemployment should be included in the model. We saw in the preceding chapters that there are arguments for including unemployment in all three equations of our model. However, we settled eventually in Chapters 2, 4 and 5 on including unemployment only in the third equation. We test this hypothesis against the inclusion of unemployment in other equations as well.

We then take the data sets one by one and discard certain variables from the full model ($(1)'''$, (2), (3)) in certain years; this process is intended to provide tighter estimates for coefficients on retained variables. We obtain in this way a final set of results for each data set which form the basis for the discussion in Chapter 7. For convenience of reference these results are presented separately as § 6.3. The chi-square value for the test of all the over-identifying restrictions (see § 5.4) is presented for each model which is estimated.

The final exercise in hypothesis testing in § 6.2 is for the equality in the equation for the recorded offence rate of the coefficients of the detection rate and the severity of punishment. The relative magnitude of these two coefficients is of particular interest since, as we saw in the appendix to Chapter 2, Becker (1968) drew some important conclusions from the assertion that offences are more responsive to detection rates than the severity of punishment and this assertion does appear to be common in discussions of policy.

In § 6.4 we present two alternatives to our model which arise from our discussions in Chapters 3 and 5. We saw in Chapter 3, § 3.2, that it is possible to argue that the severity of punishment depends on the recorded offence rate so that one should have an equation modelling the determination of this severity. We give the results from carrying out such an exercise in § 6.4. The second alternative presented in § 6.4 involves replacing indictable offences (y) and the detection rate (p) with the corresponding variables for the sub-class of property offences involving forcible entry (breaking and entering). One objective is to use a variable which allows identification of the relation modelling the determination of actual offences (see § 5.3.1). A second purpose is the examination of a more homogeneous offence type than the disparate "all indictable offences".

In § 6.5 we present the reduced forms for our main data sets. These give the so-called "impact multipliers" showing how changes in exogenous variables affect the endogenous variables (recorded offence rate, detection rate, and policeman *per capita*) taking into account all the inter-relationships of the system.

We suggested in Chapter 5, § 5.5, that an examination of the variance-covariance matrix of residuals can lead to important insights. For example, it would be of interest if randomly (unexplained by the variables we have included) high clear-up rates tended to occur in areas with randomly high (unexplained) levels of police manpower. (Note that the effect of manpower itself on the clear-up rate is included in the "explained" clear-up rate.) These matrices are presented in § 6.6 and preliminary interpretations are offered to show the reader how they should be understood. In the same section we discuss the goodness-of-fit equation by equation, that is to say our success in explaining the variation in each of the endogenous variables.

Results are presented for FIML estimates, although occasionally where there are convergence problems in the iteration procedure for the computation of FIML, 3SLS estimates are used. Thus we concentrate on full information methods (see § 5.1). In § 6.7 however we present results using ordinary least squares (OLS) and 2 SLS estimation techniques. The purpose of presenting OLS results is to indicate the difference between the mistaken single equation method and the simultaneous-equations method. The 2SLS results are of interest since the technique is one of limited information (see § 5.1). Thus in estimating the equation for the recorded offence rate we use the information that the detection rate and the number of police per capita are endogenous but not full "knowledge" of the nature of the interdependence. Where such extra "knowledge" is mistaken, 2SLS or other limited information techniques may be more reliable.

In § 6.8 we discuss briefly one extra variable which had some *a priori* plausibility as a possible explanation of the offence rate—overcrowding inside the household. Some concluding remarks are offered in § 6.9.

We present in the appendix to the chapter correlation matrices for our main (exogenous and endogenous) variables for each data set. The matrices help the reader form judgements about possible multi-collinearities and indicate results that would be obtained from naive single-variable regressions. The appendix also contains results using the full model of Table 5.1 for each data set.

For most of this chapter results are presented for the alternative measures of the detection rate: the clear-up rate and the conviction rate. The duplication is justified by the importance of the variable and the advantages and disadvantages of the two alternatives. Discussion of the difference between the two sets of results is contained in Chapter 7, § 7.4.3. We shall refer to an estimation using the clear-up rate measure by p clear-up and one using the conviction rate measure by p convictions.

The numerical results differ somewhat from those published in earlier reports on our work in Carr-Hill and Stern (1973) and (1976). There are three reasons for this. First, our earlier work did not use unemployment as a variable. Secondly, for this final report on our work we made a last check on the data, unearthing a few errors, and for 1971 used census data on socio-economic groups which were not available for our earlier work. Thirdly, for 1961 we altered the number of observations from the 64 used for Carr-Hill and Stern (1973) to 72. The reason was that the earlier study used in part data from Greenhalgh (1966); he amalgamated certain adjoining areas. We disaggregated them (since there was no consistent aggregation practice in Greenhalgh (1966)) and recollected the data from original sources (see Data Appendix). It should be noted that the previous published studies did not contain the p convictions estimates.

We define urban districts as those with 100% of their area urbanised and call other districts rural. "Urban and rural" data sets contain both types of district and are constructed by pooling the data sets from urban and rural areas. The number of observations for 1971 was too low to allow subdivision into urban and rural sets (there were only ten urban areas), given the large number of coefficients in the model. No police districts were completely rural (in any year), in the sense of 0% urbanised. The highest percentage of urbanisation amongst "rural" areas was 84% in 1961 and 1966 and 47% in 1971.

We explained in § 5.3.2 that our model for pooled "urban and rural" sets is slightly different from (1)$'''$, (2), (3) since we include the variable R—the percentage of the area which is urbanised.

The 2SLS, 3SLS and FIML results were obtained using the SIMUL programme developed by Cliff Wymer, and the OLS and correlation matrix results using the FAKAD programme of Emil van Broekhoven and Ken MacDonald. Computations were carried out on the Oxford University computer—an ICL 1906A.

The data sets used for this study are available from the S.S.R.C. Survey Archive at the University of Essex. The data have been discussed in Chapter 4 and detail is given in the Data Appendix. The data sets are as follows: 1961 Urban (72 observations), 1961 Rural (47 observations), 1961 Urban and Rural (119 observations), 1966 Urban (66 observations), 1966 Rural (44 observations), 1966 Urban and Rural (110 observations), 1971 Urban and Rural (41 observations).

6.1 THE APPROPRIATE POOLING OF THE DATA

We examine first the hypothesis that the data for different years came from the same structure. The tests we use have been described in § 5.4. Our null hypothesis in comparing urban areas in 1961 and 1966 is that each coefficient in each equation (and the variance-covariance matrix of residuals) is constant across the years. We calculate the maximum likelihood for the model when estimated for each year separately and the maximum likelihood for the estimation where data for the two years are pooled. If the logarithms of the maximum likelihoods for the two separate data sets are ℓ_1 and ℓ_2, and for the pooled data set ℓ_3, then we saw in § 5.4 that $2 (\ell_1 + \ell_2 - \ell_3)$ is asymptotically chi-square (with degrees of freedom equal to the sum of the number of coefficients and elements in the variance-covariance matrix) on the null hypothesis that the coefficients (and the matrix) are the same across the years, or less formally that the process operating in urban areas was identical in 1966 and in 1961. Tests were carried out for p clear-up only.

The results are as follows. The log-likelihood values were calculated for the model (1)$'''$, (2), (3) of Chapter 5 which is presented in Table 5.1. There are 23 coefficients (including 3 constant terms) and 6 entries in the variance-covariance matrix and thus 29 degrees of freedom for the tests. The chi-square value for the test for a structural break between urban areas in 1961 and 1966 was (using p clear-up) 73·3. With 29 degrees of freedom this would lead us to reject the null hypothesis of no structural break between 1961 and 1966 at the 0·1% level. In other words on the null hypothesis, log-likelihood values of this magnitude would be expected in repeated sampling less than one in a thousand times. Loosely speaking high chi-squared values lead to rejection of the null hypothesis. Quantities of the distribution-function of χ^2 are presented in Table 6.14 (on p. 209).

A similar test was carried out for a structural break between 1966 and 1971. Since the 1971 data consist of pooled urban and rural areas, we must use the form of the model modified for such sets (see § 5.3.2 and below). And in order to carry out the comparison with 1966 we must use the 1966 Urban and Rural data set. The modifications to the model of Table 5.1 are that r (the logarithm of the percentage of each area that is urbanised) is included in each equation and rv is dropped from the first equation and d from the third because of multi-collinearity. Thus we have one more coefficient and hence 30 degrees of freedom. The chi-square value for the test for a structural break (using p clear-up) between all police districts in 1966 and all in 1971 was 111·8. With 30 degrees of freedom this would lead us to reject the null hypothesis of no structural break between 1966 and 1971 at the 0·1% level.

These rejections of the null hypothesis are so conclusive that we did not carry out any further tests for pooling across years. These, together with the discussion of changes in the 1960s in police organisation, lead us to the conclusion that data for different years should not be pooled.

Our next decision is whether urban and rural data sets should be pooled. We use in these tests the model ((1)$'''$), (2), (3)) shown in Table 5.1. and not the % urb model. The reason is that the tests require us to estimate the same model for urban, rural, and urban and rural pooled data sets, and we cannot use % urbanisation as a variable for the urban data set since it (by definition) shows no variation from 100%. The tests were carried out for

1961 and 1966, since, as we noted above, the 1971 data set is too small to warrant further splitting. Results are again given for p clear-up only.

The chi-square value for the test for whether 1961 urban and rural areas should be pooled was 165·8. With 29 degrees of freedom this would lead us to reject the null hypothesis that they should be pooled at the 0·1% level. The corresponding chi-square value for 1966 was 93·9, which implies that we should reject the null hypothesis that urban and rural data should be pooled for 1966 at the 0·1% level.

We are thus led to the conclusion that urban and rural data sets should be kept separate and we shall, for the most part, follow that conclusion. However, aside from the formal hypothesis testing described above, the arguments that we should split urban and rural data sets are less strong than those for keeping years separate, and we shall therefore occasionally be discussing estimates from urban and rural pooled sets for 1961 and 1966. For 1971 we are obliged to use the urban and rural set for the reason already given.

Thus on the basis of both tests for pooling (urban and rural and across years) we have reached the decision that the data should not be pooled. The results were sufficiently conclusive for us not to test for the many other possible ways of pooling the data. We take it that the particular ways of pooling which we tried, and which did not succeed, were *a priori* the most promising. The results were sufficiently conclusive using p clear-up for the tests not to be repeated using p convictions.

6.2 TESTING SOME PARTICULAR COEFFICIENTS

6.2.1 *The Role of Unemployment in the Model*

The model of Table 5.1 includes the rate of unemployment as a variable only in the third equation, that for the number of policemen *per capita*. The decision to include unemployment in that equation only was taken after fairly lengthy discussion in Chapters 2, 3 and 5 and was not clear-cut. It is a variable of some importance in research into and public discussion of crime (see, for example, Fleisher (1966) and press discussion of the disturbances at the Notting Hill Carnival in London in late August 1976). We therefore subjected our hypothesis on where unemployment should appear to several tests.

The alternative hypotheses which we tried are that unemployment should appear in all three equations, the second (for p) and third (for c), and in none of the equations. The procedure is as described in § 5.4. For example, the null hypothesis that unemployment should appear in the third equation only gives a likelihood value L_r, the model with unemployment in all three

Table 6.1

Likelihood values for chi-square tests on the role of unemployment

1961	Urban (p clear-up)	Urban (p convictions)
All 3	856·67	791·61
2nd and 3rd only	856·14	791·49
3rd only	855·97	790·40
None	849·14	787·93

(i) See end of table for explanatory notes. (ii) The iterative procedure for the calculation of FIML estimates presented convergence problems for the 1961 Rural and 1961 Urban and Rural sets and the results are not presented here.

1966	Urban (p clear-up)	Urban (p convictions)
All 3	777·82	750·00
2nd and 3rd only	775·85	747·83
3rd only	774·19	747·60
None	758·89	738·06

	Rural (p clear-up)	Rural (p convictions)
All 3	558·63	544·28
2nd and 3rd only	556·28	—
3rd only	556·15	541·35
None	554·63	539·82

Rural (p convictions) 2nd and 3rd only presented a convergence problem and have been omitted.

	Urban and Rural (p clear-up) % urb. model	Urban and Rural (p convictions) % urb. model
All 3	1246·56	1217·00
2nd and 3rd only	1246·51	1216·71
3rd only	1245·33	1216·15
None	1230·15	1200·71

1971	Urban and Rural (p clear-up) % urb. model	Urban and Rural (p convictions) % urb. model
All 3	511·30	509·00
2nd and 3rd only	510·59	508·70
3rd only	509·68	508·11
None	509·22	509·19

Notes.
1. Entries in the table are twice the log-likelihood value for the model specified in the left-hand column. "3rd only" is the model as Table 5.1. "All 3" also has the rate of unemployment in the first and second equations. "2nd and 3rd only" has unemployment in the second equation as well as the third, and "None" drops unemployment from all the equations.
2. Tests are carried out by subtracting entries for different rows to give a chi-square value (see text).
3. The SIMUL programme computes the entry in the table divided by the number of observations.

equations gives a likelihood value L_u and $2 \log \dfrac{L_u}{L_r}$ is distributed asymptotically as chi-square with two degrees of freedom. There are 2 d.o.f., since to go
from the alternative to the null hypothesis we impose two restrictions—the
exclusion of unemployment from the first two equations.

The results are presented in Table 6.1. The table entries are twice the
logarithm of the likelihood values. Thus to perform a test of, for example,
the hypothesis that unemployment should appear in the third equation only
against the hypothesis that it should appear in all three equations for the
1966 Urban data set (using p clear-up), we subtract 774·19 (2 log L_r) from
777·82 (2 log L_u) to obtain a chi-square value of 3·64 with 2 d.o.f. We
should accept the null hypothesis that unemployment should appear in the
third equation at the conventional 5% level and also at the less con-
servative 10% level (the probability that χ^2 with 2 d.o.f. > 4·61 is 10%—
see Table 6.14). Loosely, high χ^2 values lead us to reject the more restricted
null hypothesis. We shall in what follows attempt to give an indication of
the size of χ^2 by presenting the nearest level at which the hypothesis is
accepted or rejected rather than referring only to the conventional 5% level.

The chi-square values are presented in Table 6.2 for the tests of "3rd
only" against "All 3" in Column 1 and "None" against "3rd only"
column 2. Low values in Column 1 lead us to accept the null hypothesis of
"3rd only", and high values in Column 2 lead us to reject a null hypothesis
of "None". "High and low" are measured on the percentiles of the
appropriate chi-square distribution.

It can be seen from Table 6.2 that, broadly speaking, our presumption in
favour of unemployment occurring only in the third equation (explaining
policemen *per capita*) is supported by the data. In all except one case the
null hypothesis of "3rd only" against "All 3" is accepted at the 20% level,
and in all cases it is accepted at the 10% level. In 50% of the cases of Table
6.2 the null hypothesis of "None" against "3rd only" would be rejected
even at the 1% level. The main exceptions to our general conclusions are
1971 Urban and Rural and 1966 Rural, where the inclusion of unemployment as an explanatory variable does not seem to have strong support. The
reader, using Table 6.1, can construct similar tests for hypotheses involving
"2nd and 3rd only". The general conclusion is again that "3rd only" is
acceptable.

6.2.2 *The Selection of a "Best" Model for Each Data Set*

The model described in equations (1)$'''$, (2), (3) of Chapter 5 and presented
in Table 5.1 is our basic, or "full model". It is not true, however, that all 20
coefficients (not counting constant terms) in that model are significantly

Table 6.2
Chi-square values for tests on the role of unemployment

	"3rd only" v. "All 3" (2 d.o.f.)	"3rd only" v. "None" (1 d.o.f.)
1961 Urban p clear-up	0·71	6·83
p convictions	1·21	2·47
1966 Urban p clear-up	3·64	15·29
p convictions	2·40	9·54
Rural p clear-up	2·48	1·52
p convictions	2·92	1·53
Urban and Rural (% urb model)		
p clear-up	1·23	15·18
p convictions	0·85	15·44
1971 Urban and Rural (% urb model)		
p clear-up	1·62	0·45
p convictions	0·86	2·95

Notes.
1. Probability that χ^2 with 2 d.o.f. $> 3·22$ is 0·20
   _____ $> 4·61$ 0·10
   _____ $> 5·99$ 0·05
2. Probability that χ^2 with 1 d.o.f. $> 1·64$ 0·20
   _____ $> 2·71$ 0·10
   _____ $> 3·84$ 0·05
   _____ $> 6·63$ 0·01
   _____ $> 7·88$ 0·005
3. A low value for column 1 is in favour of "3rd only" and a "high value" for column 2 is in favour "of 3rd only".
4. 1961 Rural and 1966 Urban and Rural were excluded from the table because of convergence problems with FIML.
5. See Notes to Table 6.1.

different from zero in all years. In order to tighten up our estimates we decided to exclude certain variables. Thus for each data set we seek a "best" model. The results of this process are set out in § 6.3. The criteria in this search were informal and are presented below. We did succeed in tightening estimates to a certain extent. However, the substantive conclusions from the results which are discussed in Chapter 7 would not be changed if we based our argument on estimates using the full model. These last estimates are set out in the appendix to this chapter.

We used four criteria in the selection of a more restricted model. First, we wished to "sharpen-up" significance levels of coefficients. Secondly, we wished to improve the probability of acceptance of the over-identifying restrictions (this refers to the test for over-all model specification—see

§ 5.4). Thirdly, we examined the test of the restricted against the full model; and fourthly we tried to avoid excluding variables of central theoretical interest. Whilst not identical the first three criteria overlap.

The restricted models, whose likelihood values are given in Table 6.3, are the outcome of a short and informal search over possible models applying these criteria. We should emphasize that the choice of restricted model is a pragmatic one and those models are not offered as theoretical alternatives to the full model.

We give in Table 6.3 for each data set twice the log-likelihood values for our "full model" (that in Table 5.1), and for a "restricted model", together with the number of extra restrictions, in the latter case as compared with the "full model". The difference between the first two columns for a given row will give the number for use in a chi-square test of the extra restrictions of the "restricted model" (the third criterion above), and the third column gives the degrees of freedom.

The results of Table 6.3 show that in all cases one would not reject the null hypothesis that the additional restrictions of the "restricted model" are

Table 6.3
Likelihood values from restricting the "Full model"

	"Full"	"Restricted"	Number of restrictions
1961 Urban p clear-up	855·97	854·84	4
p convictions	790·40	788·75	3
1966 Urban p clear-up	774·19	773·38	2
p convictions	747·60	746·77	4
Rural p clear-up	556·15	555·41	5
p convictions	541·35	537·69	5
Urban and Rural ($\%$ urb model)			
p clear-up	1245·33	1243·24	4
p convictions	1216·15	1215·75	3
1971 Urban and Rural ($\%$ urb model)			
p clear-up	509·68	508·32	5
p convictions	508·14	507·12	5

Notes.
1. The entries in the table are twice the log-likelihood value for the "full" model of Table 5.1 (or the $\%$ urb model where appropriate) in the first column, and for the "restricted" model in the 2nd column. The data set is indicated in the row headings.
2. Tests are carried out by subtracting figures in the second column from those in the first to give a chi-square value with the number of degrees of freedom specified in the third column. This number is the number of coefficients in the "full" model which are set equal to zero in the restricted model.

correct even at a significance level of 50% (see the statistical table in the appendix to this chapter). This is hardly surprising, since we have eliminated only variables already found to be insignificant.

The results for the "restricted model" for all the data sets are presented in § 6.3 and a comparison of those results with Table 5.1 shows which variables have been excluded. These "restricted model" results form the basis of the discussion in Chapter 7. We have seen that in all cases the "restricted model" would be accepted against the "full model".

We should emphasize that the extra restrictions of the "restricted model" did not in general involve radical changes in coefficient estimates from the "full model", and our conclusions in Chapter 7 could have been based on the estimates from the "full model". We choose to base them on the "restricted models", since they give better significance levels and better results in the test for overall model specification. Results from the "full model" are given in the appendix to this chapter. They add only insignificant variables to the results presented in § 6.3.

6.2.3 *Comparing the Responsiveness of Offences to the Detection Rate with that to the Severity of Punishment*

Our final set of hypotheses tests in this section concerns the comparison of the coefficients in the first equation that refer to the responsiveness of the recorded offence rate, to the clear-up rate and severity of punishment respectively. We test the hypothesis that the two coefficients are equal by finding the likelihood value when the coefficients are constrained to be equal and comparing it with the (higher) likelihood where we allow the coefficients to be unequal. For the comparison of these values we again use the chi-square test involving twice the difference of the log-likelihoods (see § 5.4).

The results are set out in Table 6.4. To aid the interpretation of the two coefficients we carry out the discussion in terms of the elasticities ε_p and ε_f (see § 5.3.0). The elasticity ε_p, for example, measures the percentage decrease in the offence rate Y resulting from a 1% increase in the detection rate P. We saw in Chapter 5 (§ 5.3.0) that our estimate of ε_p is of $-\alpha_1'$ of equation (1)$'''$ in Chapter 5 and of ε_f is of $-\alpha_3'$.

The hypothesis that ε_p is equal to ε_f is rejected by our test at a 5% significance level for 1961 Urban (p clear-up and convictions), 1966 Urban and Rural, and 1966 Urban (p-convictions). (Compare the differences between the likelihood values in each row in Table 6.4 with the number 3·84, the 5% percentile value for χ^2 with 1 d.o.f.) The hypothesis that $\varepsilon_p = \varepsilon_f$ is not, however, rejected at this significance level for 1971.

Table 6.4
Testing the hypothesis that $\varepsilon_p = \varepsilon_f$

	Allowing ε_p to be unequal to ε_f					Constraining ε_p to be equal to ε_f		
	ε_p	(t-value)	ε_f	(t-value)	Likelihood value	$\varepsilon_p = \varepsilon_f$	(t-value)	Likelihood value
1961 Urban p clear-up	0·97	(4·28)	0·12	(1·73)	854·84	0·24	(2·70)	847·09
p convictions	1·00	(3·10)	0·34	(3·15)	788·75	0·29	(3·12)	782·99
1966 Urban p clear-up	0·79	(1·55)	0·28	(2·91)	773·38	0·22	(2·61)	772·66
p convictions	0·84	(3·05)	0·27	(3·00)	746·77	0·29	(3·18)	742·23
Rural p clear-up	−0·25	(0·81)	0·27	(2·00)	555·41	0·23	(2·05)	552·85
p convictions	0·19	(0·34)	0·59	(2·49)	537·69	0·59	(2·42)	537·34
Urban and Rural (% urb model) p clear-up	0·66	(2·80)	0·16	(1·74)	1243·24	0·20	(2·27)	1238·99
p convictions	0·77	(3·25)	0·20	(2·70)	1215·75	0·23	(2·86)	1210·57
1971 Urban and Rural (% urb model) p clear-up	0·80	(1·59)	0·10	(0·84)	508·32	0·17	(1·15)	506·68
p convictions	0·69	(1·59)	0·36	(2·34)	507·12	0·32	(2·17)	506·51

Notes.

1. The numbers in brackets are asymptotic t-values.
2. The difference between the two likelihood values in a row is the chi-square value for the test of $\varepsilon_p = \varepsilon_f$ against $\varepsilon_p \neq \varepsilon_f$. It has one degree of freedom—see Table 6.2 where some percentiles are given.
3. 1961 Rural and 1961 Urban and Rural are excluded because of convergence problems with FIML.

We should emphasize two points here. We should really like to test whether ε_p is greater than ε_f, since this is Becker's assertion (1968) (see appendix to Chapter 2) and it seems to be a common view that offences are more responsive to changes in the detection rate than punishment levels. But there is no convenient test of this hypothesis that we had readily to hand and so our two competing hypotheses were $[\varepsilon_p = \varepsilon_f]$ and $[\varepsilon_p \neq \varepsilon_f]$. Secondly, proportional variations in measured f may be much larger than variations in perceived f due to the large fixed element (such as the shame of a court appearance) in all punishment. The consequences of this second point were described in the appendix to Chapter 2 and are taken up again in Chapter 7 (§ 7.2).

Our general conclusion does seem to be that, for 1961 and 1966, ε_p was significantly different from ε_f, and the estimates show that ε_p was in most cases substantially higher.

6.3 THE MAIN ESTIMATES

We present in this section the results on which our conclusions in Chapter 7 are based. These are the estimated "restricted models" using FIML. The "restricted models" correspond to the likelihood values quoted in Table 6.5 and the number of restrictions applied, as compared with Table 5.1 can be seen by comparing the variables listed in the different models in Table 6.5 with those in Table 5.1. To repeat, for each data set only insignificant variables were excluded to arrive at the "restricted models".

There are seven sections to Table 6.5, each corresponding to a data set: there are three data sets for each of 1961 and 1966 (Urban, Rural, and Urban and Rural) and just one set for 1971 (Urban and Rural). In each section results are given for p clear-up and p convictions. For the three Urban and Rural data sets the % urb model is used (see § 5.3.2) which is then restricted in a similar fashion to the "restricted models" based on Table 5.1.

For each model we give both estimates of the standard errors of each coefficient and the ratio of the estimate of a coefficient to its standard error. We call this ratio the asymptotic t-value. This term is conventionally adopted since, were the number of observations to tend to infinity the ratio would tend in distribution to the normal (analogously to the simple t-statistic in single equation multiple regression). Using the percentiles of the normal distribution, coefficients with asymptotic t-values larger than $1\cdot96$ are significant at the conventional 5% level and larger than $1\cdot28$ at the 20% level.

Table 6.5
Main estimated equations

(a) 1961 Urban "Restricted" (p clear-up)

Variable to be explained			Explanatory variables			
	p	f	w	rv	e	const.
	−0·97	−0·12	0·13	0·02	−0·30	2·56
y	(0·23)	(0·07)	(0·10)	(0·03)	(0·23)	(1·11)
	4·28	1·73	1·30	0·88	1·34	2·30

	y	c	a	w	n	v	const.
	−0·53	−0·46	−0·17	0·19	−0·06	0·07	1·34
p	(0·20)	(0·22)	(0·09)	(0·08)	(0·03)	(0·05)	(0·58)
	2·59	2·08	1·94	2·33	2·36	1·58	2·29

	y	p	m	v	q	const.
	−0·65	−0·57	−0·86	−0·05	0·09	7·14
c	(0·44)	(0·47)	(0·21)	(0·05)	(0·03)	(1·81)
	1·46	1·21	4·11	1·00	2·97	3·95

Covariance matrix of residuals

0·054		
0·034	0·026	
0·044	0·031	0·044

Variance

y 0·082
p 0·031
c 0·014

Chi-square value of log-likelihood ratio: 12·92 with 11 d.o.f.

1961 Urban "Restricted" (p convictions)

Variable to be explained			Explanatory variables			
	p	f	w	rv	e	const.
	−1·00	−0·34	0·57	0·16	0·02	−4·78
y	(0·32)	(0·11)	(0·20)	(0·05)	(0·37)	(2·56)
	3·10	3·15	2·90	3·41	0·05	1·86

	y	c	a	w	n	e	v	const.
	0·49	−1·03	−0·41	0·49	−0·10	0·68	0·26	−5·43
p	(0·43)	(0·68)	(0·28)	(0·25)	(0·07)	(0·62)	(0·16)	(3·33)
	1·15	1·53	1·49	1·93	1·50	1·11	1·65	1·63

	y	m	v	d	q	const.
	−0·34	−1·01	−0·13	0·07	0·06	6·76
c	(0·22)	(0·29)	(0·07)	(0·06)	(0·04)	(1·97)
	1·55	3·41	1·77	1·16	1·45	3·43

Covariance matrix of residuals

0·055		
0·005	0·080	
0·021	−0·010	0·023

Variance

y 0·082
p 0·058
c 0·014

Chi-square value of log-likelihood ratio: 19·07 with 13 d.o.f.

Table 6.5 *continued*

(b) 1961 Rural "Full Model" (*p* clear-up)

Variable to be explained	Explanatory variables							
	p	*c*	*f*	*a*	*w*	*rv*	*e*	const.
	—0·93	0·48	—0·11	—0·16	0·62	0·18	0·70	—6·77
y	(0·04)	(0·79)	(0·08)	(0·08)	(0·24)	(0·06)	(1·04)	(5·72)
	25·07	0·61	1·35	1·95	2·62	3·17	0·67	1·18
	y	*c*	*a*	*w*	*n*	*e*	*v*	const.
	0·23	4·46	—0·15	—0·59	0·26	4·07	1·16	—17·71
p	(0·74)	(4·17)	(0·19)	(0·94)	(0·22)	(4·09)	(0·67)	(19·24)
	0·31	1·07	0·78	0·63	1·17	1·00	1·74	0·92
	y	*p*	*m*	*v*	*d*	*q*	const.	
	—0·93	—6·24	—0·11	5·13	0·22	1·30	8·46	
c	(2·99)	(16·50)	(1·65)	(13·45)	(0·86)	(3·27)	(21·99)	
	0·31	0·38	0·07	0·38	0·26	0·40	0·38	

Covariance matrix of residuals   Variance

```
0·046                           y 0·706    Chi-square value of log-
0·018    0·164                  p 0·802    likelihood ratio: 10·63
0·148    0·146       1·267      c 0·015    with 10 d.o.f.
```

1961 Rural "Full Model" (*p* convictions)

Variable to be explained	Explanatory variables							
	p	*c*	*f*	*a*	*w*	*rv*	*e*	const.
	—0·98	—0·22	—0·31	—0·15	0·90	0·14	—0·16	—4·74
y	(0·04)	(0·85)	(0·10)	(0·08)	(0·26)	(0·06)	(1·10)	(6·05)
	23·18	0·26	3·11	1·72	3·43	2·46	0·15	0·78
	y	*c*	*a*	*w*	*n*	*e*	*v*	const.
	—0·05	4·45	—0·23	—0·06	0·26	4·09	0·87	—21·49
p	(0·52)	(3·37)	(0·18)	(0·71)	(0·20)	(3·46)	(0·48)	(17·14)
	0·10	1·32	1·24	0·08	1·30	1·18	1·84	1·25
	y	*p*	*m*	*v*	*d*	*q*	const.	
	0·96	—2·28	—1·19	2·97	—0·18	0·71	9·11	
c	(1·78)	(4·20)	(2·18)	(5·32)	(0·27)	(1·19)	(15·35)	
	0·54	0·54	0·54	0·56	0·65	0·59	0·59	

Covariance matrix of residuals   Variance

```
0·055                           y 0·706    Chi-square value of log-
0·024    0·176                  p 0·798    likelihood ratio: 9·78
0·104    0·143       0·589      c 0·015    with 10 d.o.f.
```

Table 6.5 *continued*

(c) 1961 Urban and Rural "Full Model" (p clear-up) 3SLS

Variable to be explained	Explanatory variables							
	p	c	f	a	w	r	e	const.
	−0·94	0·01	0·05	−0·14	0·36	0·15	0·18	−1·28
y	(0·04)	(0·32)	(0·07)	(0·08)	(0·15)	(0·02)	(0·38)	
	23·08	0·04	0·82	1·69	2·44	6·04	0·47	
	y	c	a	w	n	e	v	r	const.
	1·59	1·63	0·22	−1·10	−0·02	−0·61	2·25	−0·18	10·71
p	(1·44)	(1·02)	(0·13)	(0·94)	(0·06)	(0·72)	(1·22)	(0·18)	
	1·10	1·60	1·72	1·17	0·35	0·86	1·85	1·01	
	y	p	m	v	r	q	const.	
	0·26	1·13	−0·52	−0·80	−0·01	0·03	1·44	
c	(0·26)	(0·47)	(0·31)	(0·28)	(0·04)	(0·06)		
	1·00	2·41	1·68	2·86	0·30	0·46		

Covariance matrix of residuals   Variance

			y 0·381
0·053			p 0·336
−0·075	0·439		c 0·032
−0·012	−0·107	0·053	

1961 Urban and Rural "Full Model" (p convictions) 3SLS

Variable to be explained	Explanatory variables							
	p	c	f	a	w	r	e	const.
	−0·99	−0·37	−0·19	−0·11	0·61	0·20	0·31	−5·03
y	(0·05)	(0·33)	(0·07)	(0·08)	(0·17)	(0·03)	(0·36)	(2·15)
	20·23	1·13	2·55	1·42	3·71	7·28	0·85	2·34
	y	c	a	w	n	e	v	r	const.
	6·52	5·09	0·06	−4·12	0·30	−3·01	6·31	−0·78	39·42
p	(3·96)	(2·67)	(0·38)	(2·57)	(0·18)	(2·10)	(3·34)	(0·47)	(23·09)
	1·65	1·91	0·17	1·60	1·70	1·44	1·89	1·66	1·71
	y	p	m	v	r	q	const.	
	−0·18	−0·48	−0·39	0·22	0·13	0·16	1·81	
c	(0·18)	(0·40)	(0·22)	(0·42)	(0·02)	(0·09)	(1·39)	
	0·97	1·20	1·79	0·53	5·52	1·77	1·30	

Covariance matrix of residuals   Variance

			y 0·381
0·080			p 0·350
−0·293	4·702		c 0·032
0·039	−0·034	0·035	

Table 6.5 *continued*

(d) 1966 Urban "Restricted" (*p* clear-up)

Variable to be explained	Explanatory variables							
	p	*c*	*f*	*a*	*w*	*rv*	*e*	const.
	—0·79	—0·56	—0·28	0·40	0·42	0·20	0·45	—6·47
y	(0·51)	(0·94)	(0·10)	(0·17)	(0·17)	(0·07)	(0·14)	(1·82)
	1·55	0·59	2·91	2·37	2·43	2·94	3·20	3·56
	y	*c*	*a*	*w*	*n*	*v*	const.	
	0·45	—1·57	—0·51	0·11	—0·10	0·12	0·25	
p	(0·27)	(0·52)	(0·30)	(0·11)	(0·05)	(0·10)	(0·76)	
	1·65	3·00	1·69	0·94	2·04	1·23	0·32	
	p	*m*	*v*	*d*	*q*	const.		
	—0·28	—0·56	—0·01	0·04	0·06	3·99		
c	(0·16)	(0·22)	(0·05)	(0·03)	(0·03)	(1·39)		
	1·75	2·59	0·23	1·63	2·41	2·86		

Covariance matrix of residuals Variance

0·079			*y* 0·173
0·029	0·062		*p* 0·038
0·028	0·027	0·017	*c* 0·018

Chi-square value of log-likelihood ration 14·36 with 12 d.o.f.

1966 Urban "Restricted" (*p* convictions)

Variable to be explained	Explanatory variables						
	p	*f*	*a*	*w*	*rv*	*e*	const.
	—0·84	—0·27	0·41	0·44	0·18	0·39	—7·07
y	(0·28)	(0·09)	(0·15)	(0·14)	(0·05)	(0·14)	(1·72)
	3·05	3·00	2·66	3·14	3·33	2·85	4·11
	a	*w*	*n*	*e*	*v*	const.	
	—0·15	0·21	—0·02	0·09	0·29	—2·37	
p	(0·13)	(0·11)	(0·03)	(0·12)	(0·07)	(1·30)	
	1·20	1·83	0·60	0·74	4·14	1·82	
	y	*p*	*m*	*d*	*q*	const.	
	—0·05	—0·44	—0·75	0·05	0·10	4·92	
c	(0·06)	(0·17)	(0·23)	(0·04)	(0·03)	(1·41)	
	0·84	2·64	3·26	1·22	3·23	3·50	

Covariance matrix of residuals Variance

0·049			*y* 0·173
0·016	0·035		*p* 0·048
0·021	0·016	0·021	*c* 0·018

Chi-square value of log-likelihood ratio 8·97 with 14 d.o.f.

Table 6.5 *continued*

(e) 1966 Rural "Restricted" (p clear-up)

Variable to be explained	Explanatory variables						
	p	c	f	w	rv	const.	
	0·25	3·25	—0·27	0·26	0·38	—3·63	
y	(0·31)	(1·42)	(0·14)	(0·14)	(0·14)	(1·65)	
	0·81	2·29	2·00	1·82	2·80	2·20	
	y	a	w	n	e	v	const.
	—0·23	0·13	—0·14	—0·02	—0·09	0·16	1·57
p	(0·11)	(0·25)	(0·13)	(0·02)	(0·08)	(0·07)	(1·13)
	2·11	0·51	1·08	0·77	1·19	2·34	1·39
	y	m	d	q	const.		
	0·18	0·11	0·11	0·02	0·12		
c	(0·11)	(0·07)	(0·02)	(0·01)	(0·40)		
	1·65	1·61	4·66	1·53	0·30		

Covariance matrix of residuals			Variance	
0·125			y 0·054	Chi-square value of log-
—0·004	0·011		p 0·014	likelihood ratio: 12·80
—0·035	0·001	0·010	c 0·016	with 15 d.o.f.

1966 Rural "Restricted" (p convictions)

Variable to be explained	Explanatory variables					
	p	c	f	w	rv	const.
	—0·19	2·93	—0·59	0·20	0·35	—4·14
y	(0·56)	(1·44)	(0·24)	(0·34)	(0·13)	(3·02)
	0·34	2·04	2·49	0·61	2·75	1·37
	y	a	w	n	e	const.
	—0·03	0·55	0·36	—0·03	—0·00	—3·12
p	(0·17)	(0·35)	(0·19)	(0·03)	(0·10)	(1·55)
	0·16	1·55	1·86	0·78	0·02	2·01
	y	m	v	d	q	const.
	0·09	0·23	0·01	—0·11	0·02	—0·57
c	(0·12)	(0·14)	(0·02)	(0·02)	(0·02)	(0·80)
	0·72	1·68	0·40	4·41	0·92	0·70

Covariance matrix of residuals			Variance	
0·093			y 0·054	Chi-square value of log-
—0·007	0·023		p 0·031	likelihood ratio: 16·84
—0·029	—0·000	0·010	c 0·016	with 15 d.o.f.

Table 6.5 *continued*

(f) 1966 Urban and Rural "Restricted" (*p* clear-up)

Variable to be explained	Explanatory variables							
	p	*c*	*f*	*a*	*w*	*r*	*e*	const.
	—0·66	0·70	—0·16	0·79	0·09	0·43	0·21	—5·02
y	(0·23)	(0·20)	(0·09)	(0·12)	(0·13)	(0·09)	(0·10)	(1·33)
	2·80	3·40	1·74	6·52	0·72	4·70	2·03	0·67
	c	*a*	*n*	*v*	*r*	const.		
	—0·61	—0·04	—0·12	0·09	0·16	—0·27		
p	(0·32)	(0·06)	(0·03)	(0·08)	(0·10)	(0·55)		
	1·90	0·67	3·43	1·15	1 1·62	0·50		
	p	*m*	*v*	*r*	*q*	const.		
	1·02	—0·36	—0·36	0·31	0·17	1·12		
c	(0·33)	(0·31)	(0·09)	(0·07)	(0·05)	(1·70)		
	3·07	1·17	4·02	4·62	3·60	0·66		

Covariance matrix of residuals			Variance	
0·041			*y* 0·176	Chi-square value of log-
0·005	0·026		*p* 0·029	likelihood ratio: 11·92
—0·008	—0·014	0·039	*c* 0·042	with 10 d.o.f.

1966 Urban and Rural "Restricted" (*p* convictions)

Variable to be explained	Explanatory variables							
	p	*c*	*f*	*a*	*w*	*r*	*e*	const.
	—0·77	0·74	—0·20	0·81	0·24	0·43	0·17	—6·37
y	(0·24)	(0·19)	(0·08)	(0·11)	(0·12)	(0·08)	(0·08)	(1·22)
	3·25	4·00	2·70	7·61	2·00	5·46	2·05	5·20
	y	*c*	*a*	*w*	*n*	*v*	const.	
	—0·15	0·39	0·15	0·06	—0·02	0·24	—1·00	
p	(0·09)	(0·14)	(0·09)	(0·04)	(0·02)	(0·06)	(0·32)	
	1·57	2·76	1·54	1·34	1·54	3·75	3·17	
	p	*m*	*v*	*r*	*q*	const.		
	1·44	—0·02	—0·46	0·24	0·07	0·18		
c	(0·58)	(0·12)	(0·15)	(0·08)	(0·03)	(1·07)		
	2·48	0·13	3·00	2·83	2·19	0·17		

Covariance matrix of residuals			Variance	
0·035			*y* 0·176	Chi-square value of log-
0·012	0·031		*p* 0·042	likelihood ratio: 10·06
—0·013	—0·050	0·086	*c* 0·042	with 9 d.o.f.

Table 6.5 *continued*

(g) 1971 Urban and Rural "Restricted" (p clear-up)

Variable to be explained	Explanatory variables						
	p	c	f	w	r	const.	
y	−0·80	0·70	−0·10	0·22	0·08	7·96	
	(0·50)	(0·41)	(0·12)	(0·23)	(0·04)	(3·27)	
	1·59	1·69	0·84	0·99	1·84	2·43	
	c	a	n	e	v	const.	
p	−0·47	−0·25	−0·05	−0·73	0·01	13·80	
	(0·21)	(0·27)	(0·04)	(0·31)	(0·14)	(2·59)	
	2·29	0·92	1·20	2·33	0·05	5·33	
	y	p	m	v	r	q	const.
c	0·69	0·94	−0·09	−0·24	−0·01	0·03	−8·53
	(0·31)	(0·55)	(0·21)	(0·18)	(0·05)	(0·04)	(4·07)
	2·27	1·71	0·44	1·36	0·21	0·83	2·09

Covariance matrix of residuals   Variance

0·034			y 0·106	Chi-square value of log-
0·003	0·015		p 0·017	likelihood ratio: 5·71
−0·024	−0·003	0·021	c 0·032	with 11 d.o.f.

1971 Urban and Rural "Restricted" (p convictions)

Variable to be explained	Explanatory variables						
	p	c	f	a	r	const.	
y	−0·69	0·85	−0·36	0·31	0·15	−0·57	
	(0·43)	(0·27)	(0·16)	(0·28)	(0·04)	(1·56)	
	1·59	3·15	2·34	1·09	3·54	0·36	
	y	c	n	w	e	const.	
p	0·77	−1·27	−0·03	0·25	−1·20	6·70	
	(0·56)	(1·10)	(0·06)	(0·29)	(0·73)	(5·64)	
	1·38	1·15	0·49	0·86	1·64	1·19	
	y	p	m	v	r	q	const.
c	−0·36	1·12	−0·62	−0·56	0·06	0·13	0·94
	(0·93)	(1·08)	(0·85)	(0·48)	(0·12)	(0·13)	(2·56)
	0·39	1·04	0·72	1·18	0·55	1·02	0·37

Covariance matrix of residuals   Variance

0·022			y 0·106	Chi-square value of log-
−0·025	0·071		p 0·027	likelihood ratio: 3·51
0·012	−0·041	0·061	c 0·032	with 11 d.o.f.

Notes.

1. The numbers of observations are as follows: 1961 Urban 72, 1961 Rural 47, 1961 Urban and Rural 119, 1966 Urban 66, 1966 Rural 44, 1966 Urban and Rural 110, 1971 Urban and Rural 41. Notation is defined in Table 5.1.
2. Interpretations of coefficients are discussed in Chapter 7.
3. Variance-covariance matrices of residuals are discussed in § 6.6.

4. Chi-square values of the log-likelihood ratios are examined in Table 6.6.
5. "Goodness-of-fit" is discussed in § 6.6.
6. The constant terms are not comparable for different years, since they depend on the scaling of the data. On the other hand constants in Table 6.A.1 are comparable across years (see the appendix to this chapter).
7. For 1961 Urban and Rural, FIML gave rise to convergence problems, and thus 3SLS estimates are presented.
8. For 1961 Rural "full model" estimates are presented since there were convergence problems for FIML on "restricted" runs.
9. For each set of numbers under a variable name the figure in the first row is the value of its coefficient in the equation for the variable to be explained, that in the second row the corresponding standard error, and that in the third the (absolute value of the) asymptotic t-value.

The chi-square value of the log-likelihood ratio is $2 \log \dfrac{L_u}{L_r}$, where L_u is the likelihood for the just-identified model (where all the over-identifying restrictions are relaxed) and L_r is the likelihood value for the model presented in the table. A high chi-square value (relative to values for given significance levels in the chi-square distribution) indicates that one should reject the over-identifying restrictions, and a low value that one should accept them. Thus it is one indication of how well the model is specified (see § 5.4).

The variance-covariance matrix of residuals for each estimated model is also given, together with variances of the endogenous variables. Note that the residual variance of an endogenous variable can be larger than the original variance. This possibility is explained in § 5.5 and is of interest in understanding the structure of the model—see also § 6.6 where the variance-covariance matrix of residuals is discussed.

Our discussion of the consequences of these results for various theories and ideas is given in Chapter 7. Our remarks in this section are reserved for particular tests and features of the computations.

The two data sets to exhibit computational peculiarities were 1961 Rural and 1961 Urban and Rural. For both data sets convergence of the iterative procedure for the calculation of FIML estimates caused problems. For the case of 1961 Urban and Rural (see Table 6.5 (c)); this led us to use 3SLS results. Thus we did not conduct a search for a "restricted model", since we did not have likelihood values to use in chi-square tests of the restrictions. In the case of 1961 Rural (see Table 6.5(b)). FIML results are presented for the "full model" of Table 5.1. The restriction exercise was not undertaken for this case, since convergence was problematic for some of the restricted models we tried.

The very high t-value for the coefficient of p (either clear-up or convictions) in the first equation for these 2 data sets might appear a little strange. A possible line of explanation might be attempted as follows. The coefficient is close to minus one and $p = \log$ (number of clear-ups or convictions *per capita*) — *y*. Thus, if the number of clear-ups or convictions *per capita* were completely unrelated to the number of recorded offences *per capita*, we should expect a coefficient on *p* in the equation for *y* of minus one. We were led to reject this as an explanation of the phenomenon for at least three reasons. First, if the argument were correct we should also expect a highly significant coefficient on *y*, in the equation for *p*, of minus one; this does not occur. Secondly, it is implausible that areas with many more recorded offences *per capita* than others would not *ceteris paribus* have more clear-ups and convictions per capita. Thirdly, for 1961 Rural *p* clear-up and 1961 Urban and Rural *p* clear-up 1 (one) lies outside the 10% confidence interval for the coefficient. Thus we regard the high *t*-values for the coefficients on *p* in the first equation for these data sets as an unexplained feature of the rural areas in 1961.

Table 6.6
Tests of over-identifying restrictions in the models of Table 6.5

Model	Chi-square value	Degrees of freedom	B such that Probability $(\chi^2 > B) = 0.20$
1961 Urban Restricted			
p clear-up	12·92	11	14·6
p convictions	19·07	13	17·0
1961 Rural Full Model			
p clear-up	10·63	10	13·4
p convictions	9·78	10	13·4
1966 Urban Restricted			
p clear-up	14·36	12	15·8
p convictions	8·97	14	18·2
Rural Restricted			
p clear-up	12·80	15	19·3
p convictions	16·84	15	19·3
Urban and Rural Restricted (% urb model)			
p clear-up	11·92	10	13·4
p convictions	10·06	9	12·2
1971 Urban and Rural Restricted (% urb model)			
p clear-up	5·71	11	14·6
p convictions	3·50	11	14·6

Notes.
1. Where Column 3 is greater than Column 1 we accept the null hypothesis that the over-identifying restrictions taken together are correct (against the alternative hypothesis that the just-identified model is correct) at the 20% level.
2. The structure of the models in question is set out in Table 6.5.

The tests for overall model specification are summarized in Table 6.6. It can be seen that in all cases except one, the over-identifying restrictions would be accepted at the 20% level (and in the remaining one would be accepted at the 10% level). In other words, in repeated sampling, if the null hypothesis is correct, one would expect chi-square values larger than those observed at least 20% of the time. Thus the overall model specification seems quite successful.

The number of coefficients which are significant at the 10% level in Table 6.5 is fairly large for all cases except for 1961 Rural p clear-up and p convictions, 1966 Rural p convictions, and 1971 Urban and Rural p clear-up, (where by "fairly large" we mean 11 or more, in other words more than half the coefficients (excluding constants) of the "full model"). Broadly speaking then, given that the nature of the models is such that a large amount of randomness is to be expected, the exercise in terms of significant coefficients and chi-square values for overall model specification seems fairly successful. (Goodness-of-fit is discussed in § 6.6). The 1961 Rural data set seems to be problematic (for convergence of FIML computation) and some of these problems may be reflected in the 1961 Urban and Rural set. The alternative estimator 3SLS is available and was used. We regard as our "main" sets the 1961 Urban and 1966 Urban, since we have decided in general to separate Urban from Rural sets and these two sets provide the largest number of observations. However, we do not wish to imply that the results from the Rural, and Urban and Rural, sets are of little importance. In fact they play a major role in our interpretations.

6.4 ALTERNATIVE MODELS

We consider in this section results from two experiments with alternative models. The first, presented in § 6.4.1, concerns the possible endogeneity of the severity of punishment variable f (since it may depend on the level of offences). The second uses breaking-and-entering offences in place of all indictable offences and is examined in § 6.4.2.

6.4.1 *Endogeneity of* f

We saw in Chapter 5 (§ 5.3 and 5.4) that at the time computations were performed, no test was available for whether or not a variable should be deemed endogenous. Our procedure for examining the issue was the informal one of treating the severity of punishment variable as endogenous and then examining the estimated equation for f and the other equations to see if they look reasonable with respect to the theory that suggested the endogeneity of f in the first place.

The results from carrying out the estimation are presented in Table 6.7. The model is that of Table 5.1 for the first three equations (except that we think of f as endogenous) together with a fourth equation intended to explain f. We treat f as a function of the (log of) the recorded offence rate, the proportion of the population that is middle class, and the proportion of recorded offences that are violent (see § 3.2). Results are presented only for the two data sets 1961 Urban and 1966 Urban.

It can be seen that v is significant in the equation for f in all four of the models of Table 6.7 (only at the 20% level for 1961 Urban p convictions but at the 5% level for the other three). However, in each case the sign of the coefficient (negative) indicates that increases in the proportion of violent offences decreases the severity of punishment, which is counter to the direction of the theory suggesting an equation for f. In 1966 the middle-class variable is significant at the 5% or 10% levels and has the "right", positive, sign.

Table 6.7
A model with severity of punishment endogenous

(a) 1961 Urban (p clear-up)

Variable to be explained	Explanatory variables							
	p	c	f	a	w	rv	e	const.
	−0·58	−0·38	0·55	0·08	0·71	0·15	−0·21	−1·74
y	(0·37)	(0·85)	(0·74)	(0·29)	(0·41)	(0·09)	(0·50)	(3·06)
	1·58	0·45	0·74	0·28	1·73	1·62	0·41	0·57
	y	c	a	w	n	e	v	const.
	0·36	−1·34	−0·57	0·16	−0·17	0·61	0·18	−1·07
p	(0·59)	(0·74)	(0·28)	(0·27)	(0·08)	(0·50)	(0·14)	(2·52)
	0·61	1·81	2·01	0·60	2·20	1·21	1·25	0·42
	y	p	m	v	d	q	const.	
	−0·08	0·19	−0·84	−0·13	0·04	0·07	5·34	
c	(0·18)	(0·15)	(0·26)	(0·07)	(0·04)	(0·03)	(1·73)	
	0·45	1·23	3·29	1·89	0·95	2·51	3·08	
	y	m	v	const.				
	−0·69	−0·26	−0·34	0·86				
f	(0·33)	(0·70)	(0·16)	(4·85)				
	2·05	0·37	2·17	0·18				

Covariance matrix of residuals				Variance	
0·079				y 0·082	Chi-square value of log-
−0·020	0·047			p 0·031	likelihood ratio: 30·35
0·013	0·006	0·014		c 0·014	with 13 d.o.f.
−0·000	−0·002	0·020	0·107	f 0·091	

Table 6.7 *continued*

(b) 1961 Urban (*p* convictions) 3SLS

Variable to be explained				Explanatory variables				
	p	*c*	*f*	*a*	*w*	*rv*	*e*	const.
	—0·40	0·02	0·67	0·21	0·77	0·17	0·14	—4·94
y	(0·57)	(0·65)	(0·54)	(0·38)	(0·37)	(0·06)	(0·52)	(3·42)
	0·70	0·04	1·23	0·55	2·06	2·78	0·28	1·44
	y	*c*	*a*	*w*	*n*	*e*	*v*	const.
	—0·02	—0·83	—0·24	0·57	0·03	—0·27	0·21	—1·23
p	(0·47)	(0·80)	(0·25)	(0·20)	(0·08)	(0·54)	(0·12)	(2·87)
	0·04	1·03	0·98	2·88	0·32	0·50	1·70	0·43
	y	*p*	*m*	*v*	*d*	*q*	const.	
	0·21	0·08	—0·57	—0·04	—0·05	0·06	3·89	
c	(0·12)	(0·16)	(0·21)	(0·07)	(0·04)	(0·03)	(1·41)	
	1·79	0·50	2·74	0·68	1·46	1·71	2·75	
	y	*m*	*v*	const.				
	—0·01	0·41	—0·20	—4·93				
f	(0·25)	(0·59)	(0·13)	(4·01)				
	0·03	0·69	1·45	1·23				

Covariance matrix of residuals Variance

0·099				*y* 0·082	
0·003	0·048			*p* 0·058	
—0·013	0·009	0·011		*c* 0·014	
—0·063	—0·005	0·013	0·087	*f* 0·091	

(c) 1966 Urban (*p* clear-up)

Variable to be explained				Explanatory variables				
	p	*c*	*f*	*a*	*w*	*rv*	*e*	const.
	—0·07	0·79	0·50	0·55	0·43	0·15	0·42	—5·16
y	(0·29)	(0·46)	(0·35)	(0·19)	(0·17)	(0·06)	(0·17)	(1·95)
	0·23	1·72	1·41	2·83	2·46	2·73	2·45	2·65
	y	*c*	*a*	*w*	*n*	*e*	*v*	const.
	0·56	—1·51	—0·73	0·06	—0·15	0·05	0·09	0·17
p	(0·49)	(0·65)	(0·41)	(0·20)	(0·05)	(0·24)	(0·13)	(2·67)
	1·14	2·33	1·78	0·32	2·86	0·19	0·66	0·06
	y	*p*	*m*	*v*	*d*	*q*	const.	
	—0·03	0·01	—0·67	—0·14	0·04	0·13	4·77	
c	(0·05)	(0·15)	(0·24)	(0·06)	(0·04)	(0·04)	(1·51)	
	0·68	0·09	2·82	2·44	1·22	3·60	3·16	
	y	*m*	*v*	const.				
	—0·11	1·04	—0·23	—8·84				
f	(0·09)	(0·50)	(0·09)	(3·18)				
	1·22	2·08	2·54	2·78				

Covariance matrix of residuals Variance

0·063				*y* 0·173	Chi-square value of log-
—0·027	0·060			*p* 0·038	likelihood ratio: 31·82
0·000	0·015	0·013		*c* 0·018	with 13 d.o.f.
—0·036	0·002	0·006	0·057	*f* 0·070	

(d) 1966 Urban (p convictions)

Variable to be explained	Explanatory variables							
	p	c	f	a	w	rv	e	const.
	0·45	1·09	0·83	0·67	0·35	0·17	0·37	3·30
y	(1·22)	(0·62)	(1·16)	(0·31)	(0·22)	(0·09)	(0·21)	(4·37)
	0·37	1·75	0·72	2·18	1·56	1·92	1·77	0·76
	y	c	a	w	n	e	v	const.
	—0·11	0·09	—0·06	0·20	—0·01	0·14	0·29	—2·69
p	(0·31)	(0·40)	(0·26)	(0·14)	(0·02)	(0·16)	(0·09)	(1·80)
	0·37	0·21	0·22	1·43	0·50	0·90	3·19	1·49
	y	p	m	v	d	q	const.	
	—0·02	—0·44	—0·62	0·01	0·01	0·16	4·65	
c	(0·06)	(0·55)	(0·31)	(0·18)	(0·04)	(0·04)	(1·93)	
	0·41	0·79	1·99	0·03	0·15	3·63	2·41	
	y	m	v	const.				
	—0·13	0·91	—0·26	—8·07				
f	(0·09)	(0·53)	(0·10)	(3·33)				
	1·47	1·73	2·68	2·42				

Covariance matrix of residuals   Variance

0·120				y 0·173	Chi-square value of log-
—0·025	0·032			p 0·048	likelihood ratio: 29·56
—0·021	0·015	0·020		c 0·018	with 13 d.o.f.
—0·054	—0·003	0·006	0·057	f 0·070	

Notes.
1. See Notes to Table 6.5 for an explanation of the lay-out.
2. When f becomes endogenous, we have four equations instead of three. The first three equations take the form specified in Table 5.1.
3. For 1961 Urban (p convictions) FIML gave rise to convergence problems, and thus 3SLS estimates are presented in Table 6.7b.

We find that y is significant in the equation for f at the 20% level in 2 cases and at the 5% level in one. In every case the coefficient is negative. The main reason for including the extra equation was the possible dependence of f on y. In discussing such a possible dependence (see § 3.2) we started with the notion that sentencers would react to higher, recorded offence levels with higher punishment levels. The results run counter to that argument. They are not inconsistent with the notion that there is a capacity constraint c but we explained that, at least with variables one could use in our study, such constraints should appear as "noise" in the model. Thus according to our prior theory the "dependence" of f on y has the wrong sign and we regard this outcome as support for our decision to confine attention in the most part to the three-equation models. Furthermore, the inclusion of a fourth equation does not seem to improve the other equations as can be seen by comparing the significant levels of the coefficients in Tables 6.5 and 6.7. In particular (for all four cases) the sign of the co-efficient on f in the first equation becomes positive; this has the (improbable) interpretation that more severe punishment causes more offences.

6.4.2 Breaking-and-entering Offences

There are two justifications for an exercise which replaces our "all indictable offence" variable and the corresponding detection rate by the particular offence type, breaking-and-entering offences (or burglaries). The first is that this sub-class of recorded offences may be more homogeneous. Secondly, it has been argued that this type of offence has a high ratio of recorded to actual offences (see § 5.3). We showed in § 5.3 how an offence variable with a recording ratio of unity could help with the problem of "unobserved variables" and lead to the identification of parameters in an equation for actual offences.

Table 6.8
A model with breaking-and-entering offences

(a) 1961 Urban

Variable to be explained				Explanatory variables				
	p	c	f	a	w	rv	e	const.
	−5·68	−4·60	0·64	−1·94	2·55	−0·22	3·24	−18·26
y	(4·60)	(5·03)	(0·92)	(1·82)	(1·78)	(0·35)	(3·25)	(16·03)
	1·23	0·91	0·69	1·06	1·43	0·64	1·00	1·14
	y	c	a	w	n	e	v	const.
	−0·62	−0·95	−0·50	0·99	0·06	0·57	−0·27	−6·81
p	(0·44)	(0·70)	(0·28)	(0·68)	(0·07)	(0·57)	(0·30)	(4·75)
	1·42	1·35	1·80	1·46	0·83	0·99	0·92	1·43
	y	p	m	v	d	q	const.	
	−0·12	0·59	−1·04	−0·19	0·10	0·08	6·02	
c	(0·10)	(0·39)	(0·37)	(0·11)	(0·06)	(0·05)	(2·21)	
	1·13	1·52	2·81	1·69	1·57	1·60	2·73	

Covariance matrix of residuals			Variance	
1·757			y 0·192	Chi-square value of log-
0·315	0·078		p 0·055	likelihood ratio: 19·95
−0·099	−0·004	0·030	c 0·014	with 10 d.o.f.

Table 6.8 *continued*

(b) 1961 Rural 3SLS

Variable to be explained	Explanatory variables							
	p	c	f	a	w	rv	e	const.
	1·69	−2·49	−0·00	−0·21	0·73	0·07	−0·47	1·11
y	(0·45)	(1·29)	(0·10)	(0·14)	(0·44)	(0·07)	(1·69)	(9·30)
	3·73	1·93	0·00	1·48	1·68	0·96	0·28	0·12
	y	c	a	w	n	e	v	const.
	0·46	1·40	0·10	−0·30	−0·01	0·19	0·00	−1·15
p	(0·14)	(0·73)	(0·07)	(0·20)	(0·04)	(0·85)	(0·02)	(4·45)
	3·35	1·93	1·50	1·48	0·16	0·22	0·24	0·26
	y	p	m	v	d	q	const.	
	0·07	0·84	−0·40	−0·02	−0·07	0·00	3·73	
c	(0·17)	(0·24)	(0·29)	(0·02)	(0·04)	(0·05)	(2·01)	
	0·38	3·44	1·37	0·84	2·02	0·10	1·85	

Covariance matrix of residuals   Variance

0·332				y 0·135
−0·178	0·096			p 0·040
0·086	−0·048	0·028		c 0·015

(c) 1961 Urban and Rural 3SLS

Variable to be explained	Explanatory variables								
	p	c	f	a	w	r	e	const.	
	−0·96	−0·85	0·00	−0·15	0·92	0·25	0·13	−6·47	
y	(0·54)	(0·49)	(0·11)	(0·12)	(0·23)	(0·04)	(0·59)	(3·35)	
	1·77	1·75	0·04	1·18	3·98	6·10	0·23	1·93	
	y	c	a	w	n	e	v	r	const.
	0·79	0·50	0·06	−0·66	−0·18	−0·03	0·13	−0·22	4·91
p	(0·40)	(0·47)	(0·08)	(0·39)	(0·08)	(0·37)	(0·06)	(0·10)	(3·71)
	1·97	1·06	0·73	1·68	2·30	0·08	2·15	2·24	1·32
	y	p	m	v	r	q	const.		
	−0·13	0·48	−0·52	−0·05	0·11	0·09	2·85		
c	(0·09)	(0·27)	(0·22)	(0·03)	(0·02)	(0·04)	(1·47)		
	1·38	1·76	2·33	2·10	5·80	2·27	1·94		

Covariance matrix of residuals   Variance

0·135				y 0·237
−0·067	0·162			p 0·049
0·024	−0·059	0·032		c 0·032

Table 6.8 *continued*

(d) 1966 Urban

Variable to be explained	Explanatory variables							
	p	*c*	*f*	*a*	*w*	*rv*	*e*	const.
	−4·19	−5·01	−0·30	−0·16	1·20	0·26	0·89	−16·26
y	(3·33)	(5·34)	(0·18)	(0·32)	(0·46)	(0·16)	(0·38)	(6·10)
	1·26	0·94	1·61	0·51	2·62	1·62	2·35	2·66
	y	*c*	*a*	*w*	*n*	*e*	*v*	const.
	0·32	−1·41	−0·25	−0·36	−0·06	−0·23	0·25	5·17
p	(0·53)	(0·61)	(0·33)	(0·58)	(0·08)	(0·41)	(0·28)	(7·83)
	0·61	2·30	0·74	0·63	0·72	0·57	0·89	0·66
	y	*p*	*m*	*v*	*d*	*q*	const.	
	−0·03	−0·54	−0·27	0·02	0·03	0·04	1·98	
c	(0·05)	(0·23)	(0·25)	(0·04)	(0·03)	(0·04)	(1·68)	
	0·64	2·34	1·09	0·63	0·92	1·08	1·18	

Covariance matrix of residuals

1·404		
0·307	0·098	
0·208	0·051	0·032

Variance

y 0·349   Chi-square value of log-
p 0·057   likelihood ratio: 16·97
c 0·018   with 10 d.o.f.

(e) 1966 Rural

Variable to be explained	Explanatory variables							
	p	*c*	*f*	*a*	*w*	*rv*	*e*	const.
	−0·88	2·18	−0·26	−0·11	0·33	0·37	0·64	−11·06
y	(0·75)	(1·13)	(0·18)	(0·57)	(0·39)	(0·13)	(0·28)	(2·67)
	1·16	1·92	1·47	0·19	0·84	2·90	2·25	4·14
	y	*c*	*a*	*w*	*n*	*e*	*v*	const.
	−0·30	0·55	0·02	−0·16	0·04	0·36	0·15	−3·19
p	(0·12)	(0·53)	(0·40)	(0·25)	(0·04)	(0·13)	(0·10)	(2·04)
	2·50	1·04	0·04	0·66	1·07	2·81	1·51	1·56
	y	*p*	*m*	*v*	*d*	*q*	const.	
	0·01	−0·23	0·45	0·06	−0·12	0·05	−1·49	
c	(0·12)	(0·22)	(0·28)	(0·08)	(0·04)	(0·04)	(1·69)	
	0·10	1·04	1·62	0·76	2·82	1·40	0·88	

Covariance matrix of residuals

0·071		
0·025	0·026	
−0·016	0·003	0·013

Variance

y 0·118   Chi-square value log-
p 0·044   likelihood ratio: 13·09
c 0·016   with 10 d.o.f.

Table 6.8 *continued*

(f) 1966 Urban and Rural 3SLS

Variable to be explained	Explanatory variable								
	p	c	f	a	w	r	e	const.	
	—1·03	0·82	0·19	0·49	0·79	0·57	0·79	—15·81	
y	(0·37)	(0·33)	(0·15)	(0·22)	(0·22)	(0·14)	(0·19)	(2·28)	
	2·81	2·49	1·29	2·19	3·61	4·03	4·06	6·95	
	y	e	a	w	n	e	v	r	const.
	1·18	—1·56	—0·91	—1·24	—0·29	—0·61	0·44	—0·57	19·48
p	(0·86)	(0·94)	(0·58)	(0·85)	(0·13)	(0·59)	(0·35)	(0·56)	(15·17)
	1·37	1·66	1·57	1·47	2·30	1·03	1·25	1·00	1·28
	y	p	m	v	r	q	const.		
	0·01	0·37	—0·38	—0·24	0·34	0·15	0·91		
c	(0·04)	(0·17)	(0·26)	(0·06)	(0·06)	(0·03)	(1·47)		
	0·18	2·23	1·46	4·33	5·76	4·22	0·62		

Covariance matrix of residuals   Variance

				y 0·336
0·104				p 0·052
—0·075	0·260			c 0·042
—0·015	0·010	0·021		

(g) 1971 Urban and Rural

Variable to be explained	Explanatory variables								
	p	c	f	a	w	r	e	const.	
	—11·35	—0·18	0·22	—1·46	—0·76	0·00	—2·38	17·03	
y	(37·49)	(6·61)	(1·47)	(5·99)	(3·97)	(0·70)	(9·56)	(73·58)	
	0·30	0·03	0·15	0·24	0·19	0·00	0·25	0·23	
	y	c	a	w	n	e	v	r	const.
	—0·10	—0·16	—0·13	—0·01	—0·00	—0·28	—0·06	0·01	2·06
p	(0·30)	(0·90)	(0·26)	(0·32)	(0·01)	(0·56)	(0·35)	(0·08)	(4·77)
	0·35	0·17	0·50	0·04	0·12	0·51	0·17	0·15	0·43
	y	p	m	v	r	q	const.		
	1·19	3·21	—1·63	0·16	—0·08	—0·08	0·95		
c	(1·68)	(6·83)	(2·74)	(0·80)	(0·23)	(0·18)	(3·99)		
	0·71	0·47	0·59	0·20	0·34	0·47	0·24		

Covariance matrix of residuals   Variance

				y 0·191	Chi-square value of log-
4·249				p 0·037	likelihood ratio: 3·77
0·381	0·034			c 0·032	with 6 d.o.f.
—1·049	—0·094	—0·309			

Notes.
1. Variables are the same as for Tables 6.5 and 6.A.1 except for y and p which are the number per head of breaking-and-entering offences and the clear-up rate for such offences respectively. See Data Appendix for full definitions and Table 5.1 for notation.

2. See Table 6.5 for further notes.
3. For 1961 and 1966 Urban and Rural and 1961 Rural FIML gave rise to convergence problems, and thus 3SLS estimates are presented in Tables 6.8 b, c, f.

For all seven data sets, we carried out the estimation using the model of Table 5.1 or the % urb model for the Urban and Rural sets, but replacing the recorded offence rate by breaking-and-entering offences *per capita* and the overall detection rate by the clear-up rate for the breaking-and-entering offences. The results are presented in Table 6.8.

The results are similar to those in Table 6.5 in some respects but not in others, and are compared with them in Chapter 7 (§ 7.4.1). In general the significance levels of the coefficients are lower than those for our main set of estimates given in Table 6.5 (or 6.A.1). Furthermore, the coefficients, particularly the role of the number of policemen *per capita* (see Chapter 7), would not support the assumption that all breaking-and-entering offences are recorded.

6.5 REDUCED FORMS

We drew the distinction between a structural model and the reduced-form model in § 5.2. The reduced form shows how the exogenous variables determine the endogenous after taking into account all the interactions between the endogenous variables. The reduced form models for three cases, 1961 Urban Restricted, 1966 Urban Restricted, and 1971 Urban and Rural Restricted (all for p convictions) are presented in Table 6.9. Note that the endogenous variables do not appear on the right-hand side of the equations, since it is precisely to remove this interdependence that we calculate the reduced form. A coefficient in the reduced form is called an impact multiplier, since it shows the full effect on the given endogenous variable of a change in the exogenous variable in question.

Our main purpose in giving the derived reduced forms here is to focus attention on the logical difference between the structure and the reduced form, and to show how the inter-relationships between endogenous variables mean that predictions of the value of an endogenous variable require information on variables which do not directly (through the structural equation explaining the variable) influence it. We give two examples. Let us consider the role of f (severity of punishment) in the explanation of p convictions in 1971 (see Table 6.9 (c)). There is no direct effect (in our second equation) of f on p. However, f affects y and y affects p; furthermore y affects c and c affects p; and there is also the feedback of c on y which will further affect p, and so on. The coefficient of f, $-0\cdot16$, in the derived reduced form for p indicates that, after all the inter-relationships have worked through, a 10% increase in the severity of punishment

Table 6.9

Derived reduced forms

(a) 1961 Urban Restricted (p convictions)

Endogenous variables		Exogenous variables										
		f	a	w	rv	n	m	e	v	d	q	const.
y		−0·18	0·22	0·05	0·09	0·06	−0·56	−0·36	−0·22	0·04	0·03	4·12
		(0·08)	(0·13)	(0·14)	(0·04)	(0·03)	(0·37)	(0·34)	(0·10)	(0·04)	(0·03)	(3·22)
		2·36	1·69	0·33	2·29	1·68	1·50	1·05	2·16	1·04	1·11	1·28
p		−0·15	−0·23	0·53	0·07	−0·06	0·56	0·38	0·22	−0·04	−0·03	−8·90
		(0·07)	(0·13)	(0·17)	(0·04)	(0·03)	(0·37)	(0·40)	(0·09)	(0·04)	(0·03)	(3·51)
		2·14	1·68	3·18	1·90	1·68	1·54	0·96	2·47	0·99	1·12	2·55
c		0·06	−0·08	0·02	−0·03	−0·02	−0·82	0·12	−0·06	0·05	0·05	5·36
		(0·03)	(0·05)	(0·05)	(0·02)	(0·01)	(0·21)	(0·12)	(0·04)	(0·04)	(0·03)	(1·61)
		1·94	1·47	0·33	1·54	1·42	3·93	1·03	1·31	1·27	1·45	3·34

Variance

y 0·082
p 0·058
c 0·014

Covariance matrix of residuals

0·062		
−0·024	0·041	
0·009	−0·001	0·010

(b) 1966 Urban Restricted (*p* convictions)

Endogenous variables		Exogenous variables										
		f	*a*	*w*	*rv*	*n*	*m*	*e*	*v*	*d*	*q*	const.
y		−0.27	0.54	0.26	0.18	0.01	—	0.31	−0.25	—	—	−5.07
		(0.09)	(0.18)	(0.16)	(0.05)	(0.02)	—	(0.17)	(0.09)	—	—	(1.86)
		3.00	2.92	1.68	3.33	0.59	—	1.82	2.87	—	—	2.72
p		—	−0.15	0.21	—	−0.02	—	0.09	0.29	—	—	−2.37
		—	(0.13)	(0.11)	—	(0.03)	—	(0.12)	(0.07)	—	—	(1.30)
		—	1.20	1.83	—	0.60	—	0.74	4.14	—	—	1.82
c		0.01	0.04	−0.10	−0.01	0.01	−0.75	−0.06	−0.12	0.05	0.10	6.22
		(0.02)	(0.05)	(0.05)	(0.01)	(0.01)	(0.23)	(0.05)	(0.04)	(0.04)	(0.03)	(1.68)
		0.84	0.78	1.92	0.81	0.59	3.26	1.06	3.04	1.22	3.23	3.71

Variance

y 0.173
p 0.047
c 0.018

Covariance matrix of residuals

0.047		
−0.014	0.035	
0.012	0.001	0.012

Table 6.9 continued

(c) 1971 Urban and Rural Restricted (p convictions)

Endogenous variables	Exogenous variables									
	f	a	w	r	n	m	e	v	q	const.
y	−0.31	0.26	0.02	0.16	−0.00	−0.37	−0.11	−0.34	0.08	0.69
	(0.15)	(0.26)	(0.09)	(0.03)	(0.01)	(0.36)	(0.42)	(0.15)	(0.05)	(3.94)
	2.02	1.02	0.25	5.07	0.23	1.03	0.25	2.26	1.48	0.18
p	−0.16	0.13	0.11	0.05	−0.01	0.13	−0.55	0.12	−0.03	2.63
	(0.08)	(0.13)	(0.12)	(0.02)	(0.03)	(0.15)	(0.28)	(0.09)	(0.03)	(2.50)
	1.94	1.02	0.89	2.52	0.50	0.89	1.95	1.36	1.12	1.05
c	−0.06	0.05	0.12	0.06	−0.01	−0.33	−0.58	−0.30	0.07	3.63
	(0.10)	(0.09)	(0.13)	(0.02)	(0.03)	(0.30)	(0.25)	(0.10)	(0.04)	(2.21)
	0.67	0.59	0.91	2.96	0.51	1.09	2.26	3.18	1.65	1.65

Variance

y 0.106
p 0.027
c 0.032

Covariance matrix of residuals

0.043		
−0.017	0.018	
0.009	−0.000	0.012

Notes.

1. The entries under the exogenous variables are in triples: the first is the coefficient or impact multiplier, the second (in brackets) the asymptotic standard error, and the third the asymptotic t-value.

2. A dash denotes that a coefficient is identically zero.

3. "Derived" means derived from the structure, see § 5.2 where we gave examples of such derivations.

4. The derivation of standard errors is, in principle, similar but rather more complex.

5. The covariance matrix of residuals in the derived reduced form is defined in Note 2 to Table 6.10.

would decrease the conviction rate by 1·6% of its value. The negative relation here is mainly because an increase in f reduces y (1st structural equation—see Table 6.5(g)) and an increase in y increases p (2nd structural equation—see Table 6.5(g)). Secondly, let us consider f in the derived reduced form for p convictions in 1966 (see Table 6.9(b)); here the coefficient is identically zero. An increase in f reduces y, which in turn affects c (see Table 6.5(d)), but both c and y are excluded from the structural equation for p (again see Table 6.5(d)) and thus there is no indirect effect of f on p.

For each of the reduced form models in Table 6.9 we have given the variance-covariance matrix of residuals in that reduced form. We explained in § 5.5 that the residuals in the reduced form provide a natural measure of goodness-of-fit (discussed in the next section), whereas residuals in the structure cannot be so used.

The impact multipliers are in principle the relevant coefficients for predictive and policy purposes, whereas the coefficients of the structure are relevant for the understanding of individual and institutional behaviour. Given the clear change in structure between the three years of our study which we noted in § 6.1, we should not advise the use of the impact multipliers for forecasting. We regard our models as giving information on the behaviour of individuals and institutions and have therefore concentrated our discussion on structural coefficients.

6.6 VARIANCE-COVARIANCE MATRICES

We shall use the variance-covariance matrices for the structural models to try to improve our understanding of the general inter-relationships of the system and in particular the role of some missing variables such as institutional influences on the statistics. The variance-covariance matrices in the reduced-form models underlie our discussion of goodness-of-fit. The matrices for both models are set out in Table 6.10 where results for data sets are in the same order as for Table 6.5. In addition to the two matrices for each case, we provide correlation coefficients for the residuals in the structure: if σ_{ij} is the entry in the variance-covariance matrix for the structure, then the correlation coefficient ϱ_{ij} between the residuals in the ith and j^{th} equations is given by $\varrho_{ij} = \dfrac{\sigma_{ij}}{\sqrt{\sigma_{ii}\,\sigma_{jj}}}$. We include "total variance" and "explained"/total in Table 6.10 for our discussion of goodness-of-fit—see below and § 5.5.

We shall not go through each of the 14 cases in Table 6.10 in detail. We shall characterise the main conclusions which emerge and discuss one or two examples in detail to show the reader how the arguments work. We examine

Table 6.10
Variance-covariance matrices

Structure			Derived reduced form			Total variance	"Explained"/ total
1961 Urban Restricted (p clear-up)							
0·054			0·065			0·082	0·21
0·034	0·026		—0·013	0·015		0·031	0·50
0·044	0·031	0·044	0·009	0·000	0·010	0·014	0·31
ϱ_{21}	0·89						
ϱ_{31}	0·90						
ϱ_{32}	0·90						
1961 Urban Restricted (p convictions)							
0·055			0·062			0·082	0·33
0·005	0·080		—0·024	0·041		0·058	0·30
0·021	—0·010	0·023	0·009	—0·001	0·010	0·014	0·28
ϱ_{21}	0·08						
ϱ_{31}	0·58						
ϱ_{32}	—0·24						
1961 Rural Full Model (p clear-up)							
0·046			0·039			0·706	0·94
0·018	0·164		—0·012	0·035		0·802	0·96
0·148	0·146	1·267	0·001	0·001	0·007	0·015	0·57
ϱ_{21}	0·21						
ϱ_{31}	0·61						
ϱ_{32}	0·32						
1961 Rural Full Model (p convictions)							
0·055			0·037			0·706	0·95
0·024	0·176		—0·030	0·078		0·798	0·90
0·104	0·143	0·589	0·001	0·003	0·007	0·015	0·57
ϱ_{21}	0·24						
ϱ_{31}	0·58						
ϱ_{32}	0·45						
1961 Urban and Rural Full Model (p clear-up) 3SLS							
0·053			0·081			0·381	0·79
—0·075	0·439		—0·040	0·054		0·336	0·84
—0·012	—0·107	0·053	0·004	0·007	0·021	0·032	0·36
ϱ_{21}	—0·50						
ϱ_{31}	—0·24						
ϱ_{32}	—0·70						
1961 Urban and Rural Full Model (p convictions) 3SLS							
0·080			0·082			0·381	0·79
—0·293	4·702		—0·045	0·080		0·350	0·77
0·039	—0·034	0·035	0·004	0·006	0·015	0·032	0·54
ϱ_{21}	—0·48						
ϱ_{31}	0·74						
ϱ_{32}	—0·08						

Table 6.10 *continued*

Structure	Derived reduced form					Total variance	"Explained"/ total
			1966 Urban Restricted (p clear-up)				
0·079			0·050			0·173	0·71
0·029	0·062		—0·004	0·021		0·038	0·45
0·028	0·027	0·017	0·013	0·005	0·013	0·018	0·28
ϱ_{21}	0·41						
ϱ_{31}	0·76						
ϱ_{32}	0·84						
			1966 Urban Restricted (p convictions)				
0·049			0·047			0·173	0·73
0·016	0·035		—0·014	0·035		0·048	0·26
0·021	0·016	0·021	0·012	0·001	0·012	0·018	0·34
ϱ_{21}	0·38						
ϱ_{31}	0·68						
ϱ_{32}	0·60						
			1966 Rural Restricted (p clear-up)				
0·125			0·031			0·054	0·43
—0·004	0·011		—0·004	0·011		0·014	0·22
—0·035	0·001	0·010	0·003	0·001	0·011	0·016	0·34
ϱ_{21}	—0·12						
ϱ_{31}	—0·98						
ϱ_{32}	0·09						
			1966 Rural Restricted (p convictions)				
0·093			0·033			0·054	0·39
—0·007	0·023		—0·018	0·025		0·031	0·21
—0·029	—0·000	0·010	0·005	0·002	0·011	0·016	0·31
ϱ_{21}	—0·15						
ϱ_{31}	—0·92						
ϱ_{32}	—0·02						
			1966 Urban and Rural Restricted (p clear-up)				
0·041			0·048			0·176	0·73
0·005	0·026		—0·009	0·021		0·029	0·25
—0·008	—0·014	0·039	0·009	—0·001	0·014	0·042	0·66
ϱ_{21}	0·05						
ϱ_{31}	—0·06						
ϱ_{32}	—0·43						
			1966 Urban and Rural Restricted (p convictions)				
0·035			0·049			0·176	0·72
0·012	0·031		—0·019	0·035		0·042	0·16
—0·013	—0·050	0·086	0·009	0·000	0·014	0·042	0·68
ϱ_{21}	0·38						
ϱ_{31}	—0·23						
ϱ_{32}	—0·97						

Table 6.10 *continued*

Structure			Derived reduced form			Total variance	"Explained"/ total
1971 Urban and Rural Restricted (*p* clear-up)							
0·034			0·043			0·106	0·59
0·003	0·015		—0·005	0·011		0·017	0·36
—0·024	—0·003	0·021	0·008	0·001	0·012	0·032	0·64
ϱ_{21}	0·14						
ϱ_{31}	—0·90						
ϱ_{32}	—0·18						
1971 Urban and Rural Restricted (*p* convictions)							
0·022			0·043			0·106	0·59
—0·025	0·071		—0·017	0·018		0·027	0·34
0·012	—0·041	0·061	0·009	—0·000	0·012	0·032	0·64
ϱ_{21}	—0·63						
ϱ_{31}	0·34						
ϱ_{32}	—0·63						

Notes.
1. The variance-covariance matrix of residuals in the structure (Σ) also presented in Table 6.5.
2. The variance-covariance matrix of the residuals in the derived form (S) is equal to $(A^{-1})\Sigma(A^{-1})'$ where A is the (3×3) matrix of the coefficients of the endogenous variables in the structure.
3. We use the variance-covariance matrix of the derived reduced form to judge goodness-of-fit (see § 5.5) as follows. If S_{ii} is the ith diagonal entry in S, then for the first equation, for example, "Explained"/Total $= (1 - S_{11}/\text{var } y)$. Similarly for p and c.
4. ϱ_{ij} is the correlation between residuals for the ith and jth equations in the structure.

first goodness-of-fit (using the reduced form) and secondly the error terms in the structure.

The goodness-of-fit in the first equation, that for the offence rate, can be judged a reasonable success. Our measure, "explained" divided by total variance in the reduced form, is above 70% in 8 out of the 14 cases. For a cross-section sample in a system where a great deal of randomness is to be expected, 70% seems rather good (but note that the standard F test on R^2 for single equation models does not apply here). The proportion of explained variance is below 70% for 1961 Urban, 1966 Rural, and 1971 Urban and Rural (for both p clear-up and p convictions). For 1971 Urban and Rural the explained proportion is still quite good at 59% for both p clear-up and p convictions.

The fit for the second equation is not so good with 5 cases with "explained" variance as a proportion of total of 50% or above and 9 cases of 30% or above.

For the third equation we have a performance in terms of fit better than that for p but worse than that for y. For 12 of the 14 cases we have "explained" as a proportion of total variance above 30%, for 7 cases above 50% and for 4 cases above 60%.

We suppose that the very good fits for y and p in 1961 Rural and Urban and Rural are connected with the very high t-value for the coefficient of p in the first equation (see § 6.3).

We turn now to the error terms in the structure (see Table 6.10). We show how the residual variance in an equation of the structure can be higher than the total variance of the variable the equation is intended to explain. Take, for example, the case 1966 Urban, and we find that for p clear-up the residual variance in the structure is $0 \cdot 062$ whereas the total variance is $0 \cdot 038$. Consider a positive random disturbance of p. There is a strong positive correlation between the errors in structural equations (2) and (3) (see Table 6.10) so that the positive disturbances of p would be associated with a positive disturbance to c. This in turn acts to reduce p through the large negative coefficient of c in the equation for p (see Table 6.5(d)). Note that the effect is outweighed neither by the decrease in c from the negative coefficient of p in the third equation, nor by the random increase in u ($\varrho_{21} > 0$) which has a positive coefficient in the second equation. The system has therefore diminished the original random disturbance in p to produce a variation in p smaller than the original random impulse.

We have just seen that an examination of the variance-covariance matrices can give us insight into the technical side of the model. We want to know, however, why the correlations of the residuals in the structure occur. We can only speculate here but there are some interesting possibilities. Let us stay with the case of 1966 Urban (p clear-up) and the positive correlation ϱ_{32} which says that a larger c than would be suggested by the non-stochastic or systematic terms in the equation for c goes with a similarly larger p. One possible explanation is that we have an omitted variable—for example, the influence of the chief constable. A dynamic chief constable may be successful both in recruiting policemen and in raising the clear-up rate. Alternatively, he may feel that if he is successful in recruiting, he ought to produce higher clear-up rates. He can influence the clear-up rate in several ways. He could, for example, instruct his force to record (and usually clear-up immediately) more smaller offences which they may otherwise have ignored. This behaviour would be consistent with the positive correlations ϱ_{31} and ϱ_{21} (see also 1961 Urban p clear-up)—see § 7.5.2 for further discussion.

The correlation ϱ_{32} is strongly positive only for 1961 Urban and 1966 Urban p clear-up, which suggests that the behaviour of chief constables in rural areas may be different: for example, they may not be so strongly conscious of comparisons between their clear-up figures and those for other areas. It is also interesting that the effect is nowhere as strong as the two cases mentioned, when we use p convictions. This measure involves less police discretion than does p clear-up. These issues are pursued a little further in Chapter 7.

6.7 ORDINARY LEAST SQUARES (OLS) AND TWO STAGE LEAST SQUARES (2SLS) ESTIMATES

6.7.1 OLS

Ordinary least squares estimates are presented in Table 6.11 for 1961 Urban (p clear-up and convictions), 1966 Urban (p clear-up and convictions). In the first equation, for example, p and c are treated as explanatory variables for y in just the same way as w or rv and no account is taken of endogeneity.

We showed in § 6.2 that the OLS estimates in a simultaneous system could be very misleading because they are biased and inconsistent. A comparison of the results of Tables 6.11 and 6.A.1 (where estimates of the same models using FIML techniques are presented) shows that the OLS estimates are indeed misleading for our models. We give three examples.

Table 6.11
Ordinary least squares estimates

(a) 1961 Urban (p clear-up)

Variable to be explained	Explanatory variables							
	p	c	f	a	w	rv	e	const.
	—0·75	0·56	—0·14	—0·03	0·16	0·13	0·11	—1·26
y	(0·17)	(0·25)	(0·10)	(0·19)	(0·17)	(0·05)	(0·43)	(2·47)
	4·56	2·29	1·40	0·17	0·92	2·48	0·24	0·51
		$R^2 = 0.47$					$\overline{R}^2 = 0.41$	
	y	c	a	w	n	e	v	const.
	—0·24	0·01	—0·24	0·11	—0·09	0·26	0·17	0·08
p	(0·06)	(0·14)	(0·11)	(0·09)	(0·03)	(0·27)	(0·06)	(1·53)
	3·85	0·08	2·28	1·22	3·06	0·94	2·76	0·05
		$R^2 = 0.54$					$\overline{R}^2 = 0.49$	
	y	p	m	v	d	q	const.	
	0·14	0·14	—0·70	—0·07	—0·01	0·05	4·49	
c	(0·05)	(0·09)	(0·22)	(0·05)	(0·03)	(0·04)	(1·44)	
	2·54	1·57	3·24	1·38	0·04	1·50	3·11	
		$R^2 = 0.30$					$\overline{R}^2 = 0.24$	

Table 6.11 *continued*

(b) 1961 Urban (*p* convictions)

Variable to be explained	Explanatory variables							
	p	*c*	*f*	*a*	*w*	*rv*	*e*	const.
y	−0·59	0·57	−0·27	0·03	0·32	0·19	0·26	−4·69
	(0·12)	(0·24)	(0·10)	(0·19)	(0·18)	(0·05)	(0·43)	(2·44)
	4·81	2·33	2·60	0·15	1·81	3·82	0·61	1·92
			$R^2 = 0.48$				$\overline{R}^2 = 0.42$	
	y	*c*	*a*	*w*	*n*	*e*	*v*	const.
p	−0·34	0·01	−0·15	0·55	0·04	0·02	0·20	−2·63
	(0·10)	(0·22)	(0·17)	(0·15)	(0·04)	(0·43)	(0·09)	(2·40)
	3·55	0·04	0·88	3·78	0·80	0·05	2·16	1·10
			$R^2 = 0.39$				$\overline{R}^2 = 0.32$	
	y	*p*	*m*	*v*	*d*	*q*	const.	
c	0·10	0·02	−0·67	−0·04	−0·02	0·05	4·47	
	(0·05)	(0·06)	(0·22)	(0·05)	(0·03)	(0·04)	(1·47)	
	1·94	0·26	3·04	0·85	0·65	1·44	3·05	
			$R^2 = 0.28$				$\overline{R}^2 = 0.21$	

(c) 1966 Urban (*p* clear-up)

Variable to be explained	Explanatory variables							
	p	*c*	*f*	*a*	*w*	*rv*	*e*	const.
y	−0·29	0·87	−0·17	0·49	0·24	0·14	0·40	−5·21
	(0·13)	(0·19)	(0·10)	(0·18)	(0·15)	(0·57)	(0·16)	(1·76)
	2·13	4·65	1·67	2·75	1·60	2·52	2·43	2·96
			$R^2 = 0.79$				$\overline{R}^2 = 0.77$	
	y	*c*	*a*	*w*	*n*	*e*	*v*	const.
p	−0·16	0·10	−0·16	0·09	−0·10	0·27	0·15	−2·04
	(0·10)	(0·19)	(0·16)	(0·12)	(0·03)	(0·14)	(0·07)	(1·48)
	1·53	0·52	1·00	0·77	3·25	1·91	2·10	1·38
			$R^2 = 0.36$				$\overline{R}^2 = 0.28$	
	y	*p*	*m*	*v*	*d*	*q*	const.	
c	0·07	0·10	−0·47	−0·14	0·01	0·12	3·68	
	(0·04)	(0·08)	(0·26)	(0·05)	(0·04)	(0·04)	(1·60)	
	1·79	1·28	1·81	2·84	0·32	3·15	2·29	
			$R^2 = 0.38$				$\overline{R}^2 = 0.31$	

Table 6.11 *continued*

(d) 1966 Urban (p convictions)

Variable to be explained	Explanatory variables							

	p	c	f	a	w	rv	e	const.
y	−0·43	0·84	−0·18	0·50	0·31	0·14	0·38	−5·88
	(0·11)	(0·17)	(0·10)	(0·16)	(0·14)	(0·05)	(0·15)	(1·63)
	3·94	4·83	1·92	3·06	2·23	2·73	2·53	3·60
	$R^2 = 0·83$						$\overline{R}^2 = 0·80$	

	y	c	a	w	n	e	v	const.
p	−0·38	0·38	0·16	0·26	−0·02	0·20	0·26	−3·38
	(0·11)	(0·20)	(0·17)	(0·13)	(0·03)	(0·15)	(0·08)	(1·60)
	3·42	1·86	0·92	1·96	0·61	1·35	3·28	2·12
	$R^2 = 0·39$						$\overline{R}^2 = 0·32$	

	y	p	m	v	d	q	const.
c	0·07	0·04	−0·41	−0·13	0·00	0·12	3·33
	(0·04)	(0·08)	(0·26)	(0·05)	(0·04)	(0·04)	(1·62)
	1·78	0·53	1·56	2·49	0·01	3·00	2·06
	$R^2 = 0·36$					$\overline{R}^2 = 0·30$	

(e) 1971 Urban and Rural (p clear-up)

Variable to be explained	Explanatory variables							

	p	c	f	a	w	r	e	const.
y	−0·62	0·83	−0·30	0·04	−0·03	0·09	0·20	4·16
	(0·29)	(0·25)	(0·22)	(0·48)	(0·30)	(0·04)	(0·50)	(5·38)
	2·15	3·38	1·36	0·08	0·11	2·30	0·40	0·77)
	$R^2 = 0·70$						$\overline{R}^2 = 0·63$	

	y	c	a	w	n	e	v	r	const.
p	−0·18	0·28	−0·23	−0·26	−0·05	−0·33	0·21	−0·01	10·97
	(0·09)	(0·17)	(0·26)	(0·16)	(0·04)	(0·27)	(0·11)	(0·02)	(2·27)
	2·02	1·64	0·89	1·59	1·33	1·24	1·94	0·43	4·82
	$R^2 = 0·47$						$\overline{R}^2 = 0·33$		

	y	p	m	v	r	q	const.
c	0·26	0·32	−0·21	−0·26	0·04	0·07	−3·56
	(0·08)	(0·16)	(0·31)	(0·11)	(0·02)	(0·04)	(1·21)
	3·07	1·97	0·68	2·47	1·62	1·61	2·95
	$R^2 = 0·67$					$\overline{R}^2 = 0·61$	

Table 6.11 *continued*

(f) 1971 Urban and Rural (*p* convictions)

Variable to be explained	Explanatory variables							
	p	c	f	a	w	r	e	const.
	—0·95	0·72	—0·42	0·36	0·08	0·17	—0·18	0·27
y	(0·19)	(0·20)	(0·18)	(0·38)	(0·23)	(0·03)	(0·40)	(3·35)
	5·04	3·65	2·34	0·94	0·35	5·07	0·44	0·08
		$R^2 = 0{\cdot}80$					$\overline{R}^2 = 0{\cdot}76$	

	y	c	a	w	n	e	v	r	const.
	—0·42	0·30	0·42	0·14	—0·02	—0·52	0·09	0·09	2·36
p	(0·10)	(0·19)	(0·29)	(0·18)	(0·04)	(0·30)	(0·12)	(0·03)	(2·56)
	4·28	1·56	1·45	0·76	0·35	1·71	0·72	3·68	0·92
		$R^2 = 0{\cdot}57$					$\overline{R}^2 = 0{\cdot}46$		

	y	p	m	v	r	q	const.
	0·31	0·33	—0·16	—0·23	—0·00	0·06	—0·97
c	(0·09)	(0·13)	(0·30)	(0·10)	(0·03)	(0·04)	(0·34)
	3·54	2·47	0·53	2·26	0·14	1·14	2·86
		$R^2 = 0{\cdot}69$					$\overline{R}^2 = 0{\cdot}64$

Notes.
1. The table contains ordinary least squares estimates treating the "variable to be explained" as an independent variable and "explanatory variables" as dependent variables.
2. Results should be compared with those given by the simultaneous-equation techniques of Table 6.12 and 6.A.1.
3. Numbers in brackets are standard errors and below the standard errors are t-values.
4. R^2 is the "explained" divided by total sum of squares and $\overline{R}^2$ the similar quantity corrected for degrees of freedom.

Examine the estimates for 1961 Urban (*p* clear-up) in Tables 6.11(a) and 6.A.1(a). In Table 6.11 the coefficient of *c* in the first equation (explaining *y*) is positive and significant but in the corresponding equation in Table 6.A.1 it is zero. The coefficient of *y* in the third equation (for *c*) is positive and significant (at the 5% level) in Table 6.11 and negative and significant at the 20% level in Table 6.A.1. Comparing the results in the two tables for 1966 Urban (*p* clear-up), we find coefficients of *p* in the third equation (for *c*) which are significant (at the 20% level) and of opposite signs.

Most of the sign differences of estimated coefficients as between Tables 6.11 and 6.A.1. seem to be concentrated on the role of *c*. However, in other cases coefficients are significant for one method and not the other, and the magnitudes of estimated coefficients differ greatly for the two techniques.

The estimated significance levels of coefficients are, on the whole, higher for OLS than FIML. This, of course, does not provide an argument for OLS, since the OLS estimates are biased and inconsistent.

6.7.2 *2SLS*

The OLS estimates above were presented to illustrate the confusion that can arise from using a technique which ignores endogeneity. However, there is a more positive reason for presenting 2SLS results. The 2SLS technique uses the information that a variable is endogenous, but when estimating a single equation, does not use full information on which factors are determining which variable. We need to know only which exogenous variables in the system do not enter the structural equation for the variable to be explained (see Chapter 5, § 5.1).

The problem in general with using more information is that it may be mistaken, and thus 2SLS (which uses less information than 3SLS or FIML) avoids some possible errors. The 2SLS estimates are set out in Table 6.12 for the same six cases as Table 6.11. The estimates in Table 6.12 should be compared with corresponding cases in Table 6.A.1.

There are differences between the 2SLS and FIML (or 3SLS) estimates but, on the whole, the stories they tell are rather similar. The striking sign disparities which occurred when we were comparing OLS and FIML are rare.

We know that FIML, 3SLS, and 2SLS are consistent so that, as the sample size tends to infinity, the estimates should come closer together. The

Table 6.12
Two-stage least squares estimates

(a) 1961 Urban (p clear-up)

Variable to be explained		Explanatory variables						
	p	c	f	a	w	rv	e	const.
y	−0·59	0·31	−0·11	−0·01	0·20	0·15	0·22	−2·18
	(0·26)	(0·51)	(0·11)	(0·21)	(0·20)	(0·05)	(0·43)	
	2·26	0·60	1·01	0·06	1·01	2·84	0·51	
	y	c	a	w	n	e	v	const.
p	−0·06	−0·42	−0·34	0·14	−0·11	0·43	0·17	−0·69
	(0·18)	(0·29)	(0·12)	(0·11)	(0·04)	(0·30)	(0·07)	
	0·35	1·47	2·69	1·32	2·98	1·45	2·54	
	y	p	m	v	d	q	const.	
c	0·15	0·22	−0·73	−0·09	−0·01	0·05	4·54	
	(0·13)	(0·16)	(0·22)	(0·06)	(0·04)	(0·03)		
	1·15	1·39	3·25	1·54	0·20	1·55		

Covariance matrix of residuals			Variance	
0·045			y 0·082	
0·001	0·017		p 0·031	
−0·003	0·003	0·010	c 0·014	

Table 6.12 *continued*

(b) 1961 Urban (*p* convictions)

Variable to be explained	Explanatory variables							
	p	*c*	*f*	*a*	*w*	*rv*	*e*	const.
y	−0·99	−0·16	−0·26	−0·18	0·66	0·21	0·45	−7·15
	(0·44)	(0·64)	(0·13)	(0·27)	(0·34)	(0·06)	(0·48)	
	2·26	0·25	2·02	0·68	1·95	3·80	0·93	
	y	*c*	*a*	*w*	*n*	*e*	*v*	const.
p	0·29	−1·04	−0·42	0·55	−0·06	0·44	0·23	−4·23
	(0·35)	(0·55)	(0·24)	(0·21)	(0·07)	(0·57)	(0·13)	
	0·83	1·88	1·75	2·67	0·88	0·76	1·88	
	y	*p*	*m*	*v*	*d*	*q*	const.	
c	0·03	−0·23	−0·69	0·02	0·01	0·08	4·24	
	(0·13)	(0·15)	(0·25)	(0·07)	(0·04)	(0·04)		
	0·23	1·53	2·73	0·33	0·22	1·91		

Covariance matrix of residuals

			Variance
0·055			*y* 0·082
0·013	0·064		*p* 0·058
0·010	0·019	0·013	*c* 0·014

(c) 1966 Urban (*p* clear-up)

Variable to be explained	Explanatory variables							
	p	*c*	*f*	*a*	*w*	*rv*	*e*	const.
y	−0·11	0·71	−0·16	0·53	0·23	0·17	0·35	−4·67
	(0·23)	(0·34)	(0·10)	(0·17)	(0·15)	(0·06)	(0·16)	
	0·49	2·05	1·59	3·04	1·61	2·98	2·19	
	y	*c*	*a*	*w*	*n*	*e*	*v*	const.
p	0·39	−1·24	−0·52	−0·02	−0·15	0·04	0·08	0·78
	(0·33)	(0·50)	(0·31)	(0·18)	(0·04)	(0·21)	(0·11)	
	1·17	2·48	1·69	0·12	3·47	0·18	0·69	
	y	*p*	*m*	*v*	*d*	*q*	const.	
c	−0·02	−0·04	−0·52	−0·12	0·02	0·13	4·00	
	(0·05)	(0·14)	(0·28)	(0·06)	(0·04)	(0·04)		
	0·37	0·30	1·90	2·14	0·51	3·25		

Covariance matrix of residuals

			Variance
0·037			*y* 0·173
−0·016	0·048		*p* 0·038
0·003	0·014	0·013	*c* 0·018

Table 6.12 *continued*

(d) 1966 Urban (p convictions)

Variable to be explained — Explanatory variables

y	p	c	f	a	w	rv	e	const.
	—0·44	0·59	—0·18	0·51	0·32	0·15	0·36	—5·68
	(0·25)	(0·30)	(0·09)	(0·16)	(0·14)	(0·05)	(0·14)	
	1·80	1·96	1·98	3·24	2·24	2·98	2·51	

p	y	c	a	w	n	e	v	const.
	—0·00	—0·05	—0·12	0·17	—0·04	0·07	0·28	—1·82
	(0·28)	(0·43)	(0·26)	(0·15)	(0·04)	(0·18)	(0·09)	
	0·00	0·12	0·46	1·13	1·15	0·41	2·96	

c	y	p	m	v	d	q	const.
	—0·02	—0·17	—0·57	—0·08	0·02	0·13	4·24
	(0·05)	(0·36)	(0·27)	(0·12)	(0·04)	(0·04)	
	0·39	0·49	2·07	0·64	0·38	3·21	

Covariance matrix of residuals

```
0·031
0·001   0·035
0·005   0·007   0·014
```

Variance

y 0·173
p 0·048
c 0·018

(e) 1971 Urban and Rural (p clear-up)

Variable to be explained — Explanatory variables

y	p	c	f	a	w	r	e	const.
	—0·49	0·89	—0·29	0·07	—0·03	0·09	0·30	2·42
	(0·91)	(0·50)	(0·22)	(0·49)	(0·31)	(0·04)	(0·78)	
	0·54	1·80	1·34	0·14	0·09	2·20	0·38	

p	y	c	a	w	n	e	v	r	const.
	—0·20	0·51	—0·23	—0·33	—0·05	—0·22	0·28	—0·02	10·13
	(0·35)	(0·78)	(0·26)	(0·23)	(0·03)	(0·47)	(0·22)	(0·04)	
	0·55	0·65	0·89	1·40	1·32	0·47	1·30	0·50	

c	y	p	m	v	r	q	const.
	0·49	0·63	—0·18	—0·25	0·02	0·03	—6·05
	(0·28)	(0·39)	(0·32)	(0·13)	(0·04)	(0·06)	
	1·79	1·60	0·56	1·88	0·35	0·53	

Covariance matrix of residuals

```
0·032
0·005    0·010
—0·016   —0·007   0·013
```

Variance

y 0·106
p 0·017
c 0·032

Table 6.12 *continued*

(f) 1971 Urban and Rural (*p* convictions)

Variable to be explained	Explanatory variables							
	p	*c*	*f*	*a*	*w*	*r*	*e*	const.
	—1·00	0·74	—0·43	0·36	0·07	0·17	—0·21	0·40
y	(0·83)	(0·41)	(0·22)	(0·37)	(0·24)	(0·07)	(0·79)	
	1·21	1·79	1·93	0·97	0·30	2·43	0·27	

	y	*c*	*a*	*w*	*n*	*e*	*v*	*r*	const.
	0·04	—0·22	0·25	0·08	—0·01	—0·83	0·06	0·06	4·22
p	(0·51)	(1·11)	(0·37)	(0·33)	(0·05)	(0·67)	(0·31)	(0·05)	
	0·08	0·20	0·67	6·24	0·26	1·23	0·19	1·05	

	y	*p*	*m*	*v*	*r*	*q*	const.
	0·12	0·59	—0·24	—0·32	0·01	0·10	0·36
c	(0·28)	(0·31)	(0·34)	(0·15)	(0·05)	(0·06)	
	0·44	1·92	0·70	2·13	0·17	1·49	

Covariance matrix of residuals   Variance

			Variance
0·021			*y* 0·106
0·000	0·020		*p* 0·027
—0·003	—0·007	0·015	*c* 0·032

differences between the estimates in Table 6.12 and 6.A.1 occur then for two main reasons: limited size of sample, and the extra information contained in the FIML technique. The extent to which 2SLS and FIML estimates are similar (different) then increases (reduces) our confidence in our specification, and diminishes (increases) our worries about the size of sample. We are inclined to view the similarities between the estimates using the two techniques as mildly reassuring. We should stress, however, that this judgement is subjective (and our vested interest is obvious), and no precise tests of this confidence have been offered.

6.8 CROWDING IN THE HOUSEHOLD

We discussed in Chapter 2 (§ 2.3.7) theories which pointed to over-crowding as a possible explanation of the rate of offending. We used as a variable a measure which is negatively related to this concept—the proportion of households with less than ½ a person per room (*H*)—and log *H* or *h* was included in the first equation. The remainder of the model is either that in Table 5.1 or the % urb model as appropriate. The results for 1961 Urban (*p* clear-up and convictions) 1966 Urban (*p* clear-up and convictions) and 1971 Urban and Rural (*p* clear-up and convictions) are presented in Table 6.13.

Table 6.13
Overcrowding in the household

	Coefficient	t-value	Chi-square value (one d.o.f.)
1961 Urban			
p clear-up	—0·17	1·37	2·05
p convictions	—0·38	2·41	6·80
1966 Urban			
p clear-up	—0·18	1·32	1·41
p convictions	—0·27	1·93	4·47
1971 Urban and Rural			
p clear-up	—0·17	0·76	1·18
p convictions	—0·11	0·51	0·29

Notes.
1. The coefficient is that for h in the first equation (explaining the offence rate) where the model is either that in Table 5.1 or the % urb model as appropriate.
2. The t-value is the asymptotic t-value.
3. A negative coefficient indicates that more overcrowding increases offences.
4. The chi-square value is $2 \log L_u / L_r$ where L_u is the likelihood value including h and L_r is the likelihood excluding h. There is one degree of freedom. The probability that chi-square with one degree of freedom

$$> 1 \cdot 64 \text{ is } 0 \cdot 20,$$
$$> 2 \cdot 71 \text{ is } 0 \cdot 10,$$
$$> 3 \cdot 84 \text{ is } 0 \cdot 05,$$
$$\text{and} > 6 \cdot 63 \text{ is } 0 \cdot 01$$

The coefficient of h is negative throughout as would be suggested by the theory, although it is insignificant for 1971. For 1966 Urban (p convictions) the inclusion of h ruined significance levels in the second and third equations, and for 1961 Urban (p clear-up) it spoilt significance levels in the third equation and produced convergence problems. There remain therefore only two "satisfactory" cases: 1961 Urban (p convictions) and 1966 Urban (p clear-up).

On balance we decided to drop h as a variable from the other experiments. This is not a decision which we took with great confidence and that is the reason why the results using h are summarised here. We record that the coefficient had the "right" sign and postpone further discussion until Chapter 7 (§ 7.4.2).

6.9 CONCLUDING REMARKS

The interpretation of the estimated coefficients presented in the tables of this chapter follow in the next chapter. We summarize very briefly here just

Table 6.14

Quantiles of the distribution function of χ^2

(Reproduced from Table III of Sir Ronald Fisher's "Statistical Methods for Research Workers", Oliver and Boyd Ltd., Edinburgh, by kind permission of the author and publishers.)

$P=1-F$	0·99	0·98	0·95	0·90	0·80	0·70	0·50	0·30	0·20	0·10	0·05	0·02	0·01
$\nu=1$	$0{\cdot}0^3157$	$0{\cdot}0^3628$	$0{\cdot}0^3393$	0·0158	0·0642	0·148	0·455	1·074	1·642	2·706	3·841	5·412	6·635
2	0·0201	0·0404	0·103	0·211	0·446	0·713	1·386	2·408	3·219	4·605	5·991	7·824	9·210
3	0·115	0·185	0·352	0·584	1·005	1·424	2·366	3·665	4·642	6·251	7·815	9·837	11·345
4	0·297	0·429	0·711	1·064	1·649	2·195	3·357	4·878	5·989	7·779	9·488	11·668	13·277
5	0·554	0·752	1·145	1·160	2·343	3·000	4·351	6·064	7·289	9·236	11·070	13·388	15·086
6	0·872	1·134	1·635	2·204	3·070	3·828	5·348	7·231	8·558	10·645	12·592	15·033	16·812
7	1·239	1·564	2·167	2·833	3·822	4·671	6·346	8·383	9·803	12·017	14·067	16·622	18·475
8	1·646	2·032	2·733	3·490	4·594	5·527	7·344	9·524	11·030	13·362	15·507	18·168	20·090
9	2·088	2·532	3·325	4·168	5·380	6·393	8·343	10·656	12·242	14·684	16·919	19·679	21·666
10	2·358	3·059	3·940	4·865	6·179	7·267	9·342	11·781	13·442	15·987	18·307	21·161	23·209
11	3·053	3·609	4·575	5·578	6·989	8·148	10·341	12·899	14·631	17·275	19·675	22·618	24·725
12	3·571	4·178	5·226	6·304	7·807	9·034	11·340	14·011	15·821	18·549	21·026	24·054	26·217
13	4·107	4·765	5·892	7·042	8·634	9·926	12·340	15·119	16·985	19·812	22·362	25·472	27·688
14	4·660	5·368	6·571	7·790	9·467	10·821	13·339	16·222	18·151	21·064	23·685	26·873	29·141
15	5·229	5·985	7·261	8·547	10·307	11·721	14·339	17·322	19·311	22·307	24·996	28·259	30·578
16	5·812	6·614	7·962	9·312	11·152	12·624	15·338	18·418	20·465	23·542	26·296	29·633	32·000
17	6·408	7·255	8·672	10·085	12·002	13·531	16·338	19·511	21·615	24·769	27·587	30·995	33·409
18	7·015	7·906	9·390	10·865	12·857	14·440	17·338	20·601	22·760	25·989	28·869	32·346	34·805
19	7·633	8·567	10·117	11·651	13·716	15·352	18·338	21·689	23·900	27·204	30·144	33·687	36·191
20	8·260	9·237	10·851	12·443	14·578	16·266	19·337	22·775	25·038	28·412	31·410	35·020	37·566
21	8·897	9·915	11·591	13·240	15·445	17·182	20·337	23·858	26·171	29·615	32·671	36·343	38·932
22	9·542	10·600	12·338	14·041	16·314	18·101	21·337	24·939	27·301	30·813	33·924	37·659	40·289
23	10·196	11·293	13·091	14·848	17·187	19·021	22·337	26·018	28·429	32·007	35·172	38·968	41·638
24	10·856	11·992	13·848	15·659	18·062	19·943	23·337	27·096	29·553	33·196	36·415	40·270	42·980
25	11·524	12·697	14·611	16·473	18·940	20·867	24·337	28·172	30·675	34·382	37·652	41·566	44·314
26	12·198	13·409	15·379	17·292	19·820	21·792	25·336	29·246	31·795	35·563	38·885	42·856	45·642
27	12·879	14·125	16·151	18·114	20·703	22·719	26·336	30·319	32·912	36·741	40·113	44·140	46·963
28	13·565	14·847	16·928	18·939	21·588	23·647	27·336	31·391	34·027	37·916	41·337	45·419	48·278
29	14·256	15·574	17·708	19·768	22·475	24·577	28·336	32·461	35·139	39·087	42·557	46·693	49·588
30	14·953	16·306	18·493	20·599	23·364	25·508	29·336	33·530	36·250	40·256	43·773	47·962	50·892

Note.

For values of ν greater than 30 the quantity $\sqrt{(2\chi^2)}$ may be taken to be distributed normally about mean $\sqrt{(2\nu-1)}$ with unit variance.

a few of the main conclusions of this chapter which are not directly connected with the magnitudes and signs of coefficients.

We saw that the data for different years should not be pooled, since the structures for different years seem to be different. These changes over time point to the difficulties of time-series analysis, since the process of change would not be easy to model. We found also that data for urban and rural areas should not be pooled.

The goodness-of-fit, overall model specification, and number of significant coefficients seemed to be reasonably good given the nature of the theories being tested and the amount of randomness to be expected in the data. This judgement is, of course, subjective.

The experiment with modelling the determination of the severity of punishment reinforced our prior view that it should be treated as exogenous in our model. Similarly, the replacement of all indictable offences by breaking-and-entering offences was not particularly successful as an attempt to solve the recording problem. We saw that the correlations between errors were a fruitful source of hypotheses concerning influences on the statistics. The simple regression techniques of OLS produced results rather different from our simultaneous-equations techniques. Our whole approach implies, of course, that OLS procedures are misleading for our model.

It is time now to see how our estimated coefficients for structural equations presented in § 6.3 relate to the theories which we have discussed in previous chapters.

Appendix to Chapter 6

ESTIMATES OF THE "FULL MODEL" AND CORRELATION COEFFICIENTS

Table 6.A.1

The "Full model"

(a) 1961 Urban (p clear-up)

Variable to be explained		Explanatory variables						
	p	c	f	a	w	rv	e	const.
	−0·96	0·00	−0·15	−0·07	0·19	0·05	−0·27	1·86
y	(0·26)	(0·47)	(0·07)	(0·13)	(0·12)	(0·04)	(0·25)	(1·50)
	3·63	0·01	2·00	0·52	1·59	1·38	1·08	1·24
	y	c	a	w	n	e	v	const.
	−0·39	−0·56	−0·24	0·23	−0·08	0·14	0·09	0·54
p	(0·20)	(0·31)	(0·11)	(0·09)	(0·03)	(0·22)	(0·06)	(1·23)
	1·91	1·79	2·25	2·56	2·37	0·61	1·65	0·43
	y	p	m	v	d	q	const.	
	−0·54	−0·39	−0·91	−0·07	0·04	0·10	6·87	
c	(0·37)	(0·36)	(0·34)	(0·06)	(0·04)	(0·04)	(2·46)	
	1·45	1·07	2·70	1·16	0·86	2·14	2·79	

Covariance matrix of residuals   Variance

0·052			y 0·082	Chi-square values of log-
0·026	0·022		p 0·031	likelihood ratio: 17·65
0·037	0·022	0·034	c 0·014	with 10 d.o.f.

1961 Urban (p convictions)

Variable to be explained		Explanatory variables						
	p	c	f	a	w	rv	e	const.
	−0·41	−0·57	−0·39	−0·34	0·85	0·18	0·14	−6·10
y	(0·62)	(0·84)	(0·14)	(0·34)	(0·42)	(0·06)	(0·49)	(3·73)
	2·25	0·67	2·70	1·03	2·02	2·93	0·28	1·64
	y	c	a	w	n	e	v	const.
	0·50	−1·17	−0·48	0·54	−0·11	0·74	0·21	−5·76
p	(0·45)	(0·69)	(0·27)	(0·26)	(0·08)	(0·65)	(0·16)	(3·46)
	1·12	1·68	1·76	2·04	1·47	1·14	1·31	1·66
	y	p	m	v	d	q	const.	
	−0·35	0·01	−0·93	−0·15	0·06	0·07	6·26	
c	(0·23)	(0·18)	(0·31)	(0·10)	(0·06)	(0·04)	(2·10)	
	1·53	0·04	2·97	1·57	1·14	1·62	2·98	

Covariance matrix of residuals   Variance

0·086			y 0·082	Chi-square value of log-
0·031	0·082		p 0·058	likelihood ratio: 17·42
0·025	−0·009	0·024	c 0·014	with 10 d.o.f.

Table 6.A.1 *continued*

Tables 6.A.1 (b) and (c) are identical to 6.5(b) and (c) respectively

(d) 1966 Urban (*p* clear-up)

Variable to be explained	Explanatory variables							
	p	c	f	a	w	rv	e	const.
	—0·64	—0·24	—0·26	0·38	0·40	0·19	0·41	—6·12
y	(0·40)	(0·71)	(0·09)	(0·18)	(0·16)	(0·06)	(0·15)	(1·77)
	1·59	0·33	2·84	2·16	2·53	3·04	2·79	3·45
	y	c	a	w	n	e	v	const.
	0·40	—1·46	—0·56	0·12	—0·11	0·03	0·10	—0·08
p	(0·34)	(0·56)	(0·32)	(0·13)	(0·05)	(0·16)	(0·10)	(1·74)
	1·17	2·59	1·76	0·93	2·26	0·17	1·01	0·05
	y	p	m	v	d	q	const.	
	—0·05	—0·24	—0·68	—0·03	0·05	0·08	4·76	
c	(0·05)	(0·16)	(0·24)	(0·05)	(0·03)	(0·03)	(1·53)	
	0·87	1·51	2·86	0·59	1·56	2·64	3·11	

Covariance matrix of residuals

			Variance	
0·061			y 0·173	Chi-square value of log-
0·017	0·056		p 0·038	likelihood ratio: 13·55
0·024	0·024	0·017	c 0·018	with 10 d.o.f.

1966 Urban (*p* convictions)

Variable to be explained	Explanatory variables							
	p	c	f	a	w	rv	e	const.
	—0·68	0·31	—0·25	0·46	0·36	0·17	0·37	—6·36
y	(0·32)	(0·39)	(0·09)	(0·16)	(0·16)	(0·05)	(0·14)	(1·87)
	2·18	0·79	2·66	2·83	2·28	3·13	2·62	3·40
	y	c	a	w	n	e	v	const.
	0·06	—0·12	—0·17	0·16	—0·01	0·04	0·30	—1·81
p	(0·24)	(0·42)	(0·22)	(0·14)	(0·02)	(0·13)	(0·09)	(1·59)
	0·27	0·29	0·79	1·19	0·44	0·37	3·20	1·13
	y	c	m	v	d	q	const.	
	—0·05	—0·72	—0·79	0·09	0·05	0·12	5·09	
c	(0·07)	(0·70)	(0·33)	(0·23)	(0·05)	(0·05)	(2·07)	
	0·73	1·03	2·38	0·39	1·10	2·49	2·46	

Covariance matrix of residuals

			Variance	
0·037			y 0·173	Chi-square value of log-
0·009	0·038		p 0·048	likelihood ratio: 8·14
0·017	0·027	0·032	c 0·018	with 10 d.o.f.

Table 6.A.1 *continued*

(e) 1966 Rural (*p* clear-up)

Variable to be explained	Explanatory variables							
	p	*c*	*f*	*a*	*w*	*rv*	*e*	const.
	0·18	2·98	—0·27	—0·31	0·42	0·35	0·13	—5·47
y	(1·30)	(1·35)	(0·15)	(0·62)	(0·40)	(0·14)	(0·23)	(3·94)
	0·14	2·21	1·80	0·50	1·06	2·49	0·55	1·39
	y	*c*	*a*	*w*	*n*	*e*	*v*	const.
	—0·23	0·07	0·20	—0·13	—0·01	—0·09	0·16	1·45
p	(0·11)	(0·30)	(0·24)	(0·13)	(0·02)	(0·07)	(0·07)	(1·14)
	2·10	0·23	0·84	1·03	0·52	1·26	2·31	1·27
	y	*p*	*m*	*v*	*d*	*q*	const.	
	0·28	0·43	0·12	—0·07	—0·10	0·02	0·08	
c	(0·18)	(0·61)	(0·08)	(0·11)	(0·03)	(0·01)	(0·53)	
	1·55	0·71	1·52	0·59	3·84	1·23	0·14	

Covariance matrix of residuals

0·106		
—0·001	0·011	
—0·031	—0·004	0·012

Variance

y 0·054   Chi-square value of log-
p 0·014   likelihood ratio: 12·06
c 0·016   with 10 d.o.f.

1966 Rural (*p* convictions) 3SLS

Variable to be explained	Explanatory variables							
	p	*c*	*f*	*a*	*w*	*rv*	*e*	const.
	—0·79	1·39	—0·72	0·17	0·25	0·21	0·02	—4·62
y	(0·52)	(0·47)	(0·18)	(0·47)	(0·23)	(0·05)	(0·10)	
	1·54	2·99	3·99	0·36	1·09	3·87	0·19	
	y	*c*	*a*	*w*	*n*	*e*	*v*	const.
	—0·15	—0·02	0·61	0·39	—0·01	0·03	—0·05	—3·70
p	(0·15)	(0·40)	(0·35)	(0·19)	(0·04)	(0·10)	(0·09)	
	1·05	0·04	1·78	2·10	0·27	0·26	0·53	
	y	*p*	*m*	*v*	*d*	*q*	const.	
	0·14	—0·00	0·32	0·01	—0·11	0·04	—1·03	
c	(0·12)	(0·17)	(0·27)	(0·06)	(0·03)	(0·04)		
	1·15	0·01	1·20	0·18	3·87	1·01		

Covariance matrix of residuals

0·030		
0·006	0·020	
—0·012	0·000	0·010

Variance

y 0·054   *See Note 3 to Table.*
p 0·030
c 0·016

Table 6.A.1 *continued*

(f) 1966 Urban and Rural (*p* clear-up)

Variable to be explained	Explanatory variables							
	p	*c*	*f*	*a*	*w*	*r*	*e*	const.
	—0·69	0·67	—0·14	0·80	0·10	0·43	0·20	—4·99
y	(0·25)	(0·20)	(0·09)	(0·12)	(0·13)	(0·09)	(0·10)	(1·32)
	2·79	3·36	1·60	6·47	0·78	4·91	1·91	3·79
	y	*c*	*a*	*w*	*n*	*e*	*v*	*r*	const.
	—0·43	—0·00	0·34	0·06	—0·07	0·06	0·10	0·26	—1·94
p	(0·29)	(0·34)	(0·25)	(0·09)	(0·03)	(0·09)	(0·06)	(0·13)	(1·72)
	1·50	0·00	1·38	0·62	2·34	0·68	1·66	1·97	1·13
	y	*p*	*m*	*v*	*r*	*q*	const.
	0·05	1·27	—0·25	—0·40	0·26	0·18	0·84
c	(0·09)	(0·42)	(0·30)	(0·11)	(0·10)	(0·05)	(1·69)
	0·59	3·00	0·81	3·68	2·66	3·30	0·50

Covariance matrix of residuals   Variance

0·042			*y* 0·176	Chi-square value of log-
0·022	0·023		*p* 0·029	likelihood ratio: 9·83
—0·012	—0·021	0·050	*c* 0·042	with 6 d.o.f.

1966 Urban and Rural (*p* convictions)

Variable to be explained	Explanatory variables							
	p	*c*	*f*	*a*	*w*	*r*	*e*	const.
	—0·77	0·74	—0·19	0·79	0·26	0·43	0·20	—6·61
y	(0·24)	(0·19)	(0·08)	(0·12)	(0·12)	(0·08)	(0·10)	(1·31)
	3·22	3·95	2·24	6·89	2·09	5·37	1·99	5·06
	y	*c*	*a*	*w*	*n*	*e*	*v*	*r*	const.
	—0·21	0·35	0·20	0·09	—0·03	0·02	0·21	0·05	—1·61
p	(0·23)	(0·24)	(0·19)	(0·09)	(0·02)	(0·05)	(0·09)	(0·16)	(1·53)
	0·93	1·48	1·06	0·99	1·23	0·44	2·28	0·33	1·06
	y	*p*	*m*	*v*	*r*	*q*	const.
	—0·03	1·44	—0·03	—0·46	0·25	0·09	0·29
c	(0·11)	(0·61)	(0·15)	(0·17)	(0·11)	(0·07)	(1·26)
	0·26	2·35	0·20	2·80	2·30	1·24	0·23

Covariance matrix of residuals   Variance

0·035			*y* 0·176	Chi-square value of log-
0·014	0·030		*p* 0·042	likelihood ratio: 9·66
—0·012	—0·048	0·088	*c* 0·042	with 6 d.o.f.

Table 6.A.1 *continued*

(g) 1971 Urban and Rural (*p* clear-up)

Variable to be explained	Explanatory variables							
	p	*c*	*f*	*a*	*w*	*r*	*e*	const.
	—0·65	0·78	—0·05	0·09	0·19	0·07	—0·08	7·22
y	(0·60)	(0·43)	(0·10)	(0·21)	(0·23)	(0·04)	(0·35)	(6·18)
	1·08	1·81	0·56	0·44	0·83	1·81	0·22	1·17

Variable to be explained	Explanatory variables								
	y	*c*	*a*	*w*	*n*	*e*	*v*	*r*	const.
	—0·15	0·26	—0·25	—0·23	—0·04	—0·42	0·20	—0·02	11·61
p	(2·24)	(2·01)	(0·73)	(0·78)	(0·08)	(0·72)	(0·23)	(0·18)	(3·14)
	0·07	0·13	0·35	0·29	0·49	0·58	0·89	0·09	3·70

Variable to be explained	Explanatory variables						
	y	*p*	*m*	*v*	*r*	*q*	const.
	0·73	0·74	—0·11	—0·18	—0·02	0·02	—7·17
c	(0·30)	(0·48)	(0·18)	(0·17)	(0·05)	(0·03)	(3·54)
	2·42	1·54	0·61	1·07	0·40	0·66	2·02

Covariance matrix of residuals

			Variance	
0·034			*y* 0·106	Chi-square value of log-
0·005	0·009		*p* 0·017	likelihood ratio: 4·35
—0·025	—0·006	0·021	*c* 0·032	with 6 d.o.f.

1971 Urban and Rural (*p* convictions)

Variable to be explained	Explanatory variables							
	p	*c*	*f*	*a*	*w*	*r*	*e*	const.
	—0·43	0·98	—0·35	0·25	—0·07	0·13	0·23	—1·84
y	(1·18)	(0·58)	(0·25)	(0·42)	(0·32)	(0·09)	(1·02)	(5·91)
	0·36	1·69	1·38	0·59	0·20	1·34	0·23	0·31

Variable to be explained	Explanatory variables								
	y	*c*	*a*	*w*	*n*	*e*	*v*	*r*	const.
	1·07	—2·60	—0·08	0·50	—0·04	—1·96	—0·42	0·03	12·03
p	(2·04)	(4·44)	(1·04)	(0·79)	(0·10)	(2·47)	(0·98)	(0·13)	(17·49)
	0·52	0·59	0·08	0·64	0·36	0·79	0·43	0·26	0·69

Variable to be explained	Explanatory variables						
	y	*p*	*m*	*v*	*r*	*q*	const.
	—0·28	0·99	—0·55	—0·48	0·05	0·16	0·68
c	(0·80)	(0·86)	(0·84)	(0·37)	(0·11)	(0·14)	(2·10)
	0·35	1·15	0·66	1·33	0·46	1·10	0·33

Covariance matrix of residuals

			Variance	
0·026			*y* 0·106	Chi-square value of log-
—0·046	0·131		*p* 0·027	likelihood ratio: 2·49
0·014	—0·026	0·047	*c* 0·032	with 6 d.o.f.

Notes.

1. The cases in Tables 6.A.1. *a-g* are in the same order as in Tables 6.5 *a-g*.
   Cases *b* and *c* are identical in Tables 6.A.1 and 6.5 and have not been replicated here.

(continued)

2. The variables are scaled differently in different years. Since we have a logarithmic model, however, this makes only the constant terms non-comparable across years (they are comparable as between urban and rural for the same year). For the cases 1971 Urban and Rural, 1966 Urban and Rural, 1966 Urban and 1961 Urban constant terms which are comparable are given below for the "full model" for p clear-up (% urb form in the first two cases).

Comparable Constant Terms

1971 Urban and rural			1966 Urban and rural			1966 Urban			1961 Urban		
6·06	13·83	−2·24	−2·62	5·87	−1·18	6·33	20·13	15·23	17·57	14·79	22·39
(9·77)	(15·40)	(5·68)	(2·81)	(3·67)	(4·07)	(8·41)	(5·38)	(2·15)	(5·50)	(2·78)	(7·03)
0·62	0·90	0·39	0·93	1·60	0·29	0·75	3·74	7·07	3·20	5·31	3·19

3. For 1966 Rural (*p* convictions) we have given 3SLS estimates. FIML estimates were calculated but looked strange.
4. See Table 6.5 for further notes.

Table 6.A.2
Correlation matrices

(a) 1961 Urban

	y	p_{cup}	p_{conv}	c	f	a	w	rv	n	m	e	v	d	q
y	1·00													
p clear-up	−0·55	1·00												
p convictions	−0·35	0·46	1·00											
c	0·31	−0·07	−0·38	1·00										
f	−0·11	−0·01	−0·35	0·21	1·00									
a	0·19	−0·32	−0·11	−0·13	−0·19	1·00								
w	0·18	0·07	0·39	0·20	−0·42	0·12	1·00							
rv	0·42	−0·31	−0·04	0·18	0·07	0·18	0·03	1·00						
n	0·37	−0·52	−0·12	0·04	0·10	0·18	0·01	0·47	1·00					
m	−0·18	0·13	−0·06	−0·44	0·94	−0·06	−0·55	−0·04	0·09	1·00				
e	0·15	−0·18	−0·12	0·16	0·16	0·09	−0·17	0·19	0·43	0·04	1·00			
v	−0·16	0·41	0·38	−0·07	−0·20	−0·02	0·26	−0·13	−0·23	−0·09	−0·15	1·00		
d	0·36	−0·28	0·14	0·09	−0·13	0·21	0·30	0·85	0·49	−0·08	0·18	−0·03	1·00	
q	0·11	−0·33	0·25	0·30	−0·24	−0·27	0·50	0·13	0·04	−0·35	−0·26	0·16	−0·28	1·00

(b) 1961 Rural

	y	p_{cup}	p_{conv}	c	f	a	w	rv	n	m	e	v	d	q
y	1·00													
p clear-up	−0·95	1·00												
p convictions	−0·94	0·97	1·00											
c	0·08	−0·10	−0·05	1·00										
f	−0·02	0·00	−0·11	−0·35	1·00									
a	−0·12	−0·01	−0·01	0·12	0·14	1·00								
w	0·02	0·04	0·11	0·26	−0·29	−0·19	1·00							
rv	0·00	0·13	0·07	−0·52	0·39	−0·15	−0·28	1·00						
n	−0·25	0·33	0·33	−0·56	0·19	−0·13	−0·02	0·59	1·00					
m	0·02	0·09	0·05	−0·31	0·30	−0·13	−0·32	0·55	0·43	1·00				
e	−0·02	0·04	0·00	−0·65	0·27	0·01	−0·30	0·40	0·41	0·29	1·00			
v	−0·96	0·97	0·94	−0·13	0·01	0·03	0·04	0·12	0·33	0·08	0·06	1·00		
d	−0·02	0·16	0·12	−0·53	0·31	−0·18	−0·14	0·96	0·67	0·55	0·41	0·15	1·00	
q	−0·06	−0·12	0·18	0·38	−0·40	−0·21	0·48	−0·28	−0·03	−0·18	−0·39	0·03	−0·20	1·00

Table 6.A.2 *continued*

(c) 1961 Urban and Rural

	y	p_{cup}	p_{conv}	c	f	a	w	rv	n	m	e	v	d	q	r
y	1.00														
p clear-up	−0.85	1.00													
p convictions	−0.80	0.93	1.00												
c	0.36	−0.08	−0.02	1.00											
f	0.04	−0.01	−0.15	0.13	1.00										
a	−0.02	−0.04	−0.02	0.10	0.05	1.00									
w	0.09	0.03	0.16	0.19	−0.34	−0.04	1.00								
rv	0.38	−0.02	0.02	0.64	0.28	0.09	0.02	1.00							
n	−0.24	0.14	0.16	−0.52	0.01	−0.09	−0.03	−0.32	1.00						
m	0.20	0.04	0.03	0.25	0.29	−0.02	−0.30	0.65	−0.13	1.00					
e	−0.18	0.02	−0.03	−0.49	0.05	−0.03	−0.20	−0.44	0.59	−0.25	1.00				
v	−0.85	0.90	0.85	−0.25	−0.10	−0.01	0.08	−0.21	0.26	0.12	0.13	1.00			
d	0.37	−0.01	0.05	0.64	0.24	0.08	0.09	0.99	−0.32	0.66	−0.45	−0.20	1.00		
q	0.10	0.05	0.17	0.42	−0.23	−0.17	0.48	0.24	−0.14	−0.03	−0.40	−0.02	0.27	1.00	
r	0.34	0.02	0.05	0.61	0.16	0.00	0.08	0.87	0.35	0.62	−0.48	−0.18	0.89	0.24	1.00

(d) 1966 Urban

	y	p_{cup}	p_{conv}	c	f	a	w	rv	n	m	e	v	d	q
y	1.00													
p clear-up	−0.22	1.00												
p convictions	−0.27	0.57	1.00											
c	0.36	−0.11	−0.12	1.00										
f	−0.19	−0.17	−0.18	0.04	1.00									
a	0.80	−0.09	−0.05	0.07	−0.18	1.00								
w	0.27	0.07	0.20	0.01	−0.36	0.27	1.00							
rv	0.61	−0.27	−0.20	0.19	0.15	0.56	−0.03	1.00						
n	−0.03	0.44	−0.24	−0.08	0.23	−0.15	−0.11	0.27	1.00					
m	−0.24	0.14	−0.09	−0.29	0.28	−0.23	−0.49	−0.04	0.32	1.00				
e	0.72	0.01	−0.02	0.02	−0.13	0.85	0.13	−0.11	−0.11	−0.20	1.00			
v	−0.20	0.40	0.48	−0.31	−0.29	−0.04	0.17	0.48	−0.24	−0.12	−0.02	1.00		
d	0.30	−0.26	−0.16	0.13	0.10	0.16	0.17	0.80	0.41	−0.01	0.08	−0.15	1.00	
q	0.20	−0.13	0.03	0.44	−0.41	0.04	0.15	0.06	−0.14	−0.29	0.01	−0.06	0.07	1.00

(e) 1966 Rural

	y	p_{cup}	p_{conv}	c	f	a	w	rv	n	m	e	v	d	q
y	1·00													
p clear-up	−0·31	1·00												
p convictions	−0·43	0·37	1·00											
c	0·10	0·10	0·12	1·00										
f	−0·28	0·01	−0·35	−0·19	1·00									
a	−0·01	0·11	0·36	0·16	−0·30	1·00								
w	0·09	−0·11	0·39	0·25	−0·52	0·38	1·00							
rv	0·31	−0·17	−0·32	−0·50	0·40	−0·16	−0·36	1·00						
n	0·08	−0·13	−0·17	−0·48	0·31	−0·16	−0·20	0·72	1·00					
m	0·21	−0·05	−0·03	−0·18	0·21	0·01	−0·27	0·48	0·46	1·00				
e	0·06	−0·10	−0·06	−0·14	0·08	0·09	0·24	0·21	0·24	0·35	1·00			
v	0·15	0·24	−0·03	−0·08	−0·01	0·23	0·01	0·21	0·10	0·13	0·24	1·00		
d	0·29	−0·15	−0·24	−0·52	0·32	−0·12	−0·23	0·98	0·77	0·50	0·19	0·23	1·00	
q	0·12	−0·10	0·09	0·37	−0·41	−0·27	0·47	−0·38	−0·17	−0·27	−0·14	−0·08	−0·32	1·00

(f) 1966 Urban and Rural

	y	p_{cup}	p_{conv}	c	f	a	w	rv	n	m	e	v	d	q	r
y	1·00														
p clear-up	−0·18	1·00													
p convictions	−0·17	0·52	1·00												
c	0·57	−0·01	0·10	1·00											
f	−0·06	−0·12	−0·18	0·14	1·00										
a	0·62	−0·07	0·00	0·07	−0·17	1·00									
w	0·26	0·03	0·27	0·15	−0·36	0·26	1·00								
rv	0·65	−0·05	0·05	0·67	0·27	0·16	0·05	1·00							
n	−0·30	−0·30	−0·27	−0·56	0·09	−0·13	−0·19	−0·35	1·00						
m	0·23	0·08	0·03	0·30	0·32	−0·12	−0·26	0·59	0·12	1·00					
e	0·36	−0·03	−0·06	−0·18	−0·12	0·70	0·00	−0·05	0·02	−0·11	1·00				
v	−0·21	−0·03	0·29	−0·31	−0·26	−0·02	0·09	−0·20	−0·36	−0·14	0·09	1·00			
d	0·58	0·34	0·09	0·68	0·25	0·05	0·11	0·99	−0·05	0·60	−0·15	−0·19	1·00		
q	0·26	−0·10	0·09	0·43	−0·33	0·00	0·28	0·14	−0·25	−0·10	−0·09	−0·11	0·16	1·00	
r	0·56	0·07	0·10	0·65	0·18	0·02	0·07	0·88	−0·36	0·63	−0·14	−0·09	0·89	0·17	1·00

Table 6.A.2 continued

(g) 1971 Urban and Rural

	y	p_{cup}	p_{conv}	c	f	a	w	rv	n	m	e	v	d	q	r
y	1·00														
p clear-up	−0·50	1·00													
p convictions	−0·03	0·17	1·00												
c	0·72	−0·25	0·27	1·00											
f	−0·25	−0·02	−0·21	−0·20	1·00										
a	0·41	−0·33	0·23	0·35	−0·32	1·00									
w	0·55	−0·32	0·28	0·58	−0·42	0·31	1·00								
rv	0·67	−0·44	0·27	0·61	0·19	0·37	0·39	1·00							
n	−0·18	−0·06	−0·11	−0·25	0·33	−0·27	−0·42	−0·03	1·00						
m	0·16	−0·02	0·26	0·07	0·18	−0·08	0·03	0·32	0·09	1·00					
e	−0·08	−0·25	−0·39	−0·26	0·07	0·00	−0·18	0·03	0·15	−0·39	1·00				
v	−0·37	0·39	0·06	−0·48	−0·11	−0·25	−0·15	−0·32	0·09	0·18	−0·12	1·00			
d	0·69	−0·44	0·31	0·62	0·11	0·38	0·46	0·98	−0·03	0·37	0·00	−0·30	1·00		
q	0·55	−0·25	0·17	0·57	−0·36	0·17	0·57	0·32	−0·17	0·11	−0·26	−0·21	0·37	1·00	
r	0·67	−0·38	0·43	0·60	0·00	0·37	0·50	0·90	−0·01	0·44	−0·17	−0·23	0·94	0·49	1·00

Notes.

1. For definitions of variables see Table 5.1 and Data Appendix.
2. Lower case letters denote logarithms of upper case letters (thus all above variables are logged).
3. p_{cup} is an abbreviation for p clear-up and p_{conv} for p convictions.

7

Interpreting the Results

7.0 INTRODUCTION

The previous chapter contains the results from estimating the models and testing hypotheses using the techniques described in Chapter 5. In this chapter we look at the values and significance of the coefficients that have been obtained in the light of the hypotheses and theories discussed in Chapters 2 and 3. In those chapters we laid particular stress on deterrence theories of the determination of offence levels, which concentrate on incentives and disincentives, and on theories of the recording of offences and the labelling of offenders as advanced more recently by sociologists of deviance. Accordingly, in the discussion of our results we shall pay special attention to these theories, examining deterrence theories in § 7.2 and recording theories in § 7.3.

First, however (§ 7.1) we shall discuss those coefficients particularly relevant to another of the major themes in our study, the importance of analysing the determination of the detection rate and the size of the police force at the same time as the determination of the recorded offence rate. Thus we discuss the second and third equations of our model. We postpone to § 7.3, however, discussion of those coefficients which are likely to be particularly affected by recording phenomena.

Alternative models provide the subject matter of § 7.4 where we discuss the use of breaking-and-entering offences, the alternative measures of the detection rate (p convictions and p clear-up) and certain variables which were considered at an early stage in the analysis and subsequently discarded.

Coefficients are, in general, presented in tabular form so that it is easy to compare the results in the following ways: across years; in urban or in rural areas;[1] and using either p clear-up or p convictions. We then examine the stability of the various estimates obtained for a coefficient across different parts of the table. The values discussed are the coefficients reported in § 6.3, and subsequent sections, of the preceding chapter. These coefficients provide measures of the structural relationships between the dependent and independent variables in each equation. It is important to remember in interpreting these coefficients that all the variables were logged so that with a coefficient of 1·0 a change of 1% in an explanatory variable corresponds to a 1% change in the variable in that equation which is to be explained. In other words, these coefficients compare the effects of proportional and not absolute changes in the variables (justification for using the logarithms of variables was given in § 5.3).

In conformity with standard statistical practice, only coefficients reaching a certain level of significance are taken as representing non-negligible effects. The choice of levels depends on the context in which and the purpose for which the estimates are to be used. In this study we are examining processes which are likely to have a considerable amount of noise or randomness, theories which are imprecise, and we use measures which are not wholly satisfactory. We have, therefore, used both the conventional 5% level ($t > 1·96$) and the more liberal 20% level ($t > 1·28$). (Note that our estimates are asymptotically normal—see Chapter 6, § 6.3—and this is our justification for taking significance percentiles from the normal distribution.)

In the final section of this chapter (§ 7.5) we evaluate the overall performance of the model, both in explaining the observed variance in the level of recorded offences, the clear-up or conviction rate, and the size of the police force, and in helping us to understand the processes at work. The remainder of this introduction is devoted to a brief discussion of variance and covariance in the data and possible associated computation and estimation problems.

In any estimation exercise of this type, the likelihood of obtaining significant results depends not only on the worth of the model and the validity of the data in measuring the variables used in the model, but also on some statistical features of the data. One problem which can arise is insufficient variation in the data, that is when the observational points for a variable are all clustered around one value. For in this case statistical techniques of the type used here, which depend on the comparisons of differences and relative changes, can run into computational difficulties and produce unreliable estimates as a result of cumulative rounding errors. It is not easy to judge whether such errors are serious for any given combination of computer

---

[1] When discussing the results in this chapter, we shall often use the terms data and areas interchangeably. We shall not use capital letters for urban and rural since we are not concerned with formal titles.

programme and data set, but the following reasons lead us to suppose that, for our study, they are not. We have obtained identical results on both the Harwell Atlas and Oxford 1906A computers and (for 2SLS) using the FAKAD regression programme (written in Oxford by Emil van Broekhoven and Ken MacDonald) and SIMUL (written in LSE by Cliff Wymer). Further, an examination of the standard deviations of different variables in Table 7.1 indicates that they do not differ dramatically in orders of magnitude.

Table 7.1
Standard deviations of variables

	1961		1966	
	Urban	Rural	Urban	Rural
y	0·286	0·840	0·416	0·232
p clear-up	0·176	0·896	0·196	0·119
p conv.	0·241	0·893	0·218	0·175
c	0·120	0·124	0·135	0·126
f	0·301	0·356	0·265	0·162
a	0·151	0·382	0·303	0·071
w	0·181	0·131	0·185	0·139
rv	0·554	0·790	0·573	0·840
n	0·657	0·821	0·727	0·728
m	0·062	0·096	0·059	0·066
e	0·064	0·055	0·298	0·225
v	0·272	0·906	0·320	0·245
d	0·438	0·732	0·401	0·732
q	0·387	0·407	0·379	0·453

	1961	1966	1971
	Urban and Rural	Urban and Rural	Urban and Rural
y	0·618	0·420	0·326
p clear-up	0·580	0·170	0·131
p conv.	0·592	0·205	0·164
c	0·180	0·206	0·179
f	0·331	0·234	0·171
a	0·269	0·240	0·077
w	0·163	0·169	0·149
r	1·482	0·371	1·145
n	0·851	0·879	0·544
m	0·098	0·074	0·068
e	0·074	0·277	0·070
v	0·627	0·299	0·191
q	0·412	0·421	0·501

Note.
Variables are defined in Table 5.1. Lower case letters denote logarithms.

The presence of high inter-correlations between the exogenous variables in an equation can also cause problems; for the estimation process effectively partitions the variance in an equation. When two variables are highly inter-correlated, it may be difficult to differentiate between their respective contributions to the variance of the dependent variable. In fact, we have already taken account of some of these problems in the original specifications of the model in Chapters 4 and 5. Thus, we included only one age variable instead of a selection of those suggested by the theories. The variables population density (d), percentage of area urbanised (r) and total rateable value (rv) are also strongly inter-correlated—the correlation coefficient is over 0·8 in each data set, see Table 6.A.2 (r is, of course, irrelevant to the urban data sets). The effects they embody are, however, conceptually distinct. Thus, whilst the inter-correlations caused estimation problems (multi-collinearity) if two of these variables were included in the same equation we decided, for any given equation, to use the variable which was theoretically or from prior information particularly relevant to that equation. We were informed by the Home Office that population density is a factor in the allocation of police. Incentive theories suggest the use of the rateable value variable (rv) for the offence equation. For the urban and rural data sets we wished to distinguish urban and rural areas in each equation and thus we discarded both rv and d and included r in each equation.

Table 7.2 shows the cases where the inter-variable correlations are greater than 0·7 (the full correlation matrices are given in Table 6.A.2). The cut-off is arbitrary but it can be interpreted as follows. A regression of one variable on the other would "account" for half—or $(0·7)^2 = 0·49$ to be precise—of the variance of the independent variable (the distribution of correlation coefficients is discussed, for example, in Kendall and Stuart (1973) p. 308). Apart from the cases cited above of d, r and rv, the only other instances of high inter-correlations are:

(1) in rural areas in 1961 between p convictions, p clear-up, v and y;
(2) in urban and rural data in 1961 between p clear-up, p convictions, v and y;
(3) in urban data in 1966 between a, e and y;
(4) in rural data in 1966 between d and n; and
(5) in urban and rural data in 1971 between c and y.

The correlation between d and n does not pose a direct problem because the two variables do not appear in the same equation. The correlations between v and p, and between a and y and e and y, that is between a dependent and an independent variable, are only to be welcomed. The correlations between p and y and between c and y are, of course, of particular interest to our study. Yet these high correlation coefficients may be associated with

Table 7.2
Inter-variable correlations over 0·7 in the data sets

Year	Urban value	Rural value	Urban and rural value
1961	(rv,d) 0·8483	(p convictions, y) —0·94 (v,y) —0·96 (v,p convictions) 0·94 (p clear up, y) —0·95 (v,p clear-up) 0·97 (p convictions, 0·97 p clear-up) (d,rv) 0·97	(p convictions, y) —0·80 (v,y) —0·85 (v,p convictions) 0·85 (p clear-up, y) —0·85 (v,p clear-up) 0·90 (p convictions, p clear-up) 0·93 (d,rv) 0·99 (r,rv) 0·87 (r,d) 0·89
1966	(a,y) 0·80 (e,y) 0·72 (e,a) 0·85 (d,rv) 0·80	(d,rv) 0·98 (d,n) 0·77	(d,rv) 0·99 (r,rv) 0·88 (r,d) 0·89
1971			(c,y) 0·72 (d,rv) 0·98 (r,rv) 0·90 (r,d) 0·94

Note.
A line down the side denotes a linked set of correlations involving three or four variables.

convergence problems; we have already noticed that for the 1961 rural and urban and rural data sets the iteration procedure to find full information maximum likelihood estimates did not converge.

This leaves two cases: the high inter-correlation between v and y in 1961 in both rural and urban and rural data which negated the effect of a high correlation between v and p and thus reduced the significance of v in the corresponding estimates in § 6.3; and the high correlation between e and a in the urban data in 1966 which does not seem to have caused any problems. Overall the problems of inter-correlation do not seem to be too severe.

7.1 THE DETERMINATION OF THE DETECTION RATE AND THE NUMBER OF POLICEMEN

We discuss in this section the coefficients in the second and third equations of our model for p, the clear-up or conviction rate and c, the number of policemen *per capita*. Discussion of coefficients particularly affected by recording phenomena is postponed to § 7.3.

7.1.1 *Scale and Character of Police Work in Different Districts: The Determination of the Clear-up/Conviction Rate*

As explained in Chapter 3 (§ 3.1) the detection problem confronting the police was measured by the recorded offence rate (y) and the size of the district (n). The recorded offence rate is intended to measure the work-load. The size of the district, embodying any economies or diseconomies of scale in organisation could have been measured by any one of a number of parameters, which are all very highly inter-correlated: we have chosen the night-time, or residential, population.

The character of police work is difficult to quantify in the context of this equation. Clearly one could imagine any number of variables, but estimating their likely influence on the clear-up or conviction rate is another matter altogether. In the end we chose only one index, v, the proportion of all recorded indictable offences which were in Class I, "violent offences" (the choice is discussed in more detail in Chapter 3, § 3.1).

Table 7.3
Coefficients of certain variables in the second equation

Explana-tory variable	Variable to be explained	1961			1966			1971
		U	R	UR	U	R	UR	UR
y	p cup	—0·53**	0·23	1·59	0·45*	—0·23**	—	—
	p conv.	0·49	—0·05	6·52*	—	—0·03	—0·15*	0·77*
n	p cup	—0·06**	0·26	—0·02	—0·10**	—0·02	—0·12**	—0·05
	p conv.	—0·10*	0·26*	0·30*	—0·02	—0·03	—0·02*	—0·03
v	p cup	0·07*	1·16*	2·25*	0·12	0·16**	0·09	0·01
	p conv.	0·26*	0·87*	6·31*	0·29**	—	0·24**	—

Notes.
1. Coefficients are from Table 6.5 of Chapter 6.
2. p cup denotes p clear-up and p conv. denotes p convictions.
3. U denotes the urban data set, R the rural set, and UR the urban and rural pooled set.
4. A double asterisk denotes an asymptotic t-value greater than 1·96 and a single asterisk a t-value greater than 1·28. These correspond respectively to 5 and 20% significance levels from the normal distribution.
5. A "—" denotes that the variable was excluded from the equation in the "restricted" runs of Table 6.5.
6. Coefficients likely to be particularly affected by recording phenomena are discussed in § 7.3.

The results are presented in Table 7.3. The behaviour of y is erratic as between the different types of run: in 1961 its coefficient is significant negatively for p clear-up in urban areas and positively for p convictions in the pooled (urban and rural) data; in 1966 it is significant positively for p

clear-up in urban areas, negatively for p clear-up in rural areas, and negatively for p convictions in the pooled data; and in 1971 it is significant positively for p convictions. This suggests that if y correctly measures the scale of the detection task confronting the police, then overall a larger or smaller work-load does not change the detective efficiency of the police. It is perhaps more likely that the influence of y on p depends on recording phenomena in a way which is difficult to disentangle. For further discussion of the wealth of possibilities raised by recording phenomena, see § 7.3.

On the other hand, the coefficient of n in the equation for the detection rate behaves more consistently; in 1961 it is significant negatively for p clear-up and p convictions in urban areas and positively for p convictions in pooled and rural data; in 1966 it is significant negatively for p clear-up in both urban and pooled and for p convictions in pooled data; and elsewhere appears mostly negatively but not significantly. The significant coefficients are mostly negative and are mostly about $0 \cdot 1$ in absolute value. This is an interesting finding in view of the fact that one of the reasons for the administrative reorganisations of the police during this decade was precisely the amalgamation of small rural areas into larger ones, thereby forming (supposedly) more efficient police forces. This is reflected in the total number of observations which drops from 119 in 1961 to 110 in 1966 and 41 in 1971. (The main amalgamations in the decade under study took place in 1968.) Clearly we cannot conclude from our results that larger police forces are more efficient.

The insignificance of size of district, n, as a determinant of p in 1971 raises an interesting possibility when contrasted with its negative effect (for urban areas) in 1961 and 1966. It may be that the size of districts had reached the point where some of the advantages of scale, for example it allows the use of certain equipment, had started to offset the disadvantages, such as loss of contact with local populations and more rigid bureaucracies. In this case the reorganisations would have achieved a size of district of minimum efficiency.

It is interesting to note here that Popp and Sebold (1972) who investigated the relationship between *per capita* crime costs (both expenditures and losses due to crime) and a variety of inter-SMSA (Standard Metropolitan Statistical Area—thus cities or towns) characteristics for the U.S.A. concluded that there are decreasing returns to scale over the entire range of population sizes.

The coefficient of v in the equation for the detection rate was much more consistent: in 1961 positively significant in all runs; in 1966 positively significant for p convictions in both urban and pooled areas and for p clear-up in rural areas, and otherwise insignificant; and insignificant in 1971. The fairly high values of many of these positively significant coefficients suggest that the proportion of violence in total offences is a good indicator of the overall character of offences in an area insofar as that affects detection rates; it is not, of course, usually thought of as a policy variable.

Consideration of the second equation as a whole is deferred until after we have discussed the role of the police variables and those representing age and the proportion of working class in the population in § 7.3.

7.1.2 Recruiting a Police Force

We argued in Chapter 3, § 3.3.0, that the number of qualified persons offering themselves for work as police officers was, in the years under study, generally less than the number demanded—as represented by the "established strength" of the force. Supply was less than demand. We concluded that we should have just one equation (as opposed to one each for supply and demand) representing the determination of the number of officers in a force. In that equation we should represent supply factors, since we had argued that supply was the binding constraint. However, intensity of recruitment would affect supply and thus certain demand factors could be included insofar as they affect this intensity. In this manner we included:

(1) the offence rate (y), variations in which can be expected to affect the intensity of recruitment efforts and perhaps the supply of manpower (*via* the morale of existing police personnel);

(2) the clear-up or conviction rate (p) which may affect the intensity of recruitment efforts as well as supply (*via* morale again);

(3) the proportion of the population which is middle-class (m), whose influence on the attitudes of police authorities may help to spur recruitment and which may affect supply through its effect on the available pool of potential recruits;

(4) the proportion of recorded offences which are "violent" (v), which may have effects similar to y and p;

(5) the population density (d), (or the percentage of an area urbanised in the urban and rural sets) which may have a significant impact on recruitment efforts (demand) through its affect on patrolling requirements;[2]

(6) the unemployment rate (q) which may affect the supply of potential recruits.

---

[2] The reader will recall from § 7.0.1 that because of the high correlation between the two variables, d was included in the third equation in the runs using urban and rural data separately, but was replaced by r in runs using pooled data.

The description of reasons for including explanatory variables which has just been given makes it clear that it is difficult to form *a priori* expectations about the signs of the majority of the coefficients. All of the variables y, p, m, v embody competing pulls of factors tending to spur recruitment effort and those discouraging potential recruits from coming forward, or encouraging existing personnel to leave the force, and one should not necessarily expect the outcome of these competing effects to be the same for different years, or across urban and rural areas. On the other hand, it is reasonable to entertain strong expectations about the signs of the coefficients on d and q: we were told that population density is a factor in demand and one can suppose that high unemployment facilitates recruitment. We examine the variables in turn.

Table 7.4
Coefficients of all variables in the third equation

Explana-tory variable	Variable to be explained	1961			1966			1971
		U	R	UR	U	R	UR	UR
y	p cup	—0·65*	—0·93	0·26	—	0·18*	—	0·69**
	p conv.	—0·34*	0·96	—0·18	—0·05	0·09	—	—0·36
p	p cup	—0·57	—6·24	1·13**	—0·28*	—	1·02**	0·94*
	p conv.	—	—2·28	—0·48	—0·44**	—	1·44**	1·12
m	p cup	—0·86**	—0·11	—0·52*	—0·56**	0·11*	—0·36	—0·09
	p conv.	—1·01**	—1·19	—0·39*	—0·75**	0·23*	—0·02	—0·62
v	p cup	—0·05	5·13	—0·80**	—0·01	—	—0·36**	—0·24
	p conv.	—0·13*	2·97	0·22	—	0·01	—0·46**	—0·56
d/r	p cup	—	0·22	—0·01	0·04*	0·11**	0·31**	—0·01
	p conv.	0·07	—0·18	0·13**	0·05	—0·11**	0·24**	0·06
q	p cup	0·09**	1·30	0·03	0·06**	0·02*	0·17**	0·03
	p conv.	0·06*	0·71	0·16*	0·10**	0·02	0·07**	0·13

Note.
For the format of this Table see Table 7.3.

The coefficient on the recorded offence rate in the equation for the number of police *per capita* was rarely significant: in 1961 negatively for urban data; in 1966 positively using p clear-up in rural data; and in 1971 positively for p clear-up. Otherwise the coefficient showed a slight tendency to be negative but not significantly so; Bloch (1974) obtained a similar result in a case study of Washington. Overall the offence rate is not an important factor for either recruitment or supply (unless the effects happen to cancel).

The coefficient on p clear-up or p convictions in the equation for the number of police *per capita* is significant more frequently but its behaviour is erratic. Thus, in 1961 the coefficient was positive in pooled urban and rural data for p clear-up; in 1966 negative in urban data but positive in pooled data for both p clear-up and p convictions; and in 1971 positive for p clear-up.

Overall, therefore, it seems that p has a slightly positive effect on the size of the police force (and here we differ from Bloch (1974)). The effects of higher morale associated with higher p may, therefore, be of greater importance through lower police "quit-rates" or easier recruitment, than any allocation of police to areas with lower clear-up rates.

The coefficient on the proportion of population that is middle-class, m, also appeared significantly in the equations quite frequently. In 1961 it is strongly negative in urban data and less strongly negative, but still significant, in pooled data for both p clear-up and p convictions; in 1966 it is strongly negative in urban data but positive, although less strongly, in rural data for both p clear-up and p convictions; and it is not significant at all in 1971.

Overall one gets the impression of a quite strong negative effect which is mystifying in terms of the pressure for recruitment, but can be understood in terms of the potential supply. Thus we suppose that during the sixties, despite considerable propaganda, it was difficult to recruit from the middle class. A similar explanation is that m is acting as a substitute for w, the proportion of working class in the district.[3] In that case the interpretation would be that the higher the proportion of working class in the population the larger the size of the police force, again suggesting that supply factors dominate.

The coefficient on the proportion of violent in total offences, v, in the equation for the number of police *per capita*, is significant quite frequently and always negatively in 1961 for p convictions in urban areas and for p clear-up in pooled data; in 1966 in pooled data for both p clear-up and p convictions; and in 1971 not at all. Overall there seems to be a consistent negative effect which again lends support to the view that supply factors predominate.

The coefficient on population density, d, is also significant quite frequently and nearly always positively: in 1961 with pooled data for p convictions; in 1966 in all runs except that with urban data p convictions

---

[3] Note, however, that the negative correlation between m and w is never higher than 0.5; on the other hand, the near zero value of the correlation in 1971 would account for the insignificant result. (See the correlation tables: Chapter 6, Table 6.A.2.)

(although in the case of rural data for p convictions, the coefficient was, exceptionally, negative). It is not significant at all in 1971. Overall there seems to be a clear positive effect with a modal value of around $+0.1$. This result seems to support the hypothesis that an increased population density is seen as requiring more police coverage, so that recruiting efforts are intensified.

The coefficient on the unemployment rate, q, in the explanation of police manpower is frequently significant and always positively: in 1961 in urban data for both p clear-up and p convictions and in pooled data for p convictions: in 1966 in all runs, except that with rural data for p convictions; but not in 1971. The coefficient fluctuated around 0.1.

Thus, if there is high unemployment in an area then the problem of recruiting a police force is considerably eased.

A final assessment of the relative weights of factors tending to spur recruitment or to affect supply is deferred to § 7.5, where we discuss the substantive results concerning the system as a whole.

7.2 THE ECONOMIC FACTORS IN THE DETERMINATION OF OFFENCES

The review of "deterrence" theories in the first part of Chapter 2, § 2.2, showed how one might expect the disincentives and incentives to illegal activity to affect the rate of such activity. We argued there that the way in which these disincentives and incentives affect the individual propensity to offend could best be measured by the clear-up or conviction rate (p), the proportion of convictions for indictable offences where the offender was imprisoned (f), and the total rateable value per area (rv) respectively.[4] The expectation was that the coefficients of both p and f would be negative and that of rv positive. Becker (1968) has further argued that the coefficient of p should be larger in absolute value than that of f (see appendix to Chapter 9).

As can be seen in Table 7.5 below, the coefficients of p and f were significant at the 5% level in eighteen and at the 20% level in twenty-four out of twenty-eight cases in the equation determining the level of recorded offences. Thus both the detection rate, p, and the severity of punishment, f, affect the recorded offence and in the directions predicted by deterrence theories for the actual offence rate. We discuss the behaviour of the coefficients on p and f, in turn, below.

[4] The reader will recall from § 7.0 that because of the high correlation between the variables rv was included in the first equation in the runs using urban and rural data separately, but was replaced by r in runs using pooled data.

The coefficients of p were similar, whether p clear-up or p convictions were used, the largest difference between significant coefficients occurring in urban and rural data in 1966 where their values were, respectively —0·66 and —0·77. This similarity is quite surprising in view of the arguments in Chapter 2 (especially § 2.2 and 2.3) that, since area clear-up rates cannot be calculated from published data whilst court proceedings are widely publicised, one might expect the perceived probability of capture (as an element in the calculations by the potential offender) to be more sensitive to conviction rates than clear-up rates.

The coefficient of p in the determination of the offence rate varied around —0·95 in all data sets in 1961; varied around —0·75 in urban and pooled data sets in 1966 (being insignificant in rural data); and in 1971 its value remained in the same range as 1966. The effect of p on y seems to have decreased. A possible explanation is that official statistics have become more unreliable as measures of perceived probabilities of apprehension.

Table 7.5
Coefficients of "Economic" variables in the first equation

		1961			1966			1971
		U	R	UR	U	R	UR	UR
p	p cup	—0·97**	—0·93**	—0·94**	—0·79*	0·25	—0·66**	—0·80*
	p conv.	—1·00**	—0·98**	—0·99**	—0·84**	—0·19	—0·77**	—0·69*
f	p cup	—0·12*	—0·11*	0·05	—0·28**	—0·27**	—0·16*	—0·10
	p conv.	—0·34**	—0·31**	—0·19**	—0·27**	—0·59**	—0·20**	—0·36**
rv (r in UR)	p cup	0·02	0·18**	0·15**	0·20**	0·38**	0·43**	0·08*
	p conv.	0·16**	0·14**	0·20**	0·18**	0·35**	0·43**	0·15**

Note.
For the format of this table, see Table 7.3.

The behaviour of the coefficient of f varied between runs using p clear-up and p convictions, for example, in pooled data in 1961 the coefficient was positive (although admittedly small and insignificant) for p clear-up and —0·19 for p convictions. The coefficients in runs with p clear-up were considerably smaller in absolute value than those with p convictions in every case except for urban data in 1966.

Whereas the coefficients on f in the equation for the recorded offence rate do not show any systematic difference between the seven data sets, it is noticeable that the coefficients in the 1961 and 1966 pooled data sets are considerably smaller in absolute value than in the corresponding sets using urban and rural data separately. This, combined with the observation that the average value of f is smaller in rural than in urban areas in both 1961 and 1966 (see Table 7.6), lends support to the argument in § 6.1 that the urban and rural areas should be treated differently. The relationship between y and f for the three data sets is represented diagrammatically in Fig. 7.1 as follows:

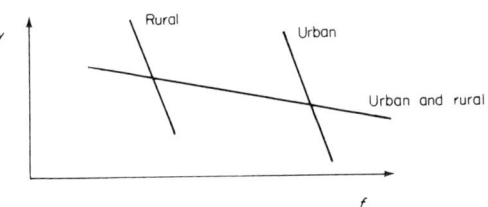

Fig. 7.1.

The figure ignores, of course, any differences between urban and rural areas associated with other variables.

Table 7.6

Average value of F—the proportion of those convicted who are incarcerated

	1961	1966	1971
Urban	0·17	0·19	
Rural	0·15	0·17	
Urban and Rural	0·16	0·19	0·15

Note.
The entry is the geometric mean of F across the sample indicated.

The tentative conclusion is, then, that the effect of imprisonment has remained quite stable over this decade. We described in Chapters 2 and 3 a number of reasons why we might observe a negative relation between recorded offences and the severity of punishment. In Chapter 2 we concentrated on deterrence theories. There is also the possibility, described in § 3.4.2, that individuals will respond to high levels of the probability and severity of punishment by taking care that their actions are not labelled as offences; and finally there is the possibility that the prevention of certain criminal acts by imprisonment contributes significantly to a negative relation.[6] We argued in § 2.2.3 that this last effect was unlikely to be significant in the interpretation of the actual offence rate.

---

[6] These do not exhaust the possible interpretations (see Gibbs (1975)) but we regard these three effects as the most important.

The magnitude of the coefficients of p and f are of particular interest for both policy and theoretical debate. The coefficient estimated for f is rarely more than 0.3 in absolute value. This seems to imply that the use of a custodial sentence *per se* does not have a very large effect on the recorded offence rate. Thus, using a coefficient of 0.25 as an example (this is close to the 1966 urban estimates), custodial measures for 24% as opposed to 20% of those found guilty would decrease the number of offences by 5%; but this implies increasing the custodial population (in an already over-crowded institutional system) by 20%. Moreover, it seems reasonable to suppose that, if a change to more custodial sentences (from non-custodial ones) does not have much effect, gradations within custodial sentences, such as variations in length, will also have little effect. On the other hand, our estimates suggest that changes in p have more substantial effects. Thus, a 10% increase in p from, say, 50% to 55% would decrease offences by 7.5%, or more. But as we shall show later, it appears difficult to know how to change p systematically.

Other studies have also shown that, if measures of p and f similar to ours are used, then both variables affect the recorded offence rate. Ehrlich (1967) concluded that the likelihood of arrest was more of a deterrent than the level of punishment (this is an unpublished paper quoted in Becker (1968)). As a result of a series of studies with others, Votey (1969) summarizes one of their main results as "The decline in police effectiveness, as measured by the ratio of offences cleared by arrest to known offences (clearance ratio) . . . . . has encouraged criminality and induced higher rates of growth in *per capita* offence rates" (p. 3). These, and several other authors used single-equation models, but Swimmer (1974) obtained a similar result with a two-equation model. There appears to be a consensus in the literature (see Silver (1974)) that p and f or similar variables constitute effective deterrents.

In our study, although y decreased as both p and f increased, the absolute value of the coefficient of p was often as much as three times or more greater than that of f. As explained in the previous chapter (in § 6.2.3) it proved possible to test statistically the proposition that the elasticity of y with respect to p was different from the elasticity with respect to f. Our test suggested significant differences between these elasticities in 1961 urban data sets, some 1966 sets, but not in 1971 sets. Thus the test gives some support to the notion that the two elasticities are significantly different.

We must take care, however, in drawing conclusions about individual behaviour and underlying utility functions from any claim on the relative magnitude of our estimated elasticities. And this is quite apart from the ubiquitous recording problem and inadequacies of our measure of punishment as imposed by the court. We noted in Chapter 2 (see § 2.2.3) that the actual penalty received in court is only a part of the punishment as seen by the individual. We quoted the work of Willcock (1974) which showed that, for a sample of adolescents, considerable weight was attached to the shame of appearance in court. And Belson (1975b) found in his study of 500 adolescents that family disapproval was a much more powerful deterrent to delinquent activity than the perceived likelihood of being caught. Accordingly we presented formally in the appendix to Chapter 2 a measure of punishment which included a fixed element "J" for the perceived costs of court appearance and public conviction. If such perceived costs were on average several times as large as those inflicted by the court, then even given our estimates, the responsiveness to perceived total punishment might indeed be greater than that to the probability of apprehension: for then the decrease in offences associated with a given percentage increase in measured punishment corresponds to a much smaller percentage increase in perceived total punishment. Thus the responsiveness to percentage changes in such punishment may be much larger than indicated by our estimates of the elasticity with respect to measured punishment (see the appendix to Chapter 2 for further discussion). And given social attitudes towards arrested persons (whatever sentences they receive) perceived costs of public convictions may be very large.

As can be seen from Table 7.5, one of the most impressive findings in the first equation was that the coefficient of rv, or of r in pooled data sets[7], was significant in every data set (except the 1961 urban set for p clear-up). The coefficient was always positive, varying between 0·08 and 0·43 in cases where it was significant. There was no systematic difference between the coefficients in runs involving p clear-up or p convictions. The estimated coefficients in runs with rural data sets tended to be larger than with urban data sets. The main differences, however, occurred between the years, since the coefficients in 1966 were considerably larger (averaging around 0·3) than those in the other two years (averaging around 0·15).

Our result is, therefore, clear: areas with relatively high rateable values have higher recorded rates of offences. Given the high inter-correlations between d, r and rv, this could be interpreted in terms of the anomic effects of overcrowding or urbanisation on the motivations to illegal activity. We are, however, inclined to a straightforward interpretation in terms of the opportunities for illegal acquisition of wealth for two reasons: first, the constancy of the effect in urban areas and rural areas, would be implausible if rv were acting as a substitute for either d or r; and secondly, our preference for using overcrowding in the home rather than d as a measure of pressures

[7] We use r rather than rv because we wanted to capture the town-country effect; we could not use both as they are closely correlated (around 0·9). Moreover, both are also closely correlated with population density, so that we cannot be sure that we are capturing the opportunity effect (of more booty available) or the pressures of urban living. (These effects are not conceptually entirely distinct, of course.)

on space as affects individuals (see § 6.8 for the results and § 2.3.7 and 7.4.2 for a discussion). The opportunity effect also seemed to be more plausible on *a priori* grounds (see Chapter 2).

We thus take our results as providing support for Wilkins' supposition (1964) that a proportion of all property transactions will always be illegal. Given that the majority of recorded indictable offences—which is our y— are property offences, the volume of illegal transactions will be then larger if the total volume of property transactions is larger in any one area. Thus, any structural shift or acceleration in the commission of property offences should be calculated over and above a "natural" rise consequent upon any increases in transactions or wealth.

Clearly enough the opportunities for offending, the probability of apprehension and its likely consequences, do have an effect which appears relatively consistently in all of our data sets. Nevertheless, doubts remain as to the appropriate interpretation of the results because of theoretical difficulties and recording problems. Thus for example, the likelihood of detection and the severity of punishment if caught, may affect the precautions which an offender takes in such a way as to affect the probability of the incident being recorded as an offence.

Discussion of recording problems is presented in the next section.

7.3 THE RECORDING PROBLEM

We have reserved for this section consideration of those variables which are particularly likely to be associated with recording phenomena. These are the following: the extent of social control, measured by the number of serving police officers per head of population (c); a measure of the resources devoted to social control (e); and the two crucial sociological variables, the proportion of young people (a) and the proportion of working-class people (w) in the local population.

These are the variables for which the results varied widely between data sets. This variation is just what was anticipated in Chapter 3. We suggested there (§ 3.5) that changes in police organisation, public attitudes and police-public relations were likely to give rise to considerable changes in recording phenomena. And we described the important changes which had taken place in the 1960s.

7.3.1 *The Criminal Statistics, Police Organisation and Police-Public Relations in England and Wales in the 1960's*

We saw in § 3.5 that there had been major changes in police organisation in England and Wales in the 1960s. Partly as a result of this, but for other reasons too, police-public relations changed considerably. We argued that these changes would imply substantial shifts in recording phenomena across years; we argued further that these recording phenomena were likely to differ considerably in their impact as between urban and rural areas. These provided important reasons for treating the data from different years separately and similarly for urban and rural areas.

We shall now examine in more detail the effect the changes in recording phenomena may have had on our coefficients. In § 3.5 and 3.6 we distinguished, as a consequence of more police in an area, three separate effects in the process of generating recorded offences. We called these creating, reporting and deterrent effects and summarised their impact on the coefficients on the number of policemen in the model in Table 3.7 which we reproduce below:

		Offence rate	Detection rate
Creating effect		+	+
Reporting effect	Urban	+	—
	Rural	+	+
Deterrent effect	Urban	—	—
	Rural	0	0

To recap, an entry in the first row, for example, of + for the offence rate and + for the detection rate means that more policemen *per capita* in an area will imply, through the creating effect, more offences and a higher detection rate. The creating effect refers to the recording of events by policemen and the reporting effect the reporting of events by the public to the police. The deterrent effect is the discouragement of offences, for a given actual detection rate, by the presence of more police through a higher perceived detection rate. Detailed justification for our assumptions on the signs in the array are given in § 3.6. We turn now to an examination of how these effects may have combined in the changing circumstances of the 1960s to produce the results which we found.

7.3.2 *The Effect of* c *and* e *on* y *and* p

The behaviour of the coefficients across years and for urban and rural areas is presented in Table 7.7. It will be seen that there are indeed sharp differences between data sets and we can point to some general patterns.

Broadly speaking, the number of policemen, c, seems to be a more important variable than expenditure on the police. The role of the latter is confined (as regards significant coefficients) to a positive effect on recorded

Table 7.7

Coefficients of police activity variables in the first and second equations

Explanatory variable	Variable to be explained	Measurement of p	1961 U	1961 R	1961 UR	1966 U	1966 R	1966 UR	1971 UR
c	y	p cup	—	0.48	0.01	−0.56	3.25**	0.70**	0.70*
		p conv.	—	−0.22	−0.37	—	2.93**	0.74***	0.85***
e	y	p cup	−0.30*	0.70	0.18	0.45**	—	0.21**	—
		p conv.	0.02	−0.16	0.31	0.39***	—	0.17***	—
c	p	p cup	−0.46**	4.46	1.63*	−1.57**	—	−0.61*	−0.47**
		p conv.	−1.03*	4.45*	5.09**	—	—	0.39***	−1.27
e	p	p cup	—	4.07	−0.61	—	−0.09	—	−0.73**
		p conv.	0.68	4.09	−3.01*	0.09	0.00	—	−0.20*

Note.

For the format of this Table see Table 7.3.

offences in 1966 and a negative one on the clear-up rate in 1971. The behaviour of the coefficients on c shows interesting changes across the years. Again speaking broadly, in 1961 an increase in the number of police in an area did not significantly affect the recorded offence rate but had a negative effect on the clear-up rate in urban areas. In 1966 more police increased the recorded offence rate, whilst more police decreased the clear-up rates; and in 1971 more police increased the recorded offence rate and decreased the clear-up rate.

The balance seems to have shifted in the way in which the available set of illegal activities is transformed into the set of recorded offences. In so far as the above distinction between "creating", "reporting", and "deterrent" effects is of value, it suggests the following: in respect of the offence rate the "creating" and "reporting" effects increased in relation to the "deterrent" effect. Thus the positive impact on the recorded offence rate of the "creating" and "reporting" effects were cancelled by the negative impact of the "deterrent" effect in 1961, but as the former two become more important during the decade, with the increased formalisation of police practice, the positive effects of more policemen on the recorded offence rate became dominant.

The effect of more police on the clear-up rate was broadly speaking negative throughout the decade. This suggests that the negative influence of the "reporting" and "deterrent" effects on the clear-up rate may have sharpened to offset the positive influences of increases in the "creating" effect. Thus, increased public awareness of the police and crime may have led to more reports of minor events which are difficult to solve or not worthwhile solving. And an increasing role for the "deterrent" effect on the clear-up rate could have been a consequence of a similar phenomenon. Recall (§ 3.6) that the strength of the "deterrent" effect is higher where a larger number of offences in the recorded statistics are contributed by the less professional offenders. An increase in this proportion over the decade is consistent with both the changes in "reporting" effects just noted, and a possible increase in care by the more professional offender to prevent his offences from being recorded.

These statements are made within the context of the historical observations made earlier. But it should be noted that our interpretation that increases in recorded crime statistics are due to changes in police practice as well as to changes in the underlying phenomena which they are supposed to denote, also accords with the findings of several other quantitative studies (as well as much of the literature cited in Chapter 3). Thus, Ahamad (1967) showed that the number of police per head of population was one of three significant variables in accounting for the increases in seventeen types of recorded crime in England and Wales from 1950 to 1967. Greenwood and

Wadycki (1973) used a 2-equation model to explain the level of expenditure (corresponding to our *e*) provided for, and the level of service (as measured by prevailing crime rates—corresponding to our *y*) provided by, law enforcement. They found that ". . . given the distribution of total crime between reported and unreported, and given the efficiency of additional police personnel in detecting relative to preventing crime, additional policemen result in an increase rather than a decrease in measured crime rates . . ." (p. 138).

The implications of such findings for researchers using published criminal statistics are examined in some detail in Chapter 8. What is clear, at this stage, is that in order to understand the effects of changes in the amount of, or expenditure on, the police force on the recorded offence and clear-up rates, we have to consider changes in the way in which (illegal) activity becomes recorded as offences.

7.3.3 Social Change and the Arrested Population

There is a variety of social trends which affect the nature of police operations. Thus there is the commonplace sociological observation that increased industrialisation and urbanisation are accompanied by looser communal networks of informal social control. It could be argued that previously deviance was either contained in fact or, if not, then absorbed into a local culture; and further that any incidents of deviance which could not be so contained were not necessarily reported to the police or that, if they were so reported, witnesses were reluctant to give evidence. In such a story, the self-policing elements in the system also become weaker: thus contacts between people become impersonal so that there are no effective ties to act as informal controls; with technological change new laws are enacted, thus drawing more activities into the criminal net; and as society develops it becomes more difficult to relate private to public interests with a consequent increase in the tolerance of illegality.

From our point of view, a loosening of these informal networks would mean two things: first, a large increase in offences reported to the police without there necessarily being any actual increase in deviance; and secondly, an increase in the likelihood of an offence being cleared-up or leading to a conviction (if we suppose witnesses become more willing to offer evidence). Since, at least according to sociological folklore, these ties were greatest in working-class areas which suffered most upheavals from "redevelopments" in the fifties and sixties, such an effect would be most noticeable in areas with a large working-class population.

Another important phenomenon was the growth of an autonomous youth sub-culture with distinctive mores and dislike of any formal authority: for example, "teddy boys" first hit the headlines in the mid-1950s and the Campaign for Nuclear Disarmament (CND), with its predominantly youthful backing, was active in 1959-62. One of the crucial features of this development was a pronounced antagonism to the police. Although the rationale for increased mobility and procedural changes in police work must also be seen in the general context of a drive for "efficiency" in government departments[8], some of the changes in police organisation (such as juvenile liaison schemes or less formal treatment of juvenile affairs) were specifically designed to improve relations with youth.[9]

We shall now try to show how the changing circumstances of the 1960s were reflected in the coefficients concerning the two socio-demographic variables we included.

7.3.4 *The effect of* a *and* w *on* y *and* p

It can be seen from Table 7.8, that, as for the coefficients of c and e, coefficients of the variables measuring the proportion of youth and working class in the population of an area (a and w) were also different for different data sets. We discuss them in turn below.

In 1961 the coefficient of a was negative and significant in the first equation in both runs in rural and pooled data, whilst it was negative and significant in the second equation in urban data, but positive and significant in pooled data for p clear-up. In 1966 in the first equation, the coefficient was significantly positive in urban areas and more strongly so in pooled data, whilst it was negatively significant in the second equation in urban data for p clear-up and positively significant in rural and pooled data for p convictions. And finally in 1971 it was not significant in either equation.

In the equation for the recorded offence rate, although there are differences between estimates using p clear-up or p convictions and between urban, rural or pooled data sets, the most striking differences are between the years. The changes in the coefficients accord partly with our expectations. Thus, the negative effect of the adolescent age structure on the recorded crime rate in 1961, which corresponds to an informality of police practice *vis-à-vis* youth in the fifties, changed into a positive effect in 1966 as a change in those police practices took place. Our attempt to look at age bands narrower than the 15-24 group used here was not particularly successful (see Carr-Hill, Hope and Stern (1972)).

---

[8] We do not want to deny the plausibility of a *post-hoc* technocratic thesis such as that of J. K. Galbraith (1967) or H. Marcuse (1964), which shows how these elements are related, but they lack the required analytic depth to account for changes in police procedures.

[9] It is true that the changes came after the Royal Commission on Police (1962) and thus represent a somewhat tardy response to the growth of youth culture.

The coefficients again cease to be significant in 1971, which within the above framework could mean one of two things:

(i) that the special antagonism between the youth and the police was fading away in the context of a general decline in relations between the police and all sections of the public; or

(ii) that the procedures developed by the police during the decade for dealing with the adolescent delinquent (a wide variety of measures ranging from the "short, sharp shock" of the detention centre to the "detached youth workers" reporting directly to the police authorities) were effective.

The first of these explanations seems to us to be rather more plausible.

In the equation for the determination of the detection rate on the other hand, the main difference is between urban and rural areas. The coefficient is generally negative in urban areas and positive in rural areas. There are two possible explanations that fit into our general scheme of interpretation. First, that clearing-up an offence involving a young lad leads to fewer associated clear-ups (e.g., *via* offences taken into consideration). Secondly, that young offenders merge more easily with others of their age group in urban areas and so are less easily identifiable.

In 1961 the coefficient of w, the proportion of working-class people in the population, was positively significant in the first equation with every data set, whilst in the second equation it was negative in both rural and pooled data (though significantly so in the latter for p convictions), but positively significant in urban data. In 1966 the coefficient of w in the first equation was positively significant in every case, except in rural data for p convictions and in pooled data for p clear-up; and in the second equation it was positively significant for p convictions in all data sets. In 1971 the coefficient was insignificant in both equations.

The effect of the proportion of working class on the recorded offence rate seems uniformly positive for 1961 and 1966, although the size of the coefficient seems to have decreased a little. This is consistent both with the theory that the working class is more criminogenic and the theory that they are more liable to be labelled as offenders. For further discussion see Chapter 8 (§ 8.1). The interpretation of the behaviour of this variable in the equation for the detection rate is complex. There was a change between 1961 and 1966 in that its significance seems to have increased. This may be explained in terms of the loosening of informal social controls in working-class areas so that there was less mutual protection. The result in 1971 is not, however, consistent with any trend. In any event it is clear that we do not have a uniform effect of the proportion of working class in a population on either the clear-up or conviction rate.

Table 7.8

Coefficients of age and social class in first and second equations

Explana-tory variable	Variable to be explained	Measure-ment of p	1961 U	1961 R	1961 UR	1966 U	1966 R	1966 UR	1971 UR
a	y	p cup	—	−0·16*	−0·14*	0·40**	—	0·79**	—
		p conv.	—	−0·15*	−0·11*	0·41**	—	0·81**	0·31
w	y	p cup	0·37*	0·62**	0·36**	0·42**	0·26*	0·09	0·22
		p conv.	0·57**	0·90**	0·61**	0·44**	0·20	0·24**	—
a	p	p cup	−0·17*	−0·15	0·22*	−0·51*	0·13	−0·04	−0·25
		p conv.	−0·41*	−0·23	0·06	−0·15	0·55*	0·15*	—
w	p	p cup	0·19**	−0·59	−1·10	0·11	−0·14	—	—
		p conv.	0·49*	−0·06	−4·12*	0·21*	0·36*	0·06*	0·25

Note.

For the format of this Table see Table 7.3.

We should now ask about the relationship between our results and findings about the social class distribution of offenders. On the one hand every investigation of arrested or imprisoned offenders shows a clear majority of lower-status individuals, but on the other, interviews of sample populations about what offences they will admit to having committed are equivocal, any difference corresponding to social status which appears is much smaller (see § 2.2.5). Quantitative studies comparable with ours have, on the whole, found a relationship between recorded offence rates and variations in the social composition of the population (for example, nearly all U.S. studies distinguish black and white populations). However, the prominent role which we have attributed to recording phenomena in our interpretation implies that, unless such phenomena are taken into account, one cannot draw any conclusions about the differences in offending behaviour of different social groups.

7.4 ALTERNATIVE MODELS

Up to now, we have concentrated on interpreting the results presented in § 6.2 and § 6.3 of the previous chapter. But Chapter 6 also presented several other sets of results which have substantive implications for both theory and policy. In this section we consider the implications of the estimates that we obtained for some of the alternative models presented in Chapter 6.

We first look at the results obtained by using breaking-and-entering offences, instead of all indictable offences, together with the corresponding clear-up rate. Breaking-and-entering offences were used for two reasons: first, because some writers have claimed that nearly all such offences are reported so that the recording problem, which has been a major theme in this book, would not arise; secondly, it might appear to avoid the criticism that no one process can be expected to generate a heterogenous phenomenon such as all indictable offences. The full estimates for this model were presented in § 6.4. Secondly, we discuss our decision to exclude unemployment from the first and second equations. This was justified theoretically in Chapters 2 and 3 and supported by the tests in § 6.2.1. We also discuss briefly another variable which was excluded from our principal model, the level of overcrowding, for which the results were presented in § 6.8.

Finally, we present an assessment of the comparative worth of models with p clear-up and with p convictions. Throughout this chapter we have discussed both in the context of each coefficient. Here we return to the basic question posed in Chapter 4, namely whether one is a better measure than the other of the likelihood of apprehension as viewed by the potential offender.

7.4.1 *Do We Avoid the Recording Problem by Using Breaking-and-Entering Offences?*

The results using breaking-and-entering offences are given in Table 6.8. Since the crux of the recording problem in our model is the behaviour of *c, e, a,* and *w,* we concentrate on the coefficients of those variables here (see Table 7.9).

The coefficients of *c* and *e* in the first equation are significant negatively in two cases in 1961, significant positively in all but one case in 1966, and not significant in 1971. As compared to the behaviour of *c* and *e* when using all indictable offences (given in Table 7.7), the coefficients fluctuate even more from year to year, going from negative in 1961 to positive in 1966 and insignificant in 1971. Within the framework presented in § 7.3, this would suggest that police concentrated their energies on breaking-and-entering offences relative to other types in the middle part of the decade but not at the beginning and the end. We are aware of no evidence which makes it possible to evaluate this possibility.

The coefficients of *c* and *e* in the second equation also vary considerably. In 1961 there is one significant negative coefficient, in 1966 there are two negative and one positive, and in 1971 none is significant. The main difference seems to be that between the significant negative coefficients estimated for all indictable offences in 1971 and the insignificant ones estimated for breaking-and-entering offences. However, as few coefficients in Table 7.9 are significant, it is perhaps unwise to speculate further.

The coefficients of *a* and *w* in the first equation behave very similarly to those in the principal model (given in Table 7.8) using all indictable

Table 7.9
Coefficients of police activity, age and social class variables
in the model using breaking-and-entering offences

Explanatory variable	Variable to be explained	U	1961 R	UR	U	1966 R	UR	1971 UR
c	y	—4·60	—2·49*	—0·85*	—5·01	2·18*	0·82**	—0·18
e	y	3·24	—0·47	0·13	0·89**	0·64**	0·79**	—2·38
c	p	—0·95*	1·40	0·50	—1·41**	0·55	—1·56*	—0·16
e	p	0·57	0·19	—0·03	—0·23	0·36**	—0·61	—0·28
a	y	—1·94	—0·21*	—0·15	—0·16	—0·11	0·49**	—1·46
w	y	2·55*	0·73*	0·92**	1·20**	0·33	0·79**	—0·76
a	p	—0·50*	0·10	0·06	—0·25	0·02	—0·91*	—0·13
w	p	0·99*	—0·30	—0·66*	—0·36	—0·16	—1·24*	—0·01

Note.
For the format of this Table see Table 7.3. *y* refers to breaking-and-entering offences only and *p* to the clear-up rate for such offences.

offences. Thus in 1961 the coefficient of a is negatively significant in one case and that of w is positively significant in all three; in 1966 the coefficient of a is positively significant in one case and that of w in two; and in 1971 neither is significant. The variation in the signs of coefficients from year to year is similar to that in the first equation of the principal model (although there are less significant coefficients) so that similar interpretations could apply.

The coefficients of a and w in the second equation diverge from those in the principal model in differing degrees. In 1961 the coefficient of a is negatively significant in one run, whilst that of w is negatively significant in one run but positively in another; in 1966 the coefficients of both a and w are negatively significant in one run, but neither is significant in 1971. Thus in the second equation the behaviour of a is similar to that in the principal model, whilst the effect of w is more negative.

Overall, although the coefficients of these four variables are not similar to the principal model (Table 7.8) in every respect in the two equations, the differences are not all that marked. Moreover, they are alike in the sense that they change sign in more or less the same way between the years. This suggests that the common belief that there is no serious recording problem for breaking-and-entering offences may be misplaced. The explanation of variation in the level of breaking-and-entering offences and related detections and apprehensions cannot be disentangled from changes in police practice, any more than for all indictable offences.

7.4.2 Overcrowding in the Household and Unemployment as Additional Variables in the First Equation

We saw in § 6.8 that the coefficient on the (log of) percentage of households with less than ½ person per room (h) when this variable was included in the first equation was always negative. We noted, however, that the effect of its introduction was to render insignificant the coefficients on some other variables, that the coefficient on h was itself not strongly significant and that one would not, in general, reject the hypotheses that h should be excluded from the model: we therefore decided that we should leave it out. We record here, however, that the sign of the coefficient is in accord with theories which suggest that overcrowding in the home can generate crime.

We argued in Chapters 2 and 3 that unemployment should be included as an explanation for the number of policemen, since it measures the availability of alternative opportunities. We argued further that it should not be included as an explanation of the recorded offence rate or the detection rate in addition to those variables already included in the model. These arguments were broadly speaking supported by the tests presented in § 6.2.1, which allowed us to accept the null hypothesis that unemployment should be excluded from the equations for the recorded offence rate and the clear-up rate. Our conclusion, then, is that unemployment does not play a significant role in the generation of recorded offences.

7.4.3 *Comparing the Clear-up and Convictions Models*

We have discussed runs using both p clear-up and p convictions because each has advantages and drawbacks as an indicator of the risk of detection as perceived by the potential offender. The central importance of this variable in our whole discussion justified this special treatment. In this sub-section we shall compare the overall performance of these indicators in their respective models in three ways. First, we shall look at the comparative value of the coefficients of p when it appears in both the first and third equations; secondly, we shall see how far it is possible to "explain" the variation in each through the reduced form of the second equation; and, finally, by comparing the overall plausibility of the two sets of results.

The coefficients of p in the first equation are, as was remarked in § 7.2.1 in our comments on Table 7.5, similar for the two measures. The most important differences occur in 1966: in rural areas both the p clear-up coefficient at 0·25 and the p convictions coefficient at —0·19 are insignificant, but they are of opposite signs; and in the pooled data the p clear-up coefficient is —0·66 and the p convictions coefficient is —0·77, both significant. The small differences observed slightly favour the use of p convictions on the grounds of stability across data sets, but this is by no means conclusive.

As can be seen from Table 7.4, the coefficients of p in the third equation are not so close. In 1961 all of the coefficients are insignificant and negative, except for the coefficient of p clear-up in pooled data, which is significant and positive. In 1966 both coefficients are negative and significant in urban data (—0·28 and —0·44) but neither appears at all in rural data, and both are positive and significant in pooled data (1·02 and 1·44), which may well reflect the sharp difference between the results for urban and rural data in 1966. In 1971 the p clear-up coefficient is significant at 0·94 but that for p convictions is insignificant at 1·12. In this case, then, there are some differences and the performance of p clear-up in terms of significant coefficients is slightly better.

In the derived reduced forms the extent to which the variables included "explained" p is given in Table 7.10.

In every case the variables included explain the clear-up rate better than the conviction rate. This is probably because the number of convictions depends not only on the police but also on the working of the judicial system for which no corresponding variables were included in the model.

Table 7.10
Proportion of variance "Explained" in the second
equation of the derived reduced form

| | 1961 | | | 1966 | | | 1971 |
	U	R	UR	U	R	UR	UR
p clear-up	0·50	0·96	0·84	0·45	0·22	0·25	0·36
p convictions	0·30	0·90	0·77	0·26	0·21	0·16	0·34

Note.

The figures in this table are taken from Table 6.10. The sense in which the figures in the table give the "explained" proportion of the variance of p is described in § 5.5.

Moreover, any variables relevant to this process are unlikely to depend on the characteristics of a particular area so that there will be a large unexplained variance.

It is noticeable that this better performance of p clear-up is not reflected in the number of significant variables which occur in the structural equation explaining p clear-up and p convictions (see Table 7.3). Indeed, although there are differences between the runs, there is not much distinction either in terms of a pattern of significant variables or more particularly in terms of the crucial endogenous variables. Thus y is significant for p clear-up in urban areas in 1961 and 1966 and in rural data in 1966 and for p convictions in the data for pooled urban and rural areas in all three years. There is a broad similarity in both the significance and the signs of the coefficients of a, c and e for particular data sets. If we confine ourselves to differences between significant coefficients, the only exception is pooled data for 1966, when the signs of the coefficients of c are in opposite directions. However, there are a number of cases where the coefficient is significant in only one of the two runs, but nothing to indicate a preference for one measure or the other.

Overall, therefore, there is very little to choose between the models involving p clear-up and p convictions. The question of which better portrays the role that the probability of apprehension plays in determining individual behaviour remains open. In certain respects, it is true that p clear-up runs behave slightly better than the p convictions, but the difference is minor.

7.5 SOME CONCLUDING REMARKS

We shall give general assessments of the theories embodied in our models in the light of our estimates in the concluding sub-section of this chapter. First, however, we look at three aspects of our models: the ways in which the imposition of a formal structure on the theories discussed in Chapters 2 and 3 has produced a useful interpretative framework; secondly, the overall explanatory power of the variables included in the model and the behaviour of the "unexplained" residuals; and, thirdly, the lessons that can be drawn for policy.

7.5.1 *The Advantages and Difficulties of a Formal Structure*

The use of a formal structure has meant that we have been able to test precisely several of the hypotheses in the literature about such matters as the comparative deterrent effects of the probability and the consequences of apprehension, the relevance of unemployment as an important determinant of offending behaviour, the factors affecting arrest rates, or the effect of police manpower. This is an important advantage which has prompted us to pose questions about the original theories themselves. But there are also difficulties associated with the rigidity which a quantitative model of this sort imposes.

First, we must ask to what extent the model is well specified: the question can be considered from several points of view. Thus there is the issue of whether or not variables chosen to represent conceptually different effects are too highly inter-correlated to make distinctions in practice.[10] The correlation matrix was presented in the previous chapter and discussed in the first section of this chapter. The only correlations high enough to present problems were between population density and total rateable value per area for urban areas, and between these two variables and percentage urbanisation for the pooled data sets. Our choice between these variables in any one equation was based on prior knowledge or theory but we did not include more than one of the three in any equation. Our success in obtaining relatively satisfactory significance levels in respect of most of the coefficients, suggests that this does not appear to have been a problem for other variables.

Another sense in which the specification of the model is important is whether or not we have chosen the "correct" set of endogenous variables. As was explained in Chapter 5 (§ 5.3), there were, at the time the computations were performed, no tests to decide the question statistically. We can assert, however, that the estimations obtained do make sense in the light of the formal model proposed. Similarly, there can be no formal test of whether a given restriction in a just-identified model is correct. We

[10] For example, inter-correlations between the proportion of young males in different age groups meant that our attempts at further disaggregation of the age structure of the population were unsuccessful (see Carr-Hill, Hope and Stern (1972)).

emphasized in Chapter 5 that we have to have the confidence, based on theory or knowledge or common sense, or whatever, to exclude explanatory variables from some equations but not from others. Without these exclusion restrictions (or other similar constraints) estimation cannot proceed. The particular restrictions used should, of course, be justified. We do not pretend to be totally happy with our solutions to the identification problems and we explained in Chapter 5 that our worries were particularly associated with the first equation, that for the recorded offence rate. We are somewhat reassured *ex post*, however, since we find that the coefficients in the first equation fit fairly well with received theory. For example, the coefficient on the endogenous variable p in the first equation was uniformly negative just as most theories discussed suggested it should be.

We note here that recently other authors have taken account of the simultaneity existing between the level of recorded offences and the efficiency of police operations (see, for example, Ehrlich (1973), Swimmer (1974) and Vandaele (1973)). None of them, however, has been careful to model formally the process of recording, to distinguish between different aspects of the efficiency of police operations, or even to analyse the different determinants of the actual level of police manpower. And our emphasis on recording phenomena has stood us in good stead in this chapter where we had to interpret superficially contradictory results and, in fact, led us to develop our understanding of the role played by the police during the sixties.[11]

7.5.2 *Size and Covariance of the Residuals*

We explained in Chapter 5 (§ 5.5) our choice of the ratio of the variance of the residual in the reduced form equation for endogenous variable to the variance of the endogenous variable itself as a measure of the extent to which we fail to account for the variance in the level of recorded offences, the clear-up or conviction rate, and the size of the police force. This proportionate residual or unexplained variance was for the offence rate around 30%, for the clear-up or conviction rate around 70% and for the number of policemen *per capita* around 50%—see Table 6.10 and the discussion in Chapter 6 (§ 6.6). For the recorded offence rate at least the explained variance would seem to be quite high.

The differences in explained variance may be understood as follows. Both the recorded offence rate and the operational police manpower are

---

[11] It is noticeable that other studies have relied on the estimates from one data set. Some of our most interesting findings come from the comparisons between the different data sets: equivalent results in different data sets also increased our confidence in their validity.

quantities subject to a number of well recognised social forces, many of whose particularities we have captured in our equations, whereas the clear-up rate depends at least in part on the discretion of the local police administration. We suppose that the exercise of this discretion varies substantially across police districts. Thus one might expect greater unexplained variance in the second equation than in the others.

The correlations between the residuals in the structural equations were discussed briefly in the previous chapter. Here we shall look more closely at the correlations above 0·7 (the choice of the value 0·7 is somewhat arbitrary but was discussed in § 7.0). The story essentially revolves around the third equation (ignoring the single instance of a high value of 0·89 for ϱ_{21} in 1961 urban data).

Table 7.11

Correlations amongst residuals for the structural equations which are above 0.7 in absolute value

	1961 U	1961 R	1961 UR	1966 U	1966 R	1966 UR	1971 UR
ϱ_{21}	0·89						
ϱ_{31}	0·90		0·74 (p conv.)	0·76	−0·98 −0·92 (p conv.)		−0·90
ϱ_{32}	0·90		−0·70	0·84		−0·97 (p conv.)	

Note.

ϱ_{ij} is the correlation coefficient between the residuals in the ith and jth equations (see Table 6.10). Results are for p clear-up unless otherwise indicated below the coefficient.

The correlations between the residuals in first and third equations are high and positive in urban data and high and negative in pooled data in both 1961 and 1966. The correlations between the residuals of the second and third equations are high and positive in urban and pooled data in 1961 and in urban data in 1966, but high and negative in rural data in 1966 and in the 1971 data set. The results suggest that the residual in the third equation is the central link, and thus that the missing common fact (which is being reflected in correlation between the residuals) is related to the role of the police in different areas.

A plausible story might be that a police force with high morale will both recruit well (giving a high positive residual in the third equation) and have the confidence to pursue its chosen policy towards the prevention of crime. Thus if it follows traditional policies in respect of its relationship with the community it will tackle minor incidents more informally, implying a negative residual in both the first and second equation. On the other hand if it pursues "modern" and more formal policies it can produce higher clear-up rates (and usually offence rates) in a number of ways. A Chief Constable can instruct his officers to record more minor offences; he can change the interpretation of his instructions as to when a case is to be regarded as cleared-up; and the practices regarding offences which are "taken into consideration" at the same time as another conviction, can be more aggressive. According to this line of argument, it would be the rural areas that adopted the informal policies, since we find only the negative correlations between the residuals in the third equation and those from the first and second in the results for rural and pooled data sets. This is not implausible, although we should not like to push the argument more strongly than that.

7.5.3 *The Policy Implications of the Model*

Our results do not offer great comfort for those who would wish to formulate policy. There are apparently several variables which affect the recorded offence rate but only p, f, c and e can, even in principle, be manipulated. We have seen that the only variables which affect p in a consistent fashion are the proportion of recorded offences which are violent, v, and the size of the district, n. The latter result would indicate that higher clear-up rates can be achieved with smaller areas. Although the number (c) and expenditure (e) on police do appear to have direct effects on the recorded offence rate, they have the effect opposite to that normally desired by the executive. This leaves only f; but the sensitivity to f is small. We gave a rough calculation in § 7.2 to show that a 20% increase in an already over-crowded prison population would reduce the recorded offence rate by 5%. Given the relatively small amounts involved in most property offences (see § 2.0) and the average cost of imprisonment, around £2,000 per prisoner per year in 1971, arguments for using extra imprisonment would appear to be weak.[12]

7.5.4 *A General Assessment of the Theories*

We consider here only received theories concerned with the generation of the recorded offence rate. There has not been much in the way of theorising on the other endogenous variables of our system—the clear-up or conviction rate and the number of policemen. The reader will recall that we put theories of offence rates into three groups: deterrence theories, which focus on possible rewards and punishment; those of the sociologists of

---

[12] What is at issue is really the marginal cost of imprisonment and the marginal offence. It is obvious there would be severe difficulties in carrying out such a calculation.

deviance which concentrate on the recording of events, by the authorities, as offences; and, finally, those of more traditional criminology which suggest certain sections of the population are more prone to offending, particularly the young and the lower socio-economic groups.

On the whole the first two groups of theories come out of our analysis rather well. The coefficients on variables which are stressed by the deterrence theorists—the probability and severity of punishment and the potential rewards to theft—emerge as significant right across our data sets and are of the sign which would be anticipated. We found also that the behaviour of the coefficients on the number and expenditure on police, the proportion of the population that is working class and the proportion of young males in the population, could not be understood without a reference to the way in which events are recorded. And the changes in coefficients across years when coupled with the changes in England and Wales in the 1960s allowed us to put meat on the bones of the sociology of deviance story. Here we found a particular advantage in working with more than one data set.

The group of theories which fares worst as a result of our estimates are those associated with more traditional criminology. The apparent importance of recording phenomena throws grave doubt on analyses of the offending population based on characteristics of convicted offenders; and similar doubt is cast by the self-report studies discussed in Chapters 2 and 3.

Whilst we have found some support for certain theories of the generation of recorded offences, we wish immediately to urge caution in the interpretation of our results and of the criminal statistics. We develop the need for care in the use of criminal statistics in the next chapter, particularly in relation to recording phenomena, and in Chapter 9 we warn against the misuse of economic models for the determination of policy towards crime which are based on deterrence relationships as estimated here.

8

Official Statistics, Recording and Policy*

8.0 INTRODUCTION

The discussion so far has been intentionally academic: that is, it has been exploring the intellectual foundations and implications of a set of assumptions and beliefs. But our motives for choosing our topic for research were not purely academic, we were concerned both about the conclusions drawn from discussions of official criminal statistics and about the revival of arguments by some economists concerning the desirability of basing sentences only on the costs and benefits of deterrence. In this and the next chapter we return, respectively, to the ideas which partly prompted this study: that the "crime wave" may be as much an artefact as real; and that the assimilation of criminology as a branch of microeconomic theory is mistaken.

This chapter concentrates on the way in which so-called findings drawn from the study of official crime statistics are used to determine—or to justify—particular policies of crime control. In fact, it would have been naive to suppose that the tentative conclusions we have reached, as to which variables are important and as to the nature of the process involved in determining the recorded crime rate, were only of academic interest. Indeed, we should claim that official statistics relating to crime and criminal proceedings are now of a much, if not more, public interest than they have ever been since the introduction of "political arithmetik" by Petty in the 16th Century.

We first of all consider the implications of our results for the hypotheses derived from labelling theories concerning the importance of the role played by the police and the differential vulnerability of different social groups (in

*Roy Carr-Hill takes particular responsibility for the views expressed in this chapter.

§ 8.1). We then construct, on the basis of what we have learnt, an outline theory of the way in which official statistics are produced and what they represent (in § 8.2). In the next section (§ 8.3) we briefly examine the way in which numerical information has become a more dominant component in public discussion and decision-making in general and then look at the case of criminal statistics in particular. The fourth and fifth sections (§ 8.4 and § 8.5) illustrate the general argument by considering two very specific topics: the evidence for, and use in policy discussion of, the "crime wave", that is, the apparently rapid rise in recorded crime since the middle sixties; and the evidence for, and the possibilities of, the effective deterrence of violent crime. In the final section (§ 8.6) we propose a possible set of indicators which could be developed and used in this area to enlighten public discussion and decision making.

8.1 THE LABELLING HYPOTHESIS

The discussion of the results in Chapter 7 relied on arguments about variations both in the reporting behaviour of the public and in the practices of the police in recording incidents as crimes, that is on the social processes involved in the production of the recorded crime rate. Such an account yielded what we regard as the most plausible of possible explanations of the otherwise anomalous behaviour of the coefficients on variables representing police manpower and expenditure (c and e) and of the variations in the importance and significance of variables representing the age and social class structure of the local area (a and w). In turn our explanations provide some support for the "labelling hypothesis" advanced by certain sociologists of deviance from two perspectives. First, we have the importance of the role played by the institutions of social control and by the members of those institutions in determining what is and what is not "crime"; secondly, who and who is not likely to be labelled as an offender.

8.1.1 *The Role of the Police*

Most studies which are designed to demonstrate or specify the labelling hypothesis concentrate on the labelling of the victim. That is they look at the consequences of the official designation of the deviant label on the career of the individual—for example, in terms of his or her employment possibilities or subsequent official consideration as a "suspect". Of course, some studies go more deeply into the processes involved in that they try to describe the precise interactions between the designated deviant and his or her immediate social environment (see, for example, Dinitz, Dynes and

Clarke (1969)). The focus is on what happens to the "deviant" and perhaps, how it happens.

In consequence such theorists have paid considerable attention to the characteristics of offenders, almost to the same extent as "traditional criminologists". But, although the characteristics of individuals (and their immediate social situation) are obviously relevant to any actions that they perform, so are the characteristics of the other actors and social institutions involved.

The concern of sociologists of deviance has, however, been rather wider than the study of the characteristics of labelled offenders. Thus they have conducted studies of the characteristics of institutions of social control; for example Goffman's study of a mental hospital (1961), the Morris' study of Pentonville (1963), and there have also been studies of the personality and socially defined role of both police (Bordua (1967); La Fave (1965); Skolnick (1966) and Westley (1953)) and social workers (Form and Bailey (1968); Meyer and Timms (1970)). However there is, for good practical reasons, very little knowledge of the way in which the characteristics of these institutions or the personality of the typical officer or worker affect their behaviour towards potential offenders (although Russell (1973) is an obvious exception here).

Our study cannot, of course, directly identify the particular processes involved but the results are suggestive. Thus we have shown that:

(a) two quantitative attributes of police forces, size and expenditure, play important and independent roles in the determination of the offence rate and the clear-up rate.

(b) a plausible explanation of the variations across data sets in the effect of some non-police variables is in terms of qualitative changes in police attitudes towards and relations with certain groups of the population, and police practice in recording and reporting incidents as offences.

The second observation suggests that the socio-demographic characterisation of recorded offenders is, to an important extent, a function of police attitudes and practices so that a study of the latter is a pre-requisite to a study of the former. Such a study or collection of studies would explain both how police officers habitually use the discretion available to them and how these habits arise. We draw attention briefly to the particular issues which shall be explored in the concluding chapter.

8.1.2 Discrimination Between Social Groups

On a slightly more aggregate level many authors have argued that the particular stereotypes held by the official agents of social control mean that they view the typical behaviour of certain social groups as more deviant than others (Chapman (1968), Russell (1973)): this is important. For it is often claimed by "traditional criminologists" that these same social groups are more "criminogenic", that is that because of heredity, up-bringing or their immediate environment, they are more likely to commit crimes than members of other social groups.

Further, just as traditional criminology goes on to explain why certain social groups are more criminogenic than others in terms of, for example, a poor socialisation, certain sociologists of deviance go on to show how the choice of stereotype is not arbitrary but serves to maintain a particular social structure. Our study, of course, cannot directly evaluate either type of argument, but we can examine the behaviour of the variables representing the proportion of working class and of youth in an area in the light of the two possibilities.

Consider the involvement of the working class in delinquent activities. Partly on the basis of casual observations of convicted offenders and partly on beliefs about social differences in behaviour patterns, it is often assumed that working-class people are more delinquent. The task of the theorist here becomes one of explaining the delinquent propensity of the working class (see, for example, Miller (1958)). If either these theories are combined with a belief that everyone has an equal chance of getting caught or one believes that working-class offenders are selected, then the coefficient of w (the proportion of working class in the population) would be positive in the equation describing the determination of the recorded offence rate. On the other hand, the belief that everyone has an equal chance of getting caught would lead us to expect that the coefficient of w would be zero in the equation describing the determination of the detection rate, whilst the belief that working-class offenders are selected would lead us to expect that this same coefficient would be positive. Thus we cannot discriminate between the two hypotheses of "no selection" and "selection" on the basis of the first equation, but we may be able to on the basis of the second.

In fact we found that the coefficient of w was positive and (statistically) significant in the equation describing the determination of the recorded offence rate in all cases in 1961, in four cases out of six in 1966 (although the coefficient was, on the whole, smaller) and not at all in 1971. In the equation describing the determination of the detection rate, w was positive and significant in two cases, but negative and significant in one case in 1961, positive and significant in three cases in 1966 and not significant at all in 1971. Thus the behaviour of the coefficient of w in the equation describing the determination of the offence rate is reasonably consistent with both the hypothesis of no selection and that of selection. The behaviour of w in the equation describing the determination of the detection rate, however, is more consistent with the hypothesis that working-class people are selected. The conclusion seems to be that the working class are discriminated against at the level of search and arrest.

A similar type of argument to that for the working class concerns the young. We start out from the casual observation that schoolchildren are often involved in minor delinquencies[1] and from beliefs about the unsettling effects of adolescence. The task of the theorist then becomes one of explaining the delinquent propensity of youth (see, for example, West (1967)). If either these theories are combined with a belief that everyone has an equal chance of being caught or one believes that the youth are selected, then the coefficient of a (the proportion of males aged 15 to 24 in the population of the area) would be positive in the equation describing the determination of the offence rate. The difference, as before, would arise in the equation describing the determination of the detection rate where the coefficient of a would be non-zero if there is some selection.

In fact we found that in the equation describing the determination of the offence rate the coefficient of a was negative and significant in four cases out of six in 1961, positive and significant in four cases out of six in 1966, and not significant at all in 1971. In the equation describing the determination of the detection rate, a was negative and significant twice and positive and positive and significant once in 1961, negative and significant once but positive and significant twice in 1966, and not significant at all in 1971. Thus in both equations the hypothesis of "no selection" obtains no support. The conclusion seems to be (as explained in Chapter 7) that police and public attitudes to youth have a large effect on whether or not they are caught and convicted.

Therefore in the cases of both the variables representing the working class or the youth in the area, we are forced to reject the hypothesis that there is no selection and accept that, at the level of police practice there is some discrimination which either protects or shields particular social groups or takes them as prime targets. Indeed, the variations across data sets that we have observed are so great that it is difficult to see how one could maintain, on the basis of official criminal statistics, that some social groups are more criminogenic than others.

8.2 ACTUAL AND RECORDED OFFENCES

Throughout the argument in earlier chapters we have frequently relied on the difference between actual and recorded offences. In our discussion of

[1] Thus, for some time after the Second World War, the "delinquent generation" was seen as a major problem (see Wilkins (1964), Rose (1968)). More generally, Little (1965) showed how the modal age for being arrested was the last year before leaving school.

the available theories in Chapter 3, however, we acknowledged that there were a range of positions advanced in the literature and that whilst some sociologists claim that there is no content to the notion of an actual level of offences, others accept the concept. From the point of view of the quantitative estimations, we showed in Chapters 4 and 5 that either interpretation could be adopted within the model we have used, since what interests us is how an incident, whether or not it is in some objective sense illegal, becomes recorded.

In other words, we started our construction of the formal model in Chapter 4 with a range of theories about the way in which an incident was recorded as a crime and tried to incorporate these theories through the variables included. After our empirical investigation we can now say more about the possible character of the recording process. We first of all draw a sketch of a rather general theory of the generation of official criminal statistics, and then we consider what evidence can be adduced from our study to support this theory.

8.2.1 *The Generation of Official Criminal Statistics*

In this sub-section we give an account of the process by which an incident is recorded as an offence or a person as an offender. This process involves factors at several different levels. We go from the most general to the particular:

(a) the type of society and the legal definitions employed;
(b) the way in which legal rules are applied and interpreted within a given social structure;
(c) the procedures and routines of police practices which lead to the formation of stereotypes;
(d) the way in which police resources and time are allocated;
(e) the public interest in reporting incidents as offences; and
(f) the determinants of individual behaviour.

Therefore this may appear to repeat some of the arguments which were considered in the second half of Chapter 3 when we were building up the model. There, however, our intention was to consider any element which might affect the recording of an incident as an offence. Here we are concerned with the structure and logic of the process and thus in showing which factors intervene, on what level and in which way, in the process of generating the observed criminal statistics.

(*a*) *Type of Society and Legal Definitions.* First, it is clear that the type of incident which becomes recorded as an offence, and to a lesser extent the type of individual who is labelled as an offender, depends on the type of society. For example, only when the institution of private transport is socially recognised can the use of a motor vehicle ever be construed as "theft"; only when society's moral codes restrict sexual relationships can, for example, homosexuality be construed as an offence. In a strictly formal sense, therefore, it is the way in which society assigns the label of criminality, rather than the activity itself which creates "the crime".[2]

Further, although most criminal codes are framed in such a way that their potential domain of applicability is universal, the way in which the particular provisions are formulated meshes with other features of the social structure. Thus laws are proposed and enacted by a group of jurists, legislators and politicians who if not members of, are mostly sympathetic to, the ruling class (see Griffiths (1977)). Such laws are, one can argue, intended by that class to serve its own interests rather than some abstract notion of justice (see Griffiths and Irvine (1978)). Thus polluting large areas of orchard is not an offence (unless criminal negligence can be shown) whereas taking an apple from a tree, though non-indictable is on the Home Office Standard List of Offences.

On a more specific level, the particular criminal code plays a role independent of the social structure. This code may, of course, result from the power of different interest groups without reflecting a different type of society. Thus the particular gambling laws in force may put one company out of business, but make another; the laws on pornography which permit the sale of certain "blue" books and films may have no, or very little, effect on the amount sold but do affect the way in which they are sold.

(b) *Application and Interpretation of Legal Rules within a Social Structure.*
Secondly, the way in which legal rules are applied will affect which types of incident or people are recorded. Thus legal rules are enforced by an institutional apparatus of social control which is recruited and trained in principle, to serve the interests of the ruling class. For instance, in capitalism, the bourgeoisie profits as much as it can from its dominant position in part by ensuring the acquiescence of the mass of workers in their own exploitation. In the legal area this implies that far more attention will be paid to the deviance of members of lower status groups than members of higher status groups, regardless of the extent or quality of the deviance in which different individuals are involved.

At the same time many activities or incidents, which might result in the attribution of a deviant label, are private or at least inaccessible to official control because of the way in which people live; and this varies considerably

[2] The emphasis here is on the legal label. We recognise that there are circumstances and moral positions under which one might want to discuss whether an incident should be called a crime whether or not it is illegal in the society concerned.

between social groups. Thus an unemployed person taking stationary from a shop is much more likely to be caught than an office worker who "borrows" from his office. Drunkenness among the poor is likely to be visible in the street; among the rich it is more likely to take place in clubs or private houses. It is difficult to evaluate the extent of this form of bias, since different social groups protect themselves in different ways (see Stinchcombe (1963) for a rare discussion). The most obviously vulnerable group is composed of those already convicted, who are watched more closely than others.

(c) *Attitudes and the Formation of Stereotypes.* Thirdly, there is the way in which the agencies of social control function inside the particular social structure. This means that, even within the range of deviant acts which might be the subject of sanctions, only some are selected for attention according to received notions of "real" damage and harm. In respect of some laws and in certain circumstances, informal social pressures or propaganda are seen as more effective than arrest in controlling the number of incidents. Accordingly the police rarely intervene in cases of larceny within a club or society, preferring to let the members sort it out for themselves. In a similar fashion some types of incident which might otherwise be classified as offences are not seen as very damaging. A good example is the police policy towards cautioning young offenders for what are seen as minor offences.

As a corollary the social control agencies develop particular images and stereotypes of "the deviant" which more or less conform to the types of deviance selected in this way. Thus Chapman (1968) and Russell (1973) both show, on different levels, how the treatment of certain types of incident as more serious than others corresponds to the treatment of certain types of individual as more delinquent than others. The subsequent concentration by the police on these character types almost certainly means that what they do is more often noticed and that they are caught more often for what they do. Although there is some evidence from psychological experiments on the formation of stereotypes (see, for example, Sherif (1967)) the fragmentary evidence with respect to the police makes it difficult to make a precise estimate of the importance of this effect. However, it certainly exists.

(d) *Allocation of Police Time and Police Procedure.* A fourth factor in the process is the way in which police effort and time is allocated between different functions. This reflects both the goals of policing and the procedural constraints placed upon the police. It can safely be assumed that the goals of policing in England and Wales are stable: thus in his retiring report Waldron could say "The prevention and detection of crime, as in 1829, is still our primary object . . ." (Report of the Commissioner of Police for the Metropolis (1972) p. 27). However, this does not give us any clear idea as to the balance between the two or how it may have changed. In a similar fashion, although it is still true to say that "a suspect is presumed innocent until proven guilty", the rules circumscribing police treatment of suspects may change. Thus the situations in which they are allowed to search or arrest without a warrant may be enlarged or restricted and, as a result, the police may expand or curtail their activities in respect of certain types of incident or potential offence. Obvious examples, in England and Wales in the sixties, were the rules about searching for and seizing suspected illegal drugs and the extent to which tape recordings were acceptable as evidence.

It is clear that the goals of policing and procedural constraints affect both the way in which police effort and time is allocated and therefore which types of incident or person receive most attention. For officers of a police force devoted to deterrence will address their attention to groups of people believed to be most likely to offend; officers of a police force devoted to prevention might be sweeping the streets or distributing copies of the Holy Bible according to the theoretical persuasion of the police commissioner; and one devoted to control will be concerned to assert police presence whenever crowds gather. That is, the overall policy constraints and goals determine in part the habitual beats and day-to-day organisation of the police force. Unfortunately for the further development of this argument, the main relevant study carried out in England and Wales (Martin and Wilson (1969)) found considerable difficulty in allocating police time according to function, motivation or reason. They eventually classified 50% of police time as devoted to "general policing".

(e) *Interest in Reporting Crimes.*   Attitudes to reporting can change quite quickly for several reasons. For example, the public may begin to believe that the police are ineffective and so be more reluctant to "waste time" reporting to them; we drew attention to this possibility earlier in Chapter 3. Thus people who suffer minor theft may estimate that the time and trouble involved is not worth the slight possibility of recovering the stolen items. Of course there are incentives to report to the police other than the possible discovery of the offender and goods, for example in the case of theft of a motor vehicle, where a successful insurance claim would depend on reporting to the police.

Another element which is important here is the way in which certain sections of the community may become estranged from the established legal and social structure and, as a result, refuse to co-operate with the police. The situation in this respect can also change quite rapidly: thus in London the Metropolitan Police set up a new Community Relations Branch in 1968 and in 1969 published an optimistic report saying that "a promising start had been made" (Report of the Commissioner of Police for the Metropolis (1969) p. 10); only three years later they were much more pessimistic and had to acknowledge the "regrettable fact that, in certain areas and among certain sections of the immigrant communities, there is considerable mistrust of the police" (Report of the Commissioner of Police for the Metropolis (1972) p. 19).

Finally, the public may simply begin not to regard certain incidents as delinquent. Changing sexual morals are an obvious recent example; but the development of solidarity among groups will also lead to circumstances where members of those groups would not pay special attention to certain activities which they might have otherwise reported to the police.

(*f*) *Parameters of Individual Behaviour.* A sixth factor is the structure of detection, punishment and opportunity facing the individual. From one point of view, the structure could simply be taken as representing the costs and benefits to the individual of different decisions and so would affect the actual rate of offending. An alternative possibility that we have already emphasized, is however, that these perceived costs and benefits may not only affect an individual propensity to perform certain activities, but also the extent to which individuals are cautious about what they do. In other words, changing the cost-benefit structure may not change the actual level of criminal activity but only the amount that is recorded.

Another "parameter of individual behaviour" which is important in determining precisely which incidents and which people are singled out, is the strangeness of the circumstances or the behaviour of the individual. Interactionist authors show how particular "abnormal" types of social situation and personality features are most likely to be among this final selection.

However, we do not wish to present a rigidly deterministic model of the recording process. Whilst the above six factors are important, some individuals are labelled as offenders because of a combination of chance circumstances. And it is clear that from like individuals placed in similar circumstances and involved in a specific kind of activity, only a proportion will be apprehended.

8.2.2. *The Evidence*

We have discussed the factors which we think affect the generation of official police statistics in six groups (see the list at the beginning of § 8.2.1). There is nothing definitive or revolutionary about this list, in fact, it corresponds fairly closely with the literature (OECD (1976)); Sellin and Wolfgang (1964); Wiles (1971)). The difficulty in evaluating the importance of these factors is, of course, that the process by which official criminal statistics are generated is very difficult to quantify. Most relevant empirical work has been on the micro level. Our study is on the macro level so that the estimated structural coefficients of the variables included in the first equation, which models the process by which the recorded offence rate is determined, can be viewed not only as an indication of the variables which enter into this process, but also as an estimate of their importance.

Of course, given the nature of our study, we cannot comment on some of the six factors which have been mentioned. Thus we have been considering only one legal structure (that for England and Wales in the 1960s). This means that we cannot comment on the effect of differences in laws on the types of incident which become recorded (the first factor mentioned above). Similarly, the nature of our data makes it inappropriate for us to use our results to comment on the way in which legal rules are interpreted or the way in which stereotypes are formed (the third factor). In the same way, we found no variables to measure public interest in reporting crimes (the fifth factor). We can therefore comment on only the second, fourth and sixth factors above.

First, consider the application of legal rules within a social structure (the second factor). The way in which the coefficients of the variables giving the proportion of young males aged 15 to 24 and the proportion of working class in the population (a and w) change between the years, gives support to the claim that the way in which the criminal code is actually applied depends on the position of the various groups within the social structure. We argued that the behaviour of the coefficient on a reflects a decline in the special antagonisms between the youth and the police which were an object of concern in the early and mid-sixties. We suggested that the behaviour of the coefficient of w in the equation for the detection rate could be a result of a loosening of informal community controls.

Next, there is the way in which police effort and time is allocated between different functions (the fourth factor). Our study, of course, provides no direct information on this point. But the fact that the variables giving the number of police *per capita* and the expenditure per policeman (c and e) played such an important role in our discussion of the results (particularly the former) suggests that, at least during the sixties in England and Wales, variations in police goals and procedure—or styles of policing—produced large effects on what appeared as official crime statistics.

Finally, we look at the parameters of individual behaviour which affect the likelihood of an incident being recorded as an offence or a person as an offender (the sixth factor). We found that variables such as the clear-up or conviction rate, the imprisonment rate, and the total rateable value per area (p, f and rv) do usually affect the rate of recorded offences. The straightforward interpretations of these coefficients is that the variables to which they correspond describe the structure of possibilities for the individual and therefore affect his or her decision to commit or omit certain acts. We argued above that the same variables would also affect, through care taken by individuals and the attitudes of the public, the likelihood of an incident being recorded as an offence.

The generation of recorded criminal statistics is complex but we hope we have shown that it is a process which can be understood. It is therefore clear that the interpretation of empirical results using criminal statistics by selecting just one view of one part of this process, for example, "deterrence" is perilous. We shall be arguing in Chapter 10 for further study of the recording process.

8.3 INFORMATION AND PUBLIC DISCUSSION

In a liberal democratic society, only certain modes of, or challenge to, the prevailing social organisation are accepted.[3] These modes of discourse are usually graced with the adjective "rational" or sometimes "reasonable" (see Pateman (1975) and Wolin (1961)).

In recent times, one can argue, belief in the virtues of rational verbal debate was at its zenith in the 19th century. Indeed, the image of parliament as a forum for solving political problems stems from the great debates of that century. It is, of course, difficult for someone writing to deny the value of a written (or verbal) culture; it is even more difficult to explain the peculiar form of rationality embodied in such a mode of communication (but see the valiant attempt by Pirsig (1974)). The main point is to recognise that the verbal and written culture is specific to a particular social context, for this focusses on the assumptions implicit in any particular mode of communicating information.

This last point is particularly important when the presentation of statistical information is at issue. For whilst there is still a premium on verbal or written persuasion, numerical and statistical argument have

[3] The predominant mode of discourse in a society may so restrict the range of possibilities that individuals feel forced to turn to violence as a means of communication. And the arguments of individuals or groups, who use or propose to use physical violence as a means of persuasion, are devalued and their proponents are, if not vilified, at least criminalised. Thus it would be difficult to find a discussion of the programme or objectives of the Provisional Sinn Fein anywhere in either the academic literature or the press in England. Yet there is a clear "rational" foundation to the activities of a group of people who, in one sense, are simply impatient with an 800-year-old dependence. Another example is the propaganda war conducted in West Germany over the supposed activities of the Red Army Fraction where the government and the press accused them of planning to massacre children, whilst their arguments about the necessity of attacking imperialism in the metropolis are unheard.

become an important part of the process of decision making. This has arisen partly because of the ever increasing number of precise decisions which are attempted in the management of the economy (and the society) and partly because of the accumulation of a mass of evidence and material which is only usable if summarized in a numerical way.

In this way, statistical techniques are being seen as relevant, and numerical expertise has developed, across a wide range of fields; but numerical and statistical information about a situation is no less partial than a verbal and written description of the same situation. The difference is that it is often more difficult for people to contest inferences drawn from a numerical and statistical description than a verbal one.

An example of this is the use of the gross national product (GNP) as a measure of economic welfare. The inadequacies of GNP as such a measure are well known to certain academics and some journalists. It includes, for example, maintenance of the nuclear deterrent, red tape and waste but not leisure or the preparation of meals, where one eats at home or with friends. However, the public at large has little idea how the index is constructed. Thus, whilst people may be quite capable of evaulating their own situation and, if not prevented by social organisation, planning its amelioration, they are rarely sufficiently skilled to argue about the implications of a movement in GNP.

Social indicators which are intended to augment economic information in the measurement of progress, the quality of life, or well-being are open to similar distortions. Thus the "social indicators movement" (called such by Moser (1970)) was seen as an attempt to enlighten public discussion and decision making by providing numerical but easily understandable, descriptions of living conditions. Yet it has become obvious that the travesties involved in apparently "simple" social indicators in hiding an ambiguous and complex social reality (and this point is elaborated in Miles (1976) and *Anon* (1978)) can be just as worrying as those described in the example of GNP above.[4]

The official crime statistics illustrate, almost too well, the above arguments. Clearly they can be seen as "purely" administrative statistics which provide a simple description of the volume and nature of work facing the police force and which could be used in the discussion of the next year's

---

[4] An example is the UN index of overcrowding "dwellings with more than one person per room" which would seem to be a clear measure of housing need with which all could agree. It has two pitfalls for someone who is not well acquainted with housing statistics. First, it excludes all non-conventional dwellings (caravans, shacks, etc.) which are almost certainly the most overcrowded. Secondly, the statistical unit is the dwelling and not the individual—who is the one concerned with being overcrowded. This can make a tremendous difference: thus in France in 1968, whilst 43% of dwellings contained less than 1 person per room, only 29% of people live in such dwellings (Nectoux, 1977).

budget proposal. However, if variations in recording are ignored, they can also be interpreted as providing an overall view of the nature and type of criminal activity.

A reading of the Reports of the Commissioner of Police for the Metropolis confirms one's worst fears. The criminal statistics are presented without comment on whether they represent the phenomenon of crime and, when suitably embellished, are used to paint a picture of violence and social instability. Such a picture is often used to justify using certain measures of surveillance which would not otherwise be countenanced in "peacetime"[5] which in turn might reassure the public that something is being done about the breakdown in law and order.

These "straightforward" interpretations and use of the official criminal statistics are badly flawed. First, we must ask *what kind of* social stability is threatened by the sorts of violent activities which are usually represented in the criminal statistics? It is easy to believe and say that no-one likes violence; it is more difficult to justify the selection of certain types of violence as targets for particularly severe judicial treatment, for example street muggings rather than others such as drunken driving causing injury. Similarly, *whose* law and order is breaking down? It is nice to be and feel secure; it is another question altogether from what or whom.

Secondly, apart from the ideological notions of law and order and social stability embodied in the criminal statistics, the previous sections showed the complexity of the process by which criminal statistics are generated. The interpretation and use (in discussions of policy) of official criminal statistics is therefore more akin to a gardener's craft—requiring an appreciation of many interconnected, often unpredictable and only vaguely specifiable factors—rather than the routine reading of a table. It is from this perspective that we examine two examples involving misuse of the statistics which are of particular importance. The first is that there has been a "crime wave" in the last two decades. The second, and related, example is that part of the reason for this "wave" is that sentences have become less severe. Both arguments have relied on empirically observed movements and changes in crime statistics; our study, since it has indicated some of the factors which affect criminal statistics, suggests alternative interpretations of the data.

8.4 THE MISUSE OF CRIMINAL STATISTICS

8.4.1 *The Crime Wave*

We stated in the previous section that Chief Constables usually base their commentaries on the state of crime in their district simply on the gross

---

[5] Cameroun (1975) describes how police activities can be viewed in terms of the conduct of a war.

figure (or figures by major offence types) for a given year as compared to the previous year(s). Journalists when reporting on crime, usually present them in the same way, suitably embellished according to the audience for whom they are writing (see the discussion in Pope (1974)). And although there has been some (academic) controversy over the interpretation of a particular rise or fall in figures (see, for example, the debate over the effects of the abolition of capital punishment, or over the Street Offences Act, 1959), there has been no general challenge to the received interpretation that the volume of crime is growing much faster than most other activities.

Indeed, this view was buttressed by a semi-official study conducted by the Cambridge Institute of Criminology in collaboration with the Statistical Department of the Home Office, together with the help of the Association of Chief Officers of Police of England and Wales reported in McClintock and Avison (1968). This group of researchers had earlier conducted studies restricted to one type of offence only, such as the study of robbery in London (reported in McClintock and Gibson (1961)). In each of these books the recording problem is discussed—indeed, a whole chapter is devoted to it in McClintock (1963)—but then ignored in the body of the text and, more importantly, in the conclusions which are drawn.

The chef-d'oeuvre is, however, undoubtedly *Crime in England and Wales* (McClintock and Avison (1968)). The authors began by saying:

> In using the statistics recorded by the police, it has to be constantly borne in mind that even today, there is not complete uniformity in police practice of accepting and recording incidents of social behaviour as crime (p. 4).

Indeed, when they are discussing detection rates, they say:

> From discussions with senior police officers . . . it can reasonably be assumed that some of the extreme variations in detection rates *can only be accounted* for in terms of variations in police practices in enforcing the criminal law and recording crime (pp. 101-2).

Yet in their conclusions in summarizing the changes in the number of recorded indictable crimes they say, ". . . this would indicate that during the last twelve years, the incidence of crime within the general population has more than doubled" {1955-1966} (p. 273). This assumes away variations in recording over time.

Moreover, even their conclusions about *recorded* crime rates are suspect. Thus they make two main points in their summary about "The phenomenon of crime" (McClintock and Avison (1968), p. 272): first that "There is no evidence to suggest that the main increase in crime can be directly attributed to the change in size or demographic structure of the population" (*op. cit.*, p. 272) and that "there is even in respect to common thefts, a clear indication of an increase in seriousness, as indicated by the value of the property which is stolen" (*op. cit.*, p. 273). These conclusions rely on particular and questionable methods of analysis and theories about seriousness as we show below.

Thus, on the first point, analysis of data over the same period by Ahamad (1967) and Willmer (1968) suggest on the contrary that changes in recorded crime could be explained, at least in part, by demographic changes. Ahamad (1967) investigated the trend in total indictable offences from 1950 to 1963. He employed a principal component analysis simultaneously on 18 different offence groups and extracted a common first principal component (that is a factor common to the changes over this period for each of the 18 offence groups). This first principal component could be approximated by the following equation: $F_{1j}{}^{***} = \dfrac{1}{1000} (-8280 + 0\cdot00390\, X_{6j})$ where X_{6j} are the numbers of individuals in the age group 13-19 for year j. Willmer (1968) went further; he investigated the trend in breaking-and-entering offences from 1952 to 1967, justifying his choice on the grounds that he expected all such offences to be reported. He obtained the equation: $y = -496\cdot9 + 0\cdot299\, x_1 + 0\cdot211\, x_2$ where x_1 (t) is the number of males in the home population aged 18-22, and x_2 (t) is the number of males in the home population aged 13-15.

Neither of these articles is without fault. For example, M. A. Walker (1967) explains the difficulty of drawing inferences from a principal components analysis which identifies variations in one series with variations in another, without any clear model of the inter-relations between the variables. Similarly, victimisation studies in the U.S.A. and our own analysis (see Chapter 7) suggest that only a small proportion of home breakings are reported. Indeed, reanalysis of figures used by Ahamad and Willmer might well reach different conclusions with respect to the important factors in generating the "crime wave" and especially the implication that the young are more likely to offend.

But the point we want to make here is that even though both these articles also ignored the recording problem, they were both suggesting that there had been no increase in the propensity to offend. McClintock and Avison (1968) seem, in fact, to have based their conclusions on the observation that the "largest change (in population between 1901 and 1961) has occurred in the older age groups, which would appear to be much less 'crime prone'" (p. 26): this seems to be largely irrelevant to changes in the period 1955-66. If we then consider that the public interest in reporting has probably increased both because of the decreasing tolerance of "violence" (see § 3.4) and because of the increasing proportion of property being insured (see below) McClintock and Avison (1968) seem to be jumping to conclusions.

McClintock and Avison (1968) also make an explicit argument that the value of property crime is increasing (see our Table 8.1). They recognise that any change over time in a given volume of property has to take into account inflation and indeed they attempted to standardize for this by using a cost of living index; but although this is the easiest correction to make, they recognise that it is unsatisfactory, since the basket of goods included in a cost of living index is not the same as the typical range of goods which are stolen.

More importantly, we would argue that, since the real interest (and the likely interpretation) is in respect of possible changes in the *propensity to offend*,[6] one should also take into account changes in the structure of real wealth. Recall that, in our study, the variable representing total rateable value per area, *rv*, was consistently significant over the years.

It is difficult to evaluate the force of these two points. However, as we can see from Table 8.1, both the number of easily stolen items and the

Table 8.1
Changes in the value of property crime relative to income and ownership

Year	1954-5/	1955	1961	1965/	1966	1971
(1) Total numbers of larcenies and breaking offences	317,158		591,407	853,787		
(2) Estimated average value of property stolen	£22.8		£35.1	£42.2		
(3) Estimated total value of property stolen	£7.2m		£20.8m	£36.0m		
(4) Retail Price Index	100		120	139		
(5) Gross National Product at Factor Cost (at Current Prices)		£17,033m	£24,472m		£33,153m	£48,216m
(6) Private car licences 1000's		3,526	5,979		9,573	12,059
(7) TV licences 1000's		5,400	11,657		13,919	15,805

Note.
The figures in rows (1) to (4) are for 1954-5, 1961 and 1965. They are taken from McClintock and Avison (1968) Tables 2.13, p. 55 and 2.14, p. 56. The figures in rows (5) to (7) are for 1955, 1961, 1966 and 1971. Row (5) is taken from *National Income and Expenditure 1972*, Table 1, p. 2; row (6) from *Highway Statistics 1971*; and row (7) from the *Monthly Digest of Statistics* No. 193, Table 167 and No. 313, Table 175.

[6] By "propensity to offend" here we mean, formally speaking, the coefficients in a structural equation for the actual offence rate.

overall level of consumption increased very rapidly during this period (and certainly faster than the Retail Price Index that they used). Thus the numbers of car and television licences more than doubled during the period they considered; the increase in GNP at current prices seems strangely parallel to the increase in the estimated average value of property stolen. We have not, however, made any corrections, since it is difficult to assess the reliability of figures on, say, television licences, and to provide a convenient definition of "easily stolen".

Neither have the arguments of critical criminology discouraged authors. Carter (1974), for instance, argued that the growth in *property crime* had far outstripped the rate of inflation and the growth in real wealth. He also disregarded the difference between recorded and actual crime. He seems to rely on the General Household Survey which showed that only a very small proportion of thefts reported to interviewers had not been reported to the police.[7] But this contradicts the results of studies of self-reported delinquency and the fact that the marjority of recorded property crime (involving forcible entry) is from institutions (business companies) rather than from individuals (in 1966 there were 83,615 housebreakings and 119, 146 shopbreakings reported to the police).

Further, McClintock and Avison (1968) and Carter (1974) have ignored a major influence on reporting behaviour, that is the growth in the practice of insurance over this period. Many insurance companies would refuse to honour a claim on stolen property unless the loss had been reported to the police as stolen. It is difficult to be precise, since there are no data available to us on the proportion of property (even of a certain type) insured, but taken in conjunction with the other arguments, it seems to us difficult to maintain that property crime has increased.

People obviously do steal from, and attack, other people. What is at issue here is how to decide whether or not such incidents have decreased or increased; and further one is led to wonder why the studies so far in England and Wales have been inadequate in observing minimal criteria in the interpretation of temporal trends. Our study has shown how a very wide range of factors affect the process by which crime statistics are generated as well as the propensity to illegal activity. Since, on an empirical basis, we have argued that the process generating criminal statistics differs substantially from year to year, it is difficult to say whether actual offences have decreased or increased.[8] The verdict must be "not proven".

[7] There are difficulties of including victimisation questions in a multi-purpose survey; thus American experience suggests that if "screening" or probing questions are asked several times (in slightly different ways) or if the interviewee is made aware of the subject matter by related questions beforehand (on, say, police behaviour), then more incidents of victimisation are reported.

[8] All this section, of course, accepts the validity of the notion of the actual offence rate.

8.4.2 *The Role of Sentences in the "Crime Wave"*

We have discussed at length the problems of interpreting studies of "deterrence". We provide an outstanding example of the naive use of criminal statistics in drawing inferences about the deterrent value of imprisonment.

Table 8.2

Convictions and imprisonment in Scotland in 1954-55 and 1961-62

Offence class	Changes in use of detention		Rise in numbers found guilty
	1954-55	1961-62	
Robbery	72·1%	84·3%	133·3%
Violence	65·7%	57·2%	110·0%
Sex	44·2%	28·9%	46·8%
Housebreaking	36·6%	34·2%	93·6%
Reset	22·8%	21·4%	50·0%
Theft	19·5%	16·7%	40·8%

Taken from the Tables 13, 20, 26, 30, 34, 39, 47 (Arnott and Duncan (1970)).

The rate of imprisonment for those found guilty had therefore dropped for every offence class except robbery. The authors conclude:

> . . . the small drop in the use of detention has occurred at a time when the grave types of crime have increased more quickly than the less serious varieties and likewise the more hardened categories of recidivists increased more quickly than the less experienced offenders (p. 138).

They imply that more experienced offenders have taken advantage of the slight drop in severity to over-indulge in offending behaviour.

Yet, even taking the above figures at their face value, they can easily be interpreted in another way. For, if we believe that the relative level of penalties affects the rate of offence for different offence types (which is one theory) what should we conclude? For offence groups (robbery and violence) with a high rate of detention in 1954-55 the numbers of persons found guilty more than doubled by 1961-62; for offence groups (reset and theft) with a low rate of detention in 1954-55 the numbers of persons found guilty increased by not more than half; and for "middle" rates of detention in 1954-55, the numbers of persons found guilty nearly doubled while the detention rate remained the same (as with housebreaking), and increased by less than half where the detention rate declined substantially (as with sex). Thus, if the detention rate was low or declining for an offence group, the crime rate increased by not more than half, otherwise it approximately doubled.[9] In other words, one might argue that high level of penalties lead to big increases in offending.

We have assumed that what is true for persons found guilty by the courts is also true for potential offenders; but this is unlikely. For example, more ambitious and slippery potential offenders who do not relish imprisonment might have crossed the border, leaving behind inadequates. Alternatively, the changing reporting practices of the public and police might mean that different sorts of offenders were being charged in the different offence groups in the two time periods. Without further material we cannot evaluate these possible explanations for the differential behaviour of offence classes. And the overall level of reporting and recording may well have changed substantially.

We have shown, through these two examples, that the official criminal statistics are very open to misinterpretation. Unfortunately these misinterpretations are not only of academic interest, since the basic data, and the way in which it is used, affect policy discussions in the area of crime and its social control (see Seidman and Couzens (1974)). The choice of an appropriate set of data for policy purposes is, therefore, ultimately political. In the next section we suggest a possible framework for collecting statistical data in this area.

8.5 INFORMATION FOR POLICY MAKING

The two preceding sections have, we hope, demonstrated the problems with using the criminal statistics for discussing policy options in respect of crime and its social control. Our argument has been that the information available leads to particular conclusions because of the way it is constructed. Thus, increases in recorded rates of crime become the "spread of lawlessness" (McClintock and Avison (1968) p. 272) so that the police force must be strengthened to maintain law and order. Similarly, where experienced offenders are supposed to take advantage of the light punishment meted out in court, penalties should be increased. In both cases, we have shown how these conclusions are based on totally inadequate evidence and that there is little to suggest either that criminality is increasing or that severer prison sentences would do much to change the situation.

[9] Someone might want to say that our "theory" was wrong or incomplete; that sentencers react to the offence rate (also a theory) so that changes in the use of detention follow (roughly) the number of persons found guilty. This is implied in one of the interpretations that the authors give to the observed variations in the use of detention in different types of areas: ". . . it is seen that consistently severe sentences are imposed in the cities. Whether this indicates that city crimes are of a more serious nature and therefore the perpetrators receive sterner penalties, or whether the sterner penalties are simply a matter of policy . . ." (p. 137).

The fundamental problem is that the recorded crime rate does not permit inferences concerning notions of the real crime rate or the real damage or suffering caused to victims by a 'breakdown in law and order'. Bloch (1958) makes a similar point: "It seems likely that official convictions do not measure the real level of delinquent behaviour in a community but merely increase the volume of traffic through the courts" (p. 309). We have criticised at length (in § 8.4) the use of official statistics in discussions of policy in the area of crime. But, as Macdonald (1976) suggests, if the public really is concerned with the level of *recorded* crime, then "any number of solutions are possible: reduction of the police force, increased emphasis on non-criminal work, greater attention to more serious crime and time consuming investigations of white collar crimes" (p. 216). To this list we might add, on the basis of our results, decreases in wealth.

We suppose, however that we do want to know the extent to which crime really is a problem in contemporary society. Macdonald (1976) suggests that crimes against property in fact cause trivial losses[10] compared to what people lose through being out of work or through being discriminated against because of sex (p. 217). She goes on to argue that rates of recorded crime are important in that they "represent the application of social control measures, the compilation of dossiers, invasion of privacy and certain real hardships. An increase in the size of the police force, [etc.] means an increase in the size of the population devoted to regulatory work. This means necessarily a detraction from productive work, or the provision of services, or both. Questions of crime in short, should not be examined in isolation and not without rather careful consideration of the costs of proposed solutions" (p. 217-8).

On the whole, we support her analysis. It poses the problem of what information, if any, should be collected to answer the questions she raises. The most radical (in the sense of root and branch) solution to the problem of presentation, interpretation and use of criminal statistics which have been exposed above, is to abolish them; and this is what one might infer from the position of some sociologists. But decisions made within any social structure will always be made on the basis of information of some type. Some believe that numerical information *per se* is inherently distorting (see Evans *et al.* (1978)). We accept that this theoretical position is tenable, although we ourselves believe that the real issue is the way in which, and by whom, information is collected, presented and used. More importantly we think that suppression of numerical information often does more harm than good, although we are not naive enough to suppose that the provision of better information will necessarily lead to better policies.

---

[10] Her estimate was £½ per person in the population in 1965.

Nevertheless, we would also accept the point that information presently available is of little use either in describing an aspect of the social situation ("criminal activity") or for evaluating social policies. It concentrates far too much on police activity and far too little on the effects on people directly involved. Supposing however that we could design from scratch, a system of numerical information which should be published about "crime" and its social control—what form would it take?

It is not obvious that the control of (legally defined) crime is a clearly delimited social policy concern. First, the police include control of traffic and various forms of registration among their duties. Yet there are several specialised units looking after traffic control and licensing (and their numbers are not counted in the figures for established police strength), although the police still intervene on many non-criminal occasions. And there are other independent agencies which monitor transgressions of the law (for example, the Inland Revenue, the Factory Inspectorate, etc.).

Secondly, if we decide that control of "real" crime is an appropriate policy goal, then statisticians have to solve or take into account the recording problem, which would appear very difficult. Indeed, it is not even clear that it is worth trying to solve, since one of the main reasons the "dark number" is so large is that not all legally defined crime *per se* is a source of anxiety. Thirdly, not all activities labelled as crime produce identifiable injuries and some, for example, those connected with certain drugs, appear to give positive pleasure. At the same time, a whole range of non-criminal activities also cause considerable harm, such as driving, smoking, the lack of control on chemical additives to foods and bad working conditions. Granted that one statistical system cannot cover every facet of everyday life, we should concentrate on the damage or harm suffered by people rather than the activities of a group of people called offenders. The main objections to taking a global view of damage or harm suffered by individuals is that people are far more concerned about harm from criminal activities than, say, from food poisoning. Whilst we might agree with this position we should emphasize the importance of separating actual harm (whatever the cause) from the fear of harm—as well as distinguishing both from general views about the relevant set of events or situations.

A general concern with actual harm would lead to the collection of information on injuries and suffering due to whatever cause. In a partial way this information is collected already in that data are published on reasons for admission of patients who are discharged from hospital (see Table 8.3). The figures certainly suggest that physical harm from criminal activity is but a small proportion of harm suffered by the population. There might, however, be some justification for treating deaths and injuries due to accidents, poisonings and violence as on a different level from those due to disease or illness. For the former are, in general, both relatively unexpected and, given particular social arrangements (working conditions, traffic management, sanitation, health care, community control, etc.) relatively unpredictable. Thus we know that people living and working under certain conditions are more likely to contract and eventually die from certain diseases rather than others: for the rich, heart disease; and for the poor, tuberculosis. To a limited extent the same is true of accidents at work, but their impact is far more democratic.

Table 8.3

Deaths and discharges from non-psychiatric hospitals in England and Wales broken down by cause

	Males			Females		
	1961	1966	1971	1961	1966	1971
Discharges and deaths						
Tuberculosis	125	83	54	79	50	35
Neoplasms:						
Malignant	472	548	622	422	511	572
Benign and unspecified	148	162	137	319	392	368
Diseases of the nervous						
system	137	165	181	136	156	174
Diseases of the heart	415	496	640	344	386	452
Diseases of the peripheral						
circulatory system	397	434	475	423	470	502
Diseases of the						
respiratory system	1153	1175	1089	885	872	781
Diseases of digestive						
system	1170	1194	1189	886	878	914
Pregnancy, childbirth						
and puerperium				2661	3191	4003
Diseases of musculo-						
skeletal system	298	322	346	306	324	402
Fractures, dislocations						
and sprains	391	414	450	266	292	336
Other injuries and						
reactions	626	718	846	324	414	567
Other causes	1921	2096	2541	2477	2787	3292
Total discharges and deaths						
(a) per 100,000 population	7252	7806	8570	9528	10721	12397
(b) thousands	1800	2021	2248	2526	2936	3447

Notes.

1. Numbers per 100,000 population (except for final row) in Great Britain.
2. Source: *Social Trends* No. 4 (1973), Central Statistical Office, HMSO, Table 79.

If we do take the consequences of accidents, poisonings and violence as a separate policy concern there would seem to be no good reason for distinguishing accidents from crimes for the purposes of such a social policy goal. First, the physical injury does not change according to the intent; and secondly, the boundary dividing criminal negligence from accidental is to a large extent arbitrary. A shop-keeper who sells adulterated food may be convicted, in the United Kingdom, under the Food and Drug Acts, even if he had no means of knowing whether it was adulterated, for example because it was tinned. Others have also argued that the appropriate measure for tapping the concern with personal safety should be "deaths, permanent impairment and injuries resulting from unexpected events" (OECD (1977) p. 123). They go on to argue that what we need is a range of information on the degree of victimisation of different types from different sources, and show how deaths and injuries attributed to criminal events form only a small proportion of all deaths and injuries from unexpected events.

On this basis a statistical system could be developed around the actual harm suffered either from any cause or just from unexpected events. In either case, we would need to know the socio-demographic characteristics of victims and the effects on their everyday lives as a result of the harm suffered. We would want to calculate not only the actual suffering, but also the distribution of risks of different types for different people.

The basic data for such a system would probably have to come from a health or victimisation survey. For hospital records of discharges (used in the illustrative table above) would only have fragmentary information on the social context or on the circumstances of the incident causing harm. Moreover, we would probably be interested in a wider range of incidents than those which require hospitalisation; for example in the case of criminal victimisation when the victim was only slightly injured, although the consequences could have been much more serious. It is important to note that incidents of criminal victimisation, although analogous, are different from actual offences (see Christie (1968)). Moreover, the factors which influence the level of criminal victimisation reported would be different and probably be even more extensive than those we have considered in Chapters 2 and 3. For these reasons, although we think that victimisation data are interesting or important, we do not agree with Birdsall and Robb (1975) in believing they can help in estimating an offences function.

The second concern above was subjective fear of harm. People are usually more worried about the likelihood of a *criminal* unexpected event than an *accidental* incident, and this probably affects their life style. One of the victimisation studies carried out in the U.S.A., showed how 37% of a non-white female sample were afraid to go out in the street at night and several respondents had recently moved home because of a fear of "crime"

(Ennis (1967) p. 73). There are two questions: how should we treat this fear of harm, how is it related to the likelihood of harm?

We have suggested in answer to the first question that this fear of harm should be treated in addition to, and separately, from, the counting of actual instances of harm. For the *ex ante* (before the event) anxiety is a loss—insofar as anxiety makes people unhappy—as well as the *ex post* (after the event) consequences. Anxiety is clearly important but it is neither easy to evaluate nor influence; and there are problems associated with trying to reduce anxiety. If we convince people that the probability of damage is small they might become careless (for example driving and road accidents).

The second question concerns the determinants of individuals' perceptions of the probability of harm. We know of very little research on this topic and further empirical work could be of great interest. This is especially important since the information the public receive concerning the probability of harm can be very misleading. Thus an announcement of 30,000 violent crimes annually, or a chance of approximately 6 per 10,000 of being attacked, sounds quite high until one realises that few people are actually hurt as a consequence and understands the contrast with deaths from industrial or traffic accidents.

8.6 CONCLUDING REMARKS

This chapter has looked at the relationship between official statistics and the notion of the real crime problem in order to draw out the implications for policy in respect of crime. Thus we first showed how our results lend support to the arguments of sociologists of deviance that there are social biases in the selection of individuals as offenders. We then went on to present an outline of how we believe incidents and individuals are chosen as recorded offences and offenders respectively.

Next, we looked at the problem of the use of numerical information in decision making in general, and in the formation of criminal policy in particular. We showed how numerical information restricts the range of options in policy-making. In particular, in the field of criminal statistics, this type of information leads to a concentration on rates of criminality as indications of a breakdown in societal control, rather than on the amount of harm suffered by individuals. We illustrated the argument in detail in the next section. First we argued that the rapid rise in recorded crime over the sixties does not imply that there has been a "crime wave". Secondly, we gave an example of the misuse of statistics in an argument about the effectiveness of deterrence. Lastly, we have looked at the problem of what information would be appropriate in order to formulate a social policy. Our earlier arguments lead us to question whether the control of crime (real or recorded) is in fact a sensible policy goal. Instead, we suggest that social policy should primarily be concerned with the extent of damage and harm suffered by people and we concentrated on unexpected events or situations. Although people's fear of harm in different kinds of situation is important, it is difficult to see how it could be available for policy.

The major conclusion from this chapter is that it is very difficult to relate administrative statistics as currently collected in the area of crime to coherent policy goals. This should not be a surprise: it has in fact been one of the thrusts of the "social indicators movement" that the choice and presentation of data in the area of social policy is ultimately a political problem. It is, however, worth emphasizing the point, since the options, and even the solutions, for policy towards crime appear to some to be so clear.

9

The Economic Approach to Crime and Punishment

9.0 INTRODUCTION

A primary objective in this book has been the estimation of relationships modelling on the one hand the effect of changes in the probability of detection and the level of penalties on the number of offences, and on the other the determinants of the probability of detection. In this chapter we wish to examine the way in which knowledge of these relationships might be used. We shall be concerned with the social choice of punishment levels. Our basic question will be: "If extra punishment deters why is punishment not increased?" This question involves a number of difficult issues but we think that the points that we shall make are straightforward. However, some of the important ones do seem to have been missed by some of those, particularly economists, who have discussed these matters.

An economist might argue that once we know the cost and effectiveness of deterrence, the formulation of policy should be straightforward. The main thrust in this chapter, however, will be that it is hard to produce arguments for the selection of policy which are based on the standard cost-benefit or utilitarian calculus familiar to economists, and which also explain punishment levels that are both observed and commonly advocated. In § 9.1 we explain this view in detail and take as our starting point the model used by Becker (1968) in his attempt to provide an economic explanation of punishment.

While his attempt is interesting we shall argue that it is, in part, mistaken. The problem is that Becker's model leads in general to the conclusion that punishment levels should be so large that the number of offences is negligible. Thus the model fails to provide an answer to the question: "If extra punishment would deter, why not apply more punishment?" We shall examine several possible "economic" answers to this question and make the suggestion that these answers are insufficient to explain punishment levels that we see or would envisage. (We classify an argument as "economic" if it is based on a comparison of costs and benefits narrowly defined—the classification is to some extent subjective). We suggest further that to understand these levels we must invoke the notion of retribution. A complete analysis of the solution in Becker's model requires a little mathematics and this is provided in the appendix to this chapter.

We use Becker's model as a vehicle to make our point, since it is the best-known and most influential of recent contributions by economists. However, the problems we shall raise are general and we should like to emphasise that Becker's model has been chosen only as a particularly clear example of a misguided notion that seems to run through many discussions of policy towards crime (see, for example Ehrlich (1975) and Stigler (1970)). This notion is that, once we have identified a deterrence function relating offences to probabilities and severity of punishment, we have made the major step to the formulation of policy, and that all that remains is to specify the damages from offences and the costs of apprehension and punishment.

In § 9.2 we give a brief discussion of the role of retribution in policy towards crime and draw the distinction between retribution and the notion of horizontal equity which is frequently used by economists.

We examine in § 9.3 the relationship between the particular models that have been used to study policy towards crime and the more general theories of externalities found in welfare economics. Each has lessons for the other. Concluding remarks are contained in § 9.4.

9.1 THE FAILINGS OF THE COST-BENEFIT APPROACH

The notation in this chapter is the same as in the appendix to Chapter 2 and not consistent with that used in the econometric models of Chapters 4-7.

The argument of this section is that the "economic" approach to crime and punishment has failed to provide a coherent account of punishment levels as we see them, and the reason is that it has failed to provide a satisfactory answer to the question of why extra punishment is not imposed if it deters. To justify this claim we must look at the detail of models which purport to account for levels of punishment: this will involve a statement in symbolic terms of the aims of the decision-making authority. A mathematical statement of the model is contained in the appendix to this chapter.

The point at issue is a simple one and we shall choose a simple model in order to make it. We follow the best-known treatment of the economic approach to crime and punishment, that of Becker (1968). Imagine a society with a fixed number of people and where there is one type of crime. The total number of offences Y is a function of the probability of detection for an offence p and the level of punishment which we suppose can be measured by the number f—we write $Y = Y(p, f)$. By taking f as a (one dimensional) number we are supposing that there is a single kind of punishment with intensity which can be summarized in one number, or that the severity of different kinds of punishment can be reduced to a common denominator. The objective of the decision maker is to manipulate p and f to give the optimum policy. The optimum is defined to be that combination of p and f which gives minimum value of a function which expresses "social loss". The function is called the social loss function and is supposed to measure net costs in terms of social welfare which result from criminal activity and the agencies set up to control that activity.

In Becker's model the social loss function has three components which we shall suppose are all measured in monetary terms: the damage from offences, a function $D(Y)$ of the level of offences; the cost of detection and trial, and function $C(Y, p)$ of the number of offences and the proportion solved; and the cost of punishment *per se*. The total number of punishments is pY (to keep things simple we make no distinction between a detection and a guilty finding in court). We suppose that we can, crudely speaking, measure the total amount of punishment by fpY, where f is the level of punishment for an individual finding of guilt. Becker then proposes a multiplier b which translate the total amount of punishment into social loss; thus b is the social loss per unit of punishment. The notion would, of course, be hard to make precise in practice, but the model requires a statement of the social loss from punishment and this is a simple form. We shall have much to say about the contribution of this term to social loss later in this section.

We have thus supposed that all relevant costs have been reduced to a common denominator and we can write the net social loss formally as $L(p, f)$ where

$$L(p, f) = D(Y) + C(Y, p) + bpfY \qquad (1)$$

The loss is to be minimised by choice of p and f. The calculations lying behind the terms in (1) would usually be based on individual costs and benefits. Thus, for example, the net damage from an offence would be based on gains to offenders and losses to victims and the costs of punishment might be based on resources used in incarceration.

It should be clear that the domain of choice in the problem described in (1) is narrow. We consider variations only in the expenditure on the formal agencies of social control and in the level of punishment. Other factors determining the level of offences are taken as fixed. For example the educational system, the distribution of wealth, recreational facilities and so on are all taken as given: they enter the model as non-varying determinants of costs and behaviour. For the moment we shall investigate the logic of the simple model.

A central topic in Becker's analysis is the case for, and the appropriate level of, fines. He argues that fines are merely transfer payments involving no real costs of resources (remember that the cost of obtaining a detection and a conviction are in the term C), and that therefore the social loss from a fine is zero and thus $b = 0$. We shall discuss further the particular proposition that there is no cost or benefit in a transfer payment in § 9.3. Note that collection costs for fines are excluded by the assumption $b = 0$ (although they are not from (1)).

If $b = 0$ the minimand becomes

$$L(p, f) = D(Y) + C(Y, p) \tag{2}$$

Remembering that Y is a function of p and f we now ask which combination of p and f minimises L in (2). In looking for an optimum combination we suppose that it is possible to vary p and f separately. At the optimum it must be true that, given p, no change in f could reduce L, and similarly for given f no change in p could reduce L. Then at an optimum the net change in L from a small increase in f, holding p constant, must be zero. For if it were positive L could be reduced by decreasing f and if it were negative L could be reduced by increasing f and so we would not have an optimum. We can see from (2) that the effect of f for the case b equal to zero operates *only* through the level of offences Y and therefore at the optimum the effect on L of a small change in Y at constant p, must be zero.

Now imagine a decrease in f which produces just one more offence. Since the net change in L must be zero at the optimum and changes in f affect L only through Y then, at the optimum,

$$\Delta D + \Delta_1 C = 0 \tag{3}$$

where ΔD is the extra damage from one more offence and $\Delta_1 C$ is the extra cost of maintaining the detection proportion at p when offences increase by one (equation (3) is, technically, the first order condition for optimum f; see the appendix to this chapter for a more formal mathematical argument).

Consider now the change in L from a small decrease in p (at constant f)

which results in one more offence. The effect on L is $\Delta D + \Delta_1 C$ from the extra offence, but in addition we have the change in C from the reduction in p which we call $-\Delta_2 C$. We write the change in costs C from the reduction in p as minus $\Delta_2 C$ since we wish the notation Δ to correspond to a change resulting from the increase in a variable. Now we saw above that the condition for the optimum choice of f is that the net change in L from an extra offence, $\Delta D + \Delta_1 C$, is zero. Hence the net effect on the minimand of the reduction in p from a position where f has been chosen optimally is just $-\Delta_2 C$. This is negative, since $\Delta_2 C$ is positive; or in words for a given level of offences, one can make a positive reduction in social loss by reducing the proportion detected. Hence if f is chosen optimally and p is greater than zero, we cannot be at the full optimum (with f and p chosen optimally) since net social loss would be reduced by reducing p.

Let us sum up the argument. If the social loss is merely the sum of damages from offences and the costs of detection, then the punishment level is set optimally where the net marginal damage of an offence is zero. If we then consider the level of detection we find that we can save on costs of detection by reducing the proportion of offences detected, with no off-setting cost from the increase in offences.

We seem to have reached a nonsensical position—if f is chosen optimally then p cannot be. The answer to the conundrum is straightforward. The above argument has made the implicit assumption that there is some positive number of offences resulting from optimum f. The argument establishing condition (3), that the marginal social loss from an offence is zero, involved the assertion that if the marginal loss were positive, then social loss could be reduced by an increase in f and a reduction in the number of offences. Such a reduction can only occur where the number of offences is strictly positive. The only alternative to the nonsensical position just described is to set f so large that there are no offences (or that further increases in f have no extra deterrent effect). This must be the optimum solution for problem (2).

Again we can summarize the argument simply. If there is no social cost from punishment (the assumption Becker makes for fines) we can reduce social loss by increasing penalties and reducing the number of offences until the penalties are so high that there are no offences.

We have found that the cost-benefit, social loss approach of Becker, in its simplest form, leads to a severe, unrealistic conclusion. It is clear that penalties in the world are not so large that there are no offences. We must therefore ask what the model leaves out in representing policy towards punishment and crime.

It may appear that the absurd conclusion of a simple model is a peculiar point from which to start a discussion of the role of deterrence in the social choice of punishment levels. We should emphasize, however, that we have merely stated formally the question which we raised at the beginning of the chapter: "If extra punishment deters why is punishment not increased?". And the model we have used captures in a simple form an important type of approach, or group of approaches, which we can call utilitarian, to the problem of optimum punishment. The Bentham (1948) discussion is based on the notion that punishment should be chosen to maximise the general good (sum of individual utilities), or equivalently, minimise the social loss. Further, the "reductivist" line of Walker (1972) fits easily into the social loss framework: he wishes to reduce offences but with some concern with the cost of so doing (for further discussion see the end of this section). Our question then is whether the cost-benefit/utilitarian/reductivist approach can be saved from the attack of the simple question as to why punishment is not raised, by a modification of the simple model from which we started.

We shall go through several possible "economic" or utilitarian answers to our question and then ask whether, collectively, these answers provide a response which is sufficient to claim that such approaches can explain punishment levels which we see. We shall suggest that they do not and that it seems that we have to invoke the concept of retribution to explain why penalties are not increased. A simple definition of retribution would be that the punishment inflicted on an offender should be closely related to the damage involved in the offence. The notion that punishment should be commensurate with the offence will, of course, give an upper limit to punishment which can provide an answer to our basic question. We defer further discussion of retribution and return to the economic argument. The reader must, of course, make his own judgement as to the adequacy of the answers to the basic question that are presented here. We have presented such "economic" answers as have occurred to us; they seem inadequate and retribution is the only real alternative explanation available.

The discussion of our arguments will proceed more easily if we have examples of certain offences in mind. We shall consider the appropriate punishment for a petty theft, say of value £10 or £20 and without forcible entry, or a minor act of vandalism, such as small damage to a telephone box. Such offences are the most important, numerically, in the crime statistics we have been examining in previous chapters. For example, in 1966 of 1,199,859 recorded indictable offences, 848,600 were offences against property without violence and of these 848,600, 60% involved property of value less than £10 (Criminal Statistics, England and Wales 1966; see § 2.0, p. 12). More serious offences are, understandably, the primary policy concern in many discussions of penalties and we shall not be able to exclude them in this discussion, but the issue we wish to look at can be examined more simply if we concentrate on minor offences as our examples. We shall be thinking of punishment by a small fine—say £30. Many of the arguments, however, will apply to the case where punishment involves prison. We return to the problem of imprisonment below.

The order of the arguments we now present is not intended to represent our view of their relative importance or plausibility. We repeat our question: "Why, if extra punishment deters, is the punishment not raised?"

We can exclude collection costs of fines from our list of arguments insofar as over some range at least, they are independent of the level of the fine. In this case such costs, although possibly large, could not provide an argument against increasing punishment over this range, although they would outside the range.

The first and second arguments explore circumstances in which the social cost of a fine may not be zero. In the third argument we examine the possibility that net marginal damages from offences are negative, that is, the marginal offence is beneficial, and in the fourth and fifth arguments we allow the possibility that offences increase with punishment. The sixth argument points to a cost of increased punishment through an increase in costs of apprehension. The seventh concerns costs of punishing the innocent, and the eighth the fear of punishment.

First, larger fines may so impoverish the finee that it can no longer be argued that the social cost of the fine, as a transfer payment, is zero. Thus the social marginal valuation of a unit of income to the finee will become larger than the value placed on an increment to government funds, so that a transfer from the finee to the government is seen as a cost. It seems doubtful that in general fines are pushed to the point where the resulting poverty of the finee is the over-riding argument against further increases. Further, there are ways of increasing fines, whilst retaining differentials between offences, which would not increase the social cost of punishment very severely. For example, one might suggest that many fines instead of being just one payment be repeated for a few years after the event, thus increasing the fine without producing penury in any year. If this decreases, by the consequent deterrence, the social loss L as modelled, it would be hard to produce an economic argument against it which was based on considerations which are embodied in the analysis up to this point.

But, such a procedure for collecting fines would almost certainly involve large collection costs which would not be independent of the level of fines. The difficulty of collecting fines from poor offenders is illustrated by the frequent use of imprisonment for defaulting finees. This difficulty appears to be taken into account in England and Wales by sentencers when fixing the fine for an individual. It does not, however, provide an argument against a small increase for a finee who is not very poor.

Secondly, one might argue that the social loss from fines is negative, because government revenue is very valuable and that fines should not be pushed so far that this revenue begins to drop off severely. We should guess that this argument would be unconvincing to many if put a little more openly, as follows: "We should not raise fines from current levels because offences would drop off so sharply that we should lose fine revenue." One could think of examples of revenue raising opportunities from fines which are not accepted. (For a discussion of some related problems see Kolm's (1973) discussion of tax evasion.)

A third argument for keeping down fines may be that at very low levels of offences, the net damage from the offences is negative. In other words, if penalties are already high, offences may only be committed by those whose personal benefit from committing the offence is very high and might outweigh, in the social calculus, the harm done to others. There are doubtless examples of beneficial offences: for example, one might argue that it is better for a speed limit to be broken to take a severely injured person to hospital than for it to be observed and the person to die. It would be difficult to argue, however, that if fines were high enough, all, or the majority of the residual offences, would be beneficial. One would have to be both a very strong believer in *homo economicus* and to argue that most personal "gains" should enter the social welfare function. In other words, one would need to argue that individuals carried out acts where (their) expected benefits exceeded expected costs and that these expected net benefits should be included in the social calculus. In the case of an assault, for example, the expected benefit is the "pleasure" the person carrying out the assault obtains from the act. Few would wish to include this benefit as a gain in the social calculus.

There may, however, be specific types of offences for which this kind of argument is appropriate: for example, a possibility would be parking offences.

If accepted, the argument would counter the suggestion that the optimum number of offences is zero. It does not, however, meet the point that whenever f is set optimally costs are reduced by a reduction in p (although Stigler (1970) p. 527 appears to think that it does). The solution would appear to be that p should tend to zero and f to infinity in just such a combination to produce the "correct" number of offences. The conclusion is clearly absurd and there seems no escape from the introduction of a cost of punishment into the model if such a conclusion is to be avoided. Note that it is the assertion that there will, in general, be damages from an offence rather than benefits that leads us to look for costs (as opposed to benefits) associated with increasing punishment.

Fourthly, one might argue that at some levels of punishment extra punishment would imply more, not less, offences. We give two possible reasons. The first relates to the post-fine wealth of the finee and the second his view of the "just" punishment. If potential offences from an individual decrease as his wealth increases, then a substantial reduction in his wealth through a fine may generate more offences. This may occur because offences are related to the distribution of incomes (see Danziger and Wheeler (1975)) and if a person is made relatively worse off he may be motivated (by jealousy or a sense of unfairness as to distribution) to commit more offences. One can also make the case without appealing to income distribution. If a person is forced by a high fine into a situation where he is without food, he may steal a loaf of bread. The second reason invokes the notion of the "just" punishment as felt by the individual. If he feels the level of his fine is "unjust" he may become hostile to the society which inflicted it and commit more offences. We return to this issue in § 9.2.

While we think that these arguments have importance for some fines and some income levels, we should suggest that the arguments are not strong for small fines (as are being considered here) or any but the lowest income levels. Ultimately the response to this fourth argument is empirical. If one can establish that in general extra punishment implies on balance less offences, then that is enough for our purpose here. We are discussing not particular cases but the general level of punishment, for a certain kind of offence.

The fifth argument concerns the effect on offences of the structure of relative penalties. If the fine for a certain offence is high an offender might be more likely to commit another and perhaps more serious offence, either instead, or in order to limit the probability of being apprehended. This argument would not be significant in the absence of upper limits to punishment, since differentials could be maintained while increasing all punishments. It assumes significance when we recognise that humanitarian considerations concerning the nature and length of imprisonment may provide an upper limit to penalties.

It is not easy to judge the quantitative importance of this argument, and for some groups of offences it may well be substantial. For example, one can argue that it is important to keep a clear difference between penalties for offences of theft with violence which do and do not involve the use of weapons. But it is hard to argue that the whole structure of offences is so finely balanced that any alteration at the lower end of the penalties for minor acts of vandalism, say increasing a fine from £30 to £45, would cause more serious offences to increase. Again this is ultimately an empirical question.

A sixth and related point is that the level of punishment might enter the C (cost of detection) function directly, in the sense that individuals have a greater incentive to take evading action, and hire better lawyers if caught, if penalties are high. Becker (1968, p. 184) refers to the possibility that punishment level may enter C through juries being unwilling to convict if punishment levels are set very high. We discuss this point in more detail in § 9.2, since it may be connected with a view of retribution, or appropriate punishment.

If the level of punishment f does enter the C function in this way then the assertion that the net marginal social damage from an offence is zero, at optimum f, fails. The net damage would not be zero but equal to the marginal apprehension cost from an increase in f.

The argument has some plausibility but we know of no empirical evidence in favour of the view that the effects indicated are substantial for the minor property offences we have in mind. Note that the possibility was excluded from the models and estimates of earlier chapters. Again, it may be a consideration of greater importance for more serious offences.

Our seventh, and penultimate consideration, concerns the cost that is associated with punishing the innocent. We include it here, since some might describe it as economic, although we should prefer to call it retributive. On a utilitarian basis one might argue that there is no extra cost associated with fining an innocent person apart from the transfer payment which has already been included in the social loss function—in (1) through b, and (2) with the assumption that $b = 0$. We therefore think that the argument should be classified as retributive, since it is based on the notion that we should punish *only* those who have done wrong. In response one might invoke, as an explanation of the feeling that there is a cost to punishing the innocent, a principle of "horizontal equity" which says that individuals of like situation should be treated similarly. Innocent individuals should therefore be treated alike and violations of this principle impose costs. This seems very close to the retributive position, since one has to argue that the over-riding sense in which people are alike is whether they are innocent or guilty. Otherwise one would not be able to argue against fining the *unique* (say) richest person in the economy for an offence he did not commit.

Leaving aside, however, the question of whether to classify the argument as economic or retributive, it does not seem powerful enough to explain why fines for minor offences are not raised. For although it is an important issue when discussing capital punishment for example, at lower levels of punishment it is the fact of convicting the innocent that is found offensive rather than precise punishment levels (note that for such lower punishments one can compensate if innocence is discovered).

The possibility of punishing the innocent raises an issue relevant to the behavioural specification of the Becker model. Under an expected utility model the decision whether to commit an offence would depend on the difference between the expected utility of being punished if innocent and the expected utility of being punished if guilty. This raises some interesting questions. For example, the granting of extra powers to the police in certain situations may increase the probability of punishing the innocent. This may increase offences unless the probability of punishing the guilty is increased sufficiently to "compensate" for increased probability of punishing the innocent (see Harris (1970) for a discussion of other problems related to the increase of police powers). The possibility of punishing the innocent is likely to affect jury behaviour too, and we return to this point in § 9.2. Thus any cost of punishing the innocent from a utilitarian view point, concerns the (possibly) reduced deterrent effect and extra cost of obtaining convictions.

Up to now our concentration has been on *ex-post* phenomena in the sense that our loss function evaluates what has happened in the society, rather than the evaluation *ex ante* of various potential outcomes with different probabilities. It seems to us that a mixture of the two approaches is needed and this provides our eighth argument: this is concerned with the fear of future punishment. It might be argued that it is "double-counting" to count as a cost both the fear of punishment and the pain inflicted by the punishment itself; and one can argue generally that, if individuals perceive probabilities correctly, the utilitarian sum *ex post* and expected utility *ex ante* are the same so that a concern with either or both yields the same policy; thus we need not bother with the distinction between *ex ante* and *ex post*. However, if individuals do not perceive probabilities correctly or if some fears or expectations are deemed to enter the social loss function and others not, then a concern with *ex ante* as well as *ex post* welfare will require a modification to our social loss function. Its relevance here to the social loss from punishment is the *ex ante* cost associated with the fear of punishment either from the point of view of the offender or the innocent. Given our subjective estimate of the sentencers' and legislators' perception of an innocent individual's fear of being mistakenly punished, and a guess at their evaluation of the loss due to the generation of fear in offenders, we suppose again that this does not explain why, in fact, fines for minor offences are not raised substantially.

We have been through eight "economic" arguments which we have introduced to try to rescue the Becker model from the absurd solution of very high punishment under the assumption of costless punishment. The absurdity arises because there is a basic asymmetry in the Becker model. Deterrence through detection has a direct cost, whereas deterrence through punishment does not. An argument which admits deterrence but which fails to meet this asymmetry, cannot save the model. The "rescue act" must proceed then, through the introduction of a cost associated with fines or through a denial of the deterrent effect. The fourth and fifth arguments above deny the deterrent effect. The third denies that offences are damaging, but we saw that this did not meet our question. The remainder introduce some direct cost associated with punishment.

We must now leave the reader to judge whether any combination of the eight arguments can save the model. In our judgement the first carries the greatest weight as an explanation of why, in fact, the punishments under consideration are not increased. However, as we explained, it is not sufficiently general to meet the question. We have suggested that, the fourth, fifth and sixth arguments do not impinge sufficiently strongly on the punishment of small offences to answer our question and that the eighth argument is unlikely to sway the magistrates who administer the punishment for these small offences. The second and third arguments were, in general, unconvincing. The seventh argument, the cost of punishing the innocent, we prefer to classify as retributive and we return to the point in § 9.2.

Our discussion and evaluation of these eight arguments leaves us with the view that the utilitarian, or cost-benefit economic calculus as exemplified by Becker cannot, even when modified in certain ways, give a full explanation of why, in practice, many fines are not increased. In many cases it seems that punishments are not changed because the level of punishment is deemed appropriate or just in relation to the damage involved: Becker (1968) attempted (see § 9.3 and the mathematical appendix to this chapter) to show that his cost-benefit approach could provide a justification for the level of the fines being set equal to the damage from an offence. We have seen that his model is flawed and we are left with the conclusion that any apparent justice in a link between the damage and penalty is based on a notion of the appropriate retribution.

We should emphasize that, while we have taken the Becker model as a starting point, the conclusion we have come to would apply to most attempts at an "economic explanation" of punishment, since we have tried to be exhaustive in considering possible economic arguments. We have excluded, in general, a discussion of imprisonment from our argument. We must acknowledge, however, for the case of imprisonment that the cost of extra punishment may be substantial and an important reason for not increasing sentences. It is enough, however, to challenge the utilitarian calculus as a general explanation of punishment levels to argue that it cannot explain the level of fines.

This is not the place for a lengthy discussion of the merits of retribution in sentencing systems, although we discuss in § 9.2 how retribution can be introduced as a criterion, or through the behaviour of individuals, into models. We have merely come to the conclusion that it does play an important role in actual sentencing systems (and, as far as we can see, in plausible alternatives). The reader can doubtless think of situations often viewed as just which seem to require retributive arguments for explanation. One example would be the notion of equality of punishment for similar offences. If individuals committing the same offence have different preferences or inclinations, the advocate of the social calculus would have to argue for different treatment. This would appear unjust to many people, not least to the offender who received the heavier punishment (see below § 9.2).

The reader is referred for further discussion of retributionism, utilitarianism and reductivism in punishment to the books by Hart (1968), Smart and Williams (1973) and Walker (1972). The distinction between "rule" and "act" utilitarianism discussed, for example, in Smart and Williams (1973) can play an important part in discussions of the appropriate enforcement of laws. The rule utilitarian position would be that where it is important, in a utilitarian sense, that behaviour in general conforms to some rule, then uniformity in treatment of transgressors may be desirable, even though special cases were made for individual exemptions. The act utilitarian looks at the net consequences of each act separately.

However, the arguments discussed above would in general apply equally to rule as to act utilitarianism.

Reductivism refers to a concern to reduce the frequency of the types of behaviour prohibited by the criminal law (N. D. Walker (1972) p. 18). Given a choice between two policies of equal cost the "economic reductivist", N. D. Walker says ((1972) p. 19), would choose that which would give the biggest reduction for the money. Reductivism is advocated by Walker, although he distinguishes it from utilitarianism "To call it 'utilitarianism' or 'Benthamism' implies more than is intended . . ." (N. D. Walker (1972) p. 18). It is clear, however, that the reductivist and utilitarian approaches are close and that our claim that the utilitarian position fails to provide an adequate explanation of actual penalties, applies also to reductivism.

9.2   THE INCORPORATION OF RETRIBUTION INTO POLICY MODELS

We begin with a brief discussion of the concept of retribution and then examine where and how retribution might be incorporated into models of the type discussed in the preceding section. Our examination of the concept of retribution is intended to clarify its possible role and we shall look a little further at the relation between retribution and horizontal equity. The incorporation of retribution into the model will be in two ways—in the social loss function and through the behaviour of participants.

We should distinguish three different ways in which retributivist considerations may be important in objectives. The first is as a "General Justifying Aim" of punishment (see Hart (1968) Essay I). That is, crudely speaking the penal system is, or should be, designed to ensure that offenders atone by suffering for their offences. There is a strong contrast between this form of guiding principle and the utilitarian principle of designing punishment to maximise total social welfare.

A more limited form is called "Distributive Retribution" (again see Hart (1968) Essay I) and refers to a concern with *who* should be punished rather than the amount. And finally there is the notion of "Limiting Retribution" (see N. D. Walker (1972) p. 30). This states that the appropriate punishment or atonement should not exceed the harm done by the offence. There are obvious problems of measurement, but the idea is that the offence itself places upper limits on punishment. One could extend the notion to include a lower limit too, and we shall use "Limiting" in this wider sense.

That there should be a special concern with punishing the guilty and not the innocent may seem trivial, but it does seem that we have to invoke it as a special principle in connection with policy towards punishment, since it cannot be deduced from, for example, either a utilitarian position or a notion of horizontal equity.

The reason a utilitarian might be concerned with punishing the guilty rather than the innocent is, as we have seen (see our discussion of the seventh argument in the previous section), deterrence will work only if one is more likely to suffer punishment if one does commit an offence than if one does not. But this does not attach any cost *per se* to punishing the innocent, and it seems that many would want to regard such punishment as a direct social loss.

A principle of horizontal equity can produce a result quite close to the notion that one should punish only the guilty but fails in an important respect. We can consider the problem of punishment in a society consisting of individuals, no two of which are alike. The notion that like individuals should be treated alike does not then yield any conclusions at all. If we argue that the over-riding sense of "like individuals" in policy towards punishment is whether or not they are guilty, we have merely re-stated the notion of "Distributive Retribution". An alternative form of the notion of horizontal equity would be that like persons should face the same probability distribution of outcomes. This principle is met here if identical innocent individuals have equal probabilities of being punished: thus some innocent individuals would be punished. Therefore, this alternative form also fails to explain a concern to punish the guilty.

We can ask now how retribution might be incorporated into models of the kind discussed in § 9.1. The incorporation of the weaker (distributive) form of retribution discussed above would require specification, not only of a cost of punishing the innocent, but also the cost of not punishing those of the guilty who "get away with it" (for an expression of the strong feelings this generates, see Mark (1973)). The stronger (limiting) version would require a cost to be attached to deviations in punishment levels from that deemed to be appropriate to the harm done. For example bf, the social cost for a punishment f in (1), might be replaced by a function $S(f)$ as illustrated in Fig. 9.1.

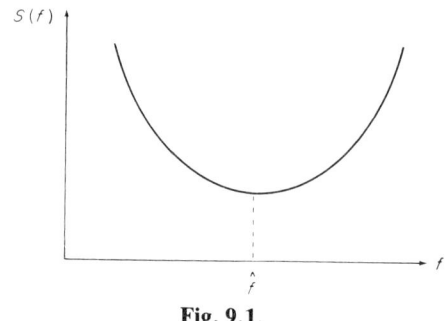

Fig. 9.1.

The minimum for $S(f)$ occurs where f is equal to $\hat{f}$ the "appropriate" punishment for the offence. Such a formulation would include both costs of punishing the innocent and not punishing the guilty: where the guilty are not punished, $f = 0$, and where the innocent are punished $\hat{f} = 0$.

We must acknowledge here that there is something rather vulgar about the attempt to combine two distinct approaches to the problem of the social choice of punishment, the utilitarian and the retributive, into one grand social loss function.

One need not discuss retribution in the model solely in terms of the minimand. It may be important to recognise retributivist feelings in participants in the system. For example, juries may be reluctant to convict if they feel prospective penalties are likely to be unjust in the strong retributive sense. This phenomenon could be modelled by introducing the level of punishment, or its deviation from the "appropriate" level, into the cost of producing convictions. The weaker notion could be important too, if the measure of reasonable doubt used by a jury is a function (however vague) of previous instances of conviction of innocent individuals.

Punishment which is seen as unjust can affect the behaviour of individuals in two ways. Someone who is subject to punishment he sees as unjust, may be so embittered that he is more likely to offend than if punishment had been lower. Thus offences may increase with punishment over a certain range. Secondly, respect for the law and willingness to accept punishment, may be functions of the degree to which penalties are seen as just. Again this could lead to offences increasing with punishment over a certain range.

In addition, there would be increased costs of obtaining convictions as punishment increases, since the public may be unwilling to co-operate if offences are seen as unjust and the individual might be particularly strongly motivated to avoid punishment.

The appearance of retribution in the behaviour of the different agents could, at least indirectly, be checked empirically. The data we have been using in this study are, however, too aggregated for one to expect to be able to detect this kind of detail.

9.3 THE ECONOMIC THEORY OF EXTERNALITIES

There is a well known result in welfare economics, which we shall explain shortly, concerning the appropriate policy towards an activity by one individual which imposes costs or benefits (externalities) on others. Examples of externalities are smoking cigarettes in crowded places or using a car, thus emitting exhaust, causing wear on roads and contributing to congestion. Under certain assumptions, which are rather strong, one can show that the optimum policy (in the sense of maximising a social welfare function where the arguments of the function are the utility levels of the members of the society) is that he should pay, in the form of a corrective tax, an extra amount over and above the costs of producing the articles used in the activity, say the cigarette, equal to the cost to others inflicted by the marginal, or last, unit of the activity. The conclusion is similar to that which Becker (1968) claimed to have obtained for the optimum fine. We shall see below that his argument was close to those which are usually employed to establish the standard result in welfare economics. Thus given the faulty logic of the Becker model, we must ask whether anything is wrong with the standard economic theory of externalities.

The answer is that there is nothing wrong with the logical structure of the theory of externalities. Any criticism of the conclusion should therefore be directed towards the assumptions on which the argument is based. These can be, or at least should be, stated clearly and to keep things simple we take the case where externalities arise only in consumption, and thus our corrective tax system applies only to consumption goods. The main assumptions relevant here are that individuals maximise their utility facing (post-tax) prices they believe are independent of the quantities they buy, that pre-tax prices reflect social costs of production (the factor and resource cost), the income distribution is as the government would wish it, there are no costs associated with the calculation or collection of taxes and that these taxes are equal to the externality costs inflicted on others.

The argument can then be sketched as follows. Suppose first there is no tax imposed to "correct" for the externality. The utility maximising individual will push an activity, or the consumption of a good to that point where the last or marginal unit is worth to him just what he must pay for it, the social cost of production. The social benefit of the last unit, which we suppose is measured by the worth to the individual, thus the price, is less than the total social cost of that unit, since to the social cost of production must be added the costs inflicted on others by the activity or consumption in question. Thus, in the absence of taxation, the net social benefit of the last unit is negative and we do not have an optimum.

The argument goes on to say that the optimum can be supported by a tax system where the individual pays for the costs inflicted on others. He then equates the value to him with cost of production, plus cost to others and the net social value of the marginal unit is neither positive nor negative.

Note that we have compared the money cost to the individual with the money cost of production and the money cost to others, and have taken no account of the revenue raised by the tax (it merely being a transfer from the individual to the government). It is here that we have to appeal to the assumption that we have an optimum income distribution since our comparisons involve the implicit assumption that a unit of income, or the willingness to pay, of one individual is worth the same as that of another. We are assuming throughout the argument that the government correctly perceives and represents the interest of the individuals on whom the externality is inflicted.

The interesting innovation of Becker's approach is that it involves the explicit introduction of the costs of collecting taxes—in his model the cost C of detecting a proportion p of offences Y. Thus, in his "solution" the optimum fine is equal to the social cost of detection plus the damage caused by the offence. Apart from the cost of detection we have a particular case of the general theory of externalities (we can see this more clearly when Becker's argument is set out formally in the mathematical appendix to this chapter). The idea is that an offender goes on committing offences (the activity of the standard theory) up to the point where the expected gain from the offence is equal to the expected fine (market price) and that this fine should be set equal to the total social damage (cost of production plus cost of the externality), where the damage is equal to the harm to the victim plus costs of detection.

Becker laid particular stress on two features of his conclusion. The first was that the fine should be independent of any attributes of the offender, and the second that the level should be directly related to the harm caused (so that we can dispense with notions of limiting retribution in justifying such fines).

Our presentation of the general theory of policy towards externalities now allows us to make several observations on the Becker theory. First, we found that in the general theory, at the optimum, the marginal net social value from the externality-producing activity is zero. The substantial difference between the plausibility of such a feature for the general theory of externalities and the particular case of crime should be clear. The activities generating the externality in the general case are usually regarded as of value in themselves to the individual performing the activity, and one can accept that this value is of a kind which should enter the social welfare function at just that value which is perceived by the individual. The purpose of the tax is to make the individual pay the cost of what he is doing. Thus the factory producing steel is producing something of value. If it also produces unpleasant smoke, we tax it, so that the price of steel takes account of the total social costs of production. Similarly the car which emits fumes, causes wear to roads, and congests, is providing its owner with transport which he regards as of value. The social decision maker formulating the social policy may see no reason to quarrel with his assessment. A tax on petrol, in lieu of car use, would face the car user with the full cost of his activity.

In the case of an act of vandalism for which the perpetrator is fined, one might argue that the psychic benefits to the individual of say smashing a telephone box, should be treated no differently for social policy from those from the use of the car. Smashing telephone boxes would have a price, like everything else, and those who liked to smash boxes would do so and pay the price in just the same manner as the motorist or the smoker. We suggest, however, that most would see the matter differently and would want to suggest that such psychic benefits should have a very low or negligible contribution to the social welfare function. In addition, some would argue that there is an explicit social cost to the illegality of the act over and above the physical damage perpetrated and any cost of apprehension. In such a case, where no positive benefits flow from an act, we cannot have an optimum situation where the net damage from the marginal offence is zero.

Becker's analysis shares with the standard theory of externalities the assumption that the income distribution is optimum. This was required in his model to give the condition that social cost of punishment is zero and to argue that the social gain from the offence accruing to the offender will just equal the fine for the marginal offence. We have seen above that many would want to ignore the gain to the offender and include a specific cost to illegality in the social calculus. If we relax the assumption that the income distribution is optimum but grant, for the moment, that there are gains from offences which are of significant value, we no longer have the conclusion that fines should be independent of the circumstances of the offender. The cost of punishing a poor offender may be seen as higher than that of punishing a rich offender, since the social value of an extra unit of income to the poor may be higher. In this case one would require a lower fine for a poorer offender (see the mathematical appendix to this chapter for further discussion).

The contribution of Becker (1968) to the theory of externalities is the explicit introduction into his model of taxation costs. There is the cost of punishment (tax) $bpfY$, which depends on the level of the punishment and is, he argued, zero for fines. In addition there is the cost of punishment (tax) which is independent of the level of the punishment (tax)—the detection cost C. Unfortunately, Becker fails to bring out the consequences of this innovation in his enthusiasm to emphasize the similarities with standard economic theory. Let us see what the model tells us.

We saw at the start of our discussion in § 9.1 that the root of the failings of the Becker model lay in the observation that if fines are set optimally, so that the damage from the marginal offence is zero, we save on detection costs by lowering the proportion detected with no offsetting social loss elsewhere. We can apply just the same argument in the general theory of externalities. Let us begin with the assumption that there are no costs associated with the enforcement of taxation. Suppose we were in a situation where everyone was made to pay a tax on a certain externality-producing good and that the tax was set at such a level that the total net social benefit from a marginal unit of the good were zero (the standard rule described above). Now suppose that a random sample of 99% of the population is made to pay the tax. The change in social welfare from the adjustment of the level of the good is zero. If we suppose that income distribution is optimum (so that the marginal worth of a pound to all individuals and to the government is equal) then there are no costs associated with loss of tax revenue. Suppose now that there are enforcement costs and that these are reduced by the change. We have shown that this change is beneficial.

It seems, then, that it will not in general be optimum to have 100% enforcement of the standard system of taxes towards externalities. We can go on to ask whether the search for a solution to the general externality problem will run into the same pitfalls as the Becker model of optimum punishment as a result of the parallel simple question as to why these taxes should not be increased. The answer is that it will not and is based on the twin observations that the contributio of externality-producing activities can be positive and that there will often be a high value on government revenue. Thus the government would, optimally, push the tax on the activity causing the externality to the point where the net benefit from the marginal unit of the activity was equal to the value of the transfer (net of collection costs) of the tax revenue from the individual to the government. To put the condition the opposite way, at the optimum a reduction in the tax would generate a little more of a valuable activity but would forego valuable taxation opportunities (for further discussion see the mathematical appendix).

9.4 CONCLUDING REMARKS

Our primary concern in this chapter has been the examination of utilitarian or cost-benefit models of optimum policy towards punishment and we paid particular attention to the formulation of Becker (1968). The reason for our concern with the issue is that these models seem to give an obvious use for the estimates of the effects of the likelihood and severity of punishment on the offence rate. Our conclusion from the examination of these models has been that they fail to explain punishment levels as we see them, since they fail to meet the simple question of why punishment levels are not raised if the consequence would be fewer offences. We discussed possible "economic" modifications to these models in an attempt to answer the question, but eventually formed the judgement that we required the notion of retribution to understand punishment levels as observed.

We discussed the manner in which retribution might enter the model both in the social loss function and the behaviour of participants. As a "General Justifying Aim" for punishment we distinguished (following Hart (1968)) a strong notion of retribution (punishment should equal damage) from retribution in distribution (concern for punishing only the guilty). The last concept was itself distinguished from horizontal equity.

The relations between the economic theory of externalities and models of crime and punishment were the subject of § 9.3. We concluded that the latter was a special case of the former apart from the introduction of enforcement costs. The logical problems of the punishment models do not undermine the general theory of externalities, since the activities causing externalities can be of value in themselves, in contrast to most offences. The lessons of the punishment model were, however, of value to the theory of externalities, since they indicate that it would not, in general, be optimum to have 100% enforcement of the standard system of taxes towards externalities.

It is time now to pull together our conclusions from this study as a whole and to make suggestions for further research.

MATHEMATICAL MODELS OF OPTIMUM DETERRENCE

9.A.0 INTRODUCTION

We argued in Chapter 9 that attempts to build models of the optimum level of punishment and probability of apprehension which are based solely on simple utilitarian or cost-benefit considerations will be likely to end in failure, in that the models will have no solution. In this appendix we begin (§ 9.A.1) with a rigorous mathematical demonstration of our argument. We comment on similar results from analyses of tax evasion and insurance schemes. It follows from the absence of a solution that, see § 9.A.2, one of the main results Becker (1968) claimed to have derived from his model—that the fine should be equal to the harm from an offence—is false. In the same section we shall show how these models relate to the standard theory of externalities which yields the apparently similar policy conclusion that the tax on an activity which inflicts damage on others should be set equal to the marginal damage from the activity. We shall discuss the relation of taxes or fines to the income of the payee. Finally (§ 9.A.3) we shall give, for easy reference, Becker's argument that, at the optimum the responsiveness to the severity of punishment should be less than that to the probability of apprehension.

9.A.1 EXISTENCE PROBLEMS

The optimisation problem as formulated by Becker (1968) was explained in Chapter 9 and we derived the expression for net social loss, which is to be minimised,

$$L\,(p,\,f) = D\,(Y) + C\,(Y,\,p) + bpfY \tag{1}$$

The notation is as used in Chapter 9. The variables which are to be chosen are the probability of apprehension p and the level of punishment[1] f. The probability p must lie between 0 and 1 and we restrict attention to non-negative fines. We therefore write the problem

$$\text{Minimise } L\,(p, f) \tag{2}$$
$$0 \leqq f$$
$$0 \leqq p \leqq 1$$

Given that all the functions in the problem are differentiable (and assuming, as is acceptable here, no problems with constraint qualifications) the optimum must satisfy one of the conditions (3), (4), (5).

$$\left.\begin{array}{l} f \geqq 0 \\ \\ L_f \geqq 0 \end{array}\right\} \text{ comp. } \quad \text{and} \quad \begin{array}{l} 0 < p < 1 \\ \\ L_p = 0 \end{array} \tag{3}$$

$$\left.\begin{array}{l} f \geqq 0 \\ \\ L_f \geqq 0 \end{array}\right\} \text{ comp. } \quad \text{and} \quad \begin{array}{l} p = 0 \\ \\ L_p \geq 0 \end{array} \tag{4}$$

$$\left.\begin{array}{l} f \geqq 0 \\ \\ L_f \geqq 0 \end{array}\right\} \text{ comp. } \quad \text{and} \quad \begin{array}{l} p = 1 \\ \\ L_p \leqq 0 \end{array} \tag{5}$$

The notation $\Big\}$ comp. denotes that the pair of inequalities bracketed together are complementary slack, that is, if one of the inequalities holds with strict inequality the other holds with strict equality. Subscripts denote partial derivatives. Thus the first of the conditions in each of (3), (4), (5) says that if the severity of punishment f is strictly positive at the optimum then the net effect of a small change in f on social loss (L_f) must be zero. For if this were not the case social loss could be reduced by a small change in f. Similarly if at the optimum L_f is strictly positive then f must be zero, else social loss could be reduced by a small decrease in f.

The second of the conditions in (3) says that if p, at the optimum, lies strictly between zero and one (we say we have an interior solution for p) then the net effect of a small change in p on social loss must be zero. The second condition of (4) says that if p is zero at the optimum, then L_p must be non-negative else social loss would be reduced by a small increase in p. The

---

[1] There are, see appendix to Chapter 2, certain problems associated with the measurement of punishment. We follow in this appendix the notation and measurement of Becker.

second condition of (5) says, similarly, that if p is one at the optimum then L_p must be non-positive; otherwise social loss would be reduced by a small reduction in p.

We shall take the case $b = 0$, which Becker argued was appropriate for fines, and examine possible values of p and f satisfying the alternative necessary conditions to see if they could be optimum. We shall show that none of the values satisfying the necessary conditions can be optimum: it will follow that no optimum exists. We suppose that Y_f is strictly negative for $p > 0$, $f > 0$ and C_p is strictly positive for $Y > 0$, $p \geqq 0$. Thus for $p > 0$, $f > 0$, extra punishment deters and for positive offences increases in the detection rate require resources, subscripts denote partial derivatives and D' is the derivative of D with respect to Y.

In the case $b = 0$ we have

$$L_f = (D' + C_Y)\, Y_f \tag{6}$$

$$L_p = (D' + C_Y)\, Y_p + C_p \tag{7}$$

Suppose we have a pair (p, f) with both p and f strictly positive. Let us ask whether such a pair could be optimum. If f is strictly positive and the pair is optimum then by the first part of each of (3), (4) and (5) we have $L_f = 0$. From (6) and $Y_f < 0$ we have

$$D' + C_Y = 0 \tag{8}$$

and hence, since[2] $Y > 0$,

$$L_p = C_p > 0 \tag{9}$$

But if p is greater than zero, as we are assuming, then L_p must satisfy either (3) or (5). Hence (9) is a contradiction and we have established that no pair (p, f) with both p and f strictly positive is optimum. Intuitively, the argument is that if f is chosen so that the net costs from the marginal offence are zero (the condition for optimum f where $f > 0$) then we save on apprehension costs by reducing p, with no offsetting social loss from any change in offences.

The remaining possibilities are first that one of p or f is zero at the optimum or secondly, that no optimum exists. Where p is zero we may suppose that there is no change in offences from altering f. With $b = 0$ this implies no change in social loss from altering f (see equation (1)) so $(0, f)$ is equivalent in welfare terms to $(0, 0)$. We can thus represent the remaining alternatives as zero punishment or that no optimum exists. Let us suppose directly that there exist configurations of p and f providing lower social loss

[2] $Y > 0$ is implied by $Y \geqq 0$ (non-negative offences) and our assumption that $Y_f < 0$.

than that where punishment is zero; that is, we can do better than the situation with zero punishment. The conclusion is that no optimum exists.

Let us examine what has gone wrong. We know in general that the problem of maximising a continuous function over a compact set does have a solution. We have continuity, since we have imposed the stronger condition of differentiability. The failure of existence here is due to the constraint set not being compact—there is no upper bound on f. If we imposed an upper bound on f, F say, so that an optimum did exist then the above argument shows that the optimum must be at F. Thus, loosely speaking, the result of the Becker model is that the punishment should be indefinitely large. The point is intuitively obvious—if offences cause damage and can be costlessly deterred (it has been assumed directly that there is no cost to changing the level of punishment) then we minimise social loss by increasing punishment until there are no offences. Where there are infinite punishments and no offences the optimum probability of apprehension is indeterminate; provided it is strictly positive the prospect of infinite punishment will deter all offences. Where the optimum number of offences is non-zero, as may be the case if certain offences are considered beneficial, the optimum policy (where we speak loosely of infinite f as optimum) is to let p tend to zero and f to infinity in such a manner (which will depend on the function $Y\,(p,\,f)$) to produce the "right" number of offences.

The basic asymmetry in the Becker (1968) model between p and f is that f does not enter the $C\,(Y,\,p)$ function in its own right; if it does the whole structure of the model changes. The first order conditions for optimum p can be obtained from that for optimum f merely by substituting p for f and the argument used above to establish that an optimum does not exist cannot be applied. The possibility that the model should contain f as an explicit argument in the C function was considered in the body of Chapter 9. Although we did not provide a full argument, we rejected it as a means of saving the Becker model (and see also § 9.A.3).

Becker seemed to realise that there may be difficulties of the kind described above at several points in his analysis—see Becker (1968) pp. 183-4, footnote 26, p. 189 ($b = 0$ and Figure 4) and p. 193 for example. He suggested that the zero offence solution (where we use the term as a short-hand for the existence problem described) was possible but considered for his analysis (for $b = 0$ and elsewhere) the case where offences were not zero at the optimum. But the zero offence solution is not merely a possibility, it is a logical necessity from the model where $b = 0$. His analysis of conditions where some other solution holds is therefore in error and irrelevant.

Problems where formally optima do not exist but where infinite penalties seem to be dictated by the formulation of the problem, have been noted in connection with tax evasion by Kolm (1973). Kolm notes, in his observations on the problem of income tax evasion as formulated by Allingham and Sandmo (1972), that the authors showed that in the determination of expected tax yield, penalties and p are substitutes. A given amount of tax revenue (which here includes penalty payments by apprehended evaders) is therefore collected at minimum cost, he remarks, by letting punishment tend to infinity and the probability of detection tend to zero (as he puts it "hang evaders with probability zero" Kolm (1973), p. 266). The reason is similar to that noted here—penalties deter at no cost, whereas detection consumes resources. Kolm proposes a maximand alternative to government revenue. This is the expected utility of income of the representative individual plus the utility from the public good on which the government is assumed to spend its revenue. He examines the possibility, which cannot be excluded, that an optimum fails to exist but seems to think that the interior solution ($0 < p < 1$ and finite penalties) is "normal" (see Kolm (1973) p. 269). Optimum policy towards tax evasion was also examined by Srinivasan (1973) and Singh (1973). The problems raised here do not appear in their models because penalties are not considered as a policy variable.

Mirrlees (1974) considers optimum insurance schemes where farmers produce and consume a crop under conditions of uncertainty. He also encounters the possibility of indefinitely large penalties. We give a brief sketch of his model. The distribution of outcomes is affected by work input. He considers a population of identical farmers. In a directed economy there would be an optimum (in the sense of maximising a utility sum over individuals) work input level—call it z^*. He shows in an example that in an economy where farmers select their own work input level subject to the crop insurance scheme selected by the government, no optimum insurance scheme exists. However, he shows also that the government can move all the farmers as closely as it pleases to z^* by imposing very heavy penalties on the few, who by chance, fall below a given output level. Thus problems of infinite penalties appearing optimum in utilitarian welfare economics are not confined to models of crime and tax evasion.

9.A.2 THE THEORY OF EXTERNALITIES AND THE RELATION BETWEEN FINES AND DAMAGE FROM AN OFFENCE

Becker (1968) claimed to have deduced the strong conclusion that fines should be set equal to the total marginal damage caused by the offences including both direct damage and resources involved in apprehension. We give his (erroneous) argument here in order to demonstrate the analogy with the theory of externalities. This will throw light both on models of optimum punishment and the theory of externalities.

Imagine, for the sake of the argument, that we did have an optimum with f strictly positive. We should require, see (6) and (8), as a condition for optimality that the marginal damage from an offence be zero, thus $D' + C_Y = 0$.

We now divide the damage from offences Y into two components, the harm done to the victims, $H(Y)$ and the gain to the offenders $G(Y)$. The net damage is then

$$D(Y) = H(Y) - G(Y) \tag{10}$$

Differentiating (10) and using (8) we have (where primes denote derivatives)

$$G'(Y) = H'(Y) + C_Y \tag{11}$$

at Becker's "optimum". At this point Becker adopts the assumption that p is equal to 1. He argues that an offender will push his number of crimes to that point where the marginal benefit to him $G'(Y)$, will be equal to the fine f. This is analogous to the standard result in the theory of demand that consumer maximisation gives price equal to marginal utility of a good divided by the marginal utility of income. We thus have, according to this line of argument, an individual who chooses Y to maximise

$$U[G(Y) - fY] \tag{12}$$

giving $\quad G'(Y) = f \tag{13}$

From (11) and (13) we have

$$f = H'(Y) + C_Y \tag{14}$$

This is the result on which Becker lays great stress (it is his (1968) equation (29))—the fine should be equal to marginal damage plus marginal cost of apprehension. If p is set to some number $\hat{p}$ below one and we suppose offenders maximise expected money gain (13) is replaced by

$$\hat{p} f = G'(Y) \tag{13'}$$

with a corresponding modification to (14). Where expected utility is maximised the individual chooses Y to maximise

$$(1 - p) U(G(Y)) + p U(G(Y) - fY)) \tag{15}$$

The basic and overwhelming objection to this analysis is that it is completely irrelevant to the optimum, since we have seen that an optimum does not exist. It has interest only if we regard the probability of apprehension as fixed and this is absurd in a model designed to explain the optimum allocation of resources to apprehension. On the other hand, we seem to have added something sensible, costs of apprehending offenders or those who inflict externalities, to a sensible, and well-accepted model in welfare economics—that which is standard in the theory of externalities. This standard representation of the theory of externalities (see, for example, Buchanan and Stubblebine (1962)) abstracts from enforcement costs, $C(Y, p) = 0$, and portrays the optimum level of externality inflicting activity, or Y, as that level where $D'(Y) = 0$ or $G'(Y) = H'(Y)$—marginal gain equal to marginal harm. One then argues, as in the above, that this is achieved where the individual pays a price or fine equal to f. It would appear that Becker has provided a generalisation which includes the standard theory as a special case. If Becker's analysis is faulty, we must ask whether the same is true of the standard theory.

But this generalisation of the standard theory of externalities allows an extra degree of freedom, the determination of the probability of apprehension and it is the two degrees of freedom together which, given the structure of the model, bring the inevitability of the existence problem. It is quite possible that the activity in question is so damaging that even with costless apprehension, one would want prices or fines to be so high that the level of the activity is zero. This kind of answer becomes, as we have seen, unavoidable when p is to be selected together with f and where apprehension requires resources. The standard theory is, in a formal sense, correct. If, however, the results change so radically when we make a natural and, apparently, simple modification, we must then ask if the theory is of value. We have seen that the problems arose because we relaxed the assumption that enforcement of taxes or fines was costless. We can restore the theory of externalities by dropping a second of the assumptions of first-best welfare economics—that lump sum taxes are possible, that is, that taxation can be levied and income redistributed costlessly or without problems of incentives. We demonstrate this claim formally below. We shall then see that the argument is not credible if applied to models of crime.

Without the assumption that the lump-sum taxes are possible we cannot argue, as we did implicitly in the above, that views about income distribution can be embodied in a redistributive tax system and so can be ignored in our analysis of externalities. Neither are we justified in arguing that a fine, as a transfer payment from individual to government, is of zero cost or benefit. If different individuals or groups have different social weights on increases in their incomes, then our analysis of policy towards externalities should take that into account.

We can proceed formally as follows. We write the minimand

$$L (p, f) = D (Y) + C (Y, p) - \alpha R (p, f) \tag{16}$$

where R is net government revenue from administering the probabilities and taxes at levels (p, f) for the externality producing activity (net of all costs not included in $C (Y, p)$). The parameter α denotes the premium (which we suppose is positive) on tax revenue, or uncommitted public income, relative to private income. We subtract αR from the minimand, since extra revenue is a gain not a loss. The use of such a premium is now standard in the literature on cost-benefit analysis—see Little and Mirrlees (1974), Sen (1968)—and arises from the recognition that since public revenue can be raised only with some cost on the margin, it will be more valuable than private income. We consider here, using α, the value of increments in public income relative to increments for a representative individual. The relative values for different individuals are considered below.

The first order condition for the optimum tax f becomes

$$(D' + C_y) Y_f - \alpha R_f = 0 \tag{17}$$

If we suppose that R_f is positive (raising taxes raises more revenue) and Y_f is negative (the taxes decrease the level of the activity) we have that, at the optimum

$$D' + C_Y < 0 \tag{18}$$

Given that $C_Y < 0$ we must have $D' < 0$. Hence at the optimum there must be a marginal benefit from the externality producing activity. It is easy to check that we cannot deduce from (17) that there is a cost reducing change in p available, as we could when α is zero and the last term is absent. There is no reason to suppose that an optimum fails to exist in this model. Tax revenue will fall if taxes are pushed too high and high taxes will also discourage activity which is of value on the margin. Hence there is a presumption that infinitely high tax rates will not be "optimum".

We can now see why this route is not really open to the Becker analysis of crime, for if D' is positive we cannot satisfy (18). We can argue that at the optimum there should be a net benefit from a factory producing a valuable commodity as well as damaging smoke (where the calculation is made before allowing for costs of collection or the revenue raised) but it is much more difficult to conceive of beneficial offences, or at least offences which governments would want to count as beneficial, given that the activity has already been made illegal.

In his interpretation of the condition that fines should be set equal to marginal damage (here (14)), Becker laid great stress on the implication that fines should therefore be independent of the circumstance of the offender, in particular whether he is rich or poor. We have seen that one cannot base conclusions on (14), since the model has no solution, but let us examine the proposition that fines should be independent of the position of the offender in an analogous model where we do have a solution.

We saw that the problem (16) would in general have a solution. Let us consider the problem (16) as applied to two groups of individuals. Incomes are equal within the groups and in all respects, other than income, the groups are identical, but one group is richer than the other. The fines or taxes for the poorer group should be lower. The reasons are as follows. First, the value of α, the premium on incremental income to the government relative to that to the individual, would be lower for the poorer group since, we suppose, the social value of increments to poorer individuals is seen by the government to be higher. It is intuitively clear and one can check formally that a fall in α will imply a lower optimum f.

Secondly, the net damage $D(Y)$ from activity level Y will be seen as lower for a poorer individual, since such gains as accrue in money terms (and we are supposing that the activities are identical for the two groups) to the poorer individual have higher value. Again one can check that a downward shift in the $D(\ )$ function implies lower optimum punishment.

Finally, the propensity to indulge in the (risky) activity (the level of the function $Y(p, f)$) will be lower for the poorer group, since we established in the appendix to Chapter 2 that given diminishing absolute risk-aversion, poorer individuals will be less likely to accept a given gamble. And one can also check that a downward shift in the Y function will involve smaller optimum punishment.

Hence the Becker proposition that fines should be independent of the circumstances of the offender which cannot be examined in his model (since it has no solution) turns out to be false when examined in a more sensible framework. And we can give a definite answer—*ceteris paribus*—fines or taxes on externality-producing activities carried out by the poor should be lower than for the rich.

9.A.3 BECKER'S RESULT ON THE RELATIVE RESPONSE TO OFFENCES TO p AND f

We discussed in the appendix to Chapter 2 the assertion that one can derive, from the observation that offences are more responsive to the probability of apprehension than the level of punishment, the conclusion that offenders are risk-preferrers so that "crime does not pay". We give briefly here Becker's derivation of the relative responsiveness as an optimality condition in his model.

Suppose an optimum to problem (1) exists with $0 < p < 1$ and f finite. The first order conditions are

$$(D' + C_Y + bpf)\, Y_p + bfY + C_p = 0 \tag{19}$$

$$(D' + C_Y + bpf)\, Y_f + bpY = 0 \tag{20}$$

Hence

$$\frac{bfY}{Y_p} + \frac{C_p}{Y_p} = \frac{bpY}{Y_f} \tag{21}$$

From (21) and using the definitions of the elasticities of offences with respect to P and f: $\varepsilon_p = -\dfrac{p}{Y}\, Y_p$ and $\varepsilon_f = -\dfrac{f}{Y}\, Y_f$ we have

$$\frac{1}{\varepsilon_p} - \frac{1}{\varepsilon_f} = \frac{C_p}{bfpY_p} \tag{22}$$

If the cost of punishment is positive ($b > 0$) the right hand side will be negative and we have

$$\varepsilon_p > \varepsilon_f \tag{23}$$

as Becker claimed.

Interpretations and consequences of this condition were discussed in the appendix to Chapter 2. We shall not comment in detail on its derivation (we have followed the Becker argument) but merely note a few points which follow from the discussion in Chapter 9 and the earlier sections of this appendix.

The result depends on the asymmetry in the model between p and f. If f is introduced into the $C\,(\ )$ function the above argument is no longer conclusive. The result depends also on b being positive. We have argued in our discussion of externalities that where lump sum taxes are impossible there may be a premium on government revenue relative to individual incomes. Where punishment is by fines this would imply that b is negative. And finally, the assumption that we have a solution with non-zero offences in this model is not one which we can regard as obvious, even where punishment is costly.

10

Conclusions

10.0 INTRODUCTION

Criminal statistics are important: they are used widely in discussion of crime and the police by politicians and journalists, by Chief Constables and academics. It is important, therefore, to understand the processes involved in the generation of recorded offences; this is not an easy or simple task. We have seen that we require theories of the way the public, the police and politicians behave; we require data and statistical methods, and we require careful interpretation of results. We have tried to use or provide all these things. The resulting exercise has been long, and occasionally difficult. We believe that these difficulties are an inherent part of our subject and the techniques required to tackle it. It is time, however, to summarize what we have learned. In so doing we shall make several suggestions for further research.

We began, in Chapter 2, by presenting the "economic" and "traditional criminological" approaches to the generation of crime. The former emphasizes the effect of opportunities for legal and illegal activity and the likelihood and severity of possible punishment in determining individual choice, and the latter notions such as family and social class background, and situations of anomie and culture conflict. We saw the theories as essentially complementary with the former stressing the perceived consequences, gains and losses, of criminal activity and the alternatives, and the latter the social factors determining the way in which different individuals perceive. This contrasts with many authors (especially Becker (1968), but see also Sullivan (1973)) who argue that the economic can replace the traditional criminological approach. We have not emphasized psychological theories since, while they may be a crucial part of any study at the level of the individual, they have nothing to add to socio-demographic theories at a macro level. Our eventual purpose, completed in Chapters 4 and 5, was the construction of a model of the generation of crime statistics.

For reasons which have been stressed throughout this book (and see, particularly, Chapter 5) we cannot study the generation of the actual number of offences in isolation. Certain variables, specifically the detection rate and the intensity of social control (the number of policemen) simultaneously determine, and are determined by, the recorded offence rate. Coherent estimation demands that we study the processes generating all three variables simultaneously. And we cannot use criminal statistics without asking how events become recorded as offences. As well as being crucial to the study of the generation of actual offences, these extra processes are of central interest in their own right as parts of an interlacing system of crime, authority and criminal statistics.

Accordingly in Chapter 3 we looked at theories and evidence of the determination of the clear-up or conviction rate and the number of policemen *per capita*. And we examined the challenge from interactionist theories to those of traditional criminology (and the challenge applies, *a fortiori*, to the economic approach) about the way in which individuals or acts become classified as criminal. These interactionist theories required further development, however, before the basic ideas could be included in the formal model which we wanted to construct; they suggest a model of the factors determining whether certain acts are classified as recorded offences and thus allow alternative interpretations of the rôle of variables such as the age structure of the population, already included, as explanatory variables for the recorded offence and clear-up rates, under the previous theories.

The models derived from the theories and findings discussed in Chapters 2 and 3 were presented formally in Chapter 4. At that stage we examined possible measures of different factors using available data. Statistical procedures were the subject matter of Chapter 5. We examined formally the problems raised by simultaneous causation and unobserved variables, and methods of testing hypotheses. We considered and rejected the possibility of a time series analysis. The difficulties of specifying lag structures and the precise way in which the system changes over time, together with very few observations on important socio-economic variables, imply that the exercise would not be worthwhile.

The results from testing the model and associated hypotheses were presented in Chapter 6. We considered whether we could pool data from urban and rural areas and from different years, and examined tests for how the model should be specified. We also considered the potential usefulness of the derived reduced form, the role of the variance-covariance matrix and the possibility of using breaking-and-entering offences as a surrogate variable for total offences. In Chapter 7 we interpreted the main results in the light of the theories discussed in Chapters 2 and 3, and compared our results with those of some other authors.

We ranged a little more widely in Chapters 8 and 9 to examine some of the implications of the economic and interactionist theories. In Chapter 8 we extended the theory of the generation of criminal statistics, concentrating particularly on the recording of offences. We then used the resulting ideas in an examination of the role of criminal statistics in policy discussions and the conclusions of certain well-known studies. We showed in Chapter 9 that "economic" theories of the optimum punishment and expenditure on police, which use functions describing the operation of "deterrence", are seriously defective as explanations of existing punishment levels. We suggested that the defects were likely to remain so long as the notion of retribution is omitted; this led to some general comments on the economic theory of externalities.

In the next section we shall summarize the methodological lessions of this study for the strategy of testing a social theory. In § 10.2 we indicate the most prominent features of our results. These results, and the theories lying behind their interpretation, suggest several possible lines of research into attitudes and organisation of the police force, and these are presented in § 10.3. The related question of the disaggregation of the statistics we used (those for all indictable offences) is discussed in § 10.4. We comment on the difficulties of using official criminal statistics and some possible alternatives in § 10.5. We discuss possible theoretical research problems in the theory of punishment, retribution, equity and externalities in § 10.6. In § 10.7 we mention briefly certain things which, with the benefit of hindsight, we might have done differently. Our concluding remarks are contained in § 10.8.

10.1 STATISTICAL METHOD

We have been concerned in this study with statistical inference in the face of two problems: simultaneous causation and unobserved variables. We trust that we do not have to argue the virtues of using models, although we hope that the clarity they force was illustrated by our discussion of the interactionist theories in Chapter 3. For the purposes of our model it was necessary to distinguish between two versions of the theories—the first where the notion of a true level of offences (whether or not recorded) is unacceptable, and the second where the true level is regarded as a concept with content, but as a number which is very large when compared with the level of recorded offences. Similarly the discussion of the role of unemployment in the literature is often rather disconnected, since different authors stress different aspects. For example, Phillips, Votey and Maxwell (1972) take the rate of unemployment as a measure of labour market opportunities in legal and illegal worlds; Glaser and Rice (1959), as a measure of available time and others simply as a measure of poverty (Thomas (1925)).

We shall not attempt to summarize our discussion of the econometric problems of simultaneous causation and unobserved variables. We shall concentrate on certain aspects which we have chosen to make a feature of our study.

The simultaneous-equations problem is that of the horse and cart: we must try to tell when the horse is pulling the cart and when the cart is pushing the horse. We hope that it is clear that the problems of simultaneous equations permeate the social sciences. We saw that the various processes had to be modelled as separate equations of the system. To treat the system as a single regression equation leads to misleading, that is inconsistent, estimated coefficients. We found that there was an "identification problem" in ascribing equations (and therefore coefficients) to processes. This problem can only be tackled by prior knowledge and theorising about the forms of the different processes.

We did not solve the problem of unobserved variables in any final sense but we showed that the difficulties it raised could be handled formally and, indeed, the formal presentation was of value both in specifying a model for estimation (which must involve observed variables) and interpreting results. Thus we included in our model at the initial stages variables on which no data were available but which were the variables implicit or explicit in the theory. For example, the economic theory of criminal activity as the response of individuals to certain expectations about possible gains and losses, applies to the actual level of offences and not just the sub-sample that is recorded. In presenting the offence equation in the original system, therefore, we view actual offences as the variable being determined; we then model the process by which offences are recorded. The final step to a model that can be estimated is to substitute out those unobserved variables. This last model is then called a "partial reduced form". The advantage of this procedure is that it exhibits clearly those coefficients which can be interpreted directly as parameters of the original system, for example giving direct impact on the actual level, and those coefficients which are an amalgam of parameters of the original system. The latter type must then be interpreted as arising from more than one process; this view proved indispensable when interpreting results.

The simultaneous-equations techniques not only give consistent estimates of coefficients, but the particular form we employed (full information maximum likelihood), was also especially convenient for the testing of hypotheses. We computed maximum likelihood estimates, and the likelihood values under different hypotheses were then compared to test one hypothesis against the other. It is in this way that we were able to test, for example, the hypothesis that the responsiveness of recorded offences to the clear-up rate is equal to that for the level of punishment, and that the rate of unemployment is a significant determinant of the recorded offence rate. And of particular importance, we were able to test whether the structure of our model, thus the behaviour of agents involved in it, remained constant during the 1960s, and whether the structure for urban and rural areas is the same.

The simultaneous-equations technique can be used to examine the inter-relations between errors in equations. This can provide ideas as to which other variables would be necessary to complete the model. An example is the role of police attitudes and practices in the recording of offences, since discretion over recording can be exercised in different ways in different areas. Such a variable was necessarily omitted from the model because of difficulties of measurement.

We should argue that the general lesson is that simultaneous-equations techniques are often required by the types of theory under examination in the social sciences and are not difficult to use, since they are available in package programmes. We were fortunate to be provided with the SIMUL package developed by Cliff Wymer at the London School ·of Economics. Further, the package provides not only parameter estimates for the equations under study but also, for example, likelihood values and estimates of the variance-covariance matrices of residuals which can contribute valuable additional information.

10.2 THE RESULTS

There were successes and failures for all three types of theory "economic", "traditional criminological", and "interactionist", under examination. Perhaps the main lesson from the examination of our estimated coefficients is that it is perilous to examine one, or just two, of the theories in isolation. All three played important roles in understanding results and the combination of the three seems to lead to interesting shifts over time in the picture they describe.

We shall not re-state the estimates presented in Chapter 6 and discussed in Chapter 7 but we will pick out certain broad features to set the scene for our discussion of further research possibilities in the following sub-sections.

We must remind the reader that the offence variable we used, all indictable offences, consisted mainly of larcenies or breaking-and-entering offences without violence to the person. Moreover, these are mainly minor acts of theft—for example, in England and Wales in 1966 of a total of 1,200,000 indictable offences, 850,000 were larcenies, and 280,000 breaking-and-entering—together 94% (figures to nearest 10,000 offences from Criminal Statistics 1966). And over 60% of larcenies and 40% of breaking-and-entering offences involved property of value less than £10. Such offences are of a regular and routine nature and one can suppose that they are likely to be related to a combination of economic and social forces of the type embodied in our model.

First, we look at those estimates which are similar for all three years. In the equation modelling the determination of the recorded offence rate, we find that the detection rate, the level of punishment and the "opportunity" variable (total rateable value per area) performed significantly and with the expected signs for all three years. The responsiveness of the recorded offence rate to the detection rate was found to be larger than that for the level of punishment. We argued caution in using this result to form conclusions about risk-attitudes of offenders, since the level of punishment measured is but a fraction (and at low levels of punishment a small fraction) of that perceived. There is, for many at least, a substantial perceived cost to court appearance and conviction *per se*, independent of the level of punishment. Thus proportional variations in measured punishment are larger than in total perceived punishment.

But we must not forget that these estimates refer to the recorded offence rate; they cannot be used to make direct inferences about the effect of these variables on actual offences. For if the probability and severity of punishment for a recorded offence is high, individuals will take care to avoid their actions being labelled as recorded offences. It is not easy however, to explain away, using recording phenomena, the positive effect on offences which we found for the opportunity variable (total rateable value per area).

The main variable in the equation for the recorded detection rate to behave in a similar manner across the years, was the size of police district. For 1961 and 1966 the larger police districts exhibit lower detection rates: this suggests that arguments for larger police districts should be scrutinised carefully. It is interesting to note, however, that the main amalgamations between police forces (during the period we studied) in England and Wales took place in 1968 precisely on the grounds of efficiency. The detection rate was also higher in districts where recorded violent offences, as a proportion of total offences, were higher. This variable was chosen as an indicator of offence mix for the second equation, since with violent offences the aggressor is often known to the victim, making detection much easier.

The number of policemen *per capita* was, for our data sets, an increasing function of the level of unemployment. We took this as confirmation of the view that demand for policemen from the central and local authorities exceeded the supply of people willing to become or remain policemen. High unemployment is favourable to the recruiting and retaining of policemen. This recruiting interpretation is corroborated by the behaviour of the variable m denoting the proportion of the population which is middle class—the number of police *per capita* decreases, for most of our cases, as m increases.

Factors which vary in their impact across the years in both the equation for the offence rate and that for the detection rate, include the social class and age structures, the number of police *per capita* and expenditure per policeman. These variations can best be understood, in our view, in terms of the way in which actual offences become recorded. Thus the positive effect of the number of policemen *per capita* on the offence rate in 1966 and 1971 is, we have suggested, the result of more policemen recording more crimes, rather than the police creating actual offences. Similarly, the negative effect of the number of policemen on the clear-up or conviction rate is better understood as a question of caution on the part of the offender faced with an apparently efficient police force, rather than as an example of the growth of bureaucracy or too many cooks spoiling the broth. The negative effect on the recorded offence rate of the proportion of young males in the population in 1961 becomes a positive one in 1966, and we suggested the appropriate interpretation was that a change in police relations with the young, becoming more formal and hostile in the mid 1960s, manifested itself in more youthful offences being recorded (this phenomenon appears to have disappeared by the end of the decade). A parallel appears with the changes in the coefficient on the proportion of working class in the population in the equation representing the determination of the detection rate. We suggested these might be understood in terms of changing attitudes and patterns of life in working-class communities during the sixties. We had in mind, in particular, that a weakening or disintegration of community spirit produced a reduced reliance on informal methods of social control.

The role of the police in the generation of the offence statistics, and particularly their relations with and attitudes towards particular groups, will be one of our major suggestions for further research in the next subsection.

We have found then some support for all the three types of theory in this study which purport to explain the offence rate. The "economic" variables, the detection rate, the punishment level and available opportunities perform consistently well as determinants of recorded offence rates. The arguments of the interactionist school were crucial in understanding the behaviour of variables describing the police force, the young and particular class groups.

The young and the working class, favourite topics in traditional criminology, do seem to play important roles in generation of offence statistics, but, as we have seen, the way in which these are mediated by the police force seems very important.

The determination of the detection rate is clearly of substantial importance, but we have found that it is hard to produce policy variables which can sensibly be used to control the detection rate: the behaviour of the size variable (large districts have lower detection rates) runs counter to the directions suggested by the particular organisational arguments which have been used to justify amalgamations, and increases in detection rates through an increase in the proportion of violent offences seem unattractive as a policy variable. Yet the direct control of the detection rate was a central feature of Becker's (1968) "economic approach" to crime and punishment. We have suggested that our difficulty with this equation is to a large extent due to variations in recording practices which we have been unable to capture.

The conclusion is that we should be catholic with our theories. When proposing one theory we should not deny the importance of others (see Becker (1968)) and we have found that there are severe handicaps in understanding data if we dismiss any of the three theories. Secondly, we have seen that we must pay special attention to the way in which the data are generated.

10.3 THE POLICE

Our variables relating to the police force have, necessarily, been rather crude. Many of our arguments have invoked particular ways in which the police influence what actions become recorded offences and which individuals become offenders. These arguments require further research in studies of police behaviour and organisation, in several directions.[1] We give examples of studies which might corroborate or refute some of the interpretations we have made. The generation of such questions was one of the outcomes to be expected from a macro-study and was anticipated in our introductory chapter.

Our offence variable was highly aggregated—all indictable offences—and we should like to see studies of particular offence types. We did, at one point, use breaking-and-entering offences in place of all indictable offences partly for this reason (the other reason being that some have argued that nearly all breaking-and-entering offences are reported, so that the recording problem is circumvented). The exercise was not particularly successful: an

[1] McCabe and Sutcliffe (1978) is a good example of the kind of work we have in mind. We learned of its publication too late for a discussion to be included here.

important reason for this, we believe, is that it was not possible to dis-aggregate other variables, especially those relating to police activity.

In fact, given the importance of police activity one would require detail of the allocation of police effort to particular tasks. Such data are not collected as a matter of routine and particular studies (see Martin and Wilson (1969)) show that the most important category of fieldwork is "general policing". This includes patrolling, prevention and, we presume, some back-sliding. Although it is difficult to see how all police activities could be allocated according to purpose, it would seem to be essential, both for administrators allocating police effort and academics and commentators trying to understand and make inferences from official statistics, to know in some detail what police do. During the "rationalising" of the police forces in the 1960s there seems to have been little data on what was being rationalised. Thus the first priority in such a study would be the collection of basic data on police activity.

Our discussion in Chapter 3 in justifying our model and in Chapter 7, when interpreting results, referred to quotes from Chief Constables on the effects of motorised police on police-public relations and our interpretation of the coefficients corresponding to the number of policemen *per capita* and expenditure per officer rested on suppositions about changing equipment, procedures and techniques. In particular we supposed that higher expenditure per officer reflected in part superior equipment. Statistics on equipment available, and information on how it is used, would be a first requirement of a study of the techniques of policing. One would then go on to examine how techniques and procedures affect, and are affected by, police-public relations and the numbers of offences of different types which are recorded.

There are several possible determinants of the attitudes and practices of individual policemen. First, these attitudes and practices would be deter-mined, in part, by the information which is available to him. We referred, for example, in Chapter 3 to Russell's (1973) work on the Sussex police and the way information available in the SUSCRO files may lead to concentra-tion on particular stereotypes of the potential offender. We mentioned in our discussion of the increased formality of police practice in the early 1960s the Offender's Index. Information will influence the allocation of attention by the police to both individuals and groups. Speed of trans-mission of information is likely to affect both detection rates and whether an offence is recorded. Again the problem is the absence of data and research studies.

Secondly, attitudes to different groups, and recording practice would also be influenced by both training and recruitment. Thus one would like to know, as part of a study of relations between police and the public, who becomes, or wants to become a policeman, how he becomes a policeman and how he is trained. The other side of the coin is the collection of reasons for which policemen leave the force. Some may be forced out or discouraged. For others it may be that pay and working conditions are crucial, and so on.

Thirdly, the policeman's practice and reactions to different situations will be determined in part by what is required by the hierarchy. The studies by Banton (1964) and Cain (1973) although valuable are not recent. Therefore we should like to know how far he is expected to produce offences and clear-ups and what are the attitudes of his superiors to different sorts of results and behaviour. Thus we should like to know the organisational constraints and incentives which he faces.

Fourthly, police attitudes and practices as well as those of the public would depend on their opportunities for social intercourse. For example segregated housing, and activities which are discouraged or forbidden may effect the view which one group takes of the other. What effect has the reduction of foot-patrolling had on police-public contact?

The above list of factors affecting police behaviour which are likely to manifest themselves in the criminal statistics is not intended to be exhaustive. They are all items which are of possible importance but on which evidence is anecdotal and meagre. The list is intended to indicate the extent of our ignorance about the way in which the police force behaves.

10.4 DISAGGREGATION

Many of the findings and hypotheses which are considered in Chapters 2 and 3 were originally concerned with a very restricted set of phenomena compared with the whole range of offences which have been the subject of our study. And indeed, at one stage, it seemed that it would be advantageous to conduct the analysis in terms of specific offence types. Similarly, many of the variables that were included in the analysis seem to hide important variations. For example, the literature suggests much more specific relationships between age and offending than is portrayed in our variable 'a', (the proportion of males aged 15-24 in the population) and elsewhere (Carr-Hill, Hope and Stern, 1972) we have tried (without much success) to exploit this.

There are three possible obstacles to detailed analyses of this sort: the lack of appropriate data, insufficient precision in the theory, and problems of interpretation of variables. This last arises because of high intercorrelation between included exogenous variables. It is only considered briefly here, partly because it is usually unavoidable in this kind of study and partly because it is not an insuperable obstacle to studies closer to the level of the individual. For extreme examples of very high inter-correlation normally only occur between variables which interlink, or overlap conceptually or definitionally.

In our study, for example, we originally wanted to include variables measuring the alienation, overcrowding and wealth of an area, suggested by different theoretical perspectives. We chose the percentage of an area urbanised, population density and rateable value per unit area as the respective measures: these measures were highly inter-correlated and not strictly separable on the interpretative level for our data.

The first problem, the lack of appropriate data, is pervasive in the social sciences. We saw in the preceding section that little is known of the allocation of police time to different activities and offences and still less for each police district of our sample. Further analyses of the kind advocated here by detailed offence class are unlikely to be worthwhile until such data appear.

The second problem noted above with disaggregation is that many of the theories are too vague to provide the material for a detailed analysis without a good deal more analytical flesh. For example, in what particular ways do alienation or anomie act so as to determine the observed levels of frauds or of sex offences? Without an explanation or account of anomie which is *activity specific* we cannot assign precise variables in a disaggregated analysis.

While it would be attractive, if the data were available, to look at more detailed offence types, we should not be dismissive about the interest in analysing the aggregate "all indictable offences". On a theoretical level, there is some coherence to the notion of an aggregate of "all indictable offences" which is not shared by a particular group of offences. For the interactionist it is the labelling of an individual as an offender, or an act as an offence, that is important rather than the particular label attached to the act. And most criminological theories have been on a rather general level and cannot be specified in terms of particular offence types. There are processes such as the effect of the level of offences on the demand for police manpower, which cannot be easily reduced to a combination of demands relating to each offence type. And, pragmatically the vast majority of all indictable offences are larcenies or breaking-and-entering offences without violence to the person (for more detail see the appendix to Chapter 4).

From the point of view of both policy and public concern it is probably offences involving violence against the person which attract the most attention. These constitute a relatively small proportion of total indictable offences (48,024) in a total of 1,199, 859 in 1966 i.e. approximately 5%). The proportion is too small to justify the use of crude measures such as the total number of police officers or expenditure per police officer. Moreover, robbery with violence contributed only 4,474 recorded cases, murder 169, and rape 644. Thus if one were to confine attention to violent offences one would be dealing with mainly assaults of various kinds without theft. The theories of behaviour involved would certainly be rather different from those analysed here—see, for example, Wolfgang and Ferracuti (1967). The inclusion of the proportion of violent in total offences in our model is as an indicator of offence mix in the determination of detection rates and the number of policemen *per capita*. We should not wish to use our type of model as one of the determination of the level of violent offences.

There remains the possibility of disaggregating within the property offence class. In particular, the sub-class of breaking-and-entering offences was used at one stage in our study partly to attempt to circumvent the recording problem. The results are presented in Chapter 6 and we saw that they did not eliminate the problem; indeed the results are, in general terms, not dissimilar from those obtained using all indictable offences. Larcenies constitute such a high proportion of all indictable offences that it is safe to assume that similar results using that sub-class would also have been obtained.

Thus of the three important sub-classes, larcenies would, we suppose give results very similar to those we have obtained, breaking-and-entering offences we have seen give similar results, and finally violent offences would require a different approach. We have reached the conclusion, then, that unless one is prepared to undertake a detailed study of a homogeneous offence class, including detailed data on police response to the particular type of offence selected, then further disaggregation, from the level we have chosen here, in the estimation of models such as ours, is not worthwhile.

10.5 THE OFFICIAL CRIMINAL STATISTICS

The recording problem has been a recurring theme throughout this book. In Chapter 8 we showed how a theory which accounted for the generation of the official criminal statistics would have to be very complex.

We showed how discussions which ignore this complexity can be faulty in their interpretations of the official criminal statistics. In particular we showed how the available data do not support the claim that there has been a "crime wave" during this period and that claims for the effectiveness of deterrence on the basis of such figures have to be viewed with circumspection.

We then went on to consider what would be an appropriate statistical system, if one were interested in the extent to which people suffer, whether from crime, accident or disease. We showed how such a statistical system should concentrate first and foremost on the amount of harm that people suffer in different circumstances. Of course, such data would look very different from the existing criminal statistics but would respond more precisely to what is usually the concern behind the fear of crime that is, security.

10.6 EXTERNALITIES, EQUITY AND RETRIBUTION

We saw in Chapter 9 that the economic theory of externalities, on which the standard (Becker) economic treatment of crime and punishment is based, is inadequate to provide a description of punishment levels as we see them set by policy makers, magistrates and judges. The model proposed by Becker has no solution other than that with zero offences. We argued that it was necessary to invoke the notion of retribution to understand these punishment levels. This argument does not by itself justify retribution (see below) but uses it to understand what we see. We argued that retribution was, in turn, similar to but distinct from the notion of horizontal equity which is sometimes invoked in economics.

While we have said that our argument does not by itself justify the retributive punishment, we do see it as a contribution to a discussion of appropriate punishment, and it raises serious questions for the utilitarian or cost-benefit position. If we are forced into the position that our current system is to a substantial degree retributive we can ask whether this is as we want it to be. If we reject the notion of retribution, then we must provide alternative criteria. We have seen the danger that utilitarian, deterrence or "reductivist" (see N. D. Walker (1972)) theories might lead us to rather large punishment levels. Further, they do not give a satisfactory explanation to our aversion to punishing the innocent.

This is not the place to try to construct appropriate or acceptable penological criteria. We hope, however, that our discussion in Chapter 9 might be a contribution in that direction. Further, we hope it will caution against believing that the estimation of responsiveness to punishment and other determinants of offence rates, recorded or otherwise, is the answer or even the major part of the answer to questions of appropriate punishment.

10.7 POSSIBLE MODIFICATIONS TO OUR MODEL

It is inevitable in a study such as this that, were we to start again, there are certain things which we should do differently. We mention some of these here. Those changes that would have been feasible would not have involved substantial changes in strategy and, we expect, would not have led to substantial changes in results. The existence of information on certain important factors would, on the other hand, have allowed a rather different approach. We have already referred to these at length in the book: examples are the allocation of police energies and time, and the measurement of public attitudes. The severity of the measurement problems in these examples is obvious. Thus major problems with the absence of data were inevitable.

The main theoretical difficulties—particularly those connected with unobserved variables and the identification problems—were also unavoidable. However, we regard the informational and theoretical problems as providing a major part of the interest of this study and hope that we may have contributed to the understanding of some of them.

But there are certain changes which we could have made. We occasionally met problems at seminar presentations because we chose "all indictable offences" to represent the outcome of the processes generating recorded offences. We have explained this choice at length in earlier chapters and commented further in § 10.4 above. We now think that confusion would have been avoided if we had dropped certain of the more dramatic violent offences such as murder and rape from our sample. The difference to the total number of offences would have been trivial (see § 10.4 and the appendix to Chapter 4).

We could also have extended our list of explanatory variables for certain of the equations. For example, variations in police organisation might have been measured in terms of the length of service of the Chief Constable; distribution of police time and effort could have been examined more sensitively through looking at the numbers of traffic wardens and non-operational staff and the amount of overtime; the provision of social services as a defensive net between the individual and the police could have been quantified; information other than simply the proportion of incarcerations could have been used as a measure of sentencing patterns; and the effect of road traffic on the nature of the policemen's task could have been taken into account. On all of these variables, some data exists. In particular, the use in the second equation of a variable based on road accidents and traffic wardens might have led to increased confidence over identification (see § 5.3).

Whilst we guess that in many or most cases the introduction of new variables would have required substantial extra work and have made little difference to our results, there are some we now wish we had tried.

10.8 CONCLUDING REMARKS

The main purpose of our study has been specific: to develop a model of the generation of criminal statistics for police districts in England and Wales in 1961, 1966 and 1971 and to estimate the model using statistical techniques appropriate to the theories under examination. Thus our book has the style of a monograph which reports in a direct way on the processes of, and conclusions from, our study.

We hope, however, that the interest of our work is rather wider than the particular time period and region under study. Chapter 2 provided a critical review of certain theories, and supporting evidence, of offending behaviour. Theories and evidence on the institutional aspects of the criminal statistics were examined in Chapter 3; and certain of the ideas and theories under examination could not be incorporated directly into our framework without further theoretical analysis.

Our use of certain econometric techniques in estimation and the detailed testing of hypotheses will, we hope, be instructive for other studies: these techniques were explained in Chapter 5. In particular we would stress the importance of simultaneous-equations methods for sociological studies, the value of handling problems of unobserved variables in a formal way, the potential of information contained in the relation between errors in different equations, and finally that hypotheses can be and should be directly tested in the model.

We argued, particularly in Chapters 8 and 9, that some previous authors had displayed a worrying lack of care in the use of models and statistics. Worrying because it can lead to strong or extreme policies which are unpleasant and are not justified by their analysis. Thus we have seen that models which are intended to provide a complete economic approach to crime and punishment lead to nonsensical results. And we emphasized that we must never lose sight of the fact that criminal statistics have been constructed by agencies which should themselves, together with their relations with the rest of the community, form part of the subject under study. It seems that quantitative analysis in this area requires particular circumspection.

A counsel of caution in the use of criminal statistics and theoretical models of the generation of, and policy towards, crime should not, however, be taken as an argument that they should not be used at all. We hope we have demonstrated both that one can learn a great deal, and that a great deal remains to be learned, from their analysis.

Data Appendix:
Definitions and Data Sources

Prepared by J. Kynch

The data are for police districts in England and Wales in 1961, 1966, and 1971. For most districts it was possible to "allocate" census data, but in certain cases this was impossible. The following districts were therefore excluded:

1961 and 1966   Metropolitan Police District, City of London, Essex County, Hertford County, Kent County, Surrey County and Tyne River Police.

1971   Metropolitan Police District, City of London, Essex and Southend-on-Sea, Hertford County, Kent County, Surrey County.

The total numbers of districts used were in 1961, 72 urban districts and 44 rural districts; in 1966, 66 urban and 44 rural; in 1971, 41 districts mixed rural and urban. A district is designated urban if 100% of its area is urbanised.

Sources of data used were
C 61   Census 1961 England and Wales. General Register Office, H.M.S.O.
C 66   Sample Census 1966 England and Wales. General Register Office, H.M.S.O.
C 71   Census 1971 England and Wales. Office of Population, Census and Surveys, H.M.S.O.
CSS 61   Home Office Supplementary Statistics relating to crime and criminal proceedings 1961.
CSS 64   Home Office Supplementary Statistics relating to crime and criminal proceedings 1964.
CSS 66   Home Office Supplementary Statistics relating to crime and criminal proceedings 1966.
CSS 71   Home Office Supplementary Statistics relating to crime and criminal proceedings 1971.
PFS 61   Police Force Statistics 1961-2. The Institute of Municipal Treasurers and Accountants and the Society of County Treasurers, County Hall, Chester.

PFS 66   Police Force Statistics 1966-67. The Institute of Municipal Treasurers and Accountants and the Society of County Treasurers, County Hall, Chester.

PFS 71   Police Force Statistics 1970-1. The Institute of Municipal Treasurers and Accountants and the Society of County Treasurers, County Hall, Chester.

RV 61   Rates and Rateable Values, Ministry of Housing and Local Government, H.M.S.O. 1961-2.

RV 66   Rates and Rateable Values, Ministry of Housing and Local Government, H.M.S.O. 1966-7.

RV 71   Rates and Rateable Values, Ministry of Housing and Local Government, H.M.S.O. 1970-1.

The data were obtained from the published forms as above, with the exception of the offences cleared-up and some of the 1971 census data. Where there were gaps in the publication of the census data at the time of collection, figures were obtained direct from the Office of Population Censuses and Surveys (OPCS), in particular those for all of the socio-economic classes in the 1971 middle class and working class. We are grateful for the co-operation of the OPCS. The 1970-71 PFS and RV data were used (instead of 1971-2) since at the time of collection for use in the calculations for conference paper at Turin in 1974 (see Carr-Hill and Stern (1976)) the 1971-2 publications were not available.

In some of our earlier studies (for example, Carr-Hill and Stern (1973)) we used data for urban areas in 1961 collected by W. F. Greenhalgh when at the Home Office Scientific Advisors' Branch and reported in Greenhalgh (1966). In this study we have recollected the data for urban districts.

The Variables

We give the definition and symbol for each variable and the sources of the data used in its measurement. The S Column number after the details of a variable refers to the position in the data file for the appropriate year in the files deposited at the SSRC data bank at the University of Essex. (When referring to columns in published tables we always use the abbreviation "col.").

Indictable Offences per Head of Population (Y)

Total indictable offences divided by total population. This is residential or night-time population here. Offence categories included in indictable offences can be found in Table 4.A.1.

1961	CSS 61.	Table 4 (a(i)). Total indictable offences	S. Column 1.
	PFS 61.	Col. 3. (Urban) Total population.	S. Column 15.
		Col. 3c. (Rural) Total population.	
1966	CSS 66.	Table 4 (a(i)). Total indictable offences.	S. Column 2.
	PFS 66.	Col. 2. Total population.	S. Column 4.
1971	CSS 71.	Table 4 (a(i)). Total indictable offences.	S. Column 1.
	PFS 71.	Col. 2a. Total population.	S. Column 10.

Breaking-and-Entering Offences per Head of Population (Y_{BE})

1961	CSS 61.	Table 4. Sum of offence types 28-32, 34.	S Column 8.
1966	CSS 66.	Table 4. Sum of offence types 28-32, 34.	S Column 17.
1971	CSS 71.	Table 4. Sum of offence types 28-31, 34.	S Column 4.
		(no offence type 32)	

Population data as above.

There was a change in the definitions of these offence types for 1971.

	1961 and 1966	1971
28	Burglary	Burglary in dwelling
29	Housebreaking	Aggravated burglary in a dwelling
30	Breaking shops, offices, etc.	Burglary in building other than a dwelling
31	Attempts to break and enter	Aggravated burglary in a building other than a dwelling
32	Entering with intent	
34	Robbery	Robbery

Clear-up Rate (P_{cup})

The fraction of known indictable offences that were cleared up. A "clear-up" is defined in Appendix A(i).

1961, 1966, 1971 Total indictable offences clearer-up provided by the kind permission of the Home Office Statistical Division.

Total indictable offences: see above.

1961	Total Indictable Offences Cleared up	S Column 22
	Percentage of Indictable Offences Cleared up	S Column 23
1966	Total Indictable Offences Cleared up	S Column 16
1971	Total Indictable Offences Cleared up	S Column 18
	Percentage of Indictable Offences Cleared up	S Column 19

The numbers of breaking-and-entering offences cleared up for each district were also supplied by the Home Office Statistical Division and are in S Column 24, 1961, S Column 18, 1966 and S Column 23, 1971.

Conviction Rate (P_{conv})

The number of persons found guilty of indictable offences divided by indictable offences known.

1961	CSS 61.	Tables 1(a-d). Total persons found guilty of indictable offences in Magistrate Courts. Col. 2, male plus female. S Column 2.
	CSS 64.	Tables 1(a-d). Total persons found guilty, in all Courts, of indictable offences, male plus female.
		Table 1(a) Cols. 2, 10
		Table 1(b) Cols. 2, 12
		Table 1(c) Cols. 2, 14
		Table 1(d) Cols. 2, 12
		S Column 4.

Tables 1(a-d). Total persons found guilty, Magistrate Courts, of indictable offences, male plus female. Cols. 2.
S Column 3.

To obtain a figure for all courts, the number of persons found guilty in Magistrate Courts in 1961 was multiplied by the reciprocal of the proportion of guilty findings that occur in Magistrate Courts. This last proportion was taken from 1964, the first year for which these data were available.

1966   CSS 66.   Tables 1(a-d). Total persons found guilty, indictable offences, all Courts. S Column 1.

1971   CSS 71.   Tables 1(a-d). Total persons found guilty, indictable offences, all Courts. S Column 2.

Severity of punishment (F)
The ratio of the number of males who received a custodial measure to the number of persons convicted of indictable offences. (Custodial measure is defined in Appendix A(ii)).

1961   CSS 61.   Tables 1(a-d). Males receiving custodial measures, Magistrate Courts.   1(a) Cols. 7, 8, 11.
                                                   1(b) Cols. 7, 8, 10, 12.
                                                   1(c) Cols. 7, 8, 10.
                                                   1(d) Cols. 7, 9.
                    S Column 5.

        CSS 64.   Tables 1(a-d). Males receiving custodial measures, Magistrate Courts.   1(a) Cols. 7, 8.
                                                   1(b) Cols. 7, 8, 9, 10.
                                                   1(c) Cols. 9, 10, 11, 12.
                                                   1(d) Cols. 9, 10.
                    S Column 6.

        CSS 64.   Tables 1(a-d). Males receiving custodial measures, all courts.
                                                   1(a) Cols. 7, 8, 18, 19, 20.
                                                   1(b) Cols. 7, 8, 9, 10, 20, 21, 22.
                                                   1(c) Cols. 9, 10, 11, 12, 21, 22, 23.
                                                   1(d) Cols. 9, 10, 18.
                    S Column 7.

To obtain a figure for all courts the number of males receiving a custodial measure in Magistrate Courts in 1961 was multiplied by the reciprocal of the proportion of male custodial measures that occurred in Magistrate Courts in 1964, the first year for which these data were available. The number of persons convicted of indictable offences was calculated in the manner described for the previous variable for all three years, 1961, 1966 and 1971.

1966   CSS 66.   Tables 1(a-d). Males receiving custodial measures, all courts.
                                                   1(a) Cols. 7, 8, 18, 19, 20.

1(b) Cols. 7, 8, 9, 10, 20, 21, 22.
1(c) Cols. 9, 10, 11, 12, 21, 22, 23.
1(d) Cols. 9, 10, 18.
S Column 11.

1971   CSS 71.   Tables 1(a-d). Males receiving custodial measures, all courts.

	Magistrate Courts	Assize and Quarter Sessions.
1(a)	Cols. 8, 9.	Cols, 6, 11, 12.
1(b)	Cols. 7, 9, 10, 11.	Cols. 6, 10, 11, 13.
1(c)	Cols. 8, 9.	Cols. 6, 8, 9.
1(d)	none	none

S Column 3

Number of Policemen per Head of Population (C)

In all cases this figure is based on average daily strength (excluding additional constables and civilian staff).

1961	PFS 61.	Col. 11. Average daily strength.	S Column 9.
		Cols. 3 and 3c. Total population.	S Column 15.
1966	PFS 66.	Col. 19. Policemen per head.	S Column 6.
	(The variable used was 1000/S Column 6.)		
1971	PFS 71.	Col. 11. Average Daily Strength.	S column 5.
		Col. 2a. Total population.	S Column 10.

Proportion of young males in the population (A)

Number of males aged 15-24 divided by total population.

1961	C 61.	County Reports. Table 6. Number of males aged 15-24. S Column 11.
1966	C 66.	County Reports. Table 6. Number of males aged 15-19. S Column 12.
		Number of males aged 20-24. S Column 13.
		Number of males aged 10-14. S Column 19.
		Number of males aged 25-29. S Column 20.
1971	C 71.	County Reports. Table 8. Number of males aged 15-24. S Column 7.

At an earlier stage we experimented with using different youth measures, or more than one youth measure, and have therefore included more detail in the files for 1966. For the total population figures see under Y above.

Proportion of the Population that is working class (W)

1961	C 61.	County Reports. Occupation, Industry, Socio-economic Groups.
		Table 5, sum of groups 7, 10, 11, 15. S. Column 13.
1966	C 66.	County Reports. Table 14, sum of groups 7, 10, 11, 15. S Column 14.

(For both 1961 and 1966 these figures are proportions.)

1971   By kind permission of Census Branch, OPCS. From Draft Table 975 the following data were extracted:
Number of economically active males in Socio-economic groups 7, 10, 11, 15.
S Column 21.
Total males economically active. S Column 20.

The proportion of working class in the population was taken to be the ratio of the two previous figures. (Before the 1971 Census Data were available we used 1966 data allocated to the new areas. The proportions of working class from that calculation are given in S Column 12.)

Proportion of the population that is middle class (M)
1961   C 61.   County Reports — Occupation, Industry, Socio-economic Groups. Table 5, sum of groups 5, 6, 8, 9, 12, 14. S Column 14.
1966   C 66.   County Reports. Table 14, sum of groups 5, 6, 8, 9, 12, 14. S Column 21.
(For both 1961 and 1966 these figures are proportions.)
1971   By kind permission of Census Branch, OPCS. Groups 5, 6, 8, 9, 12, 14 from Draft Table 975. See notes on the previous variable W. The total number of economically active males in the given groups is given in S Column 22. The proportion of the population in the given groups in 1966 is in S Column 13.

Total rateable value per area (RV)
Total rateable value (TRV) multiplied by $\dfrac{\text{population density}}{\text{total population}}$
1961   RV 61.   Table A, Col. 4 TRV. S Column 12.
1966   RV 66.   Pt. I. Table 4, Cols. 10 and 11. Table 6 TRV. S Column 8.
(In 1966 we extracted Domestic Rateable Value. Table 4, Col. 9 and Table 6, Col. 10. S Column 7.)
1971   RV 71.   Table 8, Col. 12. Table 7, Col. 11 TRV. S Column 8.
For population density see under D below, and for total population see under Y above.

Expenditure per officer (E)
1961   PFS 61.   Col. 19.   Expenditure per officer (on average daily strength). S Column 10.
1966   PFS 66.   Col. 48.   Total expenditure on police chargeable to rates and grants. S Column 3.
                Col. 19.   Policemen per head of population. S Column 6.
                Col. 2.   Population. S Column 4.
1971   PFS 71.   Col. 41.   Total expenditure on police chargeable to rates and grants per head of population (in thousands). S Column 6.
                Col. 11.   Average daily strength. S Column 10.
                Col. 2a.   Total population. S Column 5.

Proportion of violent offences in total offences (V)
"Violent" offences divided by total indictable offences.

1961   CSS 61.   Table 4. Offence types 1-26, 34, 76.   S Column 20.
1966   CSS 66.   Table 4. Offence types 1-26, 34, 76.   S Column 10.
1971   CSS 71.   Table 4. Offence types 1-26, 34, 76.   S Column 17.
For total indictable offences see Y above.

Population density (persons per acre) (*D*)

1961	PFS 61.	Col. 3 divided by col. 2 (urban).	S Column 16.
		Col. 3c divided by col. 2c (rural).	
1966	PFS 66.	Col. 3 (urban).	S Column 5.
		Col. 3b (rural).	
1971	PFS 71.	Col. 3b.	'S Column 11.

Total population (*N*)

See above under total indictable offences per head. 1961. S Column 15.

1966. S Column 4.

1971. S Column 10.

Proportion of households with less than ½ person per room (*H*)

1961	C 61.	County Reports. Table 18.	S Column 19.
1966	C 66.	County Reports. Table 8.	S Column 9.
1971	C 71.	County Reports. Table 23.	S Column 24.

Proportion of area that is urbanised (*R %urb.*)

1961	PFS 61.	For rural areas only—urban areas 100% by definition.	
		Col. 2a. total urban area.	S Column 21.
		Col. 2c. total area.	
1966	PFS 66.	Col. 3a.	S Column 15.
1971	PFS 71.	Col. 3a.	S Column 9.

Unemployment (*Q*)

The number of economically active males unemployed divided by the number of persons (males plus females) economically active.

1961   C 61.   Occupation, Industry, Socio-Economic Groups. Table 1.

Number of economically active males unemployed divided by total population,

S Column 17.

Number of economically active persons unemployed divided by total population, (observations 57-72 missing and entered as 0·0).   S Column 18.

Number of females economically active,   S Column 25.

Number of males economically active,   S Column 26.

(Hence unemployment variable used in S Column 17 × S Column 15/

(S Column 25 + S Column 26).)

(For S Column 15 see under *N* above.)

1966   C 66.   Economic Activity, County Leaflets. Table 1.

Number of economically active females unemployed,   S Column 22.

Number of economically active males unemployed,   S Column 23.

Number of economically active females,   S Column 24.

Number of economically active males,   S Column 25.

1971   C 71.   County Reports. Table 18.

Number of economically active persons,	S Column 14.
Number of economically active males unemployed,	S Column 15.
Number of economically active persons unemployed,	S Column 16.
Number of economically active males,	S Column 20.

Appendix A(i)

CRIMES 'CLEARED-UP'

This is reproduced from Greenhalgh (1966).

"A crime is 'cleared-up' when

1. a person has been arrested or summoned for the offence (this instruction is not affected by any subsequent acquittal);
2. a prisoner admits the offence and the offence is taken into consideration by the Courts (a refusal by the prisoner to admit the offence to the Court should be treated as a cancellation of any previous admission);
3. the offender has been proceeded against in another Police district for the crime;
4. the offender has died, or been removed to a Mental Hospital, before proceedings were instituted;
5. the offender has been cautioned by the police (i.e. a child handed over to parents);
6. the offender admits an offence, but there is a definite obstacle to proceedings (e.g. embezzelement, where no item of money can be specified owing to bad book-keeping);
7. the prosecutor or essential witness is dead and proceedings cannot be pursued;
8. the guilt of the offender is clear but the person offended against refuses to, or is permanently unable to, or (if a juvenile) is not permitted by whoever is in charge of him, to give evidence;
9. the offences are of "Infanticide" or "Attempted Suicide", which by the nature of the crime must be "cleared-up";
10. the offender is serving a sentence and admits the crime but it is decided that no useful purpose would be served by proceeding with the charge;
11. it is ascertained that a "crime" has been committed by a child under 8 years of age, it should be written off as "no crime" but a record of such cases should be kept.
    In cases where a warrant for the arrest of the offender, although issued, remains unexecuted, the crimes should be regarded as "undetected" until the offender is apprehended or until the case comes within the above definitions. As a general principle and apart from the particular examples given above, it should be noted that, where there is insufficient evidence for proceedings to be taken against a known and available person, the crime should be regarded as "undetected"."

Appendix A(ii)

CUSTODIAL MEASURE

A custodial measure is defined for different age groups as follows:

21 and over: Imprisonment without option of a fine.
              Corrective Training.
              Preventive Detention.
              Committal for Sentence § 29 MCA from Magistrates Court.
17-20:   Imprisonment without option of a fine.
              Detention Centre.
              Borstal Training.
              Committal for Sentence § 28 & 29 MCA from Magistrates Court.
14-16:   Remand Home.
              Detention Centre.
              Approved School.
              Borstal Training.
              Committal under § 28 MCA from Magistrates Court.
Under 14:   Remand Home.
              Approved School.

See CSS 61, 64, 66, Tables 1(a-d).

Appendix A(iii)

SOCIO-ECONOMIC GROUPS

The definitions of the socio-economic groups (SEGs) (1) to (17) are as follows. The list is taken from the 1961 census for England and Wales, Socio-Economic Group Tables p. (vii).

(1) Employers and managers in central and local government, industry, commerce etc.: large establishments.
     Persons who employ others or generally plan and supervise in non-agricultural enterprises employing 25 or more persons.
(2) Employers and managers in industry, commerce etc.: small establishments.
     As in (1) but in establishments employing fewer than 25 persons.

(3)	Professional workers: self-employed.
	Self-employed persons engaged in work normally requiring qualifications of university degree standard.
(4)	Professional workers: employees.
	Employees engaged in work normally requiring qualifications of university degree standard.
(5)	Intermediate non-manual workers.
	Employees, not exercising general planning or supervisory powers engaged in non-manual occupations ancillary to the professions but not normally requiring qualifications of university degree standard; persons engaged in artistic work and not employing others thereat; and persons engaged in occupations otherwise included in group (6) who have an additional and formal supervisory function.
(6)	Junior non-manual workers.
	Employees not exercising general or supervisory powers, engaged in clerical, sales and non-manual communications and security occupations excluding those who have additional and formal supervisory functions.
(7)	Personal service workers.
	Employees engaged in service occupations caring for food, drink, clothing and other personal needs.
(8)	Foremen and supervisors: manual
	Employees (other than managers) who formally and immediately supervise others engaged in manual occupations, whether or not themselves engaged in such occupations.
(9)	Skilled manual workers.
	Employees engaged in manual occupations which require considerable and specific skills.
(10)	Semi-skilled manual workers.
	Employees engaged in manual occupations which require slight but specific skills.
(11)	Unskilled manual workers.
	Other employees engaged in manual occupations.
(12)	Own account workers (other than professional).
	Self-employed persons engaged in any trade, personal service or manual occupation not normally requiring training of university degree standard and having no employees other than family workers.
(13)	Farmers: employers and managers.
	Persons who own, rent or manage farms, market gardens or forests, employing people other than family workers in the work of the enterprise.
(14)	Farmers: own account.
	Persons who own or rent farms, market gardens or forests and having no employees other than family workers.
(15)	Agricultural workers.
	Employees engaged in tending crops, animal, game or forests or operating agricultural or forestry machinery.
(16)	Members of armed forces.
(17)	Indefinite.
	Persons with inadequately stated occupations.

References

Adams, T. F. (1963). Field interrogation. *Police,* **7,** No. 4 (March-April).

Ahamad, B. (1967). An analysis of crimes by the method of principal components. *Appl. Statist.* **16,** 17-35.

Allingham, M. G. and Sandmo, A. (1972). Income tax evasion: a theoretical analysis. *J. Publ. Econ.* **1,** 323-338.

Amemiya, T. (1977). The maximum likelihood and the nonlinear simultaneous equation model. *Econometrica,* **45.**

Andenaes, J. (1974). "Punishment and Deterrence". Univ. of Michigan Press, Ann Arbor.

Andry, R. G. (1960). "Delinquency and Parental Pathology: a Study in Forensic and Clinical Psychology". Methuen, London.

Anon (1978). Social indicators: for well-being or social control. *Radical Statistics,* London.

Arnott, A. J. E. and Duncan, J. A. (1970). "The Scottish Criminal". Edinburgh Univ. Press, Edinburgh.

Arrow, K. J. (1971). "Essays in the Theory of Risk Bearing". North-Holland, Amsterdam.

Bailey, W. C. (1966). Correctional outcome: an evaluation of 100 reports. *J. Crim. Law, Criminol. & Police Sci.* **57,** 153-160.

Banton, M. (1964). "The Policeman in the Community". Tavistock, London.

Barnes, H. E. and Teeters, N. K. (1951). "New Horizons in Criminology", 2nd edn, and 1959 3rd edn. Prentice Hall, New Jersey.

Beccaria, C. (1769). "An Essay on Crime and Punishment" (translated from the Italian with a commentary attributed to M. de Voltaire). Printed for F. Newbery, London.

Becker, G. (1968). Crime and punishment: an economic approach. *J. Polit. Econ.* **76,** 169-217.

Bedau, H. A. (1970). Deterrence and the death penalty: a reconsideration. *J. Crim. Law, Criminol. & Police Sci.* **61,** 539-548.

Belson, W. A. (1975) a. "The Public and the Police". Harper & Row, London and New York.

Belson, W. A. (1975) b. "Juvenile Theft: the Causal Factors". Harper & Row, London and New York.

Bentham, J. (1948). "An Introduction to the Principles of Morals and Legislation" (W. Harrison, ed.). Blackwell, Oxford.

Berndt, E. K., Hall, B. H., Hall, R. E. and Hausman, J. A. (1974). Estimation and inference in nonlinear structural models. *Annls Econ. & Soc. Measmt,* **3,** No. 4, 653-666.

Biderman, A. D. (1967). Surveys of populations samples for estimating crime incidence. *Annls Amer. Acad. Polit. & Soc. Sci.* **374,** 16-53.

Birdsall, W. C. and Robb, A. L. (1975). The impact of victimisation studies on econometric explanations of crime. *Proc. Amer. Statist. Assoc., Soc. Statist. Sect.*

Bloch, H. A. (1958). Juvenile delinquency: myth or threat? *J. Crim. Law, Criminol. and Police Sci.,* **49,** 303-9.

Bloch, P. B. (1974). "Equality of Distribution of Police Services: A Case Study of Washington". The Urban Institute, Washington, D.C.

Block, M. K. and Heineke, J. M. (1975). A labour theoretical analysis of the criminal choice. *Amer. Econ. Rev.* **65,** 314-325.

Bordua, D. J. (1967). "The Police: Six Sociological Essays". Wiley, New York.

Borrell, C. and Cashinella, B. (1975). "Crime in Britain Today". Routledge & Kegan Paul, London.

Brown, W. W. and Reynolds, M. O. (1973). Crime and punishment: risk implications. *J. Econ. Theory,* **6,** 508-514.

Buchanan, J. M. and Stubblebine, W. C. (1962). Externality. *Economica,* **29,** 317-384.

Buikhuisen, W. (1975). General deterrence: research and theory. *In* "National Swedish Council for Crime Prevention (1975) *General Deterrence Conference Proceedings,* 2nd-4th June 1975, Report No. 2". Stockholm.

Burt, C. (1944). "The Young Delinquents". Univ. of London Press.

Cain, M. C. (1973). "Society and the Policeman's Role". Routledge & Kegan Paul, London.

Cameroun, I. (1975). War against crime. *Peace News,* 23rd October.

Carr-Hill, R. A. (1979). A statistical study of recorded data relating to patterns of sentencing at selected quarter sessions in 1963 and the convictions of adult males. Unpublished thesis for D.Phil., Oxford.

Carr-Hill, R. A., Hope, K. and Stern, N. H. (1972). Delinquent generations revisited. *Quality & Quantity,* **6,** 327-352.

Carr-Hill, R. A. and Stern, N. H. (1971). An econometric model for the supply and control of recorded offences in England and Wales. Paper presented to the European Econometric Conference, Barcelona, September 1971.

Carr-Hill, R. A. and Stern, N. H. (1973). An econometric model of the supply and control of recorded offences in England and Wales. *J. Publ. Econ.* **2,** 289-318.

Carr-Hill, R. A. and Stern, N. H. (1976). Theory and estimation in models of crime and its social control and their relations to concepts of social output. *In* "Economics of the Public Services (M. Feldstein and R. Inman, Eds). Macmillan, London.

Carr-Saunders, A. M., Mannheim, H. and Rhodes, E. C. (1942). "Young Offenders". Cambridge Univ. Press, London.

Carter, R. L. (1974). Theft in the market. *Hobart Paper 60.* Institute of Economic Affairs, London.

Chambliss, W. J. (1966). The deterrent influence of punishment. *Crime & Delinquency,* **2,** No. 1, 70-75.

Chambliss, W. J. and Seidman, R. B. (1971). "Law, Order and Power". Addison-Wesley, Reading, Mass.

Chapman, D. (1968). "Society and the Stereotype of the Criminal". Tavistock, London.

Christianssen, K. O. (1975). On general prevention from an empirical standpoint. *In* "National Swedish Council for Crime Prevention (1975) *General Deterrence Conference Proceedings,* 2nd-4th June, 1975, Report No. 2". Stockholm.

Christie, N. (1968). "Hidden Delinquency: Some Scandinavian Experience". 3rd National Conference on Research and Teaching in Criminology, University of Cambridge, Institute of Criminology, Cambridge.

Christie, N., Andenaes, J. and Skirbekk, S. (1965). A study of self-reported crime. *In* "Scandinavian Studies in Criminology", vol. 1. Tavistock, London.

Cicourel, A. V. (1968). "The Social Organisation of Juvenile Justice". Wiley, New York.

Cloward, R. A. and Ohlin, L. E. (1961). "Delinquency and Opportunity". Free Press of Glencoe, Illinois.

Cohen, A. K. (1955). "Delinquent Boys: the Cult of the Gang". Free Press of Glencoe, Illinois.

Cohen, A. K. (1966). "Deviance and Control". Prentice-Hall, Englewood Cliffs, New Jersey.

Cohen, S. (ed.) (1975). "Images of Deviance". Pelican, London.

Cohen, S. (1973). The failures of criminology. *The Listener,* **90,** No. 2328, 8th November, 1973.

Curtis, L. A. (1975). "Violence, Race and Culture". Lexington Books, Heath & Co., Lexington, Kentucky.

Danziger, S. and Wheeler, D. (1975). The economics of crime: punishment or income distribution. *Rev. Soc. Econ.* **33,** 113-131.

Davis, K. C. (1969). "Discretionary Justice: a Preliminary Enquiry". Louisiana State Univ., Baton Rouge.

Downes, D. (1966). "The Delinquent Solution". Routledge & Kegan Paul, London.

Dhrymes, P. J. (1970). "Econometrics". Harper & Row, New York and London.

Dinitz, S., Dynes, R. and Clarke, A. C. (eds) (1969). "Deviance: Studies in the Process of Stigmatization and Societal Reactions". Oxford Univ. Press, New York and London.

Douglas, J. D. (1967). "The Social Meanings of Suicide". Princeton Univ. Press.

Douglas, J. D., Ross, J. M., Hammond, W. H. and Mulligan, D. G. (1966). Delinquency and social class. *Brit. J. Criminol.* **6,** 294-302.

Durant, M., Thomas, M. and Willcock, H. D. (1972). "Crime, Criminals and the Law". HMSO, London.

Durkheim, E. (1966). "The Division of Labour in Society". Free Press of Glencoe, Illinois.

Ehrlich, I. (1967). The supply of illegitimate activities. Unpublished MS Columbia Univ., New York.

Ehrlich, I. (1973). Participation in illegitimate activities: a theoretical and empirical investigation. *J. Polit. Econ.* **81,** No. 3, 521-565.

Ehrlich, I. (1975). The deterrent effect of capital punishment: a question of life and death. *Amer. Econ. Rev.* **65,** No. 3, 397-417.

Ehrlich, I. (1977). Capital punishment and deterrence: some further thoughts and additional evidence. *J. Polit. Econ.* **85,** 741-788.

Ennis, P. H. (1967). "Criminal Investigation in the U.S." NORC Univ. of Chicago, Chicago.

Erickson, M. L. and Empey, L. T. (1963). Court records, undetected delinquency and decision-making. *J. Crim. Law, Criminol. & Police Sci.* **54**, 456-469.

Evans, G., Irvine, J. and Miles, I. (1978). "Demystifying Social Statistics". Pluto Press, London.

Eysenck, H. J. (1957). "The Dynamics of Anxiety and Hysteria". Routledge & Kegan Paul, London.

Eysenck, H. J. (1964). "Crime and Personality". Routledge & Kegan Paul, London.

Ferber, R. (1966). Research on household behaviour. *In* "Surveys of Economic Theory". American Economic Assoc. and Royal Economic Soc. Macmillan, London.

Ferguson, T. (1952). "The Young Delinquent in His Social Setting: a Glasgow Study". Oxford Univ. Press, London.

Fisher, F. M. (1966). "The Identification Problem in Econometrics". McGraw-Hill.

Fisher, F. M. and Nagin, D. (1976). On the feasibility of identifying the crime functions in a simultaneous model of crime rates and sanction levels (mimeo). MIT.

Fleisher, B. M. (1966). "The Economics of Delinquency". Quadrangle, Chicago.

Form, R. and Bailey, R. (1968). "Authority in Social Casework". Pergamon Press, Oxford.

Galbraith, J. K. (1967). "The New Industrial State". Hamish Hamilton, London.

Gerth, H. and Wright Mills, C. (1947). "From Max Weber, Essays in Sociology". Kegan Paul, London.

Gibbs, J. P. (1975). "Crime, Punishment and Deterrence". Elsevier, New York, Oxford and Amsterdam.

Glaser, D. and Rice, A. (1959). Crime, age and employment. *Amer. Soc. Rev.* **24**, No. 5, 679-686.

Glueck, E. T. and Glueck, S. (1950). "Unravelling Juvenile Delinquency". Harper & Row, New York.

Glueck, S. and Glueck, E. T. (1946). After-conduct of discharged offenders. *In* "English Studies in Criminal Science", vol. 5. Macmillan, London.

Goffman, E. (1961). "Asylums: Essays on the Social Situations of Mental Patients and Other Inmates". Doubleday, New York.

Gold, M. (1966). Undetected delinquent behaviour. *J. Res. Crime & Delinq.* **3**, 27-44.

Goldberger, A. S. and Duncan, O. D. (eds) (1973). "Structural Equation Models in the Social Sciences". Seminar Press, London.

Green, H. J. A. (1976). "Consumer Theory", 2nd edn. Macmillan, London.

Greenhalgh, W. F. (1966). "Police Regression Analysis". Home Office Scientific Advisors' Branch Police Rep. SA/Pol. 6.

Greenwood, M. J. and Wadycki, W. J. (1978). Crime rates and public expenditures on police protection: their interaction. *Rev. Soc. Econ.* **33**, No. 2, 138-151.

Griffiths, D. and Irvine, J. (1978). Political perspectives on a radical statistics. *In* "Demystifying Social Statistics" (G. Evans, J. Irvine and I. Miles, eds). Pluto Press, London.

Griffiths, J. A. G. (1977). "The Politics of the Judiciary". Manchester Univ. Press.

Harris, J. R. (1970). On the economics of law and order. *J. Polit. Econ.* **78**, (1) Jan/Feb 165-174.

Hart, H. L. A. (1968). "Punishment and Responsibility". Clarendon Press, Oxford.

Hausman, J. A. (1975). An instrumental variable approach to full-information estimates for linear and certain non-linear econometric models. *Econometrica* **43**, 727-738.

Hausman, J. A. (1977). Specification tests in econometrics. MIT Economics Working Paper No. 185. *Econometrica.*

Hawkins, R. (1973). Who called the cops? Decisions to report criminal victimisations. *Law & Soc. Rev.* **7**, No. 3, 427-444.

Heineke, J. M. (1975). A note on modelling the criminal choice problem. *J. Econ. Theory,* **10.**

Hendry, D. F. and Harrison, R. W. (1974). Monte Carlo methodology and the finite sample behaviour of ordinary and two stage least square. *J. Economet.* **2,** 151-174.

Hendry, D. F. and Srba, F. (1977). The properties of autoregressive instrumental variables estimators in dynamic systems. *Econometrica,* **45,** 969-990.

Henry, A. F. and Short, J. F. (1954). "Suicide and Homicide". Free Press of Glencoe, Illinois.

Her Majesty's Inspector of Constabulary. Reports for 1960, 1961, 1962, 1966, 1967, 1971, 1972 and 1973.

Hewitt, L. F. and Jenkins, R. L. (1947). "Fundamental Patterns of Readjustment". Thomas, Springfield, Illinois.

Hindness, B. (1973). "The Use of Official Statistics in Sociology: a Critique of Positivism and Ethnomethodology". Macmillan, London.

Hood, R. and Sparks, R. (1970). "Key Issues in Criminology". Weidenfeld & Nicolson, London.

Hood, W. C. amd Koopmans, T. C. (Eds) (1952). "Studies in Econometric Method". Cowles Commission Monograph No. 14. Wiley, New York.

House of Commons Estimates Committee (1966). *Police.* First Report (HC 145).

House of Commons Estimates Committee (1969). *Police.* Second Report (HC 89).

House of Commons Expenditure Committee (1974). *Police Recruitment and Wastage.* Seventh Report (HC 310).

Johnston, J. (1972). "Econometric Methods", 2nd edn. McGraw-Hill, New York.

Kendall, M. G. and Stuart, A. (1973). "The Advanced Theory of Statistics", vol. 3, 3rd edn. Griffin, London.

Kitsuse, J. I. and Cicourel, A. V. (1963). A note on the official use of statistics. *Soc. Problems,* **11,** 131-139.

Klein, R., Buxton, M. and Outram, Q. (1976). "Social Policy and Public Expenditure 1976. Constraints and Choices, a Commentary on the 1976 Public Expenditure White Paper". Centre for Studies in Social Policy, London.

Kolm, S. Ch. (1973). A note on optimum tax evasion. *J. Publ. Econ.* **2,** 265-270.

La Fave, W. R. (1965). "Arrest: the Decision to Take a Suspect into Custody". Little Brown & Co., Boston.

Little, A. D. (1965). The prevalence of recorded delinquency in England and Wales. *Amer. Sociol. Rev.* **30,** No. 2, 260-263.

Little, I. M. D. and Mirrlees, J. A. (1974). "Project Appraisal and Planning for Developing Countries". Heinemann, London.

MacDonald, L. (1969). "Social Class and Delinquency". Faber & Faber, London.

MacDonald, L. (1976). "The Sociology of Law and Order". Faber & Faber, London.

Malinvaud, E. (1970). "Statistical Methods of Econometrics", 2nd edn. North-Holland, Amsterdam.

Mannheim, H. and Wilkins, L. T. (1955). "Prediction Methods in Relation to Borstal Training". Studies in the Causes of Delinquency and the Treatment of Offenders, no. 1. HMSO, London.

Marcuse, H. (1964). "One Dimensional Man: Studies in the Ideology of Advanced Industrial Society". Routledge & Kegan Paul, London.

Mark, R. (1973). Dimbleby lecture. *The Listener*, 8th November 1973, **90,** No. 2328.

Martin, J. P. (1962). "Offenders as Employees". Cambridge Studies in Criminology No. 16. Macmillan, London.

Martin, J. P. and Wilson, G. (1969). "The Police: a Study in Manpower": the Evolution of the Service in England and Wales 1829-1965". Cambridge Studies in Criminology No. 24. Heinemann, London.

Matza, D. (1964). "Delinquency and Drift". Wiley, New York.

McCabe, S. and Sutcliffe, F. (1978). "Defining Crime: a study of police decisions". Blackwell, Oxford.

McClintock, F. H. (1963). "Crimes of Violence". Cambridge Studies in Criminology No. 18. Heinemann, London.

McClintock, F. H. and Avison, N. H. (1968). "Crime in England and Wales". Cambridge Studies in Criminology No. 22. McMillan, London.

McClintock, F. H. and Gibson, E. (1961). "Robbery in London". Cambridge Studies in Criminology No. 14. Macmillan, London.

Merton, R. K. (1938). Social structure and anomie. *Amer. Sociol. Rev.* **3,** No. 5, 672-682.

Merton, R. K. (1957). "Social Theory and Social Structure", revised edn. Free Press, New York.

Meyer, J. C. and Timms, N. (1970). "The Client Speaks". Routledge & Kegan Paul, London.

Miles, I. (1976). Numerical moralities. Paper presented to the *1st Radical Statistics* Conference, London, November 1975.

Miller, W. B. (1958). Lower class culture as a generating milieu of gang delinquency. *J. Soc. Issues,* **14,** No. 3, 5-19.

Mirrlees, J. A. (1974). Notes on welfare economics, information and uncertainty. *In* "Essays on Economic Behaviour Under Uncertainty" (M. Balch, D. McFadden and S. Wu, eds). North-Holland, Amsterdam.

Mizon, G. (1972). A test for structural change in a simultaneous equations model (mimeo). St. Catherine's College, Oxford.

Morris, T. (1957). "The Criminal Area". International Library of Sociology and Social Reconstruction. Routledge, London.

Morris, T. and Morris, P. (1963). "Pentonville: a Sociological Study of an English Prison". International Library of Sociology and Social Reconstruction. Routledge, London.

Moser, C. A. (1970). Some general developments in social statistics. *In* "CSO Social Trends No. 1". HMSO, London.

Nectoux, F. (1977). A note on the UN index of overcrowding. *Radical Statistics,* No. 10.

OECD (1976). "Data Sources for Social Indicators of Actual Victimisation Suffered by Individuals with Special Reference to Victim Survey". OECD Social Indicators Development Programme Special Studies No. 3. OECD, Paris.

OECD (1977). "Measuring Well-being: A Progress Report in the Development of Social Indicators". Social Indicators Development Programme No. 3. OECD, Paris.

Pateman, T. (1975). "Language, Truth and Politics". Stroud Pateman, Devon (private publication).

Phillips, L., Votey, H. L. and Maxwell, D. (1972). Crime, youth and the labour market. *J. Polit. Econ.* **80,** No. 3, 491-504.

Piliavin, I. and Briar, S. (1964). Police encounters with juveniles. *Amer. J. Sociol.* **70,** 206-214.

Pirsig, R. M. (1974). "Zen and the Art of Motorcycle Maintenance: An Enquiry into Values". Bodley Head, London.

Pope, L. (1974). Press representations and alternative interpretations. Unpublished dissertation for BA degree in social science, Sussex University.

Popp, D. O. and Sebold, F. D. (1972). Quasi-returns to scale in the provision of police service. *Public Finance,* **27,** No. 1, 46-61.

President's Commission on Law Enforcement and the Administration of Justice (1967). Task force report: "The Police". US Govt Printing Office.

Rainton, D. (1973). Police cautions in Sussex. Unpublished dissertation for BA degree, Sussex University.

Report of the Commissioners of Police for the Metropolis (1969).

Rose, G. N. G. (1968). The artificial delinquent generations. *J. Crim. Law, Criminol. & Police Sci.* **59,** No. 3, 370-385.

Royal Commission on the Police (1960). Interim report. Cmnd 1222, HMSO, London.

Royal Commission on the Police (1960). Minutes of evidence (Part 1). Assn Chief Police Officers England and Wales. HMSO, London.

Royal Commission on the Police (1962) Final report. Cmnd 1728. HMSO, London.

Russell, C. (1973). The formation of stereotypes by the police. Unpublished dissertation for MA degree, Sussex University.

Schafer, S. (1968). "The victim and his criminal: a study in functional responsibility". New York.

Scheffé, H. (1959). "The Analysis of Variance". Wiley, New York.

Schwartz, K. and Orleans, S. (1961). On legal sanctions. *Univ. Chicago Law Rev.* **34,** 274-300.

Seidman, D. and Couzens, M. (1974). Getting the crime rate down: political pressures and crime reporting. *Law & Soc. Rev.* **8,** No. 3, 457-493.

Sellin, T. (1938). Culture, conflict and crime. *Soc. Sci. Res. Counc. Bull.* 44. New York.

Sellin, T. and Wolfgang, M. E. (1964). "The Measure of Delinquency". Wiley, New York.

Sen, A. K. (1968). "Choice of Techniques", 3rd edn. Blackwell, Oxford.

Shaw, C. R. and McKay, H. D. (1942). "Juvenile Delinquency and Urban Areas". Univ. Chicago Press, Chicago.

Sherif, M. (1967). "Social Interactions, Processes and Products: Selected Essays". Aldine Press, Chicago.

Short, J. F. and Nye, F. I. (1957). Reported behaviour as a criterion of deviant behaviour. *Soc. Problems,* **5,** No. 3, 207-213.

Short, J. F. and Nye, F. I. (1958). Extent of unrecorded juvenile delinquency. *J. Crim. Law, Criminol. & Police Sci.* **49,** No. 4, 296-302.

Silver, A. (1974). Econometric studies in crime and deterrence: a survey (mimeo). City College, New York.

Singh, B. (1973). Making honesty the best policy. *J. Publ. Econ.* **2,** 257-263.

Skolnick, J. H. (1966). "Justice without Trial: Law Enforcement in Democratic Society". Wiley, New York.

Skolnick, J. H. and Woodworth, J. R. (1967). Bureaucracy, information and social content: a study of a morals detail. *In* "The Police: Six Sociological Essays". Wiley, London.

Smart, J. J. C. and Williams, B. (1973). "Utilitarianism: For and Against". Cambridge Univ. Press, London.

Sparks, R. F., Genn, H. and Dodd, D. (1977). "Surveying Victims". Wiley, New York.

Spergel, I. A. (1964). "Racketville, Slumtown and Haulberg: an Exploratory Study of Delinquent Subcultures". Univ. Chicago Press, Chicago.

Srinivasan, T. N. (1973). Tax evasion: a model. *J. Publ. Econ.* **2**, 339-346.

Steer, D. J. (1970). "Police Cautions: a Study in the Exercise of Police Discretion". Oxford Univ. Penal Research Unit Occasional Papers No. 2. Blackwell, Oxford.

Stigler, G. (1970). Optimal enforcement of laws. *J. Polit. Econ.* **78**, No. 3, 526-536.

Stinchcombe, A. (1963). Institutions of privacy in the determination of police administrative practices. *Amer. J. Sociol.* **69**, 150-160.

Sullivan, R. F. (1973). The economics of crime: an introduction to the literature. *Crime & Delinquency,* **19**, No. 2, 138-149.

Summers, R. (1965). A capital intensive approach to the small sample properties of various simultaneous equations estimators. *Econometrica,* **33**, 1-41.

Sutherland, E. H. and Cressey, D. R. (1966). "Principles of Criminology", 6th edn. Lippincott, New York.

Swimmer, G. (1974). The relationship of the police to crime: some methodological and empirical results. *Criminology,* **12**, No. 3, 293-314.

Taylor, I., Walton, P. and Young, J. (1975). "Critical Criminology". Routledge & Kegan Paul, London.

Thomas, D. S. (1925). "Social Aspects of the Business Cycle". Studies in Economic and Political Science, No. 80. Routledge, London.

Thomas, D. A. (1970). "Principles of Sentencing". Heinemann, London.

Toby, J. (1964). Is punishment necessary? *J. Crim. Law, Criminol. & Police Sci.* **55**, No. 3, 332-337.

Trasler, G. (1962). "The Explanation of Criminality". Routledge & Kegan Paul, London.

Turk, A. T. (1969). "Criminality and Legal Order". Rand McNally, Chicago.

Vandaele, W. (1973). The economics of crime: an econometric investigation of auto-theft in the United States (mimeo).

Vaz, E. W. (1966). Self-reported delinquency and socio-economic status. *Canad. J. Corrections,* **8**, 20-27.

Vold, G. B. (1958). "Theoretical Criminology". Oxford Univ. Press, New York.

Votey, H. L. (1969). Economic crimes: their generation, deterrence and control. US Department of Commerce (PB) Washington, DC.

Waldron, J. (1972). Introduction to "Report of the Commissioner of Police for the Metropolis for 1971". HMSO, London.

Walker, M. A. (1967). Some critical comments on "An Analysis of Crimes by the Method of Principal Components" by B. Ahamad. *Appl. Statist.* **16**, 36-39.

Walker, N. D. (1968). "Crime and Punishment in Britain", 2nd edn. Edinburgh Univ. Press, Edinburgh.

Walker, N. D. (1972). "Sentencing in a Rational Society". Pelican, Harmondsworth.

Wallerstein, J. S. and Wyle, C. J. (1947). Our law-abiding law breakers. *Probation,* **25**, 107-112, 118.

West, D. J. (1967). "The Young Offender". Duckworth, London.

West, D. J. and Farrington, D. P. (1973). "Who Becomes Delinquent?" Heinemann, London.

Westley, W. A. (1953). Violence and the police. *Amer. J. Sociol.* **59**, 24-41.

Westley, W. A. (1970). "Violence and the Police: a Sociological Study of Law, Custom and Morality". MIT Press, Cambridge, Mass.

Wiles, P. (1971). Criminal statistics and sociological explanations of crime. *In* "Crime and Delinquency in Britain" (W. G. Carson and P. Wiles, eds). Martin Robertson, London.

Wilkins, L. T. (1964). "Social Deviance: Social Policy, Action and Research". Tavistock, London.

Wilkins, L. T. (1969). "Evaluation of Penal Measures". Random House, New York.

Willcock, H. D. (1974). Deterrents and incentives to crime among boys and young men aged 15-21 years. OPCS Social Survey Division (SS 352).

Willmer, M. A. P. (1968). Is the battle being won? *Police Res. Bull.* No. 7.

Willmer, M. A. P. (1970). "Crime and Information Theory". Edinburgh Univ. Press, Edinburgh.

Wilson, J. Q. (1968). "Varieties of Police Behaviour". Harvard Univ. Press, Cambridge, Mass.

Wolfgang, M. F. and Ferracuti, F. (1967). "The Subculture of Violence: Towards an Integrated Theory in Criminology". Tavistock, London.

Wolin, S. J. (1961). "Politics and Vision: Continuity and Innovation in Western Political Thought". Allen & Unwin, London.

Zellner, A. (1971). "An Introduction to Bayesian Inference in Econometrics". Wiley, New York.

Zimring, F. E. and Hawkins, G. J. (1968). Deterrence and marginal groups. *J. Res. in Crime and Delinq.* 5, No. 2, 100-114.

Zimring, F. E. and Hawkins, G. J. (1973). "Deterrence". Univ. Chicago Press, Chicago.

Name Index

Subject Index

(Numbers in italic refer to the reference section)

QUANTITATIVE STUDIES IN SOCIAL RELATIONS

Consulting Editor: Peter H. Rossi

UNIVERSITY OF MASSACHUSETTS
AMHERST, MASSACHUSETTS

Peter H. Rossi and Walter Williams (Eds.), EVALUATING SOCIAL PRO-GRAMS: *Theory, Practice, and Politics*

Roger N. Shepard, A. Kimball Romney, and Sara Beth Nerlove (Eds.), MULTIDIMENSIONAL SCALING: *Theory and Applications in the Behavioral Sciences,* Volume I – Theory; Volume II – Applications

Robert L. Crain and Carol S. Weisman, DISCRIMINATION, PERSONALITY, AND ACHIEVEMENT: *A Survey of Northern Blacks*

Douglas T. Hall and Benjamin Schneider, ORGANIZATIONAL CLIMATES AND CAREERS: *The Work Lives of Priests*

Kent S. Miller and Ralph Mason Dreger (Eds.), COMPARATIVE STUDIES OF BLACKS AND WHITES IN THE UNITED STATES

Robert B. Tapp, RELIGION AMONG THE UNITARIAN UNIVERSALISTS: *Converts in the Stepfathers' House*

Arthur S. Goldberger and Otis Dudley Duncan (Eds.), STRUCTURAL EQUATION MODELS IN THE SOCIAL SCIENCES

Henry W. Riecken and Robert F. Boruch (Eds.), SOCIAL EXPERIMENTATION: *A Method for Planning and Evaluating Social Intervention*

N. J. Demerath, III, Otto Larsen, and Karl F. Schuessler (Eds.), SOCIAL POLICY AND SOCIOLOGY

H. M. Blalock, A. Aganbegian, F. M. Borodkin, Raymond Boudon, and Vittorio Capecchi (Eds.), QUANTITATIVE SOCIOLOGY: *International Perspectives on Mathematical and Statistical Modeling*

Carl A. Bennett and Arthur A. Lumsdaine (Eds.), EVALUATION AND EXPERIMENT: *Some Critical Issues in Assessing Social Programs*

Michael D. Ornstein, ENTRY INTO THE AMERICAN LABOR FORCE

Seymour Sudman, APPLIED SAMPLING

James D. Wright, THE DISSENT OF THE GOVERNED: *Alienation and Democracy in America*

Roland J. Liebert, DISINTEGRATION AND POLITICAL ACTION: *The Changing Functions of City Governments in America*

Walter Williams and Richard F. Elmore, SOCIAL PROGRAM IMPLEMEN-TATION

Edward O. Laumann and Franz U. Pappi, NETWORKS OF COLLECTIVE ACTION: *A Perspective on Community Influence Systems*

Eric Hanushek and John Jackson, STATISTICAL METHODS FOR SOCIAL SCIENTISTS

Richard F. Curtis and Elton F. Jackson, INEQUALITY IN AMERICAN COMMUNITIES

Richard A. Berk, Harold Brackman, and Selma Lesser, A MEASURE OF JUSTICE: *An Empirical Study of Changes in the California Penal Code, 1955–1971*

Samuel Leinhardt (Ed.), SOCIAL NETWORKS: *A Developing Paradigm*

Donald J. Treiman, OCCUPATIONAL PRESTIGE IN COMPARATIVE PERSPECTIVE

Beverly Duncan and Otis Dudley Duncan, SEX TYPING AND SOCIAL ROLES: *A Research Report*

N. Krishnan Namboodiri (Ed.), SURVEY SAMPLING AND MEASURE-MENT